MONTROSE

MONTROSE

BY

JOHN BUCHAN

*Sedulo curavi humanas actiones non ridere, non lugere,
neque detestari, sed intelligere.*—Spinoza

JAMES THIN

1979

THE MERCAT PRESS, EDINBURGH

This is a facsimile of the 1928 edition published by
Thomas Nelson and Sons, Ltd.

ISBN 0 901824 55 0

Printed in Great Britain by
Billing & Sons Limited
Guildford, London and Worcester

FRATRI DILECTISSIMO

W. H. B.

When we were little, wandering boys,
   And every hill was blue and high,
On ballad ways and martial joys
   We fed our fancies, you and I.
With Bruce we crouched in bracken shade,
   With Douglas charged the Paynim foes;
And oft in moorland noons I played
   Colkitto to your grave Montrose.

The obliterating seasons flow—
   They cannot kill our boyish game.
Though creeds may change and kings may go,
   Yet burns undimmed the ancient flame.
While young men in their pride make haste
   The wrong to right, the bond to free,
And plant a garden in the waste,
   Still rides our Scottish chivalry.

Another end had held your dream—
   To die fulfilled of hope and might,
To pass in one swift, rapturous gleam
   From mortal to immortal light.
But through long hours of labouring breath
   You watched the world grow small and far,
And met the constant eyes of Death
   And haply knew how kind they are.

▼

One boon the Fates relenting gave.
   Not where the scented hill-wind blows
From cedar thickets lies your grave,
   Nor 'mid the steep Himálayan snows.
Night calls the stragglers to the nest,
   And at long last 'tis home indeed
For your far-wandering feet to rest
   For ever by the crooks of Tweed.

In perfect honour, perfect truth,
   And gentleness to all mankind,
You trod the golden paths of youth,
   Then left the world and youth behind.
Ah no! 'Tis we who fade and fail—
   And you, from Time's slow torments free,
Shall pass from strength to strength, and scale
   The steeps of immortality.

Dear heart, in that serener air,
   If blessed souls may backward gaze,
Some slender nook of memory spare
   For our old happy moorland days.
I sit alone, and musing fills
   My breast with pain that shall not die,
Till once again o'er greener hills
   We ride together, you and I.

PREFACE

In September 1913 I published a short sketch of Montrose, which dealt chiefly with his campaigns. The book went out of print very soon, and it was not reissued, because I cherished the hope of making it the basis of a larger work, in which the background of seventeenth-century politics and religion should be more fully portrayed. I also felt that many of the judgments in the sketch were exaggerated and hasty. During the last fifteen years I have been collecting material for the understanding of a career which must rank among the marvels of our history, and of a mind and character which seem to me in a high degree worthy of the attention of the modern reader. The manuscript sources have already been diligently explored by others, and I have been unable to glean from them much that is new; but I have attempted to supplement them by a study of the voluminous pamphlet literature of the time. My aim has been to present a great figure in its appropriate setting. In a domain, where the dust of controversy has not yet been laid, I cannot hope to find for my views universal acceptance, but they have not been reached without an earnest attempt to discover the truth.   J. B.

Elsfield Manor, Oxon,
    June, 1928.

CONTENTS

INTRODUCTORY: THE EARLY SEVENTEENTH CENTURY . 15

BOOK I.—PREPARATION

I. YOUTH 33
II. THE STRIFE IN SCOTLAND 44
III. THE FIRST COVENANT WARS 77
IV. MONTROSE AND ARGYLL 106
V. THE RUBICON 136

BOOK II.—ACTION

VI. THE CURTAIN RISES 167
VII. TIPPERMUIR 178
VIII. ABERDEEN AND FYVIE 198
IX. INVERLOCHY 213
X. THE RETREAT FROM DUNDEE 229
XI. AULDEARN AND ALFORD 240
XII. KILSYTH 261
XIII. THE WAR ON THE BORDER 273
XIV. AFTER PHILIPHAUGH 291

BOOK III.—PASSION

XV. THE YEARS OF EXILE 317
XVI. THE LAST CAMPAIGN 347
XVII. THE CURTAIN FALLS 361
XVIII. "A CANDIDATE FOR IMMORTALITY" 382

APPENDIX: MONTROSE ON "SOVEREIGN POWER" . 397
INDEX 409

ILLUSTRATION

MONTROSE (from an engraving by A. Matham, forming
   the frontispiece to the 1647 Hague translation of
   Wishart)   .   .   .   .   *facing page*   274

The crown and motto on the jacket of the book are copied from
   the Declaration issued by Montrose at the beginning of his
   campaign in 1644, preserved among the papers of the
   Napier family.

MAPS

1. Campaign of Tippermuir and Aberdeen . . . 190
2. Battle of Aberdeen 200
3. Campaign of Inverlochy 218
4. Campaign of Dundee and Auldearn 238
5. Battle of Auldearn 246
6. Campaign of Alford 252
7. Battle of Alford 256
8. Campaign of Kilsyth 262
9. Battle of Kilsyth 270
10. Campaign of Philiphaugh 282
11. Campaign of Carbisdale 352

ABBREVIATIONS

A. P. S.	*Acts of the Parliaments of Scotland.* 12 vols., 1834–75.
Army of the Covenant	*Papers relating to the Army of the Solemn League and Covenant (1643–47).* 2 vols. (S. H. S.), 1917.
Baillie	*Letters and Journals of the Rev. Robert Baillie.* 3 vols., 1841.
Balfour	*Historical Works (Annales) of Sir James Balfour.* 4 vols., 1824–25.
Burnet, *Mem. of the Hamiltons*	*The Memoirs of James and William, Dukes of Hamilton,* by Gilbert Burnet, 1677.
Calderwood	*History of the Kirk of Scotland (1524–1625),* by David Calderwood (Wodrow Society). 8 vols., 1842–59.
Cal. S. P., Dom.	*Calendar of State Papers, Domestic.*
Clanranald MSS.	The narrative of Alasdair Macdonald's campaign, by a shanachie of Clanranald in the " Black Book of Clanranald." It is translated in Cameron's *Reliquiæ Celticæ,* II., 138–209 (Inverness, 1894), and the Gaelic text has been edited by Joseph Lloyd, with an historical introduction by Professor Eoin McNeill, in *Alasdair Mac Colla* (Dublin, 1914).
Clarendon, *Hist.*	*History of the Rebellion,* by Edward, Earl of Clarendon (ed. Macray), 1888.
Firth	*Cromwell's Army,* by Sir C. H. Firth, 1902.
Forbes Leith	*Memoirs of Scottish Catholics during the Seventeenth and Eighteenth Centuries,* by William Forbes Leith, S.J. 2 vols., 1909.
Gardiner	*History of England,* by S. R. Gardiner. 10 vols., 1886.
Gardiner, *Civil War*	*History of the Great Civil War,* by S. R. Gardiner. 4 vols., 1910.
Gordon of Rothiemay	*History of Scots Affairs,* by James Gordon (Spalding Club). 3 vols., 1841.
Gordon of Ruthven	*Britane's Distemper,* by Patrick Gordon (Spalding Club), 1844.
Gordon of Sallagh	Continuation (by Gilbert Gordon of Sallagh) of *A History of the Earldom of Sutherland,* by Sir Robert Gordon of Gordonstoun, 1813.
Guthry	*Memoirs of Henry Guthry, Bishop of Dunkeld.* 2nd edition, Glasgow, 1747.

Gwynne . . . . . . *Military Memoirs of the Great Civil War*, by John Gwynne (ed. Sir W. Scott), 1822.

Hist. MSS. Comm. . . . *Reports of the Royal Commission on Historical Manuscripts.*

Lang . . . . . . *History of Scotland*, by Andrew Lang. 4 vols., 1900–6.

M. & S. . . . . . Editorial matter in edition of Wishart by Murdoch and Simpson.

Mem. of M. . . . . . *Memorials of Montrose and his Times*, ed. by Mark Napier (Maitland Club). 2 vols., 1848–50.

Monteith . . . . . *The History of the Troubles of Great Britain*, etc., by Robert Monteith of Salmonet. Eng. trans., 1738. The French original, *Histoire des Troubles de la Grande Bretagne*, was published in Paris in 1661.

Napier . . . . . . *Memoirs of the Marquis of Montrose*, by Mark Napier. 2 vols., 1856.

P.C.R. . . . . . . *Register of the Privy Council of Scotland.* 2nd series, 8 vols., 1899–1908.

Rothes . . . . . *Relation of Proceedings concerning the Affairs of the Kirk of Scotland*, by John, Earl of Rothes (Bannatyne Club), 1830.

Row . . . . . . *History of the Kirk of Scotland (1558–1637)*, by John Row (Wodrow Society), 1842.

Rushworth . . . . *Historical Collections of Private Passages of State*, etc., by John Rushworth. 8 vols., London, 1721.

S.H.R. . . . . . . *Scottish Historical Review.*

S.H.S. . . . . . Scottish History Society.

Spalding . . . . . *The History of the Troubles and Memorable Transactions in Scotland and England (1624–45)*, by John Spalding (Bannatyne Club). 2 vols., 1828.

Spottiswoode . . . *History of the Church and State of Scotland (203–1625)*, by John Spottiswoode (Spottiswoode Society). 3 vols., 1851.

Wardlaw MS. . . . . . *Chronicles of the Frasers : the Wardlaw MS.*, by James Fraser (S. H. S.), 1905.

Wariston . . . . . *Diary of Sir Archibald Johnston of Wariston*, Vol. I., 1632–39 (S. H. S.), 1911 ; Vol. II., 1650–54, 1919.

Wigton Papers . . . . . "Documents from the Archives of the Earls of Wigton, 1520–1650," in *Miscellany of the Maitland Club*, Vol. II., 1840.

Wishart . . . . . *The Memoirs of James, Marquis of Montrose*, by the Rev. George Wishart, edited by Alexander Murdoch and H. F. Morland Simpson, 1893. [Wishart's narrative is referred to by its chapters, and when a page is indicated the reference is to the Latin text in this edition.]

MONTROSE

INTRODUCTORY

THE EARLY SEVENTEENTH CENTURY

IN a famous letter Keats has expounded life under
the similitude of Chambers. There is first the
Thoughtless Chamber, when man lives only for sensa-
tion; then comes the Chamber of Maiden Thought,
when he consciously rejoices in the world of sense, and
from this happy illumination acquires insight into the
human heart; thence open many doors—"but all
dark, all leading to dark passages." The simile applies
not only to individual experience, but to the corporate
life of peoples. There come epochs when a nation
seems to move from the sun into the twilight, when the
free ardour of youth is crippled by hesitations, when
the eyes turn inward and instinct gives place to questioning.

Such a period commonly follows an age of confidence
and exuberant creation. We can see the shadows beginning to lengthen in the early years of Elizabeth's
successor, and they do not lift till the garish dawn of
the Restoration. It is dangerous to generalize about
an epoch, but the first half of the seventeenth century
has a character so distinct that it is permissible to
separate certain elements in its intellectual atmosphere,
which affected the minds of all who dwelt in it, whatever their creeds or parties. Whether we study it in
the record of its campaigns and parliaments, or in the
careers of its protagonists, or in the books of its great
writers, three facts are patent in contrast with its
predecessor.

"Is not this world a catholic kind of place?" Carlyle has written. "The Puritan gospel and Shakespeare's plays: such a pair of facts I have rarely seen saved out of one chimerical generation." The greatness of the Elizabethan age was that it was catholic; that is, a number of potent, and usually conflicting, forces were held for a brief season in equilibrium. The Reformation had broken certain seals of thought, but it had not destroyed the integrity of the Church. The Middle Ages, in the monarchy and in much of the law and custom of the people, co-existed with the new learning and the adventurous temper of the Renaissance. England could conquer strange worlds and yet maintain intact her ancient domestic life. The national mood was one of confidence and ardour, so intent upon present duties and enjoyments that it could permit the latent antagonisms to slumber. But in the first decade of the seventeenth century the mutterings in sleep became a restless awaking. The monarchy, when the great figure of Elizabeth passed, was seen to be a mediæval anomaly, and prerogatives hitherto unchallenged were soon a matter of hot debate. The ecclesiastical compromise which created the Anglican Church found many critics, and even those who accepted the fact were at odds about the theory. Sanctions, which had seemed imperishable, began to tilt and crack. The old world was crumbling, and there was no unanimity about the new.

Following upon this loss of harmony in institutions came a change in the national mood, which may be described, perhaps, as a failure of nerve. The forthright enjoying temper of the Elizabethans had gone; the world was no longer so simple and so spacious; the stage had become full of questioning Hamlets. It is a mood familiar to students of classical antiquity, and may be found in high relief during the first centuries of our era. The weakening of the social fabric, and consequently of the protective power of society, increases the strain on the personality. The hopefulness of youth is succeeded by a sad acquiescence, if

not by despondency : the eye looks inward ; the soul
is disillusioned with the world, and seeks refuge elsewhere. It is the *preparatio evangelica,* for it turns the
mind to God. In such a mood religion comes to birth,
for the worldliness of youth rejoicing to run its course
is exchanged for the spirituality of those who find here
no continuing city. Life seems no longer a thing to
be shaped by man's endeavour, and in every creed,
from the predestination of the Calvinist to the mystical
Platonism of the scholar, it is conceived as a puppet-
play moved by the hand of Omnipotence. Metaphysic
has broken into a secure world, and with it have come
a sense of sin, a constant dwelling upon death, a haunting consciousness of eternity.

Something of this temper soon became dominant
in the land. Robust spirits might reject it and recover
the pagan standpoint ; wise men might struggle through
it to certainty and peace ; but the shadow of it was
universal, even in the defiance of the pagan. There was
everywhere a quickening and intensifying of certain
spiritual emotions, a sense of man's littleness and
dependence upon the unseen, a movement away from
humanism towards mysticism, a clouding of horizons
which had once been so bright and clear. The con-
gregations which listened to Donne's analysis of sin
and his pictures of the " various and vagabond heart
of the sinner " thronged to St. Paul's because the
preacher was in tune with their own thoughts. Death
was so much with them that they found comfort in
envisaging its terrors. There was satisfaction in the
belittling of life : " We have a winding-sheet in our
mother's womb, which groweth with us from our conception, and we come into the world wound up in
that winding-sheet, for we come to seek a grave." [1]
The unthinkableness of eternity hag-rode their imagination. " Methusalem with all his hundreds of years
was but a mushroom of a night's growth to this Day,
and all the four Monarchies with all their thousands of
years, and all the powerful Kings and all the beautiful

---

[1] Donne, *Deaths Duell.*

Queens of this world, were but as a bed of flowers,
some gathered at six, some at seven, some at eight,
all in one morning, in respect of this Day." [1]

A consequence of such a mood was that men believed, as in the days of St. Cyprian, that the youth
of the world had gone, and that they were living in
its old age. The new science, the new astronomy,
assisted the mood by breaking down the old comfortable,
concentric universe. " There prevailed in his (Milton's)
time an opinion that the world was in its decay, and
that we have had the misfortune to be produced in the
decrepitude of Nature. It was suspected that the whole
creation languished, that neither trees nor animals had
the height or bulk of their predecessors, and that everything was daily sinking by gradual diminution." [2] We
find the belief in Raleigh : " The long day of mankind
draweth fast towards an evening, and the world's
tragedy and time are near at an end." [3] " Think not
thy time short in this world," wrote Sir Thomas Browne,
" since the world itself is not long." [4] It is everywhere
in the sermons of the divines. Man is " an aged child,
a grey-headed infant," and but a ghost of his own
youth.[5] " As the world is the whole frame of the
world, God hath put into it a reproof, a rebuke, lest it
should seem eternal, which is a sensible decay and age
in the whole frame of the world and every piece thereof.
The seasons of the year irregular and distempered ; the
sun fainter and languishing ; men less in stature and
shorter lived. No addition, but only every year new
sorts, new species of worms and flies and sicknesses,
which argue more and more putrefaction of which they
are engendered." [6] " This is the world's old age ; it is
declining ; albeit it seems a fine and beautiful thing in
the eyes of them that know no better, and unto those
who are of yesterday and know nothing it looks as if
it had been created yesterday, yet the truth is, and a

[1] Donne, *Sermon LXXIII.*   [2] Johnson, *Lives of the Poets : Milton.*
[3] *History of the World.*   [4] *Christian Morals,* 29.
[5] Donne, *Sermon XXII.*
[6] Ibid., *Sermon XXXVI.* The same thought will be found in Donne's
" First Anniversary," *Poems* (ed. Grierson), I., 237.

believer knows, it is near the grave." [1] " The world's
span-length of time is drawn now to less than half an
inch, and to the point of the evening of the day of this
old grey-haired world." [2] The result of such a belief
was to cheapen the value of human endeavour, to show
human greatness as trivial against the vastness of
eternity. " Jezebel's dust is not amber, nor Goliath's
dust *terra sigillata,* medicinal ; nor does the serpent,
whose meat they are both, find any better value in
Dives dust than in Lazarus." [3] There was but one
paramount duty in life, to save the soul. " These are
the two great works which we are to do in this world :
first to know that this world is not our home, and then
to provide us another home whilst we are in this world." [4]
" Build your nest upon no tree here," Samuel Rutherford
wrote to Lady Kenmure, " for ye see God hath sold the
forest to death." These are more than the common-
places of theology ; they are the expression of a temper
which, by the year 1630, had become a background to
thought, an atmosphere which insensibly coloured every
man's outlook. [5]

In an age of uncertainty and change there is inevitably a craving for definition and discipline. Even
if this or that law is dubious, Law itself is regarded as
more than ever essential ; in Hooker's famous panegyric
her seat is in the bosom of God, her voice the harmony
of the world, and she is the mother of all peace and joy.
To live at all, man must make rules and keep them, and
in the prevalent flux he hankers after rigidity. The
more doubtful the political outlook the fiercer will be
the dogmas which men create and contend for ; the
more the foundations of the Church are shaken the
more high-flying and arbitrary will be the conflicting
creeds. It is an old trait of human nature, when in the

---

[1] Binning, *Sermons,* III., 372. [2] Samuel Rutherford, *Letters.*
[3] Donne, *Sermon LXXX.* [4] Ibid., *Sermon LXXII.*
[5] Even to a sporting squire like Charles Cotton, the transience of man's life
is linked with the fragility of the solid earth :

   " You and I,
  By a condition of mortality,
  With all this great and more proud world must die."

mist, to be very sure about its road. In such an era
a religious faith tends to become a complete philosophy
of life, governing also the minutest details of the secular
world. Man cries for guidance and authority, and if
he rejects one sanction he will invent others more compelling than the old. Having shaken himself loose from
history, he tends to an abstract idealism. The English
polity had been built up piecemeal by many compromises,
but its seventeenth-century critics were apt to forget
this, and to devise, like Milton, a brand-new symmetrical
structure, unrelated to the past.[1] But Milton had the
supreme merit that he always believed in the free and
rational soul of man. " He who wisely would restrain
the reasonable soul of man within due bounds, must
first himself know perfectly how far the territory and
dominion extends of just and honest liberty. As little
must he offer to bind that which God hath loosened as
to loosen that which He hath bound. The ignorance
and mistake of this high point hath heaped up one huge
half of all the misery that hath been since Adam."
The human reason was not commonly valued so high
by Milton's contemporaries, and they readily bent
themselves before authority—of king or parliament,
of bishop, Bible or congregation, or of personal revelation. Differences, which should have been discretionary,
were elevated into matters of essential principle, and men
were ready to stake body and soul on the finest points
of dogma in Church and State.

Happily these troubles of the spirit, so far as England was concerned, befell in a society nicely integrated
and fundamentally stable. Men of quick conscience and
fine intelligence, who are the shaping spirits in any era,
felt their impact, but there were in the land strong
stabilizing forces which were for long untouched by
them, and which made it certain that change would
come by slow degrees. There was not, as on the continent of Europe, a gulf fixed between the nobility and
the commonalty ; the nobles were no more than the

---

[1] See especially Milton's *Of Reformation in England, and the Causes that
Hitherto have Hindered it.*

topmost class of a great body of gentry which in the lower ranges came very near to the yeomanry, and embraced what we know to-day as the middle and professional classes. Even at the summit, the grandees of Plantagenet and Tudor origin found themselves compelled to mix with the new creations of James I. A family of Norman descent would apprentice a younger son to a trade, and marry a daughter to some new City knight or young lawyer from the Temple. Boys of ancient houses sat side by side on the grammar-school benches with the sons of farmers and tradesmen. The land was organized locally for defence and administration; an unpaid magistracy enforced the king's mandates and administered the new poor law; the ordinary citizen was the only soldier, the mediæval levy had not yet disappeared, and on the Marches manorial tenants armed with broadswords still met the judges of assize. There was little rigidity among classes, but the intensity of provincial feeling gave immense power to those local leaders who had a long tradition of popularity, so that the Lancashire gentry were accustomed to wear the Stanley livery. Shire, parish, and town were living organisms, managing their affairs with little outside interference, and to buttress their honest particularism there was a mass of hoar-ancient custom and tradition which gave a man of Gloucestershire a different outlook from a man of Devon or Kent. England still stood in the old ways, and in her affection for them lay a vast latent conservative power. But with this conservatism was joined a high measure of independence. The progress of enclosures was bringing the yeoman and the tenant-farmer into greater importance, and if each locality had its special patriotism, so had each class its own stubborn loyalties. So far as we can judge, it was on the whole a comfortable society, full of ancestral jollities, and secure, for in most parts of England a century had elapsed since the tramp of armies had echoed in their fields.

North of the Tweed the case was different. Scotland had for centuries been emptied from vessel to

vessel, and civil war was in the memories of living men.
In the Highlands the clan system still held together a
primitive society, but its Border variant had broken
down, and elsewhere no settled order of life had been
developed. The Scottish nobles had not laid aside
their ancient turbulence ; whereas in England the duel
was coming into fashion (a step towards civilization),
they still held by bravos and the " killing affray." [1]
All classes were miserably poor ; the gentry lived
squalidly in their little stone towers, the peasant was
half-starved and half-clad, and rural life had few of the
English amenities. The land was strewn with the relics
of mediævalism, and amid this lumber the spirit of
the Knoxian Reformation burned furiously, destroying
much that was ill and not a little that was good. In a
later chapter we shall consider more closely the condition of Scotland ; here it is sufficient to note that the
land was far readier for violent change than its southern
neighbour. Its conservatism was a thing of private
sentiment and passion rather than of fidelity to proved
institutions ; its history had given it a noble patriotism,
but few things to cherish beyond a savage independence,
and the cataclysmic breach with the ancient Church
had predisposed it to other breaches. At the same time
the Union of the Crowns had brought it into close
relations with England, its nobility frequented the court,
its civil and ecclesiastical policies were affected by Westminster. No overt act, no spiritual mood of England
could be without its reactions in the north, and a flame
which burned slowly amid the lush meadows and green
hedgerows might run like wildfire among the dry heather.

An era of unrest produces a thousand types, but
in the long run they range themselves in two parties,
for human nature—especially English human nature—
tends always to a dualism. It is not easy to find a
definition for either Cavalier or Puritan which shall
embrace on the one hand Suckling and Traherne, Laud
and Clarendon, Rupert and Falkland : on the other
Hampden and Barebone, Bunyan and Milton, Ireton

[1] See the case of Lord Sanquhar. Gardiner, II., 131–133.

and Lilburne. From the one party we may exclude the mere roysterers—Milton's " sons of Belial, flown with insolence and wine "—and from the other the hypocrites and the crack-brains ; every great cause has its unworthy camp-followers. The division was not a social one, for the Puritans had many of the old nobility and some of the best of the country gentry in their ranks ; and the Cavaliers had the bulk of the peasantry and a share of the trading and professional classes. The two factors in the situation were the crumbling of old things and the need of substitutes, the questioning and the demand for certainty ; the problem was how to define the fundamentals, and where to find authority. Men of the same party answered it in different and often inconsistent ways.

The stream of the Cavalier temperament was fed by many distant springs. There was the punctilio of honour, the devotion to a master, which made royalists of simple and chivalrous souls : men like Hopton and Capel, Sunderland and Sir Bevil Grenville ; men like Sir Edmund Verney, the knight marshal, from whose dying hand the standard dropped at Edgehill, though his creed was not that of the king. There were the lovers of Old England like Clarendon, its old Church, its folk religion, " its old good manners, its old good humour, and its old good nature "—things like to be destroyed by rash hands which could only offer a drab alternative. There were the believers in a central authority, and in the domain of law as against anarchy— liberal thinkers for the most part, and zealous reformers, who stood as firmly as Milton for the freedom of the human spirit, but resisted an iconoclasm which they held to be the path to servitude. Such were Falkland— who has given true conservatism its motto : " When it is not necessary to change, it is necessary not to change " —and Sidney Godolphin, who, like his friend, fell early on the battlefield.[1] There were the opportunists as

---

[1] Hobbes wrote of him : " I have known clearness of judgment and largeness of fancy ; strength of reason and graceful elocution ; a courage for the war and fear for the laws : and all eminently in one man." This " fear for the laws " was a Cavalier characteristic too often forgotten.

against the dogmatists, the men who held with Donne
that truth is not found by the straight road of an easy
revelation, but must be sought by a spiral course, and
that, as Cosin put it, " faith is not on this side knowledge, but beyond it." There were the scholars, full of
the classical Renaissance; and the Platonists, who were
not content to make the Bible the one source of truth
or to condemn as carnal what they held to be divine.
And there were the poets, who refused to narrow the
world which God had made, and, like Herbert and
Vaughan and Traherne, found everywhere " bright
shoots of everlastingness "; in such men mysticism
does not reject humanism, but enfolds and transcends it.

In this medley of types there was infinite room for
difference—Laud's theory of church government, for
example, was antipathetic to most of the party—but
under the pressure of their opponents they found
common ground, and a temperament was hardened
into a creed. That creed was, shortly, the need of
preserving a central authority in the kingship. Men
who had hotly criticized Charles's policy, who had no
love for Laud and his ways, who had sympathized with
Hampden and Eliot, found themselves ranged beside
country squires who had few ideas beyond ale and
foxes. Just as Oxford's treasures of Renaissance plate
were melted down to provide current coin for the troops,
so far-reaching doctrines were given a partial and popular
statement, and philosophies were reduced to formulas
and watchwords. In the Middle Ages treason was held
the rankest of crimes, because so little was needed to
wreck the brittle mechanism of the State. So now,
with change and anarchy in the air, lovers of order
stood by the one well-sanctioned existing authority—
the king.

In the Puritan party we find less variety of type
and a simpler temperament, but here also is diversity. The basis was in the first instance religion.[1] The

---

[1] There was also, of course, an economic basis, but I think that Mr. R. H.
Tawney (*Religion and the Rise of Capitalism*, 235) overestimates it, at least so
far as concerns the first forty years of the seventeenth century, though what he

original Puritan was one who desired to purify the
Church from all taint of Romanism, and to the end
there were Puritans who remained Churchmen. But
presently, as the difficulties of the task became apparent,
criticism of liturgical forms and of the extravagances
of episcopal power hardened with many into an opposition to all hierarchical church government, and the
acceptance of the Presbyterian doctrine of the " priesthood of all believers " and the polity of the reformed
churches in France, Switzerland, and Scotland. This
ecclesiastical preference was extended into secular
affairs, and the Puritan added to his creed a passion
for civic freedom. There were also the sectaries who
had been persecuted since the early days of Elizabeth, and who were distasteful alike to Anglican and
Presbyterian—men who were extreme individualists
in church matters, and regarded the congregation as
the divinely appointed organism.

Puritanism was neither an ecclesiastical system nor
a theological creed. Calvinism, with its doctrine of
" exclusive salvation," was, at first, the belief of Anglican
and Presbyterian alike, and it remained the prevailing creed of the Puritan party as of the bulk of their
opponents—rejected only by Laud's Arminian school,
and by sects like the Baptists and the Quakers. The
most powerful statement of Puritan theology will be
found in Anglican divines like Donne ; no Scottish
Covenanter ever dwelt more terribly upon original sin,
the torments of hell, and the awe of eternity.[1] Nor
was the Puritan either a very learned and subtle theologian, or a profound expositor of his own ecclesiastical
tastes. When a man of Milton's genius embarks upon
doctrinal questions [2] he is " in wandering mazes lost,"
like the evil spirits in *Paradise Lost*, who sat on a hill
and debated predestination. For wisdom, breadth of
knowledge, and logical acumen, no Puritan champion

says is true of post-Restoration nonconformity. The clash was far more one
of political and theological theories than of " contradicting economic interests
and incompatible conceptions of social expediency."

[1] See especially *Sermons I., XIII.,* and *LXVI.*
[2] In his *Treatise of Christian Doctrines.*

can vie with Hooker, Chillingworth, John Hales, and
Jeremy Taylor—few even reach the standard of Laud.

Puritanism was above all things the result of a
profound spiritual experience in the Puritan. It is to
John Bunyan and George Fox that we must go if we
would learn the strength of the faith. The questioning
of the epoch resulted for such men in an overwhelming
sense of sin and an overpowering consciousness of God ;
their knowledge, in Cromwell's famous words, was not
" literal and speculative, but inward and transforming
the mind to it." Unless we realize this primary fact
we cannot explain why so many diverse creeds were
ultimately conjoined to form one conquering temperament. Inevitably the faith and the practice narrowed
and hardened. Sunday, the day on which Calvin
played bowls and John Knox gave supper parties,
became the Jewish Sabbath, and the Mosaic law in
many of its most irrelevant details was incorporated
with the Christian creed. Toleration was impossible
for men who saw life as a narrow path through a land
shaken by the fires of hell ; only kindred communions
were tolerated, save by those few sects who, from hard
experience, had learned a gentler rule. A limited
number inclined to a complete separation of Church
and State, but the majority desired a purified State,
which would be the ally and the servant of the Church.
They rejected the world of sense, for there could be no
innocency in what had been corrupted by Adam's sin,
and their eyes were fixed austerely upon their own souls.
The strength of Puritanism lay in its view of the direct
relation of God and man ; its weakness in the fact that
this relation was narrowly and often shallowly construed. The Puritan became, by his severe abstraction,
a dangerous element in society and the State, since
human institutions are built upon half-truths, oppor-
tunisms, and compromises. He was pre-eminently a
destructive force, for he was without the historical
sense,[1] and sought less to erect and unite than to pull

---

[1] The Puritan statesmen were often zealous collectors of precedents, but
their legal antiquarianism was not the same thing as a sense of history.

down and separate. Milton's words might be taken as
his creed : " By His divorcing command the world first
rose out of chaos ; nor can be renewed again out of
confusion but by the separating of unmeet consorts." [1]

With the Puritans, as with the Cavaliers, many
streams from remote wells were in the end canalized
into a single channel. The mood of those who accepted
the natural world as the gift of God was set against
that which saw that world as conceived in sin and
shapen in iniquity : the ancient institutions of the
realm, which to the mind of the Cavalier should be
reformed, but in substance retained, were opposed to a
clean page on which men could write what they pleased ;
the conception of the State as a thing of balances and
adjustments was met by a theory of government as
an abstract ideal to be determined mainly by the half-
understood words of an old book : the free exercise
of men's conscience in religion was confronted with a
denial of freedom except to those of a certain way of
thinking. The truth is that the Puritan was hampered
both in civil and ecclesiastical statesmanship by that
intense individualism which was also his strength. His
creed was not social or readily communicable—

" . . . a dark lanthorn of the spirit,
Which none see by but those who bear it."

To him, as to Newman in his youth, the world was
narrowed to " two, and two only, supreme and lumin-
ously self-evident beings "—himself and his Creator.

If we put the contrast thus, it would seem that
generosity and enlightenment were predominantly on
the side of the Cavaliers. But it must not be forgotten
that, owing to the spiritual atmosphere of the age and
the tendency in such a conflict to narrower and yet
narrower definition, the common creed of Puritanism
did not fairly represent the best men in its ranks. Had
Hampden and Falkland ever argued on fundamentals
they might well have found themselves in substantial

[1] *The Doctrine and Discipline of Divorce.*

agreement. The difference, as the struggle progressed, came to lie far less in creeds than in the moods behind them, and the Puritan mood, solemn under the Almighty's eye, austere, self-centred, unhumorous, unbending, was more formidable and more valuable than their crude apologetics. Its spiritual profundity was as rich a bequest to the future as the saner and sunnier temper of the Cavalier. The difference between the best men of the two parties was a fine one—the exact border-line between the king's prerogative and popular liberties in Church and State; but most great contests in the world's history have been fought on narrow margins. And in practice the narrowness disappeared, and the divergence was glaring. For the Cavalier, with his reasoned doctrine of a central authority based on historical sanctions, had to define that authority as the king, and that king not an ideal monarch, but an actual person then living in Whitehall. The Puritan, who might have dissented reluctantly from the abstract argument, was very ready to differ about Charles.

The conflict which we call the Civil War took place under the shadow which overhung the thought of the first half of the seventeenth century. In that gloom, as we have seen, men were predisposed to define arbitrarily and fly to rigid dogma as to a refuge, for in such a constriction they found peace and strength. Those who maintained the integrity of the spirit, and refused to blindfold their minds, cloistered themselves, or, if they ventured on a life of action, were as a rule Verneys or Falklands, heartsick, distracted, " ingeminating Peace." The effective protagonists were those Cavaliers whose loyalty knew no doubts, and those Puritans who were strong in the confidence of their Lord.

It is the purpose of this book to trace the career of one whose campaigning ground was Scotland, where antagonisms were fiercer and blinder than in the south ; one who did not drug his soul with easy loyalties, but faced the problem of his times unflinchingly, and reached conclusions which had to wait for nearly two hundred years till they could be restated with some hope of acceptance; one who, nevertheless, had that single-hearted gift for deeds which usually belongs to the man whose vigour is not impaired by thought. Montrose has been called by Carlyle the noblest of the Cavaliers, yet clearly he was no ordinary Cavalier; for at the start he was a Covenanter and in rebellion against the king—rebellion of which he never saw reason to repent, and to his dying day he remained a convinced Presbyterian.

BOOK I
PREPARATION

CHAPTER 1

YOUTH

(1612–36)

I know the ways of pleasure, the sweet strains,
The lullings and the relishes of it ;
The propositions of hot blood and brains ;
What mirth and music mean ; what love and wit
Have done these twenty hundred years and more ;
I know the projects of unbridled store :
My stuff is flesh, not brass ; my senses live.

GEORGE HERBERT.

THE Highland Line in the Scottish mainland, though variously determined at times by political needs, has been clearly fixed by nature. The main battlement of the hills runs with a north-easterly slant from Argyll through the Lennox, and then turns northward so as to enclose the wide carselands of Tay. Beyond lie the tangled wildernesses stretching with scarcely a break to Cape Wrath ; east and south are the Lowlands proper—on the east around Don and Dee and the Forfarshire Esks : on the south around Forth and Clyde, and embracing the hills of Tweed and Galloway. Scotland had thus two Borderlands—the famous line of march with England, and the line, historically less notable but geographically clearer, which separated plain from hill, family from clan, and for centuries some semblance of civilization from its stark opposite. The northern Border may be defined in its more essential part as the southern portion of Dumbarton and Lennox, the shire of Stirling, and the haughs of the lower Tay. There for centuries the Lowlander looked out from his towns and castles to the blue mountains where lived his ancestral foes.

Dwelling on a frontier makes a hardy race, and from this northern Border came famous men and sounding deeds. Drummonds, Murrays, Erskines, and Grahams were its chief families, but most notably the last. What the name of Scott was in the glens of Teviot, the name of Graham was in the valleys of Forth and Earn. Since the thirteenth century they had been the unofficial wardens of the northern marches.

The ancient nobility of Scotland does not show well on the page of history. The records of the great earldoms—Angus, Mar, Moray, Buchan—tell too often an unedifying tale of blood and treason, and, after the day of the Good Lord James, St. Bride of Douglas might have wept for her children. But the family of Graham kept tolerably clean hands, and played an honourable part in the national history. Sir John the Graham was the trusted friend of Wallace, and fell gloriously at Falkirk. His successors fought in the later wars of independence, thrice intermarried with the royal blood, and gave Scotland her first primate. In 1451 the family attained the peerage. The third Lord Graham was made Earl of Montrose, when the short-lived Lindsay dukedom lapsed, and the new earl died with his king in the steel circle at Flodden. A successor fell at Pinkie ; another became Chancellor and then Viceroy of Scotland when James the Sixth mounted the English throne. The Viceroy's son, the fourth earl, apart from a famous brawl in the High Street of Edinburgh, lived the quiet life of a county laird till, shortly before his death he, too, was appointed Chancellor. He was a noted sportsman, a great golfer, and a devotee of tobacco. His wife was Lady Margaret Ruthven, a daughter of the tragically-fated house of Gowrie, who bore him six children, and died when her only son was in his sixth year. The family was reasonably rich as the times went, for the home-keeping Earl John had conserved his estate. They owned broad lands in Stirling, Perth, and Angus, and wielded the influence which the chief of a house possesses over its numerous cadets. They had three principal dwellings—the tower of Mugdock in Strathblane; the fine castle of Kincardine in Perthshire, where the Ochils slope to the Earn; and the house of Old Montrose, which Robert Bruce had given to a Graham as the price of Cardross on Clyde.

James Graham, the only son of the fourth earl and Margaret Ruthven, was born in the year 1612, probably in the month of October [1]—according to tradition, in the town of Montrose. The piety of opponents has surrounded his birth with omens; his mother is said, with the hereditary Ruthven love of necromancy, to have consulted witches, and his father to have observed to a neighbour that this child would trouble all Scotland.[2] Like Cromwell, he was the only boy in a family of girls. Of his five sisters, the two eldest were married young—Lilias to Sir John Colquhoun of Luss, and Margaret to a wise man of forty, the first Lord Napier of Merchiston. Their houses were open to him when he tired of catching trout in the little water of Ruthven, or wearing out horseshoes on the Ochils, an occupation to which the extant bills of the Aberuthven blacksmith testify. There was much in the way of adventure to be had at Rossdhu, Lady Lilias's new dwelling, and there the boy may have learned, from practising on the roebuck and wild goats of Lochlomondside, the skill which made him in after years a noted marksman.

At the age of twelve Lord Graham was entrusted to a certain William Forrett, master of arts, to be prepared for the college of Glasgow. Thither he journeyed with a valet, two pages in scarlet, a quantity of linen and plate, a selection from his father's library, and his favourite white pony. He lived in the house of Sir George Elphinstone of Blythswood, the Lord Justice Clerk; it stood near the Townhead, and may have

---

[1] In October 1632 he signed a large number of charters, conveyances, and other documents, which suggests that in that month he entered on his twenty-first year, and began, as in these days often happened, to exercise the rights of a major.

[2] *The Staggering State of Scots Statesmen*, by Sir John Scot of Scotstarvet, 14. Scotstarvet adds that the infant " is said also to have eaten a toad whilst he was a sucking child "—a tale told about the Regent Morton in the previous century.

1624-26 been one of the old manses of the canons of the Cathedral. The avenues to learning must have been gently graded, for he retained a happy memory of those Glasgow days and of Master Forrett, who in later years became the tutor of his sons. He seems to have read in Xenophon and Seneca, and an English translation of Tasso ; but his favourite book, then and long afterwards, was Raleigh's *History of the World*, the splendid folio of the first edition.

In the second year of Glasgow study the old earl died, and Lord Graham posted back to Kincardine, arriving two days before the end. Thither came the whole race of Grahams for the funeral ceremonies, which lasted the better part of three weeks. Prodigious quantities of meat and drink were consumed, for each neighbour and kinsman brought his contribution in kind—partridges and plovers from Lord Stormont, moorfowl from Lawers, a great hind from Glenorchy— the details are still extant, with the values of woodcock and wild geese, capercailzie and ptarmigan, meticulously set down. If such mourning had its drawbacks, at any rate it introduced the new head of the family to those of his name and race. He did not return to Glasgow (though five years later he showed his affection for the place by making a donation to the building of the new college library), and presently was entered at St. Salvator's College, St. Andrews, of which one of his forbears had been a founder. Master Forrett brought his possessions from Glasgow, and the laird of Inchbrakie bestowed these valuable items, the books, in a proper cabinet.

We have ample documents to illustrate his St. Andrews' days.[1] The university, the oldest and then the most famous in Scotland, had among its alumni in the first half of the seventeenth century men so diverse as Montrose and Argyll and Rothes, Mr. Donald Cargill and Sir George Mackenzie. His secretary was a Mr. John Lambie, and Mr. Lambie's accounts reveal the academic life in those days of a gentleman-commoner.

[1] *Mem. of M.*, I., 156–201.

In sport his tastes were catholic. He golfed, like James Melville a century before, and paid five shillings Scots for each golf ball. His rooms at St. Salvator's were hung round with bows, and in his second year he won the silver medal for archery, which to the end of his college course he held against all comers. Argyll, who was some years his senior, had carried off the same trophy. He was an admirable horseman, and he seems to have hunted regularly ; it is recorded in the accounts that after a day with hounds his horse was given a pint of ale. He was fond of hawking, and he went regularly to Cupar races, handing over, according to the excellent statute of 1621, his winnings beyond one hundred marks to the local kirk session for the relief of the poor. His chief friends of his own order seem to have been Wigton, Lindsay of the Byres, Kinghorn, Sinclair, Sutherland, and Colville, and he varied his residence at St. Andrews with visits to his brother-in-law (the hills of Rossdhu, complains his steward, wore the boots off his feet), the cadet gentry of his name, and Cumbernauld, Glamis, Kinnaird, Balcarres, and the other country-houses of his friends. In October 1628 he gave a great house-warming at Kincardine, which lasted for three days. In the March following he visited Edinburgh, where he appeared in gilt spurs and a new sword, and was lent the Chancellor's carriage. The picture which has come down to us of the undergraduate is that of a boy happy and well-dowered, popular with all, eager to squeeze the juice from the many fruits of life. Nor was he above youthful disasters. When his sister Dorothea married Sir James Rollo, there was huge feasting in Edinburgh and Fife, and the young earl returned to college only to fall sick. Two doctors were summoned, who charged enormous fees, and prescribed a rest cure—strict diet, and no amusements but cards and chess. The barber shore away his long brown curls, and " James Pett's dochter " attended to the invalid's food. The régime seems high feeding for what was probably an attack of indigestion—trout, pigeons, capons, " drapped eggs," calf's-foot jelly, grouse (out of season), washed

1626–28 down by " liquorice, whey, possets, aleberry, and claret."

From the accounts preserved we can trace something of his progress in learning.　He began to study Greek, and continued his reading in the Latin classics, his favourites now being Cæsar and Lucan, in his copies of which he made notes.　He can never have been an exact scholar, and it is probable that the wide knowledge of classical literature which he showed later was largely acquired from translations.　For it was the day of great translators, and at St. Andrews he had at his service North's *Plutarch*, Philemon Holland's *Livy* and *Suetonius*, Thomas Heywood's *Sallust*, and the *Tacitus* of Sir Henry Savile and Richard Grenewey.　Nor did he neglect romances, and he made his first essays in poetry.　To this stage may belong the lines ascribed to him by family tradition, in which the ambitious boy writes his own version of a popular contemporary conceit ; but he does not end, like the other versions, on a note of pious quietism :

> " I would be high ; but that the cedar tree
> Is blustered down whilst smaller shrubs go free.
> I would be low ; but that the lowly grass
> Is trampled down by each unworthy ass.
> For to be high, my means they will not doe ;
> And to be low my mind it will not bow.
> O Heavens ! O Fate ! when will you once agree
> To reconcile my means, my mind, and me ? " [1]

He had a touch of the bibliophile, for he had his copies of Buchanan and Barclay's *Argenis* specially bound. To poor authors he was a modest Mæcenas.　The accounts show a payment of fifty-eight shillings Scots to " ane Hungarian poet, who made some verses to my lord."　He subscribed for the travels of the fantastical William Lithgow, and was good-humoured enough to read and advise upon a poem in manuscript by the same

---

[1] The first four lines, in a different form, are included in the *Compleat Angler*, where they are ascribed to Donne or Sir Henry Wotton.　They have also been credited to Henry King and Sir Kenelm Digby.　For the variants see Donne's *Poems* (ed. Grierson), I., 466 ; II., 269.

hand which bore the unsavoury title of " The Gushing *1629* Tears of Godly Sorrow." [1]

In those days the business of life crowded fast upon boyhood. After the university came marriage as the next step in a gentleman's education. Not far from Old Montrose stood the castle of Kinnaird, where Lord Carnegie [2] dwelt with six pretty daughters. There Montrose had often visited, and there he fell in love with Magdalen, the youngest girl. The match was too desirable for opposition either from the Carnegies or from the young lord's guardians, and the children —Montrose was only seventeen—were married in the parish church of Kinnaird on November 10, 1629. In the marriage contract Lord Carnegie bound himself " to entertain and sustain in house with himself, the said noble earl and Mistress Magdalene Carnegie, his promised spouse, during the space of three years next after the said marriage." [3] Accordingly the young couple remained at Kinnaird for a little over three years, until Montrose came of age, and there two of their four sons were born. [4] They were years of quiet study, the leisurely preparation which is all too rare in youth for the necessities of manhood ; and they were the only season of peaceful domestic life which Montrose was fated to enjoy. The famous Jameson portrait, given by Graham of Morphie as a wedding gift to the young countess, shows him in those years of meditation, when he was scribbling his ambitions in his copy of Quintus Curtius. It is a charming head of a boy, with its wide, curious, grey eyes, the arched, almost fantastic, eyebrows, the delicate mobile lips. Life was to crush out the daintiness and gaiety, armour was to take the place of lace collar and silken doublet ; but one thing the face of Montrose never lost—it had always an air of hope, as of one seeking for a far country.

[1] It was published in 1640 at the Edinburgh press of R. Bryson.
[2] David Carnegie, created Lord Carnegie of Kinnaird by James I. in 1616, and Earl of Southesk by Charles I. in 1633.
[3] *Hist. MSS. Comm.*, 2nd Report, 168.
[4] They had five children : John, who died on active service with his father (see p. 232) ; James, the second marquis ; David, who died in infancy ; Robert; and one daughter, Jean. See Balfour Paul, *The Scots Peerage*, VI., 254–255.

In June 1633 Charles came to Scotland to be crowned. Such an occasion was well suited for the introduction of a young nobleman to the court, for in that year Montrose attained his majority, his father-in-law was high in the royal favour, and his brother-in-law Napier was one of the four peers chosen to hold the canopy over the king's head. That the world expected his presence is shown by his friend William Lithgow's recommendation of his merits in the pre-posterous poem, " Scotland's Welcome to her Native Son and Sovereign Lord, King Charles." But when midsummer came he was on a foreign shore. The reason may be traced in the scandal connected with his sister's husband, Sir John Colquhoun, which in the beginning of that year was the talk of Scotland. The laird of Luss, in company with a German necromancer of the name of Carlippis, had fled from his lawful wife, carrying with him his sister-in-law, the little Lady Katherine, who had for a time been Montrose's companion in his Glasgow lodgings. The malefactor was outlawed and excommunicated, returning fourteen years later to be received into grace by Church and State ; the unhappy girl disappears from history. With such a family horror on his mind, Montrose sought the anodyne of new scenes and fresh faces.

We know little of his travels. He started probably in the beginning of 1633, accompanied by his secretary of St. Andrews days, John Lambie, and young Graham of Morphie. According to Burnet, his travelling companion was Basil Fielding, Denbigh's son and Hamilton's brother-in-law, who flung in his fortunes later with the Puritan party. He financed his journey by drawing bills on William Dick of Braid through the latter's " factors " in Paris. The winter of 1633–34 was spent at Angers, where he no doubt was a pupil of the famous school of arms. In the old library at Innerpeffray there is still preserved a French Bible which he bought on his travels, scribbled throughout with mottoes which had caught his fancy, such as " Honor mihi vita potior " and " Non crescunt sine spinis." In Rome he met Lord

Angus, the future Marquis of Douglas, and others of the 1633–36
Scots nobility, and dined with them at the English
College there. He studied all the while—" as much of
the mathematics as is required of a soldier," wrote his
faithful adherent Thomas Saintserf, " but his great
study was to read men and the actions of great men."
It is a phrase which aptly describes the attitude of high
dedication in which the young man passed his youth.
He went gravely about the business of life, and already
had made certain of renown, though careless enough
of happiness. Long afterwards, to foreign observers like
the Cardinal de Retz, he seemed like one of the heroes
of Plutarch, and there was something even in his boyish
outlook of the high Roman manner. It was at this
time that his interests began to move strongly towards
the military art. Europe was in the throes of the
Thirty Years' War, half its gentry were in arms, the
great Gustavus was but two years dead, and in court
and college the talk was all of leaguers and campaigns.

The descriptions of his person and habits at this
date are familiar ; of middle stature and gracefully
built, chestnut hair, a clear fresh colour, a high-bridged
nose, keen grey eyes ; an accomplished horseman, and
an adept at every sport which needed a lithe body and
a cool head.[1] On his manner all accounts are agreed,
and most accounts are critical. He was very stately
and ceremonious, even as a young man, in no way
prepared to forget that he was a great noble, except
among his intimates. To servants and inferiors he
was kindly and thoughtful, to equals and superiors
a little stiff and hard. Burnet says of him that he
was " a young man well learned, who had travelled,
but had taken upon him the port of a hero too
much." [2] " He was exceedingly constant and loving,"
a friend wrote, " to those who did adhere to him,

---

[1] See Saintserf, *Relation of the True Funeralls*, 1661, his dedicatory epistle to
the second Marquis of Montrose appended to the translation of Marmet's
Entertainments of the Course, 1658, and the additions (probably by Saintserf) to
Montrose Redivivus, 1652. A description, different in some respects, is given
by Gordon of Ruthven, 76.
[2] *Hist. of his Own Time* (ed. 1724), I., 30. For Clarendon's judicious
estimate on similar lines see *Hist. of the Rebellion*, XII., 142.

1636 and very affable to such as he knew; though his carriage, which indeed was not ordinary, made him seem proud." One is reminded of Sir Walter Raleigh, whose " næve," says Aubrey, " was that he was damnable proud." Adventurous and imaginative youth is rarely free from the fault ; its sensitive haughtiness is both defensive armour and a defiance ; it believes itself destined for great deeds, and a boyish stateliness is its advertisement to the world of the part it has set itself to play.

Montrose returned home in 1636, in his twenty-fourth year—a figure of intense interest to the Scottish faction-leaders, and of some moment to the king's court. He was altogether too remarkable to please the Marquis of Hamilton, who was the interpreter of Scottish business to the royal ear, and for the first time he came into conflict with one with whom he was to fight many battles. James, third Marquis, and soon to be first Duke, of Hamilton, was not the least futile of the many schemers of his day. A vain, secret being, a diligent tramper of backstairs, and a master of incompetent intrigue, he is throughout his career the sheep in wolf's clothing. He looks at us from the canvas of Vandyck, a martial figure, grasping a baton, but in his face we can detect what Sir Philip Warwick noted—" such a cloud on his countenance that Nature seems to have impressed *aliquid insigne* "—something crack-brained, uncertain and tortuous, a warning that this was no man to ride the ford with. The royal blood in his veins gave him high ambitions, and his fierce old mother, Ann Cunningham of Glencairn, strongly coloured these ambitions, so that he was for ever halting between King and Covenant, dreaming now of winning Scotland for his master, and now of reigning himself in some theocratic millennium. His life was one long pose, but the poses were many and contradictory, and the world came to regard as a knave one who was principally a fool. Burnet, the Hamilton champion, has done his best for his memory, but the verdict of history has been written by Clarendon, who was no ill-wisher to his

house. " His natural darkness and reservation in his
discourse made him to be thought a wise man, and his
having been in command under the King of Sweden,
as his continual discourse of battles and fortifications,
made him to be thought a soldier. And both these
mistakes were the cause that made him to be looked
upon as a worse and a more dangerous man than in
truth he deserved to be." [1]

When Montrose reached London he appeared at
court, and naturally asked Hamilton to be his sponsor,
announcing his wish " to put himself into the king's
service." Hamilton did his best to dissuade him by
representing Charles as the foe of Scottish rights, and
then promptly sought out the king to tell him that
Montrose, by reason of his royal descent, was a danger
to the royal interests, and should be discouraged. The
upshot was that the traveller was received by Charles
with marked coldness. The king spoke a few chilly
words, gave him his hand to kiss, and turned away.
It was enough to discourage the most ardent loyalist,
and the rebuff made it certain that personal affection
for his monarch would play no part in determining the
young man's conduct on his return to his own country.

[1] Clarendon, XI., 262; Burnet, *Mem. of the Hamiltons*; Sir Philip
Warwick, *Memoirs of the Reign of King Charles I.*, 1701. The evidence for
Hamilton's conduct to Montrose is Heylin's *Life of Laud,* and his *Commentary
upon L'Estrange*—a good authority, for Heylin tells us that he had much of
his information from Lord Napier, who, more than any other man, was in
Montrose's confidence.

CHAPTER II

THE STRIFE IN SCOTLAND

(1636–38)

It is bad policy to represent a political system as having no charm but
for robbers and assassins, and no natural origin but in the brains of fools or
madmen, when experience has proved that the great danger of the system
consists in the peculiar fascination it is calculated to exert upon noble and
imaginative spirits.   COLERIDGE, *The Friend.*

TO understand the decision with which Montrose
was confronted on his return, we must examine
the elements of the storm which was now gathering to
a head in the north, and to this end cast our eyes back
over a tangled century of Scottish history.

I

The Reformation in Scotland has been often mis-
conceived as a sudden and universal turning from an
old way of life, and as sudden a birth of Presbytery
fully matured in creed, discipline, and constitution. In
reality it was a slow and halting process, where at the
start only one thing was determined—the breach with
Rome ; and the positive structure suffered long delays
and hesitations. The masculine genius of Knox was
better fitted for action than for constructive thought ;
he knew when to defy and when to yield, for, in F. W.
Maitland's phrase, a shrewd worldly wisdom underlay
his Hebraic frenzies ; but he was nobly inconsistent,
his views passed through baffling permutations, and,
in spite of the acumen of his mind, the fabric he reared
was neither well planned nor soundly masoned. But

on the negative side his work was final. The old building had been razed to the ground, so that in Scotland
there was at no time the remotest chance of a counter-
Reformation. The faults of the pre-Reformation Scottish Church have doubtless been too darkly painted.
In many ways its rule was beneficent, and it was rarely
oppressive, but it had little hold upon the mind of a
people which, in the Middle Ages, was notably careless
about Rome. When Scotland found religion, she found
it in a form which made her historic Church seem the
flat opposite of the commands of Omnipotence. Moreover, the Renaissance came to her mainly through the
Reformation, and, besides the religious impulse, there
were stirrings towards democracy and freedom of
thought which were satisfied by her new creed. Also
there was her ancient dislike of foreign meddling.
Rome became a hissing and a reproach, though men
might differ hotly about what should take its place.
When Knox thundered against the " diabolical,"
" rotten," and " stinking " ritual which had once been
a familiar and comforting part of the people's life,
when he declared that the mass was more odious in
God's sight than murder, he had the assent of the bulk
of the nation. " They think it impossible to lose the
way to Heaven," wrote Sir Anthony Weldon of the
Scots, " if they can but leave Rome behind them."
On the destructive side the work was complete.

We may date the Scottish Reformation from the
first " Band " of December 1557, which denounced the
abuses of Rome and demanded the introduction of the
English Prayer-book ; but it was not till the Edinburgh
Parliament of 1560 that we see the dawnings of Presbytery. Presbyterianism, as we understand the word
to-day, is distinguished by its theory of church government, its ritual, and its creed. In each domain its
special principles were slow to establish themselves.

Take the matter of church government. The cardinal doctrine of the priesthood of all believers was no
doubt there in germ from the beginning, but at first
there was little besides. The Presbyterian belief in the

equality of ministers came neither from Calvin nor
from Knox; Knox's "superintendents," as diocesan
chiefs, were strangely like bishops, and the first reformed
Scottish Church was a limited episcopacy. It was
Andrew Melville who introduced the doctrine of ministerial parity, and made bishops an offence not only
against the Scriptural conception of the Church, but
against the new notion of democracy. " Ye may have
bishops here," the minister of Dunfermline told King
James, " but ye must remember to make us all equal;
make us all bishops, else will ye never content us." [1]
The first Book of Discipline of 1561 accepted a hierarchy;
the second Book of Discipline twenty years later swept
it away. But the battle was not won; its fortunes see-
sawed during the reign of James, according as the
monarch felt his power, for he had reached the firm
conclusion that a hierarchy was a necessary protection
for the throne against the potential anarchy of Presbytery. In 1584 came the Black Acts, and a short-
lived royal triumph; in 1592 the king was forced to
accept a full Presbyterian polity; by 1600 he had won
again, and bishops sat in Parliament. His accession
to the English throne gave him a new authority, the
Melvilles were exiled, and, by means of packed ecclesiastical conventions, which he called General Assemblies,
he had the Act of 1592 repealed and episcopacy established by law. But it was no more than a parliamentary
episcopacy, scarcely affecting the life of the people,
since kirk sessions, presbyteries, and synods continued
to meet, and a staunch Presbyterian could write in
1616 : " At that time I observed little controversy in
religion in the Kirk of Scotland, for though there were
bishops, yet they took little upon them." [2] In the
early years of the reign of Charles I. the familiar Presbyterian régime was the rule in Scotland, with bishops
affixed to it as a meaningless adminicle.

In the same way the General Assembly—that
palladium of the new Church—was slow to come to

[1] Row, *History of the Kirk of Scotland* (Wodrow Society), 418.
[2] Blair's *Life* (Wodrow Society), 12.

maturity. When it was introduced in 1560, it was a copy of the national synod of the French Church. It was not a gathering of ecclesiastics, but representative of the whole religious life of the people, containing both clergy and laity popularly elected. From the start it possessed a representative authority which was lacking in the Scottish Parliament, and it presently became its rival. In the confused early years of James it wielded great powers and interfered much in secular policy—not without reason, for at the time every political problem had a religious connotation. But after the king's victory in 1597 its influence declined, and before the end of his life it became an instrument in his hands. Andrew Melville had stated its claims so high that the civil authority could not choose but oppose them. "Thair is twa Kings and twa Kingdoms in Scotland," he had told his master. "Thair is Chryst Jesus the King and his Kingdom the Kirk, whase subject King James the Saxt is, and of whase Kingdom nocht a King nor a Lord nor a heid but a member. And they whom Chryst has callit and commandit to watch over the Kirk and govern his spirituall Kingdom has sufficient power of him and authoritie sa to do." This might seem a reasonable statement of spiritual independence, were it not that the particular Assembly to which James objected had been called to discuss a question of secular politics.

We see, indeed, through the whole period between 1560 and 1638 the hardening and the magnifying of the claims of the new Church in other than legitimate matters of spiritual doctrine and discipline. It was this arrogance that made James and Charles desire a system which would bring the ecclesiastical leaders directly into the body politic, and so make them responsible to their sovereign ; the trouble was that the real leaders saw that their power lay in being detached from King and Parliament, the chiefs of an *imperium in imperio*. There is no warrant for this separation to be found in Calvin. A preacher at Nîmes took to overthrowing images and altars, declaring that it was a matter of con-

science. " God," said Calvin, " never commands any one
to overthrow idols, except every man in his own house,
and, in public, those whom He has armed with authority.
Let that firebrand show me by what title *he* is lord of
the land where he has been burning things." [1] This was
also the view of Knox, though he spoke at different times
with different voices. He bade his Berwick congregation give due obedience to magistrates, however un-
godly, without tumult or sedition, and " not to pretend
to defend God's truth and religion, ye being subjects,
by violence or sword, but patiently suffering what God
shall please be laid on you for constant confession of
your faith and belief " ; seven years later he was advising the faithful in England that " a prince who erects
idolatry . . . must be adjudged to death." But his
considered view seems to have been that in a Christian
state the last word, even in religion, lay with the civil
authority. " The ordering and reformation of religion
doth especially appertain to the Civil Magistrate. . . .
The King taketh upon him to command the Priests." [2]
The true father of the doctrine of the divine right of
Presbytery was Andrew Melville, and under his influence
the new presbyter became, in the extravagance of his
claims, but too like the old priest. When ministers,
called to account before the Privy Council for preaching
civil sedition, declared that they could only appear
before a Church court, they were laying down a principle,
ancient indeed, but none the less destructive of civil
society. Elizabeth in England saw what was coming,
and in 1590 counselled her brother of Scotland : " Let
me warn you that there is risen, both in your realm
and mine, a sect of perilous consequence, such as would
have no kings but a presbytery, and take our place while
they enjoy our privileges, with a shade of God's Word,
which none is judged to follow right without by their
censure they be so deemed." [3] The comparative impotence of the Scottish Kirk in the early years of

[1] Quoted from the *Corpus Reformatorum* (*xlvi.*, 609; *xlvii.*, 409–11) by
Lang, *John Knox and the Reformation*, 113.
[2] *Works* (ed. Laing), IV., 486, 488, quoted by Lang.
[3] *Letters of Elizabeth and James VI.* (Camden Society), 63.

Charles I. should not blind us to the fact that in the minds of some of its ablest divines there was developing a perilous doctrine of spiritual despotism.

The question of ritual was also unsettled. The first reformers in Scotland had no objection to the use of settled forms in public worship : none of them would have understood the objection of later Covenanting extremists even to the Lord's Prayer. In 1557 the Second Book of Edward VI. had been recommended, and was generally used in churches, till Knox secured its supersession by the Genevan Book of Common Order. The abhorrence of prescript prayer came into Scotland from the English Puritans. Knox disliked many things in the English Prayer-book, for it was his business to magnify differences between the old worship and the new, so as to stimulate Protestant fervour. He objected to kneeling at communion, because he believed—without historical warrant—that the first disciples sat, but he told his Berwick congregation that they might kneel if the magistrates commanded it, and made it clear that it was not retained for " maintenance of any superstition," like " the adoration of the Lord's Supper." Later his attitude stiffened, and he considered that kneeling at the Lord's table, responses, singing of the litany, services on saints' days, and the use of the cross in baptism were " diabolical inventions." But these were personal opinions ; he disliked equally the imposition of hands at the ordination of ministers, which has long been a settled Presbyterian usage. The Scottish Kirk was content to have a liturgy, but it wanted its own Genevan version, and had the authorities been wise they might have found a method of reuniting the worship of both sides of the Tweed by some such eirenicon as John Hales dreamed of—a public form of service embracing only those things upon which all Christians were agreed.[1] Scotland was willing to accept a ritual, but it must not be too suggestive of the Roman, and it must be her own and not an imposition from England. The five Articles of Perth, ratified by Parliament in

[1] See Hales's anonymous *Tract concerning Schisme*. London, 1642.

1621, enjoined kneeling at communion, the private administration of the sacrament to the dying, baptism in private houses, the confirmation of the young, and the keeping of certain church festivals—all English practices and foreign to the Genevan code : Scotland disliked them, but when they became law there was no further trouble, and, since they were not strictly enforced, they might soon have perished from desuetude. James, indeed, seems to have regarded the Perth Articles as the most he was prepared to demand, and to have guaranteed no increase of English innovations.[1] Scotland had, therefore, a legal ritual, which was imperfectly observed [2] because it was out of tune with the spirit of the Kirk, but not overtly opposed, because it had been established by means of her own law. The real strife would begin if the monarch should arbitrarily impose further Anglican forms upon her, for that would call to arms not only the Genevan purism of the Kirk, but the sleepless nationalism of the people.

At the time which we are now considering only one of the Kirk's foundations had been securely built— her dogmatic creed, which was the Calvinism of Knox's Confession of Faith, accepted by the reforming Parliament of 1560. That stood without cavil, though in the interpretation of its articles there was considerable difference of emphasis. For the rest, the Kirk was a nominal episcopacy, but the bishops were impotent, and the discipline was in substance Presbyterian : her General Assembly was in abeyance owing to royal encroachments, but it was an integral and established part of her, so that at the right moment it could be revived ; she had moved far from the moderate Erastianism of Knox, and had come to regard herself as a self-governing commonwealth, wholly independent in all things which by any stretch of language could be called spiritual, and entitled to interfere even in secular politics; her worship was in the main according to the Genevan form, but not universally regular owing to James's ill-obeyed

---

[1] Hacket, *Life of Archbishop Williams*, 64.
[2] Calderwood, VII., 611.

decrees. She was a living organism, the only institution which commanded the loyalty of the majority of the people, and she was a national thing—for she was neither Genevan, Gallican, nor Anglican, but Scottish.[1] Among the mediæval lumber of Parliament, Lords of the Articles and Privy Council, the Kirk stood out like a throbbing power-house among tombs. Whether the land were ill or wisely guided, the chief part of the guiding must be hers.

II

The ecclesiastical structure is much, but we must look closer at that more vital thing, the spirit which inspired it.

The essence of the Reformation was simplification. The great organism of the Catholic Church, with all its intricate accretions of fifteen centuries, was exchanged for a simple revelation—God speaking through His Word to the individual conscience. The Bible was its palladium, but the question presently arose as to how the Bible was to be construed, once the authority of the Church had been rejected. If the individual soul was the basis of the new creed, so apparently must be the individual judgment. That way lay anarchy and anabaptism, and it was necessary, before the Reformed Church could come into being, to establish some canon of interpretation, otherwise Protestantism would go to pieces. The liberal theologians of the seventeenth century held that the Bible was subject to the ultimate tests of conscience and reason. "The authority of man," said Hooker, "is the key which openeth the door of entrance into the knowledge of the Scriptures." To him the Bible was not a cyclopædia of all knowledge

---

[1] It is too often assumed that Scottish Presbytery was a wholesale borrowing from Geneva. As a matter of fact, while professing to follow only the Scriptures, it was highly composite in origin. "There is evidence of the formative influences of Lambert's Hessian constitution, of the Swiss, and especially of the Genevan reformation, of the foreign churches of a'Lasco and Pullain in England, with some slight influence of the Edwardian Church of England itself, and of close study of the new French ecclesiastical polity." See Miss J. G. Macgregor, *The Scottish Presbyterian Polity : a Study of its Origins*, Edinburgh, 1926 ; and F. W. Maitland, *Cambridge Modern History*, II., c. 16.

and all truth. " Admit this and mark, I beseech you,
what follows. God, in delivering Scripture to His church,
should claim to have abrogated amongst them the law
of nature, which is an infallible knowledge imprinted
in the minds of all the children of men, whereby both
general principles for directing of human action are
comprehended, and conclusions derived from them;
upon which conclusions groweth in particular the choice
of good and evil in the daily affairs of this life. Admit
this, and what shall the Scriptures be but a snare and
a torment to weak consciences, filling them with infinite
perplexities, scrupulosities, doubts insoluble, and extreme despairs." [1] This was the creed of Laud and
Chillingworth, of John Hales and Jeremy Taylor, and
from it followed the view that, if human reason were
the ultimate guide to interpretation, diversity of opinion
was inevitable and indeed essential. But such a foundation was too insecure on which to found a militant
church. Calvin took a bolder course. We know that
the Bible is God's Word, not because of the authority
of an historic church, but because of the revelation of
the Holy Spirit. This revelation must be systematized
and made explicit by God's servants, so that the way-
faring man may understand. From this it is a short
step to the foundation of a church which is the direct
medium of the Holy Spirit, and a repository of inspired
interpretation. The second edition of Calvin's *Institutes*
—he was only thirty when it was published—definitely
claims to be the canon of Scripture teaching; from it
alone the reader may learn what Scripture means.
Already the Bible is in a secondary place, and we are
not far from Tertullian's doctrine that the *regula fidei* is
not Scripture but the creed of a church.

Calvin was perhaps the most potent intellectual
force in the world between St. Thomas Aquinas and
Voltaire. Though he rejected in his system whatever
the Bible did not warrant, and not, like Luther, only
what the Bible expressly forbade, he was in many ways

[1] *Ecclesiastical Polity.* See also Laud's controversy with Fisher, Jeremy
Taylor's *Liberty of Prophesying,* and Clarendon on Hales.

nearer to Catholicism than the German reformer.
Like most great men, he was greater than the thing he
created. He was a profounder statesman than his
followers, and far less of a formalist. He could be so
inconsistent as to be accused of heresy : he saw the
dangers into which his church might drift, and declared
that he had no desire to introduce " the tyranny that
one should be bound, under pain of being held a heretic,
to repeat words dictated by some one else " ; a man
to whom Plato was of all philosophers *religiosissimus
et maxime sobrius*, had more affinities with humanism
than is commonly believed. But a law-giver must be
dogmatic, and the founder of a church must narrow his
sympathies. He faced the eternal antinomies of thought
—the reign of law and the freedom of the human spirit—
and provided not a solution but a practical compromise.
He begins with the conceptions of an omnipotent God of
infinite purity and wisdom, of man cradled in iniquity,
and of salvation only through God's grace. The sinner
is foreordained—since God orders all things—alike to
sin and to destruction. It is the omnipotence of God
that he stresses, rather than the fatherhood, for he
faces the problem from another angle than Luther : the
triviality of the created and the majesty of the creator ;
the eternal damnation of man unless lifted out of the pit
by God's election.

These doctrines and this angle of vision were not
new. Origen and Gregory of Nyssa might preach a
milder code, but they were the orthodox creed of the
Fathers of the Church. Men like Tertullian exulted in
contemplating the tortures of the damned. Unbaptized
infants, a span long, would burn for ever in hell, in
spite of the fact that their creation and death were
the direct acts of their Maker. It was the universal
mediæval belief, in spite of the questioning of a Socinus ;
it was the common doctrine of all the Reformers except
Zuinglius. " This is the acme of faith," said Luther,
" to believe that He is merciful who saves so few and
who condemns so many ; that He is just who, at His
own pleasure, has made us necessarily doomed to

damnation. . . . If by any effort of reason I could
conceive how God could be merciful and just who shows
so much anger and iniquity, there would be no need for
faith." [1] On such a view man's reason and man's moral
sense must alike be discarded as temptations of the
devil.

This was the creed of Augustine, stated by him
more passionately and harshly than by any Reformer ;
from him Calvin largely derived his dogmas, but he
took the doctrine and discarded Augustine's church.
Its central principle, the inexorableness of law, the
impossibility of free will, has been held by many secular
thinkers from Spinoza to Mill, who would have rejected
its theological implications. It was the creed of William
the Silent and Coligny and Cromwell, of Donne and
Milton and Bunyan—men in whom both conscience and
intellect were quick. Only by a noble inconsistency
and a tacit forgetfulness could it be a worthy rule of
life, and this was in fact what happened. Calvin was
greater than Calvinism, and the Calvinist was a humaner
and a wiser man than his creed. But with all its per-
versities it put salt and iron into human life. It taught
man his frailty and his greatness, and brought him into
direct communion with Omnipotence. It preached un-
compromisingly the necessity of a choice between two
paths ; in Bunyan's words the mountain gate " has
room for body and soul, but not for body and soul and
sin." It taught a deep consciousness of guilt, and a
profound sense of the greatness of God, so that they
who feared Him were little troubled by earthly fears.
Historically its importance lay in its absoluteness, for
a religion which becomes a " perhaps " will not stand
in the day of battle. It claimed to be truth, the whole
truth, when everything else was a conjecture or a lie.
" In God's matters," said Samuel Rutherford, " there
be not, as in grammar, the positive and comparative
degrees; . . . there are not here true, and more true, and
most true. Truth is an indivisible line which hath no

---

[1] *De servo arbitrio*, I., c. 23. For Calvin's view see *Institutes*, III., c. 21–23,
and his tract *De æterna Dei predestinatione.*

latitude and cannot admit of splitting." [1] It brigaded
men into serried battalions ; the free-lance disappeared ;
Mr. Haughty, in the *Holy War*, who declared " that he
had carried himself bravely, not considering who were
his foes, or what was the cause in which he was engaged,"
was duly hanged by the men of Mansoul. A creed
which was fighting for its life could not afford to be
liberal. " On such subjects, and with common men,
latitude of mind means weakness of mind. There is
but a certain quantity of spiritual force in any man.
Spread it over a broad surface, the stream is shallow
and languid." [2]

Calvin's fame rests rather on the church which he
created than on the creed which he gave it, for he was a
greater legislator than a theologian. It was not in
belief alone that safety was to be found, but in belief
within a church ; in his own words, " Beyond the bosom
of the Church no remission of sins is to be hoped for
nor any salvation "—a strange return to the ecclesi-
asticism which he had rejected. He might have said,
in the words of a recent Vatican decree, " La Chiesa non
è un credo; la Chiesa è un impero, una disciplina."
John Knox considered the Genevan Church " the most
perfect School of Christ that ever was on earth since
the days of the Apostles," and this was the view taken
by his successors of the quasi-Genevan edifice which he
erected in Scotland. It was divine, guided and inspired
by God, and not to be judged by human standards.
It could not err, though that fallible thing the human
conscience might regard certain of its actions as im-
moral. [3] It was a complex legal machine, for it was
not for nothing that Calvin, like Knox and Donne,
was bred to the law, and legal phraseology became the
fashion among the divines. [4] Wielding the most awful
powers and penalties, acting under the most august

---

[1] *The Due Right of Presbyteries*, 1644.
[2] Froude, *Short Studies*, I., 180.
[3] See Calvin's Machiavellianism in his *Commentary on Joshua*.
[4] *Cf.* Donne, *Sermons I.* and *XXXIV.*, and the constant use of law terms like
" surety," " cautioner," " dyvours," " bond," " articles," and " writs " in
Covenanting sermons.

sanctions, inspired by a narrow and absolute creed, cunningly articulated so that the whole nation was embodied under its dominion, the Kirk in Scotland was well able to speak with its adversaries in the gate.

In principle it was a noble democracy. The Kirk made no distinction of class; the ministry was not a hierarchy, but issued from the ranks and could be reduced to them again; an educated laity therefore became the pre-condition of an educated ministry. In Scotland, with its decrepit Parliament, which was no better than a machine for registering the edicts of other people, the pulpit was the sole organ by which public opinion could be expressed. Only by means of it could the masses scrutinize the conduct of their rulers. It gave expression to the very ancient and stubborn sense of liberty in the Scottish people, and to their jealous nationalism. The doctrine of divine right had never come to birth north of the Tweed; the Scots were ready to fight for their king, unless they happened to be fighting against him; the monarchy was a useful institution, and their own, but it was hedged about with no divinity. The Reformation had come about through the strife of sovereign and nobles, and the new clergy, already in opposition to the throne, when they came to quarrel with the nobles were compelled to throw themselves upon the people. Scotland had learned from Knox and George Buchanan [1] that the king derived his power from a contract with the nation, and if that contract were broken might be deposed and slain. The passive obedience which Jeremy Taylor preached in his *Ductor Dubitantium*, and which captured many of the best minds in contemporary England, was a plant which did not flourish on Scottish soil. The claim of Presbytery to authority became yearly more arrogant. There was justice in the complaint of Charles I. : " The nature of presbyterian government is to strike or force the crown from the king's head, for their chief maxim is (and I know it to be true) that all kings

[1] *De Jure Regni apud Scotos*, 1579.

must submit to Christ's kingdom, *of which they are the sole governors*."

But by its very nature the Kirk could not remain a democracy. The theocratic conception is inconsistent with the democratic doctrine of majority rule, for, as Selden pointed out, it is blasphemous to identify the odd man with the Holy Ghost.[1] Buckle has declared that the paradox of seventeenth-century Scotland was that the same people were liberal in politics and illiberal in religion, but the theological narrowness was soon to counteract the political liberalism. Holding the creed they did, the ministers gradually came to rule the nation, and, if it was largely a willing servitude, how could it be otherwise when they possessed such crushing spiritual sanctions ? Calvinism, as interpreted by Knox and Andrew Melville, involves a theocracy, and the plain man, out of fear of hell fire, will surrender his conscience and his judgment as absolutely to his minister as any Catholic to his priest. A Kirk so inspired will find itself claiming powers which only supreme genius could wield without disaster, and the atmosphere will not be favourable for the presence of genius. Its leaders are more likely to be of the type which Lord Morley has drawn in Lilburne—" the men whom all revolutions are apt to engender : intractable, narrow, dogmatic, pragmatic, clever hands at syllogism, liberal in uncharitable imputation and malicious construction, honest in their rather questionable way, animated by a rather pharisaic love of self-applause which is in truth not any more meritorious nor less unsafe than vain love of the world's applause ; in a word, not without sharp insight into theoretic principle, and thinking quite as little of their own ease as of the ease of others, but without a trace of the instinct for government or a grain of practical common sense." [2]

The prime defect of the Kirk was intolerance. It shared this fault with many other communions, but then no communion, save the Church of Rome, claimed its absolute powers. There was no " liberty of cult "

[1] *Table Talk :* Council.   [2] *Cromwell*, 291.

in Elizabeth's Prayer-book, which laid down the only
lawful form of worship; and Nowell, Dean of St.
Paul's—Izaak Walton's "good old man and honest
angler"—could clamour for the death of the Marian
bishops as savagely as any Scots reformer. Laud was
tolerant enough about creeds, but not about church
government. In England only the rare few, like Hales
and Falkland and Chillingworth, attained to that true
toleration which is based not on indifference but on
spiritual humility; [1] only a few asserted with Milton
the right of private judgment—" if a man believe things
only because his pastor says so, . . . though his belief
be true, yet the very truth he holds becomes his heresy." [2]

The question must be viewed in its due historical
perspective. The nursing-ground of intolerance is a
complete dogmatic certainty about the ordering of the
world. To the modern mind, accustomed to think of
man as a clot of vivified dust, set on an inconsiderable
planet which revolves with an infinity of others in the
immensity of space, conscious, too, that human life has
relations through countless æons with lower existences,
and is kin alike to the brutes and to the stars, it is
hard to understand the habit of thought which about
everything can pronounce unhesitatingly that here is
final truth. Such cosmic assurance requires a simple
cosmogony, and this—save in the case of a few advanced thinkers—the seventeenth century possessed.
To it the earth and all therein were made purposely by
God for man, and man's journey heaven-ward or hell-
ward was the essential purpose of creation. It held
that a few thousand years earlier the universe had been
fabricated out of chaos in six calendar days, that all
history antecedent to our era had been a preparation
for the coming of Christ, and that, the supreme sacrifice

---

[1] " He therefore exceedingly detested the tyranny of the Church of Rome
more for their imposing uncharitably upon the consciences of other men, than
for the errors in their own opinions; and would often say that he would re-
nounce the religion of the Church of England to-morrow if it obliged him to
believe that any other Christians should be damned; and that nobody would
conclude another man to be damned who did not wish him so." Clarendon on
Hales. *Life* (ed. 1759), 27–28.

[2] *Areopagitica.*

having been accomplished, at any moment the skies might open, and the trumpets sound, and the short story of the earth be closed. There were mysteries indeed, stupendous mysteries, but, if their content was unplumbed, their limits could be exactly defined. Such a cosmos was both intimate and simple, made according to man's scale and for his uses; it was without blurred lines or shadowy corners, and the mind which accepted it was ready to pronounce upon its problems as upon matters of ascertained fact.

If the nature of the popular cosmogony predisposed men to dogma, so did the quality of the revelation that illumined it. That revelation was absolute; its acceptance gave eternal life, its neglect eternal torment. Toleration is a high virtue, when it springs from humility and is regarded as in itself a religious act; but it is important to remember that in certain mental states it may be a vice, a synonym for spiritual apathy and moral sloth. "What," St. Augustine asked, "can be more deadly to the soul than the liberty of error?" The doctrine of exclusive salvation, honestly held, involves intolerance, and finds its logical consequence in persecution. If a man believes that his heart is desperately wicked, that he is doomed to eternal fires but for the interposition of God's grace, and that to walk in grace it is necessary to observe literally the precepts of the Scriptures without any attempt to rethink them in the light of new conditions—nay, that such an attempt is in God's eye the unpardonable sin—tolerance must be only another name for lukewarmness, and reason only the temptation of the devil. If he is right, all those who differ from him must be wrong, and it is his duty to enforce his faith with fire and sword. What suffering that man can inflict is comparable to the eternal misery of those who embrace false doctrine? This was the creed alike of St. Augustine and St. Thomas Aquinas; it was an integral part of seventeenth-century Protestant theology: in a milder form it will be found in more than one Papal bull of the nineteenth century. Even a liberal thinker like Richard Baxter pronounced

toleration to be " soul murder," and in that era only
Cromwell in practice, and men like Harrington, Milton,
Jeremy Taylor, and Chillingworth in their writings,
propounded a gentler doctrine. It is unhappily true
that in such an age the best men, in whom religion is
a living fire, are apt to be the narrowest. " The only
true spirit of tolerance," Coleridge has written, " consists in conscientious toleration of each other's intolerance. Whatever pretends to be more than this, is
either the unthinking cant of fashion or the soul-palsy-
ing narcotic of moral and religious indifference." [1] But
before such a mood can be attained, there must be a
critical breaking-down of the adamantine bulwarks of
dogma. Charles James Fox was right when he said
that " the only foundation for toleration is a degree of
scepticism." [2] Only the rare few could conceive of a
tolerance which was not indifferentism, but a supreme
religious duty.[3]

The Scottish Kirk held the current doctrine in its
extremest form, and for a manual of practice had
recourse to the Bible. She interpreted it arbitrarily
and literally, forgetting Donne's pregnant saying that
" sentences in Scripture, like hairs in horses' tails,
concur in one root of beauty and strength, but, being
plucked out one by one, serve only for springes and
snares." Finding little warrant for force in the New
Testament, her divines had recourse to the Old Testament, where they discovered encouraging precedents in
the doings of Elijah and Hezekiah and Josiah. This
constant resort to the Mosaic dispensation encouraged
a stiff and autocratic temper. Cromwell's famous
appeal—" We should be pitiful . . . and tender towards all though of different judgments. . . . Love all,
tender all, cherish and countenance all, in all things

---

[1] *The Friend*, I., 123.   [2] Rogers, *Recollections*, 49.
[3] The authorities on this point will be found in Lecky, *Rationalism in
Europe*, c. 4. See also Harrington, *Political Aphorisms*, and *A System of
Politics*, in his *Works* (ed. Toland, 1700); Milton, *Areopagitica*; Jeremy Taylor,
Liberty of Prophesying; Chillingworth, *The Religion of Protestants*; Southey
on Bogue's *History of Dissenters* in *Quarterly Review*, October 1813; Coleridge,
Notes, Theological, Political, and Miscellaneous, 319–321; Morley, *Cromwell*,
163–168.

that are good. . . . And if the poorest Christian, the
most mistaken Christian, shall desire to live peaceably
and quietly under you—I say, if any shall desire but to
lead a life of godliness and honesty, let him be protected "—would have sounded in their ears like a fearful
blasphemy. Their church was a theocracy, and that
involves both a claim to infallibility and a meticulous
physical discipline applied in the spiritual sphere.
They held the keys of heaven and hell, and had power
to deliver the erring over to Satan and to anticipate by
exemplary punishment in this world the torments of
the next.[1]

With such a creed there could be no real delimita-
tion between the spiritual and the secular, between
Church and State. The right of the Kirk to dominate
personal and family life was soon extended to the duty
of interference with civil government. Indeed, the rejection of toleration and the belief in uniformity led
inevitably to a usurpation of civil power. The Kirk
believed, as Catholicism believed, in a single church, a
complete and exclusive system to which a single separ-
atist was anathema. In her zeal for uniformity she in
no way differed from Laud, though she preferred another pattern. The secularization of politics did not
fully come about till the toleration of religious variety
had first been established. When the Kirk usurped
powers which seem to us in no way to belong to her
province, she was following the prevailing tendency of
the age. She was true to the mediæval idea of one
church, one rule. Against the universal claim of Rome
it was necessary to establish a counter-universalism.
Presbytery professed, as Rome professed, to be based
upon *jus divinum*, and therefore there could be no limits
to its sovereignty. With Catholic and Anglican it
waged truceless war, but it drew, like them, from the
Middle Ages, and accepted the same kind of dogmatic
sanction. High Cavalier and high Covenanter talked
the same language, though with different applications,
and divine right was the watchword of both. To each

[1] See the notes to Buckle, *History of Civilization*, c. xix.

the man who looked upon the world with a cool secular
eye and talked sober reason was worse than their
avowed opponents; he was a heretic in the fundamentals, the ultimate blasphemer.

The Scottish ministers have fared ill with later
historians, except in the copious literature of their own
communion. The wisest and greatest, Robert Leighton,
belongs to a later date, and soon deserted the manse of
Newbattle. They have been represented as violent and
illiterate peasants, mob-orators rather than divines.
As a matter of fact, they sprang either from the landed
gentry and the clergy, or from well-to-do burgher
families. Robert Traill had for his father a gentleman
of the Privy Chamber to Prince Henry; Robert Blair
was the son of an Ayrshire laird, and his mother was a
Mure of Rowallan; James Durham was an Angus
proprietor; Robert Baillie was of the Baillies of Lamington; Robert Douglas was a son of that George
Douglas who helped Queen Mary to escape from Loch-
leven; James Guthrie was a son of Guthrie of that ilk.
Almost all had received a sound education in the
humanities as well as in theology, and some, like Robert
Boyd and Alexander Henderson, Hugh Binning and
Samuel Rutherford, were notable scholars. Among
them, too, were many types of mind and temperament,
from the political shrewdness of Robert Baillie and the
quaint humanity of William Guthrie of Fenwick to the
fanatic hardness of Nevoy and the oriental lusciousness
of Samuel Rutherford.[1]

They preached a creed which, in most of its details,
is now forgotten, and the language of which is fantastic
or ridiculous to our ears. They laid down as the
necessary and universal progress towards salvation a
rigid curriculum of experiences—" exercise," " law-
work," " discovery of interest," " damps," " challenge,"
" outgate," " assurance." Well might a later seventeenth-century Scotsman exclaim: " I doubt it hath
occasioned much unnecessary disquiet to some holy per-

---

[1] *The Commissions of the General Assemblies* (S.H.S.), III., Introd.;
Howie, *Scots Worthies.*

sons that they have not found such a regular and orderly transaction in their souls as they have seen described in the books. . . . God hath several ways of dealing with the souls of men, and it sufficeth if the work be accomplished whatever the methods have been." [1] But behind their narrowness and their legal jargon we can see in many the true exaltation of the saint. Among the crudities and absurdities of their sermons and biographies there are passages of apostolic power, visions such as George Fox records in his journal, which led them to an ecstasy of praise, moments of deep tenderness towards the souls of their flocks. They must be judged by their work, and beyond doubt they gave to the Scottish people a moral seriousness, a conception of the deeper issues of life, and an intellectual *ascesis*, gifts which may well atone for their many infirmities.

Yet there is much to be atoned for, and the immediate result of their predominance was not less disastrous than beneficent. " Deliver me, O Lord," was the cry of Archbishop Leighton, " from the errors of wise men, yea, and of good men." [2] They perverted the Gospel into a thing of subtle legal conundrums ; they made morality difficult by destroying its rational basis ; they took the colour out of life for their people by condemning the innocencies of the world with a more than monastic austerity ; they inflamed the superstitions of the country by peopling it with a fanciful pandemonium. If any one has the patience to labour through a dozen volumes of their sermons, he will be aghast at the childishness and irreverence of much of their teaching. Like an African witch-doctor, they " smelled out " offenders, and they were the principal upstay of witch-burning. Miracles and portents adorned their path, and natural laws were suspended to point their lessons. They magnified their office till they hedged themselves round with a false divinity. The clouds of their dogmatic terrors darkened the world for

---

[1] Scougal, *The Life of God in the Soul of Man,* 65.
[2] *Commentary upon the First Epistle of St. Peter.*

their hearers, and condemned weak spirits to religious
mania. Their neurotic supernaturalism, which saw
judgments and signs in the common incidents of life,
weakened in the people the power of rational thought.[1]
If they gave manhood and liberty to Scotland, they
did much to sap the first and shackle the second.
Condemning natural pleasures and affections, they
drew a dark pall over the old merry Scottish world,
the world of the ballads and the songs, of frolics and
mummings and " blithesome bridals," and, since human
nature will not be denied, drove men and women to
sinister and perverted outlets. In a word, they established over the whole of human life, alike in its public
duties and in its most intimate private affairs, a harsh
and senseless tyranny, and against them, as the delegates of heaven, there was no appeal. Tougher spirits
might emerge unscathed and even fortified, but the frail
were warped and demented. Yet it was the strongest
thing in Scotland, and presently in all the Lowlands it
had made good its sway over every class of the people;
ruere in servitium consules, patres, eques.

III

To balance the claims of the Kirk there was no
strong apparatus of secular government. The so-called
Parliament, with its three estates of clergy, tenants-in-
chief, and burgesses, delegated its power in the Lords
of the Articles, who had the sole right to initiate business,
and the selection of whom was controlled by the king.
It was neither representative nor free. " The Crown
manipulated elections, determined the composition of
the committee through which all business must pass
before it reached the throne, sternly limited the time
allowed for the discussion of the committee's report,
forced a long series of measures through the House at
a single sitting, and cajoled or threatened opponents." [2]

---

[1] " Away with such rash and bold conceits : the love of God either to
causes or persons is not to be measured by these external and outward
accidents." Spottiswoode, III., 183.
[2] Rait, *The Parliaments of Scotland*, 62.

The Privy Council, the equivalent of the Cabinet, was almost identical with the Lords of the Articles. The Convention of Royal Burghs was a kind of minor parliament charged with burgh concerns, and its existence did much to distract the interest of burgess members from national affairs. In all this mechanism there was no authority which could act as a makeweight to the growing popular authority of the Kirk, guard the liberties of Scotland against royal encroachment, or, on behalf of the nation at large, control the traditional high-handedness of the nobility.

The Scottish nobles from the fourteenth to the sixteenth century were probably the most turbulent, rapacious, and ignorant in Europe. Resolute champions of indefensible privileges, they resisted all the reforming efforts of their kings, and were the death of more than one sovereign. They had not even the merit of patriotism, for often they were in arms against their own land, and Scottish history is stored with ugly tales of treason. Their prime foes had been the king and the church, and they had always cast longing eyes at the fat abbeys and the rich glebes of their clerical rivals. The Reformation gave them their chance. Two-thirds of the church plunder fell into their hands, and their Protestantism was mainly determined by self-interest. Knox complained, not without reason, that in all the Lords of the Congregation there was not one righteous man. A few became dogmatic enthusiasts, but the majority cared as little for the difference between priest and minister as for the Ten Commandments. Nor were they, like many of the great families of England—like Pembroke in Wiltshire, or Stanley in Lancashire, or Beaufort on the West Marches—magnates who performed useful duties of local administration. Their mediæval satrapies were antagonistic to the first principles of a modern state. Knox had struggled to win from the old church property reasonable endowments for his new Kirk, but the tithes and the lands went to the nobles and barons, who were determined not to disgorge. Their opposition to the Anglicanism of Charles was largely due to the fact that

it involved sooner or later a redivision of ecclesiastical
plunder; they would vehemently oppose any church
except one which they could starve.

At first sight it would seem that there could be little
in common between a proud Kirk, with a great popular
following, laying down the austerest rule of life, and a
nobility which was irreligious and oppressive, which
clung to wealth which Knox had destined for the Kirk,
and of which the Kirk was sorely in need. Indeed it
was only the blundering of the king that prevented a
breach between the two, with the clergy for once on the
royal side. The tithe had become a crying scandal, for
the feudal lords, to whom it had passed, could levy it
in kind much as they pleased and when they pleased,
so that the tenant could not get in his harvest till the
lord had taken his toll. In 1625 Charles undertook the
work of reform. He removed the judges from the
Privy Council, that they might have time for their
proper business of the Court of Session, and by the Act
of Revocation of 1625 he attempted to recover as much
as he could of the old church property for national uses.
In the most modern way he appointed a royal commission
to work out the details; the teinds were to afford a living
wage to the ministers, and the holders of church lands
were in future to pay rent to the Crown. Mr. Gardiner
calls the measure the "one successful act of Charles's
reign," and considers that it "weakened the power of
the nobility, and strengthened the prerogative in the
only way in which the prerogative deserved to be
strengthened . . . by the popularity it gained through
carrying into effect a wise and beneficent reform."[1]
But no popularity followed. Perhaps the money-
getting motive was too clear in the reform, for it was
instituted after the English Parliament had refused to
grant adequate supplies; perhaps the royal interference
with property suggested further revolutionary designs.
At any rate the king got no gratitude from the Kirk,
and he incurred the deadly displeasure of the aristocracy.
The way was prepared for an alliance between the two

[1] *Hist. of England*, VII., 279–280.

contraries, who were agreed only in their stubborn conservatism—nobles desperately intent on holding what their fathers had won, and churchmen desperately in earnest about their spiritual prerogatives. It was a very pretty powder-magazine for the inevitable spark.

The time was one of deep poverty for the common people. The bonnet-lairds and the tacksmen, the labourers and shepherds, the petty craftsmen in the villages, even the burghers in the little towns, lived very near the edge of destitution. The rudimentary and wasteful system of agriculture, with its sodden in-fields and its rank out-fields, its wretched grain, its shallow ploughing, placed the farmers at the mercy of an indifferent climate and a poor soil—for the richer valley bottoms were uncultivable from lack of drainage. Stock was in no better case, for the cattle were stunted and perpetually lean, and the sheep were moving masses of tar and vermin. At the close of each winter the spectre of starvation came very near to man and beast. Idyllic pictures have been drawn of the Covenanting peasant as a stalwart fellow in good homespun clothes and blue bonnet, and of his house as a snug dwelling like an illustration to *The Cotter's Saturday Night*. The truth seems to be that the physique of most was early ruined by poor feeding and incessant toil, that they had small regard for bodily cleanliness, that their clothes were coarse at the best and generally ragged, and that their dwellings resembled a Connemara cabin. Recurrent plagues carried off their thousands, and foul habits and a diet of thin brose and bannocks weakened the survivors. Nasty, brutish, and short was the life of the seventeenth-century Lowlander. Education did something to counterbalance the economic defects, but it is easy to exaggerate the extent of Scottish education at this era. Kirkton, indeed, records that before 1660 " every village had a school, every family almost had a Bible, yea, in most of the country all the children of age could read the Scriptures " [1]; but Kirkton was *laudator temporis acti*, and his testimony

[1] *History of the Church of Scotland*, 64.

is not borne out by parish and burgh records. Knox's great scheme remained largely an unrealized ideal; the report of the commission of 1627 reveals very many parishes in the Lowlands and the Borders without school or schoolmaster; and the remedial Acts of 1633 and 1643 were for the most part a dead letter. The fact that the new religion was based on private Bible-reading was indeed an inducement to literacy, but in the very places where theological interest was keenest we find a surprising proportion unable to write, while Wodrow was told by his father that in his day " the generality by far in the country . . . could not read." [1]

There was no middle-class to act as a force of social persistence and a sober nursery of new civic ideas, like the great bourgeoisie which was the strength of English Puritanism. Scottish commerce was a petty thing; her *noblesse de robe* were reactionary manipulators of a reactionary law; her burghers and bonnet-lairds were too near the peasant; she had no parallel class to the yeomanry and merchantry of England. If strife came it would be conducted between king, nobles, and Kirk, with the bulk of the people obedient under the spiritual narcotics of the last. There was little hope for that fruitful political dispute which is the basis of a free polity, but for wild and barren explosions there was an uncomfortable amount of powder.

IV

The spark came from a blundering king. Charles had been born in Scotland, and, according to Clarendon, was " always an immoderate lover of the Scottish nation "; but he had not his father's knowledge of the national temperament, and he had for his advisers on Scottish affairs men altogether out of touch with the people. When he came to Scotland in the summer of

---

[1] *Report of Parishes in 1627* (Maitland Club); Wodrow, *Life of Professor Wodrow*. At Dalmellington, in Ayrshire, a Covenanting stronghold, the Solemn League and Covenant was subscribed by 222 people, 179 of whom could not write.

1633 to be crowned, he had already estranged the
nobility by his perfectly just and reasonable treatment
of the tithes question. The visit revealed the existence
of an opposition even in the packed Scots Parliament,
and, since Laud was in his company, the coronation
ceremonies roused suspicion in Presbyterian breasts.
In August of that year Laud became Archbishop of
Canterbury, and entered upon the policy of reclaim-
ing Scottish barbarism to his ideal of ecclesiastical
decency. A year later the Court of High Commission
was established by royal warrant, and the number of
bishops in the Privy Council was increased to seven.
In January 1635 Archbishop Spottiswoode was made
Chancellor in succession to Kinnoull, the first time since
the Reformation that the office had been given to a
churchman.

The Scottish hierarchy of the time has been portrayed, perhaps, in darker colours than it deserves.
Spottiswoode himself, and men like Forbes and Maxwell,
Sydserf and Wedderburn, were liberal in doctrine and
exemplary in private life, and saintliness was the prerogative of neither party. But the bishops for good
and ill were out of tune with their countrymen ; they
represented a theological creed which was in advance
of their age, and an ecclesiastical creed which lagged
behind it, for they did not appreciate the passion for
spiritual autonomy which had become part of the
national mood.[1] They were impossible as mediators,
since the best of them talked a language unintelligible
to that age, and the worst of them shared in Laud's
perilous hieratic dreams. They might be intellectually
tolerant like their leader, but they were ecclesiastically
dogmatic. Their sudden rise to political power roused
the extreme suspicion of the Kirk, it offended the pride
of the nobles, and it stirred the opposition of even the
staunchest moderates. " That Churchmen have com-
petency," wrote Montrose's guardian and brother-in-
law, Lord Napier, " is agreeable to the law of God and

[1] For what can be said in defence of the bishops see W. L. Mathieson,
Politics and Religion in Scotland, I., c. x.

man; but to invest them into great estates and principal offices of the State, is neither convenient for the Church, for the King, nor for the State. . . . Histories witness what troubles have been raised to kings, what tragedies amongst subjects, in all places where Churchmen were great. Our reformed Churches, having reduced religion to the ancient primitive truth and simplicity, ought to beware that corruption enter not into their Church in the same gate." [1]

In the year 1635 the royal blunders multiplied. A temperate protest by Lord Balmerino against certain recent acts came into Spottiswoode's hand, and thence to the king's. It was construed as high treason, and in March 1635 the writer was put on trial, convicted by a majority of one, and condemned to death. He was presently pardoned, but the affair deeply impressed his countrymen; it was the bishops' doing, and it seemed as if the old liberty was now dead in the land. A crisis had been reached when a man like Drummond of Hawthornden, no lover of the Kirk, was forced into vigorous remonstrance, and could advise his sovereign to study Buchanan's *De Jure Regni apud Scotos*.[2] In May a royal warrant authorized a new book of canons to regulate the government of the Church of Scotland, and the book was published in January 1636, prepared by a committee of the Scottish bishops and revised by Laud and Juxon. It re-enacted in substance the Articles of Perth, which had become a dead letter, prohibited extempore prayer, allowed confession, and claimed for the king supreme authority in ecclesiastical causes. More ominous still, it promised a service book, or liturgy, and threatened in advance excommunication against all those who should not accept it. It would be hard to conceive of a more foolish provocation. The book had no authority except the royal *ipse dixit*, and yet many of the canons dealt with civil as well as with ecclesiastical law.[3] It challenged not only religious but political liberty.

---

[1] Napier, I., 104.
[2] Masson, *Drummond of Hawthornden*, 237-241.
[3] Row, 393.

The promised liturgy appeared in an atmosphere *1636-37* already superheated. In November 1636 Charles wrote to the Privy Council, ordering that the new " Book of Public Service " be used, and that each parish provide itself with two copies before the following Easter. But it was not till 1637 that the book was published. It is probable that the Scottish bishops had little to do with it, for even the most sacerdotal among them hesitated before this monstrous innovation.[1] Laud and his English colleagues took the English Prayer-book, made a few changes which the Scottish hierarchy had suggested, and made many others in the direction of a more exacting ritual. " The book, with the canons which preceded it, had no ecclesiastical sanction, either of all the bishops, or of a General Assembly. The imposition was an act of sheer royal autocratic papacy ; the book, being English, insulted Scottish national sentiment ; the changes from the English version were deemed to imply a nearer approach to Rome. Protestantism was in danger. The landowners suspected that Charles meant to recover some of their old ecclesiastical estates for the rebuilding of cathedrals and cleaning of churches ; and thus, from the ' rascal multitude ' upwards, through every rank and condition of his subjects, he gave intolerable offence, and caused extreme apprehension. He lost three kingdoms and his head, not for a mass, but for a surplice." [2]

The tumult was instant and universal. The devout women of Edinburgh rose in their wrath, and the first attempt to read the new service-book in St. Giles's church was the signal for a riot.[3] The flame ran fast over Scotland, for the offence was grievous ; to endure such interference with private worship was to stultify the whole Reformation principle, and to sit quiet under flagrant illegality was to sacrifice the ancient liberties

---

[1] See for a full study of its antecedents Sprott, *Scottish Liturgies*, Introd., and Hill Burton, *History of Scotland*, c. lxviii.

[2] Lang, III., 25–26.

[3] See the account in Rothes, *Relation of the Affairs of the Kirk*, App. ; Gordon of Rothiemay, I., 7–11 ; Wariston, *Diary*, I., 265 ; and for the general situation, Baillie, I., and Balfour, II. The king's statement of his case will be found in the *Large Declaration*, 1639.

1637 of the realm. Every post to England carried a supplication or remonstrance to His Majesty.[1] The Privy
Council, divided between the lay lords and the bishops,
was helpless; it suggested deputations which Charles
would not receive, and meantime it was being flooded
with petitions from every part of the Lowlands. The
king's proclamations only made matters worse, and by
October public meetings were being held everywhere,
bishops were being rabbled, and the pacific Mr. Robert
Baillie was writing : " No man may speak anything in
public for the king's part, except he would have himself
marked for a sacrifice to be killed one day. I think
our people possessed with a bloody devill." [2]

On 15th November an important step was taken.
With the sanction of the Lord Advocate, Sir Thomas
Hope, the malcontents organized themselves into a
body of commissioners—four committees of nobles,
lairds, burgesses, and ministers, henceforth to be known
as the Tables. It was in substance a provisional government, and behind it was all Scotland, except the
remoter Highlands and Aberdeen. In opposition to
the king stood the solid phalanx of the Kirk, led by
Alexander Henderson of Leuchars, the ablest statesman
among the ministers; the burgesses were unanimous
on the same side, as were also the lawyers; the lairds
were represented by such names as Stirling of Keir,
Hume of Wedderburn, Douglas of Cavers, Fraser of
Philorth, Mure of Rowallan, and Agnew of Lochnaw;
among the nobles were Sutherland, Cromartie, Ruthven,
Eglinton, Wemyss, Lothian, Home, Loudoun, Lindsay,
and Yester. The peerage and the lesser baronage of
Scotland were united as they had never been before
and were never to be again. Even the Lords of the
Council were inclining to the malcontents, and the
bishops had withdrawn from that uneasy assembly.

At the meeting of petitioners on 15th November
the young Montrose was present. In September leading

---

[1] Montrose signed the document entitled " Scotland's Supplication and
Complaint against the Book of Common Prayer, the Book of Canons, and
the Prelates," of October 18, 1637. See Dr. Hay Fleming's paper in *Proceedings
of the Society of Antiquaries of Scotland*, LX., 314-383.   [2] I., 23.

ministers had been appointed to secure adherents for the opposition, and Mr. Robert Murray of Methven was nominated for Perth and Stirling. Montrose at a later date named Mr. Murray as " an instrument of bringing me to their cause." [1] Along with Rothes, Loudoun, and Lindsay of the Byres he was appointed to the Table of the nobility.

The unrest could have only one consequence. Traquair, the Treasurer, got no comfort at the royal court ; indeed, in a proclamation which he brought back in February 1638, Charles took complete responsibility for the new liturgy, and required all petitioners to disperse on pain of treason and not to reassemble without the Council's consent. On February 22, 1638, when that proclamation was made in Edinburgh, a public protestation was read by Wariston, and one act of war was met by another. On that day Montrose was among the protesting leaders, mounted in boyish enthusiasm on a barrel, so that the prophetic soul of Rothes was moved to observe : " James, you will never be at rest till you are lifted up above the rest in three fathoms of a rope." [2] The Tables decided to revive the Covenant of 1581 against popery, and to add their own grievances, and Alexander Henderson and Wariston drafted the new version. It was an old device, for when the Scottish nobles chose to walk in the path of rebellion it had been their fashion to enter into " ane band." This was, however, to be a legal act, and to make the Almighty a party; in Wariston's word it was " the glorious marriage day of the Kingdom with God." [3] The first part repeated the Covenant of 1581 against Rome ; the second part recited the acts of Parliament passed since the Reformation in favour of the Kirk ; the third part pledged its signatories to defend their religion against all innovations not sanctioned by Parliament and Assembly, and to " stand to the defence of our dread sovereign the King's Majesty, his person and authority, in the defence and preservation of the foresaid true religion, liberties, and laws of

[1] Napier, I., 136.   [2] Gordon of Rothiemay, I., 33.   [3] *Diary*, I., 322.

1638 this Kingdom." It was a candid and straightforward document, temperately expressed and accurately directed to the grievances which it was designed to remedy. The claim was to both spiritual and civil freedom, and the formidable sanction behind it was at once ecclesiastical, feudal, and democratic. On the last day of February it was read in Greyfriars' church in Edinburgh, with its solemn appeal that "religion and righteousness may flourish in the land, to the glory of God, the honour of the King, and the peace and comfort of us all." On that and succeeding days it was signed amid scenes of deep popular emotion, and in subsequent months copies were carried far and wide through the land, and even overseas to Scots serving in foreign wars.

On the first day Montrose subscribed his name. According to Baillie he was brought in " by the canniness of Rothes." John Leslie, sixth Earl of Rothes, was an adroit diplomat, and had an old grievance against the Act of Revocation. He was disliked by Charles, and probably returned the dislike. He was little of a precisian in character, for he is described by Clarendon as "very free and amorous, and unrestrained in his discourse by any scruples of religion, which he only put on when the parts he had to act required it, and then no man could appear more conscientiously transported"; nor was he extreme in politics, and Clarendon believed that but for his early death he would have gone over to the king's side.[1] Doubtless Rothes desired to strengthen the movement by the adhesion of the representative of an historic house, who was still an attractive mystery to his countrymen; doubtless Montrose was not insensitive to the persuasive charm of one who was much his elder and was the most generally popular man in Scotland. Talks with Rothes and Mr. Robert Murray, and the fact that the Fife nobles with whom he had spent much of his time during his St. Andrews years were among the promoters of the new Covenant, may have predisposed him to the popular side.

[1] *History*, I., 171; III., 38; IV., 23, 250. *Cal. S. P., Dom.* (1641–43), 105–107.

But indeed Montrose required no " canniness " of *1638*
noble or cleric to help him to a decision. There were
those among the protagonists of the Covenant who may
have been antipathetic to him—Loudoun, his colleague
on the Tables, who had been a Campbell of Lawers and
was trusted by no man ; Wariston, that strange youth
of twenty-seven, a devotee in a lawyer's gown, who
would forget time in prayer and be on his knees for
fourteen hours at a stretch, and often, as his nephew
Burnet tells us, slept but three hours in the twenty-four.
But all Scotland was in the bond, except a few Catholic
nobles and Aberdeen doctors, and in it were the companions of his youth, and Napier, his most trusted
counsellor. The Covenant was legal, pronounced to be
so by the Lord Advocate and by the bulk of the judges,
and Montrose from his youth was a lover of legality.[1]
Further, the main issues were not yet confused. There
was no attack upon the king's authority ; indeed, the
royal sovereignty was vehemently asserted. The bishops
were unpopular, but there was as yet little of that morbid
hatred of the very name of episcopacy which followed
later, when dislike of the thing done became detestation
of the suspected means. In 1637 Baillie could still
write: " Bishops I love ; "[2] and there must have been
many in Edinburgh to relish the dialectical triumph of
the Episcopalian vintner over the Presbyterian shoe-
maker, recorded by James Howell in his letter to Lord
Clifford.[3] The true point of conflict was far greater
than any squabble about niceties of church government.
It was the right of Scotland to her ancestral liberties,
the confinement of prerogative within its legal limits,
the keeping of churchmen out of civil offices. To a
young man nourished on Plutarch and Thucydides and
familiar with the current political thought of Europe,
to one who at no time in his life could tolerate the
ecclesiastic in politics, to a Scotsman who had his full
share of the national pride, the cause of the Covenant

---

[1] Lord President Inglis has also defended its legality in his article, "Montrose
and the Covenant of 1638," in *Blackwood's Magazine*, November 1887.
[2] L., 2.   [3] *Epistolæ Ho-elianæ*, I. 36.

was the cause of the patriot, the philosopher, and the well-wisher to the king.

That February noon in Greyfriars was one of the most momentous in our history, for it was the first step in a conflict which did not end till the December day, half a century later, when a king of England became an exile. To Charles it may at first have seemed but another spasm of recalcitrance which would be presently forgotten—a matter less important than the impending judgment of the Exchequer Chamber in the ship-money case. But when the news out of Scotland came, after many days, to the ears of a certain middle-aged Huntingdonshire grazier, who had lately removed to Ely, it may have caused deeper reflections. For this grazier, in the intervals of examining the work of God in his soul, had a quick eye for public portents, and he had won so much prestige as the defender of the rights of the fen commoners, that he might hope to be sent to Westminster, should the king call another Parliament.

CHAPTER III

THE FIRST COVENANT WARS

(1638–39)

As for discontentments, they are in the politic body like to humours
in the natural, which are apt to gather a preternatural heat and to inflame.
And let no prince measure the danger of them by this, whether they be just
or unjust; for that were to imagine people to be too reasonable who do often
spurn at their own good: nor yet by this, whether the griefs whereupon they
rise be in fact great or small; for they are the most dangerous discontentments
where the fear is greater than the feeling. *Dolendi modus, timendi non item.*
BACON.

In 1639 even the most obscure woods began to be penetrated with
flashes. *Memoirs of Colonel Hutchinson.*

I

THE National Covenant was based upon sound *1638*
constitutional law, but the form of the protest—
the " band " borrowed from the Middle Ages—and
certain passages in the document were of dubious
legality. Especially ominous was the clause which
bound the signatories to mutual defence " against all
sorts of persons whatsoever," which might be interpreted
as including the king. There were many irregularities
in the obtaining of signatures, for in certain districts it
was " obtruded upon people with threatenings, tearing
of clothes, drawing of blood." [1] Moreover, to Charles
in Whitehall it might have seemed that there had been
already overt acts of revolution. The new Committee
of Sixteen, the Tables, had set about organizing a
provisional Government. As early as February 1638
steps had been taken to raise a revenue. In March a

---

[1] Gordon of Rothiemay, I., 53–56. Napier, I., 142–144.

1638 " voluntary " tax was levied in every shire of one dollar for every thousand merks of free rent ; the Covenanting lords subscribed largely, and twenty-five dollars was Montrose's contribution ; there were signs that presently the levy would cease to be optional, and that non-Covenanters would be mulcted.[1] It all looked suspiciously like the creation of a war-chest. It was certain, too, that the movement would not remain within the four corners of the Covenant, but was capable of indefinite extension. The country was on fire, and every Sunday the ministers were fanning the flame. Wariston records a sermon in Edinburgh on 1st April, when the preacher, Mr. Rollock, after reading the Covenant, requested the nobles present—Montrose, Boyd, Loudoun, and Balmerino—to hold up their hands and swear by the name of the living God : " at the which instant of rising up, and then of holding up their hands, there rose sic a yelloch, sic abundance of tears, sic a heavenly harmony of sighs and sobs, universally through all the corners of the church, as the like was never seen nor heard of." [2] Scotland was in a high-strung and perilous mood.

The wise course for Charles would have been to withdraw the service book and to give assurance that he would meddle no more with property and heritable jurisdictions ; in that way he would have driven a wedge between those unnatural allies, the nobles and the Kirk. But from this course he was estopped by his passionate desire, fostered by Laud, to establish a uniform standard of worship throughout his realm, and the fear that such a concession would weaken his cause in the quarrel now drawing to a head with the English Parliament. He would fain have acted as he did in the ship-money case, and have secured a condemnation of the Covenant in the law courts, but the whole Scottish bench and bar believed in its legality.[3] He had for a moment hopes of organizing a royalist opposition in Scotland, with the help of the Highland clans and

---

[1] Rothes, 72, etc. ; Baillie, I., 213.   [2] *Diary*, I., 331.
[3] See two letters of Traquair in *Hardwicke Papers*, II., 103–104.

possibly of Irish troops under Antrim, but he abandoned
the project when he realized that, except for Huntly
and the Gordons, and the doubtful cases of Hamilton, Lanark, Traquair, and Roxburgh, he had at the
moment no Scottish supporters. Yet the king, who
had at times no mean capacity for judging a situation,
arrived at a shrewder estimate of the Scottish situation
than his advisers. If he was to win his will force must
be used, and to collect that force he must have time.
The Privy Council had sent the Justice Clerk to court
to expound the true state of Scotland. The king was
impressed, and summoned Traquair and Roxburgh
to advise him; Spottiswoode, too, and certain of the
Scots bishops; likewise Lord Lorn, who had not
signed the Covenant, and whom Baillie thought the most
powerful subject in the kingdom.[1] The outcome of
this consultation was that the Marquis of Hamilton
was appointed a special royal commissioner to Scotland, with authority to treat with the malcontents.

It is clear that Charles was only playing for time,
and his unfortunate envoy knew well the futility of his
errand. Scotland, as he once told the king, he hated
" next to hell," and he had no liking for a task where
success and failure would be alike without profit to
himself. He arrived in the north on 7th June, to
find sullen looks and little of the welcome due to a
royal commissioner. He brought with him two proclamations, which promised that the canons and the
service book would not be pressed " except in such a
fair and legal way as should satisfy all our loving subjects "; one demanded that all copies of the Covenant
should be surrendered, which the other did not; he
was to use one or other according to his discretion.
Traquair and Roxburgh had already warned him that
a demand to give up the Covenant would wreck his
mission; and, since the tenor of the first proclamation
had become known, his diplomacy was prejudiced from
the start. He saw Rothes, and the Tables appointed a
committee of three ministers and three nobles to confer

[1] I., 146.

1638 with him, one of whom was Montrose. Things had moved fast during the previous months. Henderson and Wariston had prepared " articles of peace," which went far beyond the mere matter of the liturgy. The Committee of the Tables asked for the withdrawal of the obnoxious canons and service book, but they also demanded the summoning of a free General Assembly, and, finally, of a Parliament to decide all the questions at issue. The Scottish Church was to shape its own ecclesiastical policy, and a Scottish Parliament was to give such policy the validity of the civil law. It was an honest assertion of a justifiable nationalism.

Hamilton hummed and hawed, promised and withdrew, and finally left Edinburgh in despair. While negotiating with the Covenanters, he had been discussing secretly with his master the possibilities for the use of arms in Scotland—the chance of help from the Highland clans who hated Lorn; the best base to hold, since Edinburgh castle was in Covenanting hands. Charles was adamant on the question of giving up the Covenant ; otherwise, he said, he " had no more power than the Duke of Venice," and he intended " not to yield to the demands of those traitors, the Covenanters." [1] With such terms in his instructions no emissary had a chance. The king was negotiating only to gain time, and the duplicity of the monarch was matched by that of his commissioner. For we know, on Montrose's evidence, that Hamilton privately told the Covenanters, " as a kindly Scotsman," that if they took a firm stand they were likely to win.[2] Then ensued a war of king's proclamations and Covenanting protests. Hamilton fluttered between London and Scotland, carrying royal concessions—lavish concessions which meant nothing, since Charles had already determined to appeal to the arbitrament of war. In any case they came too late. The king proposed a new covenant of his own, the chief point of which was the abjuration of popery ; but the Covenanting leaders, whose detestation of Rome needed no advertisement, not unnaturally described it

---

[1] Burnet, *Mem. of the Hamiltons*, 43–59.　　[2] Guthry, 40–41.

as a " mockery of God." Their aim was now nothing less than the complete suppression of episcopacy
in Scotland. But the General Assembly was granted,
and Hamilton had succeeded in some degree in sowing
suspicion between the nobility and clergy by warning
each of the danger to be apprehended from the other.

During the absence of the royal commissioner from
Scotland in July, the Tables made a great effort to win
Aberdeen and the Gordon country to the Covenant's
side. Huntly himself would have none of it. His
house might be perverse and uncertain, but it never
lacked a high spirit and a wild chivalry, and he went
his own way contemptuous of Lowland fashions. The
Tables sent Colonel Robert Monro, an old soldier of
Gustavus, to ask him to subscribe the Covenant, promising to give him first place in the command of their
forces ; but Huntly replied nobly that his family had
risen by the kings of Scotland, and that if the king
were to fall he was resolved to bury his life, honour,
and estate under the rubbish.[1]   But something might
be done in the city and its environs, though Knox's
disputation in 1561 with the Aberdeen professors was
not an encouraging precedent. Montrose, with three
ministers in his suite—Mr. Alexander Henderson, Mr.
David Dickson, and Mr. Andrew Cant—arrived on
20th July, bearing a letter from Rothes to his cousin
the provost, Patrick Leslie. " Do ye all the good ye can
in that town and in the country about—ye will not
regret it—and attend my Lord Montrose, who is a
noble and true-hearted cavalier." [2]   Montrose had been
made a burgess of Aberdeen nine years before, and he
and his retinue were hospitably welcomed. But he
seems to have been in an unbending humour. He
declined the proffered banquet until the authorities
submitted to the Covenant, whereupon the provost
and the bailies distributed the wine among the poor.[3]
On the Sunday the three ministers proposed to occupy
the city pulpits, but the Aberdeen clergy were not to
be ousted. The missionaries were accommodated in a

---

[1] Gordon of Rothiemay, I., 49.   [2] Napier, I., 148.   [3] Spalding, I., 57.

1638 yard attached to the Earl Marischal's town-house, where
his sister, Lady Pitsligo, was then dwelling. The three
preached in turn from a wooden gallery, and on the
Monday repeated the performance, amid the ribaldry of
certain scoffers in an adjoining building.

Thereafter the envoys proceeded into the neighbouring villages, where they met with more success.[1] The
Aberdeen ministers presented fourteen " demands," and
there followed a wordy warfare of " answers," " replies,"
and " duplies," in which the Covenant champions did not
get the best of the argument.[2] Aberdeen declared that
it adhered to the discipline of the reformed Kirk of Scotland, but refused to condemn episcopacy or admit " the
immutability of presbyterial government." [3] It is to be
noted that, in asking for subscriptions to the Covenant,
Montrose drew up and made his colleagues sign an
emphatic declaration " that we neither had nor have
any intention but of loyalty to his Majesty, as the
Covenant bears." [4] He was interpreting what he then
believed—and the bulk of Scotland with him—to be
its spirit. But the incident is piquant when we remember who were his ministerial companions. Henderson, the wisest head and the purest character in the
Kirk, was five years later to make the last attempt
to hold him to the Covenant's side, and Dickson and
Cant were to be the central pillars of the theocracy
which he sought to overthrow. Perhaps on that
northern journey he may have found in their hearts
that which gave his enthusiasm pause, and developed
those scruples which made Baillie complain that he was
" hard to be guided," and " capricious for his own
fancies." [5] He returned to Edinburgh at the end of
July with but little to show for his labours. His future
visits to Aberdeen were to be to better purpose.

[1] Guthry, 39. Spalding, I., 59. Gordon of Rothiemay, I., 84–85.
[2] Gordon of Rothiemay, I., 86–95.
[3] Burnet. *Mem. of the Hamiltons*, 86.
[4] Spalding, I., 58.
[5] L., 247.

II

The Assembly which met in Glasgow in November *1638* was a legal gathering, sanctioned by the king, and duly presided over by Hamilton, the royal commissioner. The issues between sovereign and people had been narrowed.   Charles had surrendered all the earlier objects of strife—the liturgy, the book of canons, and an irresponsible episcopate.   It appeared that he was prepared to accept a moderate episcopacy responsible to a General Assembly, the original constitution of the Reformed Kirk in Scotland.   But with the people at large the controversy had now gone far beyond the articles of the National Covenant.   Episcopacy in any form had become suspect, because it had been made the instrument of an assault upon both civil and religious freedom.   To Charles, as to Hamilton, some form of episcopate was an essential corollary of a monarchy. To them it appeared that the control over the Kirk given by bishops appointed by the king was the only safeguard against an anarchical theocracy; to the Scottish people it seemed that so long as this channel for arbitrary government was left unblocked there was no security against further encroachments upon their liberties.   The historian may admit that there was reason in both views, but it was certain that the Assembly, the first held for twenty years, would demand the complete removal of the latter menace.

It met on the 21st day of November, in the old Cathedral of Glasgow, one of the few ancient churches in Scotland which had escaped the destroying zeal of the Reformers.   Glasgow was then a clean little city of some 12,000 inhabitants, clustered about its college and cathedral above the shining links of the Molendinar burn.   The Assembly was a packed one, since the Tables, as appeared during the proceedings, had exercised a rigorous veto over the delegates.   Of these there were some 240, 142 being ministers, and 98 laymen, ruling elders appointed by presbyteries.   The Privy Council attended, and there were numerous assessors.

1638 Hamilton had striven to regulate the body by a proclamation—completely disregarded—against the presence of retainers and the bearing of arms. The nobles and barons appeared each with his usual " tail," and not a few of the clerical members had swords and pistols, ostensibly to defend themselves on the journey against a certain John Macgregor, a bandit who professed a distaste for the Covenant and a liking for the king.[1]

The crowd at the opening was so great that the town guard had the utmost difficulty in opening a way for the members to their seats. The Glasgow populace attended in great numbers, and their behaviour in the kirk shocked the decorous soul of Mr. Robert Baillie. " It is here alone where, I think, we might learn from Canterbury, yea, from the Pope, from the Turks, or pagans, modesty and manners. . . . Our rascals without shame, in great numbers, made such dinn and clamour in the house of the true God, that if they minted to use the like behaviour in my chamber, I could not be content till they were down the stairs." [2] Hamilton sat uneasily on a high chair of state, and below him the Lords of the Privy Council—conspicuous among them the lean aquiline face and the red hair of Lorn, now, by his father's death, Earl of Argyll, and a figure of interest to every man, since he had not declared himself. In front of them was a chair for the Moderator, and a table for the Clerk. Then came a long bench at which were seated the nobles and barons elected by the presbyteries, and at which sat Montrose as an elder, representing his own presbytery of Auchterarder. At the end of the church a platform had been erected for the eldest sons of peers, and in tiers on both sides were the seats of the clerical and burgess members. The " rascal multitude," including many women, occupied the aisles and galleries. It was a strange form of ecclesiastical assembly, for among the black gowns of the ministers were the slashed and laced doublets of the laity, and the gleam of many swords.[3]

[1] Wariston, I., 399. *Large Declaration*, 232, 385.
[2] I., 124. [3] Gordon of Rothiemay, I., 157.

Alexander Henderson was unanimously elected Moderator, and Wariston, Clerk. The first step was to verify
the commissions of the members, and Hamilton found
cause to question the legality of many. His objection
to the presence of laymen was without substance, as
their admission was in accordance with the letter and
spirit of Presbyterianism. With better reason he protested against the method of electing these laymen, and
the way in which the Tables had supervised the appointments. A test case was that of Lord Carnegie, Montrose's brother-in-law, who had been nominated by the
presbytery of Brechin, but disallowed by the Tables,
and Erskine of Dun named in his stead. Montrose had
been the chief mover in the matter, and, when Wariston
inadvertently read the letter of the Tables, Hamilton
seized upon the irregularity. Montrose hotly defended
it, and thereby came into conflict not only with Southesk,
his father-in-law, but with Mr. David Dickson, who
questioned his action. The young man was in a high
temper, and in the cause he had chosen was prepared to
respect neither kinsman nor cleric.[1]

The Assembly waved aside the royal commissioner's
doubts as to its competence and constitution, and proceeded to the business at the back of every member's
head—the abolition of episcopacy. The bishops had
refused to acknowledge the court or to appear before it,
and, when their formal declinature had been handed in,
Hamilton decided to dissolve the Assembly. On the
morning of 28th November, after recapitulating the
king's concessions, he declared the Assembly illegal
owing to the method of its election, and " discharged
their further proceedings under pain of treason." He
was answered in moderate language by Rothes and
Henderson, but the latter refused to accept the dissolution. " All that are here know the reasons of the
meeting of this Assembly, and, albeit we have acknowledged the power of Christian kings for convening of
Assemblies, yet that may not derogate from Christ's
right ; for He has given divine warrants to convoke

[1] Gordon of Rothiemay, I., 152. *Large Declaration*, 240.

Assemblies whether magistrates consent or not." Then arose Mr. David Dickson, who said, looking towards Hamilton, "that that nobleman was very much to be commended for his zeal and faithfulness to his master the king, and sticking close by what he thought for his credit and interest; and he craved leave to propose his example for the Assembly's imitation. They had a better master, Christ the King of Kings, to serve, and his credit and honour to look after according to their commission and trust; and therefore he moved that, having this in their eye, they might sit still and do their Master's work faithfully." [1] In this high mood the Assembly saw Hamilton depart. It was a moment which von Ranke has compared to that scene a century and a half later, when the new French National Assembly for the first time withstood the commands of its king. [2]

Before leaving for the south, Hamilton summoned the members of the Privy Council together and counselled them to do their duty by the king. One or two withdrew, declaring that they were on the popular side, and among them was Argyll, who, the day before, when Hamilton dissolved the Assembly, had defended the legality of the lay element and announced his adhesion to the Covenanting cause. [3] Hamilton wrote to Charles and to Laud announcing the failure of his mission, and urging the necessity of speeding on the armed preparations. In his letter to the king of 27th November he provided his master with certain character-studies of the Scots nobility. Two of his comments are worth noting: Argyll " will prove the dangerousest man in this state "; of the Covenanting leaders there was " none more vainly foolish than Montrose." [4]

The Assembly resumed its sittings on the 29th, with Argyll as the solitary Privy Councillor. It sat till 20th December, and, says Burnet, " went on at a great rate, now that there were none to curb them." It pronounced the last six General Assemblies invalid; condemned the

[1] Wodrow, *Analecta*, II., 116.   [2] *History of England*, II., 116.
[3] Gordon of Rothiemay, I., 192.   Baillie, I., 144.   Burnet, *Mem. of the Hamiltons*, 106.   [4] *Hardwicke Papers*, II., 113, 121.

service book, the book of canons, and the Court of High   *1638*
Commission; annulled the Articles of Perth; declared
episcopacy to be utterly abjured and cast out of the
Kirk; established a press censorship, under the control
of Wariston; and, in a mood of startling enlightenment,
prohibited salmon-fishing on Sundays.[1]

The whole Scottish hierarchy was deposed, and most
of its members excommunicated as well. The bishops
had declined to appear, so there was no defence; the
Aberdeen doctors were not there to raise their voices,
which Baillie thought might have induced a more
moderate temper. Undoubtedly there had been much
laxness of conduct on the part of the bishops, and certain
scandals; but many of the charges were absurd, and
few were supported by evidence which would have
satisfied a court of law. The fact of holding episcopal
office was held sufficient to afford presumptive proof
of moral delinquencies. Episcopacy and its ministrants
were abolished root and branch, and certain dubious
historical dogmas were affirmed, against which Baillie,
to his honour, protested.[2] He had been impressed by
Hamilton's conduct in the commissioner's chair, and
had wept at his withdrawal; he may be taken as the
type of the moderate Covenanter, who was against
episcopacy as a system, but did not think it necessarily
forbidden by the reformed faith. But the ministerial
leaders, with the support of the lay members, would
be content with no half-hearted condemnation. On
the day when the prelates were sentenced, Henderson
preached the sermon, long known as " The Bishops'
Doom"; but the passage of Scripture selected by the
reader may have had an ominous ring in other ears
than Mr. Robert Baillie's. " These things I have spoken
to you that you should not be offended. They shall put
you out of the synagogue; yea, the time cometh that
whosoever killeth you will think that he doeth God
service."

The Assembly had clearly gone beyond its legal
powers. When the king's commissioner dissolved it,

---

[1] Gordon of Rothiemay, II., 162.   [2] Ibid., II., 108.   Baillie, I., 177, etc.

1638 under the Act of 1592, it ceased to exist at law. Henderson's act had all the significance which von Ranke has claimed for it; in the words of his most recent biographer, it " spelt revolution." [1] The Assembly claimed to repeal the laws of the land, and it proceeded to carry its edicts into action. The treatment of the bishops was as harsh as it was irregular, but revolutions are not considerate of individual rights. Our judgment of its doings must be based upon the assumption that it was a definite revolt against the king's authority. It sought, indeed, to be a modified revolution. A treasonable sermon by Mr. George Gillespie was condemned by implication by the Moderator; Argyll warned them, and Henderson repeated his warning, against any disrespect to " so good and gracious a prince "; and at the end an address was drawn up to his Majesty, humbly asking him to confirm their acts in the Parliament presently to be summoned. But a revolution is a hard thing to delimit, and it has a fatal habit of producing a reaction in kind. The doings of 1638 were exactly paralleled by the Act Rescissory of 1661, which blotted out twenty-three years of legislation and re-established episcopacy. One form of violence was to be matched by another.

> " The Gods alone
> Remember everlastingly; they strike
> Remorselessly, and ever like for like.
> By their great memories the Gods are known."

Yet to judge the protagonists at Glasgow with the cold-blooded retrospective reason of history is to do grave injustice. The implications of their actions were not present to the minds of the best of the clergy and laity. These revolutionaries were still royalists almost to a man. They opposed, not the monarchy, but the dogma of " no bishop, no king," which would impair the royal authority by making it dependent upon a particular ecclesiastical form. Their mark was Laud rather than Charles. Among them were many fanatics

[1] Orr, *Alexander Henderson*, 182.

of Presbytery, but there were also those who were
lukewarm enough towards Presbyterian claims, but
enthusiastic for Scottish liberties, and who considered
that the people should have the church they wanted.
Such men had a well-founded distrust of an episcopate
as the gate by which autocracy had often entered the
sheepfold. It is to be remembered that few Scots believed in divine right, that the nation had never known
an unquestioned monarchy like that of the Tudors in
England, and that they had been in the habit of fre-
quently taking up arms to read their kings a lesson.
While professing in all honesty their love for Charles,
they were prepared to chasten him. They demanded
that the nation's liberties should be safeguarded, and
the proof of that would be the grant of the Kirk the
nation preferred. On such a policy it was possible
to unite for the moment the gross and wary sagacity
of Rothes, the young enthusiasm of Montrose, and the
profound and subtle ambition of the latest convert,
Argyll.

III

To one who studies such portraits as exist of the
chief figures in the Scotland of that epoch, there must
come a sense of disappointment. Few convey the impression of power which is found among the Puritans
and Cavaliers of England. There is Hamilton, self-
conscious, arrogant, and puzzled ; Lanark, his brother,
dark, sullen, and stupid ; Huntly, a peacock head
surmounting a splendid body ; Rothes, heavy-chinned,
goggle-eyed, Pickwickian ; Glencairn, weak and rustical ;
old Leven, the eternal bourgeois ; the Border earls, but
one remove from the Border prickers ; Wariston,
obstinate and crack-brained ; James Guthrie, lean and
fanatical. But there are three exceptions. One is the
haunting face of Montrose, whose calm eyes do not
change from the Jameson portrait of his boyhood to the
great Honthorst of his prime. The second is the face of
Alexander Henderson, yellow from the fevers of the
Leuchars marshes, lined with thought, and burning with

a steady fire. The third is that of Archibald, eighth Earl of Argyll. We see him at nineteen, in his marriage clothes, his reddish hair falling over his collar, his grey-blue eyes with ever so slight a cast in them ; we see him in his twenty-fourth year, with the air and accoutrements of a soldier ; in the Castle Campbell portrait, unfortunately burned in the Inveraray castle fire of 1877, he is in armour, but the face has a scholar's pallor and a curious melancholy ; in the familiar Newbattle picture, painted in his late forties, he is in sober black with the skull-cap of a divine on his head, the features are drawn with ill-health and care, the mouth is compressed and secret, the nose is pendulous, and the cast in the eyes has become almost a deformity. But at whatever period we take it, it is a face of power, with intellect in the broad brow, and resolution in the tight lips and heavy chin.[1]

In every national crisis there is some personal antagonism, where the warring creeds seem to be summed up in the persons of two protagonists—Cæsar and Pompey, Pym and Strafford, Fox and Pitt. So were to stand those present allies, Montrose and Argyll, secular types of conflicting temperaments and irreconcilable views. The head of the great house of Campbell was now some thirty-four or thirty-five years of age, eight years the senior of Montrose. He had the widest possessions of any Highland chief except Huntly, and at his back by far the most powerful clan, for he lived close to the Lowlands, and could put 5,000 men into the field. His father, to whom the sobriquet of Gilleasbuig Gruamach—" Gillespie the Sullen "—properly belonged,[2] was an odd character and led an odd life. He was defeated at Glenrinnes in 1594 by the Gordons, but later added to his possessions by subduing the Macdonalds of Islay and Kintyre. But his fortune was not commensurate with his lands, he fell deeply into debt, married a Catholic second wife, joined the Church of Rome, and had to flee the country. He was permitted

---

[1] See Willcock, *The Great Marquess* (Edinburgh, 1903), a careful and temperate biography. [2] Ibid., 6.

to return, and lived some ten years in England before *1638*
his death. His first wife was a daughter of the house
of Morton, so his son had in his veins the unaccountable
Douglas blood. Like the father, the son had an unhappy childhood, for he lost his mother in his infancy,
and during his youth was perpetually at variance with
his wandering sire. He had to fight hard during his
minority for his rights, and the experience must have
made him wary and distrustful, and taught him
diplomacy and dissimulation. Charles is said to have
assisted him against his vindictive parent, and Clarendon
reports some dubious gossip about the old man warning
the king against his son, " for he is a man of craft,
subtlety, and falsehood, and can love no man, and if
ever he finds it in his power to do you a mischief, he
will be sure to do it." [1]

What is clear is that in his youth he was deeply
in debt, and found his great estates less of a boon
than an incumbrance. He determined to husband and
increase his fortune, and there is record of a curious
venture to annex an imaginary island beyond the
Hebrides.[2]   He took his part in policing the Highlands, and in 1636 brought to justice the outlaw Patrick
Macgregor, who is famous in balladry as Gilderoy. With
high politics he did not meddle. He defended the
laird of Earlston against the Bishop of Galloway, and
befriended Samuel Rutherford when brought before the
Court of High Commission, but his motive may well
have been only friendship to his kinsfolk, the Kenmures.
These incidents did not predispose him to love the
bishops, and in 1637 he convened a meeting of Rothes,
Traquair, and other noblemen, to protest against the
" pride and avarice of the prelates seeking to overrule
the haill kingdom." [3]   But up to 1638 we may regard
him as principally occupied with family troubles and
the care of his estates, a little suspect by Presbytery as
the son of a Catholic and the brother-in-law of Huntly,

---

[1] Willcock, 22. Clarendon, *History*, II., 58. Clarendon is apt to report
gossip about Scots affairs which he had no means of verifying.
[2] *Hist. MSS. Comm.*, 6th Report, 631.
[3] Spalding, I., 79.

well regarded by the king in spite of his father's warn-
ings, and with no special predilection towards the Kirk.
He was one of the few nobles who, in the summer of
1638, took the king's alternative covenant at the request of Hamilton.

In this mood he attended the Glasgow Assembly.
There it would appear that he underwent a profound
spiritual experience, and in the theological sense was
" converted." It was the habit of Alexander Henderson
during the sittings to hold meetings at night for prayer
and counsel. " I find," says Wodrow, who must have
been repeating a tradition handed down in the ministry,
" that their meetings were remarkably countenanced
of God, and that the Marquis of Argyll, and several
others who sometimes joined in them, dated their
conversion, or a knowledge of it, from those times." [1]
It was this change of heart, and not the discovery that
the Covenant was the side of the majority, that determined Argyll's course. He was an acute judge of
popular opinion, but it was something more than policy
that took him over to the Covenant side. For from
that day this man, who in the past had been wholly
concerned with his worldly possessions, and had held
himself conspicuously aloof from the Kirk, became a
religious enthusiast, a fanatic ; and no mortal, however
consummate an actor, could simulate such enthusiasm
as Argyll revealed during the remainder of his troubled
life.[2]

In assessing his character we have therefore to start
from the fact that in religious matters he was most
deeply in earnest, that he had the same proselytizing
zeal, and the same complete assurance that the armies
of Heaven were on his side, as Wariston and James
Guthrie. To this add his Campbell and Douglas ancestry. He had the chief's love of power, and it is
possible that, as in Hamilton's case, visions of a crown
may have haunted one who boasted that he was the

---

[1] *Historical Fragments*, 81.
[2] See for his personal piety, Wodrow, *Analecta*, I., 22. At Inveraray he
always wrote the sermons which his chaplain preached.

" eighth man from Robert Bruce." Such dreams were *1638*
common among the higher Scots nobility. His bitter
youth had left him suspicious and aloof, without warmth,
with few friends and fewer intimates. He could not
charm easily; he must win his way by patience,
assiduity, and talent; but he learned in time a grace
of manner to which even the hostile Clarendon bears
witness. He was, so far as can be judged, without
any interest in humane letters; his mind was mediæval
in its cast, holding firm by law and scholastic divinity.
Hence it is vain to look to him for any profound ideal
of statecraft. He was essentially a politician, a shrewd
judge of character and opinion, able to use both the
raw material of fanaticism in the ministers and of gross
self-interest in the nobles to further his ends, because he
shared the one and wholly understood the other. There
was no quicker brain in Britain to probe the possibilities of a situation. Mr. Gardiner thinks him as much
superior to Montrose as a statesman as he was inferior
in the art of war; [1] and Clarendon, after remarking
that Montrose despised him, " as he was too apt to
contemn those he did not love," adds that Argyll
" wanted nothing but honesty and courage to be a
very extraordinary man, having all other good talents
in a great degree." [2]

Honesty and courage are difficult matters upon
which to dogmatize. Argyll was a poor soldier, because
he lacked the power of grasping a tactical or strategical
problem—a gift as specialized as that for poetry or the
higher mathematics—and because he had not the kind
of personality which can impress itself upon large
bodies of men under arms. But it is idle to deny courage,
even of the rude physical kind, to a man who time and
again risked his neck, who was prepared to meet an
enemy in a duel, and who went without a tremor to
the scaffold. As for honesty, there is little enough of
the high and delicate kind at any time in the political
game, and, if we define it as scrupulous loyalty to cause
and colleague, it was a fruit which scarcely grew in

[1] *Great Civil War*, I., 126. [2] *History*, XII., 142.

seventeenth-century Scotland. In that mad kaleidoscope Argyll had as much of the rare commodity as most of his contemporaries. His troubles came primarily from a divided soul—a clear, practical intellect pulling against an obscurantist creed, the Highland chief at variance with the Presbyterian statesman, a brain, mediæval for all its powers, fumbling with the half-understood problems of a new world. With such a one subtlety will appear as irresolution, perplexity as cowardice, and a too quick mind will seem to argue a dishonest heart.

Such a man will be a power among fanatics and self-seekers, for he can read the souls of both. But there will be one chink in his armour. He will not comprehend so readily other motives, and, in failing to understand, he will miscalculate and undervalue. Single-heartedness will not come within the scope of his capacious understanding. Sooner or later Argyll was bound to find in Montrose his stark opposite, by whom he was both puzzled and repelled—one who, in the common sense of the word, had no personal ambition, who was a civic enthusiast as Wariston and Guthrie were religious enthusiasts, and who would force the appeal to that which Argyll hated and feared —the sword.

IV

Charles had much ado to raise that army which for the past nine months he had regarded as his ultimate argument. England was apathetic, and a growing proportion of her people looked askance at episcopacy. There had been no Parliament for ten years, so there were scanty supplies. The train-bands were called out, and the nobles were summoned to perform their feudal duties, but the first were half-hearted and ill-equipped, and the second was at the best a patchy volunteer service. On paper the king had some 21,000 men— 14,000 foot and 2,000 horse, and about 5,000 under Hamilton. The cavalry was under Lord Holland, and the infantry under the Catholic Lord Arundel, neither of

whom had much military experience. The plan was
an advance to the Border by the main forces, while
Hamilton should join hands with Huntly in the north
and threaten the Covenanters' rear. Meantime it was
hoped that Antrim, with his Irish, would land in Argyll,
and Strafford in the Firth of Clyde. Unless the mere
threat of an advance brought the Scots to terms, there
was little hope in the scheme, for the main army was too
weak for an invasion of Scotland, an Irish landing was
improbable, and the exchequer was too low to permit
of a waiting campaign. With the king went many
distinguished figures : Sir Edmund Verney, already in
two minds about the merits of the cause ; Falkland,
whose departure was attended by eulogistic poems from
Cowley and Waller ; Sir John Suckling, who from his
own purse equipped a troop of horse clad in white and
scarlet which, by the testimony of his own pasquil,
had no stomach for a fight.

The Scots were in a better case. The provident
Tables had already created a war-chest by voluntary
assessments ; their cause was supported by a widespread
popular enthusiasm ; the troops they could raise were
of a more martial stamp than the unwilling English
levies, and they had commanders of far higher talent
than Holland and Arundel. For, in Spalding's words,
" there came out of Germany hame to Scotland ane
gentleman of base birth born in Balveny, who had
served long and fortunately in the German wars, and
called to his name Felt Marshall Leslie, His Excellency." [1]
Alexander Leslie, now a man of fifty-seven, had risen
high in the service of Gustavus, and at Stralsund had
been a match for Wallenstein himself. So great was his
professional repute that he was given at once the unquestioned control of the Covenant forces. " We were
feared," Baillie wrote, " that emulation among our
nobles might have done harm, . . . but such was the
wisdom and authority of the old, little, crooked soldier,
that all, with ane incredible submission, from the
beginning to the end, gave over themselves to be

[1] L., 87.

guided by him, as if he had been Great Solyman." [1]
With Leslie had come over many Scottish mercenaries
of the Dugald Dalgetty type, who, finding their occupation gone on the Continent, welcomed the chance of
turning an honest penny in their native land. Such
men, as a rule, cared as little about prayer-books and
General Assemblies as they cared for the international
quibbles of a German princeling, but they were to
provide the Covenant with that which it sorely needed
and which England as yet did not possess—a body of
experienced and cool-headed professional officers.

The Tables were no laggards in war. Edinburgh
castle, which Hamilton had bought from Mar, was
surprised and taken; Dumbarton and Dalkeith followed, and soon in the south of Scotland only the castle
of Caerlaverock remained hostile. The three Lowland
noblemen who were still nominally on the king's side—
Traquair, Roxburgh, and Douglas—could do nothing
in Clydesdale and Tweeddale. Argyll was given the
wardenship of the west, and presently, by his seizure
of Hamilton's castle of Brodick and his garrisoning of
Kintyre, closed the door by which Antrim and Strafford
might have entered, while, with the unexpected assistance of the Camerons, he ravaged Huntly's Badenoch
domains. The immediate danger lay in Aberdeen, for
Charles's march from the south would be slow. Should
Hamilton's 5,000 sail north and join Huntly—now appointed royal lieutenant over all the country between
the North Esk and Caithness—the Covenant would
have to fight with a conflagration in its rear. Montrose
was appointed to deal with the situation, and Leslie,
whose formal commission as commander-in-chief was
not issued till May 9, 1639,[2] was sent with him to correct
the inexperience of this general of twenty-seven.

In January 1639 and the beginning of February
Montrose was busy beating up recruits in his own braes
of Angus, where he had high words with Southesk, his
father-in-law, who had not forgotten the dispute at
the Glasgow Assembly, and, in a sudden fit of royalism,

[1] I., 213.   [2] Terry, *Alexander Leslie*, 51.

refused the warrant of the Tables.[1] He had summoned
the northern Covenanters—the Frasers, Keiths, Crichtons, and Forbeses—to meet him at the little town of
Turriff in Aberdeenshire. Huntly heard of the rendezvous, and, resolved to prevent it, marched thither with
2,000 of his clansmen. But Montrose was to give the
first proof of his speed. Getting word of Huntly's
intention, he rode through the Grampian passes with
200 horsemen, and was joined at Turriff by 800 men.
Huntly, when he arrived, found the churchyard walls
lined with muskets, and Montrose and his friends
ensconced in the church. He had much the larger
force, but he had been forbidden to fight without
Hamilton's instructions, so he could only " glare at "
his enemies and withdraw to Strathbogie.[2] His orders
were not to take the offensive till the king had reached
the Border.

But he could fortify Aberdeen, and this it was
Montrose's business to prevent. Presently Leslie arrived with the rest of the army, and, with a force of
from 3,000 to 4,000 men, Montrose advanced on the
city. Huntly, with instructions at all costs to win time,
tried to make an arrangement with Montrose, but the
latter had his clear instructions from the Tables, and
on 30th March he entered Aberdeen. Ever in love with
the spectacular side of life, he found a rival colour for
the royal scarlet which the young Gordons wore, and
decorated his men with knots of blue ribbon. It is
curious to note that the Covenant received its famous
blue badge from the man who was to prove its chief
opponent. The city, deserted by Huntly, had no power
of resistance. The Aberdeen doctors fled by sea, and
some of the more martial citizens departed to join the
king, while the Covenanting chaplains improved the
occasion by pointing out in their discourses that upon
Aberdeen had fallen the curse of Meroz. Montrose im-

---

[1] In the commission to Montrose to be colonel in the shire of Perth, dated
May 2, 1639, Atholl is a signatory, and the similar commission for Angus
(7th May) is signed, among others, by Lord Carnegie—which shows the political
confusion of the time. *Hist. MSS. Comm.*, 2nd Report, 175.
[2] Spalding, I., 93. Gordon of Rothiemay, II., 212.

posed on the city a fine for recusancy, and appointed Kinghorn to the command, while he rode west to look for Huntly.[1]

Now follows a curious tale on which it is hard to form an opinion. Various intermediaries had been busy, and in the first week of April Huntly met Montrose in the latter's camp at Inverurie. Huntly signed a modified version of the Covenant, binding himself " to maintain the King's authority, together with the liberties both of Church and State, Religion and Laws " —probably a version dictated by Montrose himself, whose principles it exactly represented. The Gordons would be allowed to sign the Covenant if they pleased, and the Catholic members of the clan were to be protected so long as they stood by the laws and liberties of Scotland. When Huntly came again to Inverurie, he found the camp full of his hereditary enemies, Frasers, Forbeses, and Crichtons, and sent his friend Gordon of Straloch to Montrose to warn him that any attempt to carry him south as prisoner would be hotly resented by the countryside. Montrose, in reply, declared that he would stand by Huntly—" but there is this difficulty, that business here is all transacted by vote and a committee, nor can I get anything done of myself."

Montrose returned to Aberdeen, where he was joined by other of the Covenanting nobles. A council was held, and the general was severely chidden for his leniency towards Huntly. Apparently his command in the field did not carry any superior authority at the council board, for Huntly was promptly summoned to attend under a safe conduct, for which Montrose made himself specially responsible. The latter had promised more than he could perform, and the chief of the Gordons found himself in a trap. He was asked to pay certain expenses, bring in certain prisoners, become reconciled to Crichton of Frendraught, and naturally refused. He was then told that he must accompany the Covenanting lords to Edinburgh. He asked if he was to go as a prisoner or as a free man. Montrose bade him

[1] Spalding, I., 104, etc. Gordon of Rothiemay, II., 221.

take his choice, and the marquis replied that he would *1639*
go as a volunteer. This is the account of Spalding,
who makes Montrose throughout the leader in the sorry
business; Gordon of Rothiemay, who had reason to
know, since he was Straloch's son, assigns the chief part
to Leslie;[1] Monteith says that Montrose opposed the
breaking of the parole with all his power.[2] Huntly
and his heir, Lord Gordon, were carried to Edinburgh,
and his suspicions proved only too well founded. He
refused to subscribe any other covenant than that
which he had taken at Inverurie, and he and his son
were consigned to Edinburgh castle. According to his
fashion, he signalized the event by a piece of noble
declamation. " Whereas you offer me liberty, I am
not so bad a merchant as to buy it with the loss of my
conscience, fidelity, and honour. I have already given
my faith to my Prince, upon whom now this crown by
all laws of nature and nations is justly fallen. . . . I
am in your power, and resolved not to leave that foul
title of traitor as an inheritance upon my posterity.
You may take my head from my shoulders, but not my
heart from my Sovereign."[3]

It is the judgment of Mr. Gardiner that in all this
affair Montrose " played but a mean and shabby part,"
that it was " the only mean action of his life." But the
thing is too intricate for such a summary judgment.
Montrose was clearly, in matters of policy, only one
vote among many, and, moreover, he was in all major
matters subordinate to Leslie.[4] Huntly's treatment
was probably by Leslie's order, whether or not he was
present at the final meeting in Aberdeen, and it is
significant that in England it was attributed to him.[5]
Moreover, it is by no means clear that Huntly, in spite
of his rhetoric, was an unwilling captive. Why did he

---

[1] Leslie, with most of the foot and artillery, left Aberdeen on Good Friday,
12th April (Spalding, I., 119), and the interview with Huntly took place on the
13th. It is possible that Leslie waited a day or two in Aberdeen before over-
taking his army.

[2] *History of the Troubles*, 47.

[3] *The Marquis of Huntly, his Reply*, etc. (printed by Robert Young, the
King's Printer for Scotland. 1640).

[4] Gordon of Rothiemay, II., 205.   [5] *Cal. S. P., Dom.* (1639), 39.

1639 open negotiations with Montrose ? Why did he sign a
covenant at Inverurie ? He did not want a Covenant
army ravaging his lands, while he waited for instructions
from Hamilton which never came. What honour was
there in being the royal lieutenant when he was under
a superior officer who sent neither troops nor commands ? He was in an impossible position, and may
have welcomed a simple way out of it ; otherwise,
knowing how many of the foes of his house were assembled at Aberdeen, he would scarcely have put his
head into the lion's mouth. It is to be noted that he
was no sooner safe in Edinburgh castle than Charles
wrote to Hamilton describing him as " feeble and false." [1]
It is only on some such supposition that we can explain
Montrose's conduct. Had the facts been as Spalding
relates them, one so scrupulous of the point of honour
would assuredly have laid down his commission. Lord
Gordon shared Huntly's captivity, and he was soon to
be Montrose's closest friend ; it is hard to believe that
a flagrant wrong done to the father could so soon have
been forgotten by the son. But it is certain that Huntly
himself was aggrieved, and never forgave Montrose ; it
may be because Montrose was a witness of his weakness
and humiliation. " He could never be gained to join
cordially with him, nor to swallow that indignity, . . .
whence it came to pass that such as were equally
enemies to both . . . in the end prevailed so far as to
ruinate and destroy both of them, and the king by a
consequent." [2]

On the day that Montrose reached Aberdeen Charles
entered York. On 7th April he issued a proclamation
to his rebellious subjects in Scotland, inviting them
to come in and be punished. It was a blunder which
he repaired by a later proclamation of 7th May, in
which he announced that he would give his people all
just satisfaction in Parliament as soon as the present
troubles subsided, that he would not permit the Scots
to invade England, but that he did not propose to

[1] *Hist. MSS. Comm.*, 11th Report, App. VI., 102.
[2] Gordon of Rothiemay, II., 238.

invade Scotland, " if all civil and temporal obedience **1639**
was shown him." This last clause seemed to open a
way to negotiation.   But Leslie, on whose head a price
of £500 had been set,[1] took no risks; he mustered his
army on the links of Leith, and before the end of the
month was encamped at Dunglass, on his way to the
Border.   Meantime, on May Day, Hamilton had arrived
in the Forth with nineteen ships of war and 5,000 men,
to find the approaches to Edinburgh strongly fortified,
and both shores of the firth in arms.   His mother, the
terrible old dowager-countess, arrived from the west
with pistols in her holsters and the resolve to shoot her
son if he set foot on Scottish soil.   The king's commissioner proved as futile in war as in diplomacy.   He
contented himself with landing his men on the islands
of the firth, paying secret visits to Covenanting lords,
and writing melancholy letters to his master.

But up in the north the Gordons and certain local
barons—Ogilvies, Urquharts, and Setons—had taken
matters into their own hands.   In a one-sided engagement, called the Trot of Turriff, they drove out a small
Covenanting garrison under the Master of Forbes, and
marched on Aberdeen, which they occupied on the
15th of May.   Meantime Huntly's second son, Lord
Aboyne, had made his way to Charles at Newcastle,
and had offered his sword to the royal side.   He was
sent back to Hamilton for troops, but Hamilton gave
him nothing but a few field-pieces and the services of a
certain Colonel Gun, who had fought in the German
wars.   There was a chance now for a real diversion,
but Hamilton did not take it ; he sent two of his three
regiments to the king, and himself remained snugly
in the Forth.

Montrose was in Edinburgh on 18th May when he
got word of the doings in the north.   Hastily collecting
a force of some 4,000, he reached Aberdeen on the 25th,
to find that the barons had marched westward to get
Highland support, and that the young Earl Marischal
had occupied the city.   Some of his colleagues pressed

[1] *Cal. S. P., Dom.* (1639), 81.

him to make an example of the place, but he summarily declined.[1] The next day was Sunday, and while the officers were in church the soldiers made short work of any dog that had been decked in scorn with the blue ribbon of the Covenant. They also came to blows with the fisher-folk over sundry essays in salmon-poaching, forgetful of the sound resolution of the Glasgow Assembly.[2] But beyond a fine of 10,000 merks levied by the visitors, Aberdeen suffered little.

On the 30th of May Montrose marched into the Gordon country and laid siege to the castle of Gight. But two days later he had news which changed his plans. He heard that Aboyne, with a large force, was on the sea, and he assumed that Hamilton was with him. At all costs he must keep his communications open, so after a day's rest in Aberdeen he hastened south. On the 5th of June Aboyne arrived, with Tullibardine and Glencairn, two field-pieces, and Colonel Gun. His brother, Lord Lewis Gordon, who had attained the mature age of thirteen,[3] rode into the city with 1,000 of his clan, and so aroused the spirit of the burghers that by the 14th of June Aboyne had 4,000 men at his back.

Montrose had joined Marischal,[4] the head of the house of Keith, at Stonehaven, and when word came of Aboyne's landing, he went north to meet him. Aboyne's following showed the inclination, common to all Highland levies, to melt mysteriously away, but he had 600 Gordon cavalry, and he had the citizen forces of the twice-captured Aberdeen, who could expect little mercy if the war went against them. He had a strong position, for the Dee was in flood, and the narrow bridge might be held by resolute men against great odds. Had all the officers been of the stamp of Colonel

---

[1] Baillie, I., 205.
[2] Spalding, I., 141.
[3] It was a war of youth, for Aboyne was nineteen, and Marischal twenty-three.
[4] Marischal had an odd career. As we shall see, he was a signatory to the Cumbernauld Bond, but afterwards became a Covenanter, and was with Argyll at Fyvie, where his brother was killed. He opposed Montrose after Inverlochy, but later became an Engager, and was out in Pluscardine's rising.

Johnston, the provost's son and a professional soldier, it
would have gone ill with Montrose. The muskets at
the bridge-head bit fiercely into the Covenant ranks,
the spirit of the townspeople was high, and the fighting
of the first day, 18th June, left the defences intact.
But in the night Montrose brought up his heavier cannon
from Dunnottar, and at daybreak feinted with his
cavalry, sending them upstream towards an impossible
ford. Gun fell into the trap, and drew off the Gordon
horse to follow them, and in their absence the Covenanters made a general attack. Gun, having made
nothing of his ride, fell into a panic, which communicated
itself to the rest. The Gordons fled, with the unwilling
Aboyne, to their own country, and the citizens, deprived
of their allies, broke at last.

So ended Montrose's first serious essay at command
in the field. Marischal and others of his colleagues would
have burned and pillaged the city, but Montrose pled
for a respite,[1] and, fortunately for Aberdeen, events
had taken place in the south which made the truce a
peace. While Leslie was at Dunglass, the king sent
scouting parties across the Border, so the Scots moved
to Duns Law, a strong strategic position. That remarkable camp, where good provender was abundant, and
the sound of prayer and psalm rose morning and evening,
and at each captain's tent-door flew a banner with the
legend " For Christ's Crown and Covenant," and the
Lowland peasants stared, open-mouthed, at Argyll's
plaided and kilted Highlanders, may be read of in the
vivid pages of Baillie.[2] The spirit of the troops, says
that chronicler, was " sweet, meek, humble, yet strong
and vehement." The same could not have been said
of the royal army, which was ill-fed, ill-paid, ill-guided,
and sorely troubled by a species of vermin which
they called " Covenanters." Both sides had their
doubts and troubles, and the time was ripe for negotiation, since Charles could not defeat Leslie, and Leslie
at the moment did not desire to defeat Charles. A

---

[1] Gordon of Rothiemay, II., 281. Guthry, 57. Baillie, I., 222.
[2] I., 211, etc.

conference was arranged, and ultimately Charles assented to the principle that General Assemblies should deal with ecclesiastical questions and Parliament with civil, and that a free General Assembly and a free Parliament should be convened for the coming August. The king made a good impression upon the sensitive Baillie, who had been impressed by Hamilton the previous November; he thought him " one of the most just, reasonable, sweet persons they had ever seen." On this understanding it was agreed to disband both armies, and the Covenanters seem to have been so strangely confident that they had found a lasting basis of peace, that they prepared to send Leslie with a Scottish army to the help of the Elector Palatine. Yet the main point was evaded. The Covenanters held by the findings of the Glasgow Assembly, with its abolition of episcopacy and its excommunication of the bishops; the king might consent to a free General Assembly, but he would never consent to its decrees if, as it was certain to do, it reaffirmed the doings at Glasgow.[1]

That hollow treaty, variously called the Pacification of Berwick and the Pacification of Birks, was signed on the 18th of June. Montrose, when the news of it arrived, imposed a further fine upon Aberdeen, released his prisoners, and dismissed his men to their homes. A few days later he himself left with Marischal—" to post to Duns," says Baillie, " to have their part in the joy, as well they did deserve, in the common peace; where they were made most welcome both to their comrades and their king." [2]   He had won his first battle and proved his gift for war; but as he journeyed southward he can have had little of the joy of victory in his heart. The affair with Huntly, and his experience of the mediæval temper of Huntly's enemies, must have taught him how remote was his point of view from that of the colleagues whom fate had given him. He was no professional soldier like Leslie, but a perplexed and

---

[1] See, for the details of the terms, Burnet, *Mem. of the Hamiltons,* 140, etc., Lang, III., 62, etc.
[2] I., 223.

patriotic statesman, and by now he must have begun *1639*
to realize how precarious was the future of the loyalty
and the liberty which were the twin principles of his
life. To Baillie he seemed a " generous and noble
youth," whose discretion was too great. There were
soon to be harsher words used about that discretion.

CHAPTER IV

MONTROSE AND ARGYLL

(1639–42)

> If my name were liable to fear,
> I do not know the man I should avoid
> So soon as that spare Cassius. He reads much :
> He is a great observer, and he looks
> Quite through the deeds of men ; he loves no plays,
> As thou dost, Antony ; he hears no music ;
> Seldom he smiles, and smiles in such a sort
> As if he mocked himself, and scorned his spirit
> That could be moved to smile at any thing.
> Such men as he be never at heart's ease.
>
> *Julius Cæsar.*

I

1639 THE hollowness of the settlement between king and Covenant was soon to be revealed. On 1st July proclamation of the coming Assembly was made in Edinburgh, and to the consternation of the people the prelates were summoned to attend. Legally, Charles was in the right ; if the hierarchy was formally to be abolished, it had the right to be present and to defend itself ; but to the Covenanters it seemed to prove that the king had not accepted the policy of the Glasgow Assembly, and was determined to find some way of perpetuating the episcopate. In this the popular instinct was partly correct. Charles, with England in view, was not prepared to assent to the wholesale condemnation of episcopal principles which the majority in Scotland desired.[1] But if the king was unwilling to abide by the understanding of the treaty which he must have known was in the mind of the Covenant

---

[1] See the instructions to Hamilton, Burnet, *Mem. of the Hamiltons*, 149, etc.

leaders, these leaders had already broken its letter. *1639*
They did not dissolve the Tables, or disband the army,
or dispense with Leslie, or return the stores and ordnance
to Edinburgh castle, which was now in Ruthven's
hands. Riots broke out in the Edinburgh streets on
3rd July, and Traquair, Kinnoull, and Aboyne were
roughly handled by the mob. Loudoun was sent to
Berwick to apologize, but the king, not unnaturally,
demanded more—the presence of fourteen of the
Covenant leaders to discuss the situation. Some of
them, like Argyll, refused; others were forbidden by
their colleagues to attend;[1] five stalwarts only were
permitted to go—Montrose, Loudoun, Lothian, Rothes,
and Dunfermline—accompanied by Mr. Alexander
Henderson, who had not been bidden. The discussion
was a fiasco. Rothes quarrelled with the king, and
warned him that, if bishops were not abolished in
Scotland, the Scots would join with the Puritans in
attacking them in England. Charles, deeply offended,
gave up his intention of attending the forthcoming
Assembly in person, and on 3rd August returned to
London.

But this farcical conference had a profound effect
on one man. He who embarks on the tide of a popular
revolution is carried insensibly in a direction and at a
speed which he has not foreseen, and it demands a
scrupulous moral and intellectual integrity to keep true
to his first purpose. Montrose had found himself in
full agreement with the National Covenant, but the
boisterous flood which now bore him along was very
different from the even and disciplined stream for
which he had hoped. He had opposed churchmen in
politics, but the governance of Scotland was now
slipping into the hands of the Kirk; he had condemned
the king's breaches of law and constitution, but in this
respect the Covenant looked as if it would soon be as
flagrant a sinner; on behalf of the commons of Scotland he had fought the power of nobles like Hamilton
and Huntly, but there were others in his own faction

[1] Guthry, 61. Balfour, II., 341.

with the same ambitions. Above all, he had made a
central and inviolable sovereignty the foundation of
his creed, and he saw this sovereignty dissolving in
confusion. To this period, when his doubts first became insistent, we may perhaps assign these verses :

> " Can little beasts with lions roar,
> And little birds with eagles soar ?
> Can shallow streams command the seas,
> And little ants the humming bees ?
> No, no—no, no—it is not meet
> The head should stoop unto the feet."

Already his path had begun to diverge ever so little
from the broad road of the Covenant. The divergence
was slight, and to the world he still seemed to be
marching in its company, but the angle must widen,
for he was aiming at a different goal.

In those July days at Berwick Montrose had his
first true meeting with the king. Charles was no
longer the formal and distant monarch who, under
Hamilton's influence, had received coldly his boyish
offer of service. He was a man in deep distress, who
had just been successfully defied by his subjects—a
king without an army or a war-chest, who had insults
for his daily bread, and no counsellor who was not a
broken reed. That singular character is one of the
paradoxes, but not one of the enigmas, of history, for
its weakness and strength are abundantly plain. His
mild but immovable fanaticism, his lack of any quick
sense of realities, his love of wooden intrigues, his
defect in candour, his inability to read human nature,
his incapacity to decide swiftly and act boldly—they
are as patent as his piety, his fortitude, and his fidelity
to what he held to be right. But he had in the highest
degree the charm of his race, and could cast a glamour
over the most diverse minds. It was those who knew
him best who were most under his spell, so that Clarendon could describe him as " the worthiest gentleman,
the best master, the best friend, the best husband, the
best father, and the best Christian," and Sir Philip
Warwick could write : " When I think of dying, it is

one of my comforts that, when I part from the dunghill *1639*
of this world, I shall meet King Charles." [1]

In Montrose, the sight of his king in straits which
were not kingly may have awakened a chivalrous loyalty
to the person of his sovereign.   Moreover, since he was
not cognizant of Charles's secret dealings with Hamilton
and Traquair, he must have considered that the king
had thus far kept his part of the bargain better than
the Covenanters, and had granted all that the National
Covenant demanded.   Burnet will have it that he
" was much wrought upon, and gave His Majesty full
assurance of his duty in time coming, and upon that
entered in a correspondence with the king," [2] but this
story of a sudden conversion was probably Covenanting
gossip of a later date, when the breach had widened and it
was necessary to find some easy explanation. [3]   Montrose
was still a Covenanter, and resolute to complete the work
which had been begun on that spring morning in Greyfriars the year before ; but he had come to think
somewhat less well of his colleagues, and, after the
meeting at Berwick, somewhat better of his sovereign.

The General Assembly met in Edinburgh in the east
kirk of St. Giles on 12th August, with Traquair as the
royal commissioner and Mr. David Dickson of Irvine
as Moderator.   The previous Assembly at Glasgow was
not officially mentioned, but all its work was re-enacted
" at a gallop." [4]   Episcopacy was abolished in Scotland,
and the terms used, in spite of Traquair's advice, were
made as offensive as possible to the king ; episcopal
government and the power of churchmen were held
not only " unlawful to this Kirk," but " contrary to the
Word of God." [5]   The *Large Declaration*, the statement
of the king's case, written by Dr. Balcanquhal, the
Dean of Durham, was condemned in violent language,
and the Privy Council was prayed to order that the
National Covenant should be signed by every dweller
in Scotland, " of what rank or quality soever in time

---

[1] Clarendon, *History*, XI., c. 243.   Warwick, *Memoirs of the Reign of King
Charles I.*, 331.
[2] *Mem. of the Hamiltons*, 149.   [3] Guthry, 65.
[4] Gordon of Rothiemay, III., 63.   [5] Ibid., III., 47.   Guthry, 62.

1639 coming." This piece of intolerant coercion was presented by a committee, which had Montrose and Alexander Henderson among its members,[1] and duly embodied in an Act of Council. Traquair, as royal commissioner,. assented to the various proceedings, and the session closed in an atmosphere of unwonted peace. To old and staunch Presbyterians, who had fought for the Kirk as Andrew Melville conceived it, it seemed that the day of miracles had come, and a certain Mr. John Wemyss, an aged minister, speaking with difficulty, "for tears trickling down along his grey hairs, like drops of rain or dew upon the top of the tender grass," spoke a moving *nunc dimittis.* " I do remember when the Kirk of Scotland had a beautiful face. I remember since there was a great power and life accompanying the ordinances of God, and a wonderful work of operation upon the hearts of the people. This my eyes did see—a fearful defection after procured by our sins. And no more did I wish before my eyes were closed but to have seen such a beautiful day, and that under the conduct and favour of our King's Majesty." [2]

The Parliament, which met on 31st August, was a very different gathering. A more momentous Parliament had never sat in Scotland, for until it ratified the acts of the Assembly these had no legal validity, and the Kirk had no security. The first difficulty that arose was constitutional. One of the estates, the clergy, had dissolved itself, since the bishops had fled the country. In choosing the Lords of the Articles, it had been the custom for the nobles to elect the representatives of the church, and the bishops to elect the representatives of the nobles, while both together chose the representatives of the lairds and burgesses, while the king added eight nominees of his own. By means of the bishops the Crown could in this way ensure a majority. Charles desired to fill the vacancy left by the bishops by fourteen ministers chosen by the Crown, or, in the alternative, by fourteen laymen; [3] but the ministers suspected a

---

[1] Gordon of Rothiemay, III., 57.   [2] Peterkin, *Records of the Kirk,* 251
[3] Burnet, *Mem. of the Hamiltons,* 150.

trap, and the nobility were jealous of the ministers, so this scheme fell to the ground. Under protest from Argyll a temporary arrangement was come to. Traquair himself chose the nobles,[1] who in turn chose the lesser barons and burgesses. This provisional Committee of the Articles set to work, and its reach was long. It ratified the acts of the recent Assembly, and proceeded to remodel the constitution of Scotland. It whittled away the royal prerogative, by transferring the control of the Mint and the appointment of great officers of state to Parliament, and, by one vote, passed Argyll's motion that each estate, nobles, barons, and burgesses, should elect its own lords.[2]

To this sudden essay in parliamentary government Montrose was opposed, and there were many other doubters in the Covenant ranks. It must be clearly understood that Argyll's proposal, for all its modern sound, was not an early stirring of democratic ideals. The common people of Scotland had no say in the government of the country, and were to have none for many a year, except through the General Assembly. It was a provision aimed directly against the royal prerogative, and, considering the recent use made of that prerogative, it had its justification. But such a change was not a reassertion of ancient liberties, but a wholly new departure, and so violent an innovation roused suspicion. The new régime would throw the government of Scotland into the hands of him who was the most adroit electioneer, and in this connection all men's thoughts turned to Argyll. It altered, but it did not seriously liberalize, the basis of representation. Moreover, it was a demand which struck at the whole conception of monarchy as then existing. At one stroke it reduced the king to a cypher in matters in which hitherto he had been all-powerful. To Montrose it seemed to weaken sovereignty, the central sanction of law, without putting a reasonable equivalent in its place, for, if the king had his faults, a legislature of factious

---

[1] Huntly, released from Edinburgh castle, was one.
[2] Gordon of Rothiemay, III., 66. *A. P. S.*, V., 252, etc., 303.

lairds and nobles was not without them. Further, it had no finality. If the king assented, he would be pressed to greater concessions, and the foundations of order would crumble. This was also the doubt of Mr. Robert Baillie. " Whatever the Prince grants, I fear we press more than he can grant ; and when we are fully satisfied, it is likely England will begin where we have left off."

It was the turning-point of Montrose's political career. His enthusiasm for the National Covenant had made him an active member of the late Assembly, as an elder from Auchterarder, and he had supported the compulsory signature of that Covenant—an extreme step for one of his beliefs. At the moment he had no quarrel with the Kirk. He was prepared to accept every act of the Assembly, even its wholesale condemnation of episcopacy as hostile to God's Word. Two months later, when the king summoned him to London, he asked to be excused, after consulting with the Covenant leaders, on the ground that at such a time his going to court would be misconstrued—conduct which Wariston lauded as " noble." [1]   To the clerical side of the movement he was still profoundly sympathetic. But the proposed constitutional revolution made him pause, and presently sent him into opposition, for of the two sections in his party he distrusted the nobles more than the ministers. Six years later he put his position before his countrymen. " Members of the said Parliament, some of them having far designs unknown to us, others of them having found the sweetness of government, were pleased to refuse the ratification of the acts of Assembly with the abjuration of episcopacy and the Court of High Commission introduced by the prelates, unless they had the whole alleged liberty due to the subject ; which was in fact intrenching upon authority, and the total abrogation of his Majesty's royal prerogative ; whereby the king's commissioner was constrained to rise and discharge the Parliament." [2]   Men

[1] Napier, I., 228–229.
[2] "Montrose's Defence and Remonstrance," 1645. *Mem. of M.*, I., 215.

began to whisper that the young Covenant general had 1639
been seduced by the royal blandishments at Berwick,
and a paper with the words " *Invictus armis verbis
vincitur* " was presently found pinned to his chamber
door.[1]

Traquair, who had been severely censured by
Charles for his conduct as commissioner to the Assembly,
refused, on the king's instructions, to accept the decisions
of Parliament. The ostensible ground, in which Montrose ingenuously believed, was the attack on the prerogative ; the true reason was the ratification of the
Assembly's abolition of episcopacy. With England in
view, Charles could scarcely be expected to assent to
the condemnation of episcopacy as " unlawful," though
he might admit it to be contrary to the constitution of
the Kirk ; he clung to his intention to restore the
bishops at some later date, and therefore would not
assent to the act rescinding the old acts which had
established them.[2] On 14th November Parliament,
after it had protested against the illegality of the proceeding, was prorogued till the following June.[3] On
the part of Charles it was a grave blunder, for the people
of Scotland were not slow to grasp the true explanation.
He could have found some support for the defence of
the prerogative ; he could even have mustered to his
side tender consciences like that of Mr. Robert Baillie,
who was not prepared to condemn episcopacy as in
itself unlawful ;[4] with these points, if honestly stated,
he might have driven a wedge into the Covenant party.
As it was, a conviction that the king was playing fast
and loose with them on the main question of the episcopate, and dislike of the egregious Traquair, rallied the
doubters for the moment. Napier, the typical moderate, sat on the committee which represented the
prorogued Parliament. As for Montrose, we have seen
his refusal to go to court in December, and we find him

---

[1] Guthry, 65. I see no reason for Lord Stanhope's suspicion of this story,
in his *Historical Essays*, 131.
[2] See the king's letter to Traquair in Burnet, *Mem. of the Hamiltons*, 158-159.
[3] Rait, *The Parliaments of Scotland*, 63.
[4] See Baillie's letter to Loudoun, *Letters and Journals*, I., 181.

1640 a signatory, along with Loudoun and Leslie, of a letter
addressed to the King of France, representing to Louis
the " candour and ingenuity " of the Covenanters towards their king.[1]

II

With the abortive Parliament of 1639 went one of
the last embankments of the old régime, and henceforth
the tide of revolution runs fast. Parliament had been
prorogued that the king might muster his forces, and
the Covenanters did not let the grass grow under their
feet in a similar duty. It was clear that the Covenant
could only be defended on the field of battle. Through
the early months of 1640 levies were being raised and
drilled throughout the Lowlands, and on 17th April
Leslie was given his commission as commander-in-chief.[2]
In the same month Charles in England, in desperation for supplies, summoned the Short Parliament, but
no supplies were forthcoming, and in three weeks he
dissolved it. The Covenanters were much heartened
thereby, for it was plain that England in the coming
war was not behind the king. By the end of the summer
Leslie had under him some 22,000 foot and 3,000 horse,
and by freewill offerings, and offerings not so free, a
considerable war-chest had been created. Charles could
only scrape together less than half these numbers of ill-
disciplined and reluctant recruits, and after trying every
device, legal and illegal, he was still lamentably short of
money. Strafford had come over from Ireland to advise
his master, and on Strafford's counsel the Short Parliament had been summoned. But Strafford misread the
temper of England no less than Charles, and his plan of
using an Irish army in Scotland (which, misunderstood

---

[1] Rushworth, III., 1,120. *Cal. S. P., Dom.* (1640), 19–20. For the other
negotiations of the Covenanters with France at this date, see Gardiner, IX., 91,
etc. One curious result was the raising of a regiment of 2,000 Scots under
Irvine, Argyll's half-brother, which, in 1643, fought under Condé at Thionville.
See Montereul (Montreuil), *Corr.*, II., 604. The negotiations with France must
have been begun before Huntly's imprisonment in Edinburgh castle, for he
mentions them as one of the arguments used to persuade him. See pamphlet
cited on p. 99.

[2] *A. P. S.*, V., 285.

by Vane, was to be damning evidence against him **1640**
at his trial) was not accepted. With a starved and
slender force, and lacking the goodwill of the country
which formed his base, the king went out to war
against what was virtually a united nation in arms.

The prorogued Parliament of Scotland was due to
meet on 2nd June. Charles, by a proclamation in May,
prorogued it for a further month, but the proclamation
was disregarded. There was some technical informality
about it, which the acute Covenanting lawyers were
not slow to seize upon.[1] But the Parliament which met
was clearly unconstitutional, for there was no royal
commissioner; it constituted itself a Parliament by its
own act, and appointed Lord Burleigh its president;
but it still maintained a show of loyalty, declaring that
it acted by his Majesty's "tacit consent" and "presumed allowance," and that it was only "receiving and
making use of that benefit which his Majesty, in his
justice and goodness, had publicly granted to us and
never recalled." It was the fiction which the Long
Parliament in England was presently to adopt and
maintain for seven feverish years. The true state of
the case was summed up in a phrase which was probably
Argyll's, "to do the less was more lawful than to do
the greater";[2] the alternative to holding an unauthorized Parliament was to depose the king. Having
embarked upon this bold course, the new Parliament
did not lag. It ratified all the acts of the previous
Assembly, created free parliamentary committees in
place of the old Committee of the Articles, organized
the military preparations against the king, and passed
a triennial act. In five weeks it had accomplished a
huge body of legislation, which must have been carefully prepared beforehand, and thereafter it prorogued
itself till the following November.

Revolution had thus been openly declared, for by
no ingenuity of argument could these proceedings be
defended as constitutional. Montrose opposed them to

---

[1] Burnet, *Mem. of the Hamiltons*, 167. Rait, *The Parliaments of Scotland*,
65–66.   [2] Napier, I., 234, 236.

1640 the utmost of his power, but his was the only voice;[1] since war was declared against the sovereign there was less need to be scrupulous about minor prerogatives. But his opposition made him a marked man. A Committee of the Estates was appointed with dictatorial powers to act as a Government while Parliament was not sitting, and to this body, which was virtually a Committee of Public Safety, and consisted of "about forty members, from earls to tailors and saddlers,"[2] Montrose was appointed, no doubt with the intention of paralyzing his opposition. There was no alternative before him but to accept. He still held the greater part of the Covenant creed; he was in favour of the coming war, believing that it was necessary to open the king's eyes to the anti-episcopal resolution of Scotland; had he resigned he would have been impotent, and must either have fled to the king, like Airlie, or, like Huntly, hidden himself in northern fastnesses. The moment had not yet come for the final breach. Argyll was not a member of the Committee; that lover of secret power was happier pulling the wires behind the scenes. Besides, he had much business in the west, on the watch for Strafford's army. His countrymen did not attribute his abstention to modesty. "All saw he was *major potestas*, and, though not formally a member, yet all knew that it was his influence that gave being, life, and motion to these new-modelled governors; and not a few thought that this *juncto* was his invention."[3]

The first care of the Covenanting lords, as in the former war, was to prevent trouble in their rear. Angus, the Gordon country, and the Atholl domains in Perthshire were something less than lukewarm for the Covenant, and to Argyll was given the congenial task of taking order not only with the enemies of true religion, but with the ancestral foes of his house. For this commission of the Committee of Estates Montrose must share the responsibility, and his name was the first

---

[1] Wariston to Hepburn of Humbie, Napier, I., 236.
[2] The Committee included at least three men of Montrose's views, Napier, Wigton, and Stirling of Keir.   [3] Gordon of Rothiemay, III., 182.

appended. He realized the need in war of safeguarding the country behind an army, and he recognized that gentler means than a commission of " fire and sword " would scarcely suffice. Argyll was authorized to pursue the clans " until he should either bring them to their bounden duty, and give assurance of the same by pledges or otherwise, or else to the utter subduing and rooting them out of the country." [1]

He was not slack in the execution of his warrant. With 5,000 of his clan he left Inveraray on 18th June, entrapped Atholl by a ruse similar to that employed by Montrose's army with Huntly a year before,[2] and presently arrived in the lowlands of Angus, where the Campbells were regarded with the same detestation and fear as was felt elsewhere for Antrim's Irishry. Airlie was in England with the king, and his son, Lord Ogilvy, was persuaded by Montrose to surrender Airlie castle for "the use of the public." [3] Montrose accordingly wrote to Argyll saying that his presence in Angus was needless, but Argyll was not minded to take instructions from Montrose when an ancient enemy was at his mercy. He burned the " bonnie house o' Airlie," and the other Ogilvy dwelling of Forthar in Glenisla ; and from the latter Lady Ogilvy was driven, so the story goes, in circumstances of extreme barbarity. He then carried fire and sword into Lochaber, and completed his commission to the satisfaction of the Estates.[4] In it all he

---

[1] *A. P. S.*, V., 398.   [2] Guthry, 75. Spalding, I., 271.
[3] Napier, I., 245.

[4] Argyll was granted an act of indemnity for his conduct by Parliament in November 1641, when the king was present (*A. P. S.*, V. 399). The comprehensive list of offences indemnified, which included " all manner of burnings and the putting of persons to torture and death," sheds some light upon his doings. At his trial in 1661 he denied ordering the burning of Forthar, but his instructions to his lieutenant are extant (Gardiner, IX., 167, *n.* 3. *Hist. MSS. Comm.*, 6th Report, 616). Sir James Balfour (II., 380–381) says that the expedition was conducted with an exact discipline, but there may be disciplined barbarism. For the treatment of Lady Ogilvy, the chief authority is Gordon of Rothiemay (III., 165), who, however, gets his dates into confusion. In this kind of war many atrocities must occur, and many more will be invented. The popular mind, as shown in the ballad of *The Bonnie House o' Airlie*, had no doubts on the subject. For Montrose's behaviour, see Lord Ogilvy's answer to interrogatories, and the libel against Montrose in 1641. *Mem. of M.*, I., 264, etc. ; 328, etc.

1640 had behaved like the ordinary feudal baron with grievances to avenge. This zealot of the Kirk had conducted a Highland campaign according to the most ruthless traditions of the past, and had thereby compiled against himself a reckoning which Highland memories were not likely to forget.

In July Montrose marched south with his contingent to join Leslie's army, which now lay in camp near the town of Duns. He had with him the Stirling and Strathearn levies—2,500 men, says Napier, 1,600 the English spies reported. In the camp the breach with Argyll widened. Argyll accused him of undue lenity in his recent work in Angus, and of needless delay in moving his regiments; but he was absolved from blame by Leslie and the other members of the Committee. But his distrust of Argyll promptly received a full justification. The Committee of Estates was too large and heterogeneous to be an effective instrument in time of war, and proposals were being privately made to narrow it. This was common sense, but the actual scheme took an ominous form. There were already stories abroad that in his recent northern foray Argyll's soldiers had declared that they were not King Stewart's but King Campbell's men, and a Gaelic song was made of which a verse ran: " I gave Argyll the praise, because all men say it is truth, for he will take gear from the Lowland men, and he will take the Crown perforce, and he will cry king at Whitsunday." [1] The throne, as we have seen, was never far from the imagination of the great Scots nobles who had the blood of Bruce in their veins. But that was for the future; for the moment the proposals were more modest—that one man, Argyll, should be made responsible for the country north of Forth, and two men for the country south of it. Montrose protested, and had the draft commission for the north altered, so that beside Argyll's appeared his own name, with Mar, Cassilis, and others. [2]

But, alarmed by the incident, he posted back to

---

[1] *Mem. of M.*, II., 477.
[2] Montrose's own account at his trial in May 1641. Napier, I., 255.

Edinburgh, where he met his old college friend, Lord **1640**
Lindsay of the Byres, and heard of a scheme to
make " a particular man " dictator of all Scotland,
after the Roman fashion. The man, in view of
Lindsay's antecedents, could only be Argyll. To
check this intrigue, before returning to the army,
Montrose summoned a meeting of his friends at Lord
Wigton's house of Cumbernauld, near Glasgow, and
signed an agreement to resist "the particular and in-
direct practising of a few." The Cumbernauld Bond
bound the signatories to uphold the letter and spirit of
the National Covenant "to the hazard of our lives,
fortunes, and estates," and concluded with words not
usually found in Scottish " bands," for they swore
to adhere to each other " so far as may consist with
the good and weal of the public." [1] Among others,
Marischal, Wigton, Kinghorn, Home, Boyd, Atholl, Mar,
Seaforth, and Almond (Leslie's second in command)
appended their names. None, except Montrose, were
men of power ; they were the moderates, the Girondins,
of the revolution, and of little moment compared to
the " lawless resolutes " who opposed them.

Though the Bond was kept secret, the general
antagonism to Argyll's project was known, and this
was sufficient for the moment to defeat it. Montrose
returned to the army at Duns, and Leslie prepared for
the invasion of England—the ostensible purpose being
merely to present to the king a petition praying that
the recent acts of Assembly and Parliament be ratified.
The armed petitioners at once took the offensive. On
20th August, the day on which Charles left London to
assume the command of his army with Strafford as his
lieutenant-general, Leslie crossed the Tweed at Cold-
stream, by the very ford which Scott makes Marmion ride
on the eve of Flodden. His Lowlanders were in hodden-
grey with blue caps, and each, in the ancient Scottish
fashion, bore oatmeal in a haversack. The Highland
contingent were scantily clad, and carried broadswords

---

[1] The Bond was burned, but Napier discovered a transcript in the handwriting of Sir James Balfour. Napier, I., 269-270.

1640 and bows and arrows.[1] The colours of the foot had the motto " Covenant for Relligion, Crowne, and Country." [2] " We are sadder and graver than ordinary soldiers," Lothian wrote, " only we are well provided of pipers." They had fiddlers, too, but these were " intolerably given to drink." [3] By a curious fate the privilege of leading the van fell by lot to Montrose. Tweed was in high flood, so he first forded it alone on foot, and then returned to encourage his men.[4]

The campaign was short and inglorious. Conway, at Newcastle, had a force far inferior to Leslie's in both numbers and quality, and he was an indifferent general. " I am teaching cart-horses to manage," he wrote, " and making men that are fit for Bedlam and Bridewell to keep the Ten Commandments, so that General Lesley and I keep two schools : he has scholars that profess to serve God, and he is instructing them how they may safely do injury and all impiety ; mine to the utmost of their power never kept any law of God or the king, and they are to be made fit to make others keep them." [5] " I fear," he wrote also, " unpaid soldiers more than I do the Scots, and the devil to boot." [6] He had cause for his forebodings. Leslie marched without opposition to the ford of Newburn, four miles above Newcastle, the crossing of which would not only give him command of the Tyne, but enable him to attack Newcastle on the unfortified side. There Conway attempted a stand, but on 28th August he was blown out of his position by the Scottish guns. His cavalry fled to Durham, while his foot fell back on Newcastle, which next morning surrendered. It was, Clarendon wrote, " the most shameful and confounding flight that was ever heard of." A battle, which played a major part in our constitutional history, and which was to Charles what Bouvines was to King John, was won in an afternoon with a loss of a dozen to the victors and sixty to the

---

[1] *Cal. S. P., Dom.* (1640), 615.   [2] Gordon of Rothiemay, III., 261.
[3] *Earls of Ancrum and Lothian,* I., 103, etc.
[4] One of them was drowned. Napier, I., 271. Terry, *Alexander Leslie,* 108
[5] *Cal. S. P., Dom.* (1640), 268.
[6] Ibid., 548.

vanquished. Charles fell back on York; he could not *1640*
do otherwise, for he had no force which could have withstood Leslie for an hour.

The Covenanters' occupation of Newcastle, with the
surrounding district, gave them a powerful lever in subsequent negotiations, for they controlled the supply
of coal to London, and thereby £50,000 of the king's
revenue.[1] They behaved discreetly, for they had
no desire to antagonize the English people. The
first problem was that of subsistence, and Charles
consented to their raising a daily levy from the four
neighbouring counties. Negotiations began at Ripon,
and were presently transferred to London, but it was
not till August 7, 1641, that the dispute, mainly finan-
cial, was finally settled. Meantime his difficulties forced
Charles to call a Parliament, and on November 3, 1640,
as a direct result of the Scottish invasion, the Long
Parliament assembled. Already many communications
had passed between the English malcontents and the
Covenanters, beginning with Lord Savile's assurance,
with its forged signatures, in June 1640, when Leslie's
army was mustering. Now, with London as the venue
of discussion, Covenanters like Henderson and Wariston
were brought into close touch with Pym and the Puritan
leaders, and we find the idea first mooted of the forcible
introduction of Presbytery into England. Wariston
had suggested something like it to Savile in June 1640,
and Henderson, in London, came to believe that the
one hope of safeguarding Presbytery in Scotland was
by securing its establishment south of the Tweed. The
Scottish commissioners were instructed to table, as one
of their propositions, " a desire for unity in religion and
uniformity in Church government as a special means of
conserving the peace between the two countries," and
they found much support in Parliament. The London
" root and branch " petition for the abolition of episcopacy was presented to Parliament on 11th December,
and others flowed in from the shires. Parliament for
the moment rejected the Scottish plan, but the Scottish

---

[1] *Cal. S. P., Dom.* (1640), 116.

1640 commissioners continued to hope. The papers drafted at that time by Henderson on the subject contain the policy which, two years later, bore fruit in the Solemn League and Covenant. " Nothing so powerful to divide the hearts of people as division in religion ; nothing so strong to unite the hearts of people as unity in religion ; and the greater zeal in different religions the greater division, but the more zeal in one religion the more firm union. In the paradise of Nature the diversity of flowers and herbs is pleasant and useful, but in the paradise of the Church different and contrary religions are unpleasant and hurtful." [1]

That was one omen for those who had eyes to read it ; the Scots, who had at the moment the vantage, were suggesting a higher price for peace than the bills of expenses which Leslie was patiently presenting. Another was the swift movement in Parliament to exact retribution from those who, like Strafford and Laud, were commonly held to be the pillars of monarchical policy. There was a third—most fateful of all; for the Huntingdonshire grazier, who had been so active in defending the rights of the fen commoners, was now at Westminster. On a certain November day, at the opening of the session, a young courtier, Sir Philip Warwick, very proud of his fine clothes, found a member speaking in the House whom he did not know, a gentleman in a plain suit made by a bad country tailor, his linen not very clean, and a speck of blood on his little band. " His stature was of a good size, his sword stuck close to his side, his countenance swollen and reddish, his voice sharp and untunable, and his eloquence full of fervour." [2] This was he of whom John Maidston, his servant and no flatterer, wrote that " a larger soul hath seldom dwelt in a house of clay." Oliver Cromwell had set his foot upon the road which was to lead him to the mastery of England.

[1] *Arguments given in by the Commissioners of Scotland unto the Lords of the Treaty*, 1641. See also Baillie, I., 269, 274, 275, 287, 305, etc.
[2] *Memoirs of the Reign of King Charles I.*, 247–248.

III

Montrose may have hoped to find a solution of his *1640* doubts in swift action in the field, but the easy victory of Newburn brought no comfort. Of his part in that campaign we know nothing, except that in his opponents' eyes he was one of the Covenanting leaders, and that Strafford hastened to report from Darlington to the king the false rumour that he had been killed by Wilmot.[1] A man of active temper and complete honesty, if he cannot see his way plain, is apt to make a sorry business of waiting. Perplexities thickened about the path of the undecided Montrose. He saw clearly the necessity of asserting and safeguarding the central authority, the king's, if Scotland was to be saved from anarchy, and he saw no less clearly the direction of Argyll's thoughts ; but he still believed that the Covenanters as a whole were willing to listen to moderate counsels, and that if he bided his time he might yet lead his countrymen into reasonable ways. After the fiasco of Newburn and the ready capitulation of Newcastle, he may have argued that Scotland had sufficiently vindicated her rights against Charles, and that the time was ripe for insisting that the royal rights in turn should be safeguarded. He did not know how closely the interests of the Covenant were linked with Pym and his followers in the English Parliament, whose maxim it was rapidly becoming that the king could do no right. Nor did he realize the direction of the thoughts of the Scottish commissioners and their grandiose scheme for imposing Presbytery on England. He looked about for like-minded associates, and found few. He was not a simple-souled royalist like Airlie, who saw the problem as a plain choice between honour and dishonour, or a mediæval satrap like Huntly, who thought in terms of family pride and ancestral enmities. He had a philosophy of politics, which we shall presently consider, and he explored the nobility of Scotland to see if he

---

[1] *Cal. S. P., Dom.* (1640), 649.

could find others, besides Napier, who subscribed to it. So he became zealous in discussing public affairs, and thereby played into Argyll's hand.

Suspicion of him had grown among the Covenanting leaders, and he was closely watched. From Newcastle he wrote to the king a simple protestation of loyalty, and the letter came to the knowledge of the Committee —picked up by accident, says Burnet; disclosed by spies in the royal bedchamber, says Wishart. He was accused of " having intelligence with the enemy," and made the unanswerable reply that the king, against whose person and authority any aspersion was made treason by the articles of war, could not be " the enemy." [1] In Baillie's report of the incident he is spoken of as one " whose pride long ago was intolerable and meaning very doubtful." November found Montrose back in Scotland, summoned to explain the Cumbernauld Bond, the contents of which had come to Argyll's ear through hints dropped by Lord Boyd on his deathbed. The Committee of Estates called before them the signatories, who acknowledged and justified their action. Some of the ministers demanded the death of the accused, but these were too powerful to receive more than censure, since some of them commanded regiments, and all were territorial magnates. " They consulted to patch up the business after a declaration under their hands that they intended nothing against the public, together with a surrendering of the bond, which the Committee, having gotten, caused it to be burned." [2] The breach between Montrose and his former allies had become very wide. He returned to the army, and his indignation made his tongue run loose. In January 1641 he told Colonel Cochrane, in the presence of old Leslie, that he could prove that certain leaders in Scotland were scheming to depose the king, and he left no doubt in the mind of his embarrassed hearers that he referred to Argyll.[3]

In the beginning of 1641 it would appear that Mon-

---

[1] Baillie, I., 262. Burnet, *Mem. of the Hamiltons*, 228. Guthry, 87–88. Wishart, c. i. Napier, I., 271–273
[2] Guthry, 90. Spalding, I., 376.   [3] Napier, I., 276–277.

trose and his few friends decided upon a policy. They *1641*
must induce the king to come to Scotland and satisfy
every reasonable Covenanting demand ; that done, he
would be able, with the country behind him, to resist
the follies of fanatical preachers, to check the aggression
of selfish nobles, and above all to curb the ambition of
Argyll, whose treason they would be in a position to
prove. In a letter to Charles, written in the early
months of the year, Montrose offered wise advice to his
sovereign.

" Your ancient and native kingdom of Scotland is in a mighty
distemper. It is incumbent on your Majesty to find out the disease,
remove the cause, and apply convenient remedies. The disease in
my opinion is contagious, and may infect the rest of your Majesty's
dominions. It is a falling sickness, for they are like to fall from
you, and from the obedience due to you, if, by removing the cause,
and application of wholesome remedies, it be not speedily prevented.
The cause is a fear and apprehension, not without some reason, of
changes in religion, and that superstitious worship shall be brought
in upon it, and therewith all their laws infringed and their liberties
invaded. Free them, sir, from this fear, as you are free from any
such thoughts ; and undoubtedly you shall thereby settle the State
in a firm obedience to your Majesty in all time coming. They have
no other end but to preserve their religion in purity, and their
liberties entire. That they intend the overthrow of monarchial
government is a calumny. They are capable of no other, for many
and great reasons ; and ere they will admit another than your
Majesty, and after you your son and nearest of your posterity, to
sit upon your throne, many thousands of them will spend their
dearest blood. You are not like a tree lately planted, which oweth
a fall to the first wind. Your ancestors have governed theirs,
without interruption of race, two thousand years or thereabouts,
and taken such root as it can never be plucked up by any but yourselves. If any others shall entertain such treasonable thoughts,
which I do not believe, certainly they will prove as vain as they are
wicked.

" The remedy of this dangerous disease consisteth only in your
Majesty's presence for a space in that kingdom. It is easy to you
in person to settle their troubles, and to disperse these mists of
apprehension and mistaking—impossible to any other. If you send
down a commissioner, whatever he be, he shall neither give nor get
contentment, but shall render the disease incurable. The success
of your Majesty's affairs, the security of your authority, the peace
and happiness of your subjects, depend upon your personal presence.
The disease is of that kind which is much helped by conceit [1] and the

---

[1] Imagination.

presence of the physician. Now is the proper time and the critical days. For the people love change, and expect from it much good— a new heaven and a new earth ; but, being disappointed, are as desirous of a re-change to the former estate.

"Satisfy them, sir, in point of religion and liberties, when you come here, in a loving and free manner ; that they may see your Majesty had never.any other purpose, and doth not intend the least prejudice to either. For religious subjects, and such as enjoy their lawful liberties, obey better and love more than the godless and the servile, who do all out of base fear, which begets hate. Any difference that may arise upon the Acts passed in the last Parliament, your Majesty's presence, and the advice and endeavour of your faithful servants will easily accommodate. Let your Majesty be pleased to express your favour and care of your subjects' weal by giving way to any just notion of theirs for relief of the burdens these late troubles have laid on them, and by granting what else may tend to their good ; which your Majesty may do with assurance that therein is included your own.

"Suffer them not to meddle or dispute of your power. It is an instrument never subjects yet handled well. Let not your authority receive any diminution of that which the law of God and Nature and the fundamental laws of the country alloweth ; for then it shall grow contemptible : and weak and miserable is the people whose prince hath not power sufficient to punish oppression and to maintain peace and justice.

"On the other side, aim not at absoluteness. It endangers your estate and stirs up trouble. The people of the western parts of the world could never endure it any long time, and they of Scotland less than any. Hearken not to Rehoboam's counsellors. They are flatterers, and therefore cannot be friends ; they will follow your fortune, and love not your person. Pretend what they will, their hasty ambition and avarice make them persuade an absolute government that the exercise of the same (may be put) on them, and then they know how to get wealth . . .[1]

"Practise, sir, the temperate government. It fitteth the humour and disposition of the nation best. It is most strong, most powerful, most desirable of any. It gladdeth the heart of your subjects, and then they erect a throne there for you to reign. *Firmissimum imperium quo obedientes gaudent.* Let your last act there be the settling the offices of State upon men of known integrity and sufficiency. Take them not upon credit and other men's recommendation ; they prefer men for their own ends and with respect to themselves. Neither yet take them at a hazard, but upon your own knowledge, which fully reacheth to a great many more than will fill those few places. Let them not be such as are obliged to others than yourself for their preferment ; not factious nor popular ; neither such as are much hated ; for these are not able to serve you well, and the others are not willing if it be prejudice to those upon

[1] Gap of two lines in MS.

whom they depend. They who are preferred and obliged to your *1641* Majesty will study to behave them well and dutifully in their places, if it were for no other reason yet for this, that they make not your Majesty ashamed of your choice.

" So shall your Majesty secure your authority for the present, and settle it for the future time. Your journey shall be prosperous, your return glorious. You shall be followed with the blessings of your people, and with that contentment which a virtuous deed reflecteth upon the mind of the doer. And more true and solid shall your glory be than if you had conquered nations and subdued a people.

> " . . . . *pax una triumphis*
> *Innumeris potior.*" [1]

This sagacious letter might be elaborately annotated from contemporary history. There was no sentence in it which future events were not to justify abundantly, save that optimism about Scottish opinion which was to prove to Montrose a deceptive light. What could Argyll offer on the other side ? It would be a mistake to take too seriously the gossip about his monarchical ambitions. The chief of the Campbells was far too shrewd a man to let a glittering dream divert him from a practicable purpose. His aim was to be dictator of Scotland, and his abilities were adequate to the task. Had he had military genius, he might well have played in Scotland the part of Cromwell, and wholly upturned the old foundations of sovereignty. But what had he to put in its place ? Another autocracy without the sanctions of the old. He had made the cumbrous mediæval Parliament a more efficient and representative thing, but this reform merely strengthened the hands of the new oligarchy. He was sworn to the creed of intolerant Presbyterian domination in its extremest form. Above all, he was the clan chief, who supported his friends and did not forgive his enemies. To Montrose the alternative was unthinkable, for it would bring to Scotland not peace but a naked sword. He himself, in his young enthusiasm for the national religion and liberties, had been led into courses which were alien to his beliefs. He had assented to the constraint of

---

[1] Napier, I., 311-313.

1641 private consciences, when he approved of the compulsory
signature of the Covenant; he had given his approval
to feudal barbarities when he signed Argyll's commission for the subjection of the North. But his eyes
were now opened, and he hastened to draw aside from
that perilous road.

Montrose was an ingenuous conspirator, for in his
eagerness to discover like-mindedness and make con-
verts he talked freely to the wrong people. At Scone,
during a visit to Lord Stormont, he heard from Atholl,
Stewart of Grandtully, and John Stewart of Ladywell,
the commissary of Dunkeld, reports of treasonable
speeches made by Argyll during the Perthshire expedition of the previous year. He spoke of them to his
friend, Mr. Robert Murray, the minister of Methven,
who mentioned them to Mr. John Graham, the minister
of Auchterarder, who repeated the story to the Auchterarder presbytery, whence it came to the ear of Argyll.
Graham and Murray were asked for their authority,
and they named Montrose, who accepted responsibility
and in turn cited his evidence. His witnesses, he said,
were Lindsay of the Byres, Cassilis, Mar, and Stewart
of Ladywell. The witnesses were summoned before
the Committee of Estates, and proved unsatisfactory.
Lindsay remembered the conversation, but said that he
had not named Argyll. Ladywell stood by his words,
signed a written statement, and was thereupon, on
31st May, sent to Edinburgh castle.

There something happened. Either Ladywell's nerve
broke down, or he was worked on by friends of Argyll,
like Balmerino; for next day he saw Argyll, recanted
the charges against him, and declared that he had
forged them out of malice. He did more, for he confessed that he had been privy to discussions between
Montrose, Napier, his nephew Sir George Stirling of
Keir, and Keir's brother-in-law, Archibald Stewart of
Blackhall, and that, acting on their instructions, he
had sent a report of Argyll's treason to the king. The
messenger who carried it was a certain Walter Stewart
of the Traquair family, and on the return journey he

was captured by the Committee. Among the papers **1641** found on him was a short note from the king to Montrose about his coming to Scotland, to which no exception could be taken, and certain papers written in a strange jargon, which was in all likelihood the product of Stewart's own half-witted fancy, but which to the Committee had an ugly look of a secret cypher. Stewart was ready with a confused but dark-sounding interpretation, and on this document Montrose, Napier, Stirling, and Stewart of Blackhall were arrested and confined in separate rooms in the castle.[1]

It is not likely that Ladywell's first story was true. Argyll was too cautious a man to speak rashly on such matters in uncertain company; if he talked of the deposition of kings, it is probable that it was as an abstract proposition of kings in general. Nor did he show the desire of the rest of the Committee for the summary punishment of Ladywell—which would have been natural if Ladywell had been an inconvenient witness whom it was politic to silence. We know from Guthry, a hostile witness, that he consulted the Lord Advocate to see if a more lenient sentence could not be imposed.[2] The wretched man was duly convicted under the old Scottish statute of "leasing-making,"[3] and publicly beheaded in Edinburgh on 28th July.

Meantime there was the far graver business of Montrose. Argyll could afford to neglect the wild gossip of the commissary of Dunkeld, but it was another matter to have responsible Scottish nobles, with influence in the army, negotiating behind his back with the king. Napier was offered release as a favour, but declined to accept it; he declared that if any one was guilty he was, and he would not be separated from his companions. Montrose refused to answer any question before the Committee, and demanded a public trial

---

[1] Napier, I., 295, etc. Guthry, 92, etc. Spalding, II., 47, etc.
[2] Guthry, 94.
[3] Acts of 1584, cap. 134; and of 1585, cap. 10. The punishment was reduced by 6 Geo. IV., cap. 47, and abolished by 7 Will. IV., cap. 5. According to Baillie it had never been put in force before (I., 381–382). These were the Acts under which Mr. Oldbuck, in *The Antiquary*, threatened vengeance against Mrs. Macleuchar, the proprietrix of the Queensferry diligence.

1641 by his peers. Traquair angrily denied any complicity with his preposterous kinsman, Walter Stewart. The king wrote on 12th June to Argyll to clear himself; his letter to Montrose was " fit for me to write, both for the matter, and the person to whom it is written; "[1] he had made no promise to any one as to the distribution of offices; he was coming to Scotland for no other purpose than to settle the affairs of the kingdom " according to the articles of the treaty." This might seem sufficient to clear Montrose, but his opponents, having got him under duress, did not intend to let him readily go. His house was broken into and his papers ransacked, but nothing more dangerous to the peace of the realm could be found than a paper justifying the Cumbernauld Bond, and " some letters from ladies to him in his younger years, flowered with Arcadian compliments."[2] On 27th July he was brought before Parliament, and declared that he had nothing to confess or to defend. " Truth doth not seek corners, it needeth no favour." He awaited their lordships' questions or commands. " My resolution is to carry along with me fidelity and honour to the grave."[3] They could make nothing of such a man, and sent him back to prison. He was brought again before Parliament on 6th August, and a third time on 14th August.[4] On the evening of the latter day the king arrived in Edinburgh.

Charles's determination to come to Scotland, so puzzling to Clarendon, was due to the belief that he had still a powerful following in that kingdom, which needed only to be heartened by his presence. But a few days in Edinburgh were sufficient to disillusion him. With Lennox and Hamilton as his companions he recovered neither popularity nor authority. He had come north largely in the hope of securing part of Leslie's army for use in the struggle which he saw to be imminent in England, and for this he was prepared to pay a high price. He paid the price, but he did not secure his end, for Leslie's army was disbanded. Non-Covenanting

---

[1] Napier, I., 314–315.   [2] Guthry, 112.
[3] Napier, I., 346.   [4] Balfour, III., 38.

nobles like Lennox, Hamilton, Morton, and Roxburgh were compelled to take the Covenant. Hamilton, always, as Charles said, " very active in his own preservation," made his peace with Argyll. Henderson became the royal chaplain, and the king was obliged to listen to many sermons and attend endless services conducted under the austerest Presbyterian forms. He was prepared to ratify the Acts of the unconstitutional Parliament of 1640, but he was not permitted. These Acts, he was curtly informed, were already valid, and he was instructed merely to sanction their proclamation.[1] Parliament demanded, and he granted, a control over the executive and judiciary far more complete than anything claimed by the English Parliament at Westminster.[2] Its triennial meeting was guaranteed, independent of the royal assent. Loudoun was nominated Chancellor; for Treasurer, the king's suggestions first of Morton and then of Almond were vetoed, and the office was put into commission. There was no proposal of the Covenanters, however drastic, to which the king did not assent. In return he received much lip loyalty and many fine speeches, but no general popularity or confidence. As was his fatal habit, he had been too late in his concessions, and what, if voluntarily given, might once have re-established his power, now, taken by force, left only distrust and contempt.

Meanwhile, what of Montrose, now fast in prison ? Was he to go the way of Strafford ? There was an ominous sentence used by Argyll at the opening of Parliament in his reply to the speech from the Throne, when he spoke of the State as a ship in distress and the need of casting out "some of the naughtiest baggage to lighten her." [3] The old statute against " leasing-making " might be used as a weapon against nobler game than the humble commissary of Dunkeld. On 15th September Sir Patrick Wemyss wrote to Ormonde that the king had promised Montrose not to leave

[1] Rait, *The Parliaments of Scotland*, 68, etc.   [2] Balfour, III., 65.
[3] Ibid., III., 40.

1641 Scotland till he was brought to trial, " for, if he leave
him, all the world will not save his life." [1]   On 28th
August the four prisoners were called before Parliament,
when the king nodded friendlily to Napier, [2] but their case
was postponed. It would have been highly inconvenient
to Argyll and Hamilton to have Montrose at this juncture
pleading his cause before his peers.

Back again in the castle, Montrose was in a state of
miserable anxiety and impotence. He heard of the new
Act making the choice of Ministers dependent upon the
will of Parliament—a piece of constitutionalism which,
lacking the machinery and safeguards of modern government, was simply a premium set upon faction and sectarian tyranny. He heard of the decision that no one who
had shown himself active on the king's side should be
eligible for office. He must have exclaimed with Perth:
" If this be what you call liberty, God give me the old
slavery again." [3]   He heard that among the nobles
there were many who, whatever their past attitude,
now saw with alarm the road which Argyll was taking.
His one hope was Charles. He alone, if he clearly
understood the situation, had the power of making it
clear to Parliament and checking this drift towards
oligarchy. Twice he wrote from prison praying for an
interview with the king, that he might reveal matters
" which not only concerned his honour in a high degree,
but also the standing or falling of his crown." [4]   These
matters could only have been Hamilton's previous
duplicity and Argyll's present ambitions. The third
time he put his cards on the table, and on 11th October
offered to prove a clear case of treachery to the commonwealth. Charles was impressed, and prepared to lay
the business before the Chancellor and others of the
Privy Council.

But in the meantime there had begun the curious
performance known to history as the " Incident "—a
thing as obscure in its origins as the Popish Plot. For
some weeks there had been a mysterious influx of armed

[1] Carte, *Ormonde Papers*, I., 4.   [2] Napier, I., 355.
[3] Gardiner, X. 19.   [4] *Mem. of M.*, II., 5.

men into the capital, against which Loudoun, on 5th
October, had warned Parliament.[1] We know that
Hamilton and Argyll had 5,000 of their friends, and in
the other faction Lord Ker, Roxburgh's son, had 600
Borderers. On the evening of 11th October, the day
on which Montrose's third letter was received, Hamilton
went to the king in the garden of Holyrood, complained
of being traduced, and asked permission to leave the
court.[2] Next day Charles told this story to Parliament,
but on that morning Hamilton, Argyll, and Lanark had
retired to the Hamilton house of Kinneil, near Bo'ness.
Their story was that they had learned through Leslie
that there was a plot against their lives.[3] For a day
or two king and Parliament faced each other in a strange
mood, the former protesting with tears against the
insult done to his honour, the latter in complete be-
wilderment. A Committee of the Estates investigated
the business, and Montrose's correspondence with the
king was laid before them; but no definite conclusion
was reached, and the truth must remain one of the
secrets of history.

Charles was clearly innocent; so was Montrose, who
at the time was close in prison. No doubt there were
nobles, such as Ker and Crawford, with bands of
retainers at their heels, who would gladly have taken
the old Scots way of settling matters with their enemies.
There were others, such as Carnwath, who made no
secret of their view that there were now three kings
in Scotland, and that two of them could be dispensed
with. But the study of the confused evidence leaves
a strong impression that the whole affair was a trick,
a device of Hamilton's and Argyll's to escape from
the difficulties in which Montrose's third letter might
have placed them. Argyll was a master of electioneering
ingenuities, and he knew that the suspicion of being in
peril is a supreme asset to a leader. The impression
abides, too, that there was an *agent provocateur* at work

---

[1] Balfour, III., 90.　　　　　　[2] Ibid., III., 95.
[3] Leslie, however, declared afterwards that he had considered it " a foolish
business." *Cal. S. P., Dom.* (1641–43), 137, etc.

1641 behind the scenes, and this may well have been William
Murray, a gentleman of the king's bedchamber, the
son of the minister of Dysart and the nephew of Montrose's friend, the minister of Methven. Beginning as
the king's whipping-boy, he was to finish his career as
Earl of Dysart, and the father-in-law of Lauderdale.
By general consent he was one of the most degraded
characters of the age, and he was already suspect of
meddling with the king's letters; it is at least possible that the Incident was mainly his work, a bogus
conspiracy staged to give Hamilton the chance of
discrediting his opponents.[1]

On 28th October, while the Incident was at its
height, the king was playing golf at Leith, when a letter
was put into his hands. It contained the news of the
outbreak of the Irish rebellion. In a week the atmosphere in both England and Scotland had become
tense and ominous, fear of popery spread like a flame,
and the king's enemies had no need to create suspicion,
for suspicion rose like a mist from every corner of the
land. Charles could not linger in the north. On 18th
November, at eight o'clock in the morning, he rode
south, leaving for ever the country which he had so
loved and misgoverned. He departed with a lavish
shower of honours. Henderson was made dean of the
Chapel Royal at Holyrood, Wariston was knighted,
Loudoun and Leslie [2] became earls, and Argyll was

---

[1] This is Mr. Lang's view, III., 99. The depositions taken at the inquiry
may be read in *Hist. MSS. Comm.*, 4th Report, 163–170. See also Balfour, III.,
94–137. In the first edition of Clarendon's *History* (Oxford, 1702–4), Montrose
is accused of offering to the king, at a private interview, to make away with
Hamilton and Argyll (see Macray's ed., IV., c. 20). This story was repeated
by most historians, though discredited by Hume on general grounds. The
passage, so inconsistent with Clarendon's general view of Montrose, seems to
have been some rough notes for his *Life*, which somehow became mixed up
with the *History*, based perhaps, as Mr. Gardiner suggests, on the confusion
of Montrose and Crawford. In an appendix to the new edition of Clarendon,
collated with the original MSS. in the Bodleian, and published in 1826, a revised
version of the story is given which exonerates Montrose. This Clarendon
perhaps intended to replace the faulty passage. See Napier, I., 359–363.
Gardiner, X., 26. For William Murray, see Guthry, 117, Clarendon, IV.,
15, *n.*

[2] Apparently the new Earl of Leven gave the king an undertaking that
he would not in the future serve against him. See Terry, *Alexander Leslie*,
158 *n.*

made a marquis.[1] The day before the king left, Mon- *1641-42*
trose and his friends were released on probation, and in
March 1642 the case against them was finally closed.
The four gentlemen, who had been five months in
prison without trial, were informed that they owed
their escape only to the clemency of Argyll. Montrose
had engaged, ingenuously and amateurishly, in the
difficult game of subterranean Scottish politics, and had
taken a heavy fall. The new marquis could afford to
be generous to an antagonist whom, in the business of
plots and counterplots, he had so signally outplayed.

[1] Gordon of Ruthven (*Britane's Distemper*, 57) says that there was an ancient
prophecy that a red-haired and squinting Argyll would be the last earl, and
that the marquisate was accepted to avert the curse.

CHAPTER V

THE RUBICON

(1642–44)

In all questions of wide and deep interest it is scarcely less than a fatal necessity that the best cause should be the worst defended ; the consequence of which is, the temporary victory of the false and the superficial, and its establishment in the chair of learned as well as popular opinion. The cause is in the instinct of the mind to aim at the highest in the first instance—and hence with imperfect means, and in the absence of all the main conditions of its attainment.

COLERIDGE, *Notes, Theological, Political, and Miscellaneous.*

I

1640–41 DURING these years of ineffectual politics, Montrose, in his long journeys and in quiet hours of retreat at Kincardine, was steadfastly endeavouring to clarify his own mind. Some time between the autumn of 1640 and the summer of 1641 he set down his views on the principles of government in a letter to a "noble sir," who may have been Lord Napier or Drummond of Hawthornden. The paper was found by Mark Napier in a small quarto in the handwriting of Robert Wodrow, and is among the manuscripts in the National Library of Scotland.[1] It is one of those confessions of faith by which, at all periods in history, sorely perplexed men have striven to ease their souls. The seventeenth century saw no more searching political treatise, for it reveals a capacity for abstract thought rare at any time in a man of action, and especially rare in an era when, as soon as the lists were set, half-truths were vested with the authority of Sinai.

[1] It is printed in Napier, I., 280–289, *Mem. of M.,* II., 43–53, and in the appendix to this volume.

He begins by laying down a doctrine of Sovereign
Power. If a land is to be stably governed there must
be some unquestioned centre of authority which he calls
Sovereignty, " a power over the people, above which
power there is none on earth." It is limited indeed—by
the laws of God and nature, the laws of nations, and the
fundamental laws of the country ; but these limitations
are moral, religious, and constitutional, and inherent
in its very being ; it cannot be limited by division
among competing authorities. Springing ultimately
from a free people, it may in practice be delegated to a
king, as in Britain ; a council of nobles, as in Venice ;
or the estates of the people, as in ancient Rome. It
" cannot subsist in a body composed of individuities " ;
if it is " divided amongst several bodies there is no
government, as if there were many kings in one kingdom
there should be none at all."

Montrose holds no brief for monarchy, except in
so far as it is the form of sovereignty which has been
accepted by the British people. He proceeds to analyse
the nature of kingship. It is strong when it is temperate
and recognizes its moral and constitutional limitations.
" It is weak . . . when it is extended beyond the laws
whereby it is bounded ; which could never be at any
time endured by the people of the western part of the
world, and by those of Scotland as little as any." But
the ills flowing from undue restraint are not less than
the ills which spring from undue extension. No section
of the people can seize a part of sovereignty, for, if
sovereignty be divided, there follows anarchy, " the
oppression and tyranny of subjects, the most fierce,
insatiable, and insufferable tyranny in the world." He
desires free and frequent parliaments and stern dealing
with any law-breaking king ; but he insists that, when
sovereignty has been granted on conditions, it must be
inviolable so long as these conditions are observed.
Parliaments are guardians of the subjects' liberties,
but not less of the delegated rights of the sovereign
king.

He passes to the menaces to sovereignty—and there-

1640–41 fore the causes of anarchy—and he finds them in " the ambitious designs of rule in great men, veiled under the specious pretext of religion and the subjects' liberties, seconded with the arguments and false positions of seditious precedence : first, that the king is ordained for the people, and the end is more noble than the means ; second, that the constituter is superior to the constituent ; third, that the king and people are two contraries, like the two scales of a balance—when the one goes up the other goes down ; fourth, that the prince's prerogative and the people's privilege are incompatible ; fifth, that what power is taken from the king is added to the Estates of the people." On this text he preaches an acute sermon. The two first points, as he explains them, do not mean that he holds that there is any absolutism in a free monarchy, but that, the choice of monarchy having been made by the people, such monarchy, which is their own creation, must be reasonably exalted, since in its exaltation lies their security. With the fear of the encroachments of the nobility and the Kirk in his mind, he appeals to the commons of Scotland :

" And you, ye meaner people of Scotland—who are not capable of a Republic, for many grave reasons—why are you induced by specious pretexts, to your own heavy prejudice and detriment, to be the instruments of others' ambition ? Do you not hear, when the monarchial government is shaken, the great ones strive for the garland with *your* blood and *your* fortune ? Whereby you gain nothing ; but, instead of a race of kings who have governed you for two thousand years with peace and justice, and have preserved your liberties against all domineering nations, shall purchase to yourselves vultures and tigers to reign over your posterity ; and yourselves shall endure all these miseries, massacres, and proscriptions of the Triumvirate of Rome—(till) the kingdom fall again into the hands of One, who of necessity must, and for reasons of State will, tyrannize over you. For kingdoms acquired by blood and violence are by the same means retained." [1]

It is the old profound lesson of history, eternally taught and eternally forgotten. After anarchy comes

[1] There is an even more remarkable forecast of Cromwell in Drummond of Hawthornden's " Address to the Noblemen, Barons, etc.," of May 2, 1639. *Works* (1711), vii.

the dictator; the successors of the Gracchi are the **1640-41**
Cæsars; the fury of the French Revolution is stamped
out by Napoleon; the confusion of a Russia emancipated
from her old masters is imperfectly disciplined by a
harsher tyranny. In the England of that moment the
" One " of whom he prophesied was already walking
about in his sober country clothes and great buff boots.
Montrose, it is to be noted, preaches the organic nature
of the State to the common people, but to the Kirk and
the nobility he addresses a different argument. He only
warns them that their ambition will fail—the preachers,
that the nobles will use them for their own interest, " as
a cunning tennis-player lets a ball go to the wall where
it cannot stay, that he may take it at the bound with
more ease "; the nobles, that, like Æsop's dog, they
will lose the substance for the shadow in the well.
It would seem that he had made up his mind that the
Kirk and the aristocracy were no longer amenable to
reason.

We must be on our guard against reading into this
philosophy of politics more than Montrose intended. If
he saw beyond his age, he was also the child of that age.
Much in his creed is not new. Fortescue in the fifteenth
century had laid down the doctrine of constitutional
monarchy. " The King of England cannot alter nor
change the Lawes of the Realme at his pleasure; for
why, he governeth his people by power, not only royall
but politique." The Tudor monarchs had established
the principle of an indivisible sovereignty by suppressing
local immunities and crushing all rival authorities. But
Montrose shows in many respects a startling originality,
especially as contrasted with the writers of his own
political party. He does not, like James I., identify
sovereignty with monarchy;[1] he is willing to accept
any form of government, provided it fulfils the requirements which are indispensable in all governments.
Unlike his friend Drummond of Hawthornden, he has
none of the contemporary belief in Divine Right, and he

---

[1] *Works* (1616), 193. *Cf.* the broadmindedness of the *Scots Confession* of
1560, Article XXIV., Dunlop, *Collection of Confessions*, II., 90.

1640-41 is no advocate of passive obedience.[1] He is primarily
a realist, and he is curiously free from mediæval ideas
on monarchy or on religion. His central principle may
deduce from Bodin, but its application was based upon
his personal observation of Scots affairs.

To orientate his political creed in relation to his age
would require a treatise. Many philosophers of diverse
schools, like Hobbes and Milton, accepted his doctrine
of sovereignty. Montrose did not go into the meta-
physics of political origins, the question which has
agitated thinkers from Aristotle to Rousseau, whether
the title to rule be natural or conventional. He would
have accepted Hooker's view that sovereignty should be
founded on consent, and while agreeing with Milton
that sovereignty is from the people, he would have
shrunk from Milton's addendum that the popular liberty
of decision is only to be respected so long as the people
accept a particular creed.[2] In the realism of his method
of thought he has affinities with Hobbes, but not in his
conclusion : he has much in common with Samuel
Rutherford, whose *Lex Rex*, published in 1644, lays
down the thesis that sovereignty comes from the people,
who may, in time of extreme necessity, resume this
power, and nothing in common with Sir George Mackenzie, whose reply to Buchanan's *De Jure Regni*[3] is
a proof of the extravagant lengths to which a Scot could
go in defending the alien dogma of Divine Right. His
doctrine of sovereignty is at the opposite pole from that
of Strafford, who believed that the security of a nation
depended in emergencies upon an executive authority
above and outside the ordinary law, an inalienable and
overriding prerogative—a view which in one form is a

[1] Drummond's view will be found in his *Irene* (*Works*, 163). Professor
Masson, in his *Drummond of Hawthornden*, 346, etc., fails to distinguish the
completely different points of view of the two friends. If Montrose had any
mentor in his political philosophy, it was Lord Napier. See *Mem. of M.*, I., 70.

[2] See Milton, *A Ready and Easy Way to establish a Free Government*. The
doctrine of the popular origin of sovereignty had become a commonplace in
France, both among the Huguenots and their opponents. Cf. *Vindiciæ
contra Tyrannos*.—"Regis nomen non hereditatem, proprietatem, usumfructuum,
sed functionem et procurationem sonat." The close connection of Scotland
and France popularized this view, but it was also deep in Scottish history.
Cf. John Major, *Hist. of Greater Britain* (S.H.S.), 213, etc.   [3] *Works*, II., 472

truism to-day, but which in the seventeenth century, if
generally accepted, would have put an end to popular
liberties.

But Montrose is not a metaphysician. He is a
student of history and an observer of facts. His inquiry
is a practical one—how to stave off anarchy, and the
maxims which he offers have their direct contemporary
applications. He is modern in his doctrine of the
organic unity of the State, but in two matters he is
very clearly of his age.

The first is his attitude towards parliamentary
government. " It is curious to observe," says Coleridge
of the early seventeenth century, " that the thinner the
realm was (the less both in wealth and influence, and
the less they were diffused) the greater was the division
of power." [1] In the constitution of that age there was
no clear determination of function between the executive,
the judiciary, and the legislature. " The ' rule of law,'
which the power of the state existed to enforce, worked
through no specialized machinery, the organization was
still fluid, only here and there hardening into conventions. . . . The conception of an exclusive sovereignty,
inherent in any one branch of the Constitution, was still
far distant." [2] In strict theory, the true sovereign was
the law fundamental, the " law of the land," which was
regarded as beyond the reach of legislative change.
Magna Charta had been a solemn embodiment of one
portion of that law. In 1604 the Speaker of the House
of Commons divided the laws into (1) the Common law,
not mutable ; (2) the Positive law, to be altered by the
occasion of the times ; (3) customs and usages which
have time's approbation. The distinction appears in
Sir Walter Raleigh's *Prerogative of Parliaments* ; Sir
Edward Coke maintained that the function of king and
parliament was not *jus dare* but *jus dicere*—to declare
the law ; in 1659 Nicholas Bacon told Richard Cromwell's Parliament that, as regarded bicameral government, " long usage hath so settled it, as Acts of

---

[1] *Notes, Theological, Political, and Miscellaneous,* 206.
[2] Feiling, *History of the Tory Party, 1640–1714,* 33.

Parliament cannot alter it." The doctrine of the legislative supremacy of Parliament was still in the womb of time.[1]

Montrose held firmly to this conception of a law immutable and fundamental ; it was the code to which both he and Charles appealed at their trials, and it moulded his view of sovereignty. With this adamantine sanction in the background, which no other power could change, he was compelled to think of a constitution as a thing of delicate balances, of authority as a commodity scrupulously weighed out and studiously limited, and of a central delegated sovereignty as inhering in a monarch rather than in any Parliament. National health, he maintained, depended, like bodily health, upon each member playing its own part without encroachment. The monarchy seemed to him the most vital part of a nicely adjusted mechanism, since upon its proper functioning the working of all other parts specially depended. He places the emphasis on the Crown, though he gives it no autocracy. He could not foresee that this delicate adjustment would end in stagnation, and that in a later age it would be necessary to aggrandize the power of one part in order to make the wheels revolve. It was difficult for any thinker of his time to accept the legislative sovereignty of Parliament, to which the Long Parliament tried to feel its way—the notion of the " law fundamental " forbade it ; but it was doubly difficult for Montrose. For the Parliament which he knew was the Scots Parliament, with its bad traditions of incompetence and servility. It may be that Argyll had a vision of parliamentary government denied to his contemporaries, but it was a vision, for a sober survey of the facts seemed to render it impossible. A wise and impartial king might hold the balance between conflicting interests, but the Scots Parliament, swung alternately between Kirk and nobles, would, if unfettered, produce only despotism or anarchy.

The second matter in which Montrose is a man of his

[1] For the " law fundamental," see C. H. McIlwain, *The High Court of Parliament*, 1910.

time, is his attitude towards what we call democracy.
He believed that from the whole nation came the
sanction of sovereignty, but he was not a democrat in
the modern sense, for the common people in his day
were scarcely conscious of political rights, and asked
rather to be wisely protected than to be endowed with
ill-understood duties. But, both in his theory and in
his practice, he was more democratic than most of his
generation. He held that the laws were the only
safeguard of the plain man, the true monarch of which
the king was but the creature. He saw that any disturbance of the equipoise in the distribution of public
duties would not add to popular liberties, but, by
increasing confusion, would augment the power of this
or that oligarchical faction. He held—and what student
of the period will dissent ?—that the contemporary
commons of Scotland were " more incapable of sovereignty than any other known." The people, as a
political force, did not come within the imagination
of seventeenth-century Britain. " They care not what
Government they live under," said Haselrig, " so as they
may plough and go to market." [1] The proletariat was
as meaningless a thing to Cromwell and Vane as it was
to Strafford and Clarendon, and the creed of the
Leveller was as hateful to the Puritan as to the Cavalier.
Indeed it may be said that the silent masses had more
to gain from king than from Parliament, for it was the
Crown which, in Star Chamber and Council, did its best
to check enclosure, protect tenant right, and maintain
wages. Montrose, with his doctrine of the organic
unity of the State, and his constant appeal to the
" mean people," came nearer democracy, it may be
argued, than most of his contemporaries. [2]

The purpose of human government is to give to the
citizen a free, a secure, and an ordered life. The means
of effecting this purpose will vary from age to age and
from nation to nation, but one essential will always

[1] Burton, *Diary*, III., 257.
[2] There is an interesting study of Montrose's political philosophy by Arch-
deacon Cunningham, *S.H.R.*, July 1917.

remain—an effective central power "to unite and incorporate the members into one body politic that, with joint endeavour and abilities, they may the better advance the common good," and this central power must spring from the goodwill of the people at large. Montrose found it in a constitutional monarchy such as he conceived it. "He who keeps watch and ward for freedom," Coleridge has written, "has to guard against two enemies, the despotism of the few and the despotism of the many." [1] The second peril in Montrose's day had not arisen, but the first was an ever-present menace, whether it took the form of an aristocratic or an ecclesiastical junta. The truth of his doctrine is not affected by the fact that Britain found a solution by other methods than those which he foreshadowed. The hope of a popular monarchy shipwrecked on the character of Charles, and a religious quarrel in which civil politics were fatally compromised. If Montrose did not foresee either modern parliamentaryism or modern democracy, he foresaw the principle which alone gives them value. They are but means to an end, and to-day, when parliamentary government has lost much of its glamour, and criticism is revealing as mere expedients certain democratic dogmas which once seemed eternal truths, we are being driven back again to the fundamentals.

Open Burke anywhere. "I see no other way for the preservation of a decent attention to public interest in the representatives, but the interposition of the body of the people itself, whenever it shall appear, by some flagrant and notorious act, by some capital innovation, that the representatives are going to overleap the fences of the law, and to introduce an arbitrary power." [2] It is Montrose's defence, first for signing the National Covenant, and then for taking up arms against the Covenanters. "Here it says to an encroaching prerogative, 'Your sceptre has its length, you cannot add a hair to your head or a gem to your crown but what an eternal law has given to it!' Here it says to an

---

[1] *The Friend*, I., 94.
[2] *Thoughts on the Causes of the Present Discontents.*

overweening peerage, ' Your pride finds banks that it
cannot overflow.' Here to a tumultuous and giddy
people, ' There is a bed to the raging sea.' " [1]   It is
Montrose's conception of constitutional law.   Or again,
" If civil society be the offspring of convention, that
convention must be its law.   That convention must
limit and modify all the descriptions of constitutions
which are formed under it.   Every sort of legislative,
judicial, or executive power are its creatures.   They
can have no being in any other state of things ; and
how can any man claim, under the convention of civil
society, rights which do not so much as suppose its
existence—rights which are absolutely repugnant to
it." [2]   It is Montrose's case against the encroachments
of the Kirk.   He saw that in a stable government the
supreme power, while it must be delegated, cannot be
made divisible.   The Kirk was willing enough to accept
the doctrine of popular sovereignty, but it did not grasp
the inevitable conclusion—that the people cannot en-
trust this power to two conflicting authorities which
may both claim to represent them.   Church and State
cannot rule conjointly over the same sphere and under
the same sanctions.   Montrose took the historical as
opposed to the metaphysical view of human institutions,
and, moreover, in his practical interpretation he curiously anticipated the modern attitude.   He could have
little part in an age when most men believed that kings
and churches and aristocracies were mystically ordained
of God.

From his first entry into public life Montrose was at
variance with the bulk of the Scottish nobility, but it
seems certain that he began with a real enthusiasm for
the Kirk, of which he was a ruling elder.   So long as it
stood for spiritual freedom he was its fervent champion,
and this championship, as we have seen, led him occa-
sionally into courses which were contrary to his political
creed.   He had a reverence for godliness, and from

---

[1] *Speech in the House of Commons on Constitutional Reform*, May 7, 1782.
[2] *Reflections on the Revolution in France.*

such a man as Alexander Henderson he differed with profound reluctance. His personal religion was the Calvinism of his age, but he had reached it, not by the rigid schedule of grim " experiences " laid down by the Scottish divines, but by the gentler Platonic method, whereby God reveals Himself insensibly through the riches of His world, and piety crowns like a flower the natural growth of mind and soul.[1] He had the latitude of Hales or Chillingworth about inessentials, and his creed was that of the great saying of Symmachus : " Uno itinere non potest pervenire ad tam grande secretum." His condemnation was reserved for those who forgot the spirit in the letter and made religion a thing of scholastic subtleties. His affinities were with men like the Cambridge Platonists, whose Calvinism was mellowed and warmed by the love of humanity and of all things true and beautiful. He would have agreed with Whichcote that Christ is *magister vitæ non scholæ*, and that he is " the best Christian whose heart beats with the truest pulse towards heaven, not he whose head spinneth out the finest cobwebs." He had Whichcote's stalwart respect for the freedom of the mind. When later he criticized the teaching of the Scottish divines, it was on the ground of their narrow legalism and their spiritual pride.[2]

The event which compelled his final breach with the

---

[1] In the accounts of the undergraduate Montrose for 1628 there is an item, " For Mr. William Struther's ' Meditations.' " Struther, who had been tutor to Montrose's cousin, Lord Wigton, published two " centuries " of "Christian Observations and Reflections " in 1628 and 1629, and his teaching must have influenced Montrose's youth. Robert Baillie thought him " the most eloquent and gracious preacher that ever yet lived in Scotland."

[2] *Cf.* John Smith of Cambridge : " I doubt sometimes some of our dogmata and notions about Justification may puff us up in far higher and goodlier conceits of ourselves than God hath of us ; and that we profanely make the unspotted righteousness of Christ to serve only as a covering wherein to wrap up our foul deformities and filthy vices ; and when we have done, think ourselves in as good credit and repute with God as we are with ourselves ; and that we are become heaven's darlings as much as we are our own. . . . God respects not a bold, confident, and audacious faith that is big with nothing but its own presumptions. . . . It is not all our strong dreams of being in favour with heaven, it is not a pertinacious imagination of our name being enrolled in the book of life, or of the debt-books of heaven being crossed, or of Christ being ours, or of the washing away of our sins in His blood . . . it is not, I say, a pertinacious imagination of any of these that can make us the better."—*Discourse of Legal and Evangelical Righteousness*, chs. iv. and v.

Kirk was its growing alliance, under Henderson's leadership, with the Parliamentary party in England, of which the price was to be the establishment of Presbytery south of the Tweed. The policy, which culminated in the Solemn League and Covenant, is capable of defence from the point of view of the perplexed Scottish divines. The Kirk held that Presbytery was a *jus divinum*, and it had the mediæval belief in religious uniformity as the foundation of political unity. It had suffered grievously from prelatical encroachments, and the impetus for such encroachments had come from England ; its liberties could only be safeguarded if England were brought to its own way of thinking. Moreover, the Counter-Reformation was making huge strides on the continent of Europe, and it could be resisted only if there were the closest unity among all the reformed Churches ; and this seemed to involve the abolition of Anglican anomalies and the reshaping of English Protestantism according to the universal Protestant pattern.

A man like Henderson was too wise to believe that he could force Presbytery upon an unwilling England. " We do not presume," he wrote, " to propose the government of the Church of Scotland as a pattern for the Church of England, we do only represent in all modesty these few considerations according to the trust committed to us." The change must come willingly from within, and he believed that the greater part of the Anglican Church desired it.[1] He was misled by his English correspondents ; he did not—he could not— realize that the great bulk of the English people disliked Laud and the Anglican extremists, but were attached to a moderate episcopacy, that the Presbyterian majority in Parliament was not the English nation, that English Presbyterianism was very different from Scottish, and that even among the declared opponents of the king and the bishops there were many stalwart Erastians of the Selden type, who would not suffer an ecclesiastical discipline uncontrolled by the civil law.

[1] See Orr, *Alexander Henderson*, 287, 312, etc.

1640-42 Had Henderson had this knowledge, it is certain that one who sought above all things the unity and peace of the two peoples would have refrained from a policy which was to be the fruitful mother of strife. But there were few ministers with Henderson's sagacity. To most, the bringing of England into conformity with their own communion was a direct command of God, and they devoted themselves to the task with a fanatic missionary zeal. The new Covenant became a mystical compact with the Almighty, its acceptance the test of holiness, its rejection or breach a certain proof of damnation. It was to be attended by " the voice of harpers harping with their harps, which shall fill the whole island with melody and mirth." Civil statesmanship disappears in such a mood, and all that remains is a frantic theocracy.[1] The Kirk, whose spiritual rights had been threatened by Charles, was now, in the enthusiasm of a regained independence, proposing to encroach upon the sphere of secular government.

To Montrose, with his modern conception of the State, both Kirk and nobles seemed to be marching the straight road to anarchy. The National Covenant had been an assertion of unquestioned civil and religious liberties, a united nation, with a reverent acknowledgment of their Maker, recalling their king to the true doctrine of kingship. But, in the Solemn League now preparing, the Kirk had gone far beyond her lawful sphere. He knew the people of England, and realized that the acceptance by the English Parliament of Henderson's scheme could only be a price paid for alliance in rebellion. His way and the Kirk's had come to a sharp parting. The king, in spite of former

---

[1] This misunderstanding of England's attitude led to an extreme bitterness between the two peoples, the very result which Henderson hoped that the Solemn League would prevent. Compare, for example, Mr. John McClelland : " Englishmen shall be made spectacles to all nations for a broken covenant. . . . If all England were as one man united in judgment and assertion, and if it had a wall round about reaching to the sun, and if it had as many armies as it has men, and every soldier had the strength of Goliath, and if their navies could cover the ocean, and if there were none to peep out or move the tongue against them, yet I dare not doubt their destruction when the Lord hath sworn by His life that He will avenge the breach of covenant." Howie, *Scots Worthies* (1838), I., 200.

blunders, was now constitutionally in the right, and if war came it was for Montrose, and for all lovers of law and liberty, to support the central power against anarchic usurpation. If he erred in his view of Charles's character and aims, the error was justifiable, for in the past three years the king had appeared to yield all that the National Covenant had demanded, and to have assented to that historic constitutionalism which Argyll and the Kirk were now denying by word and deed.

The alternative, as Montrose saw it, was a theocracy on a feudal basis, an omnipotent Kirk and a free license to a corrupt and turbulent aristocracy, provided that aristocracy remained orthodox. How would the " mean people " of Scotland fare under such a régime ? *Quicquid delirant reges, plectuntur Achivi.* He looked around, and saw the wretchedness of their condition. Throughout all his writings and declarations there rings a note of pity for the common folk, who had to bear the brunt of their rulers' folly. " Ye have oppressed the poor, and violently perverted judgment and justice "—so ran his last tremendous indictment. Public morals were at a low ebb ;[1] nor was there any revival of true spiritual life, such as had at other times attended a season of religious wars. The hungry sheep were fed with windy politics. Let us take one witness, the celebrated Mr. Robert Law, a stout Covenanter who was ejected from his church in 1662 after the Restoration. " From the year 1652," he writes, " to the year 1660, there was great good done by the preaching of the Gospel in the west of Scotland, more than was observed to have been for twenty or thirty years before ; a great many brought in to Christ Jesus by the saving work of conversion, which was occasioned through ministers preaching nothing all that time but the Gospel, and had left off to preach up parliaments, armies, leagues, resolutions, and remonstrances." [2] The use of the Lord's Prayer was condemned by some zealots as being too

---

[1] See, for Berwick and the Lothians, a letter of an English soldier in Scotland (Sept. 1650), quoted by Lang, III., 204 ; for godly Fife, the evidence of Robert Baillie and the St. Andrews Kirk Session (ibid., III., 102).

[2] *Memorials* (ed. by C. Kirkpatrick Sharpe, 1812), 7.

1642 much of a " set form." [1] Private meetings for devotion
were discouraged as savouring of schism—a strange
policy for a church which owned Livingstone and
Samuel Rutherford. Religion was in danger of ceasing
to be a quickening spirit, and of becoming a *hortus siccus*
of withered pedantries. Of the Kirk now dominant in
Scotland, Cromwell, after Dunbar, had certain truths
to proclaim. " By your hard and subtle words," he
told the ministers, " you have begotten prejudice in
those who do too much in matters of conscience—
wherein every soul has to answer for itself to God—
depend upon you. Your own guilt is too much for
you to bear. . . . Is it therefore infallibly agreeable to
the Word of God, all that you say ? I beseech you in
the bowels of Christ, think it possible that you may be
mistaken. There may be a Covenant made with Death
and Hell." [2]

As his path became clearer before him, Montrose,
after his fashion at a crisis in his life, was moved to one
of his rare exercises in verse. He had much leisure
during these months, and spent it at his house of Kincardine with his wife and his sons, of whom the eldest
was now a boy of twelve. Thither came a pleasant
company of neighbours and kinsfolk, Napiers, Erskines,
and Stirlings, and the old hall by the Ruthven
Water heard for the last time the sound of young
voices and children's play. At this period he must
have written the lyric by which his name is best
known in our literature. It is a love song, but it is
addressed to the eyebrows of no mortal Sylvia. In
his youth ladies had written him verses, but his marriage was the one romance of his life, and, in spite
of the jealous inquisition of the Kirk, no affair of gallantry was ever linked with his name. In his ballad
the ardour of the patriot is joined to the passion of the
lover in singing of his mistress, Scotland, and what he
will do for her if she trusts him. It breathes the same
spirit as his " Discourse of Sovereignty," a hatred of

sectarian war, a plea for the unity which had long fled
from his distracted land. Almost every metaphor is
drawn from the language of contemporary politics, but
that language is warmed and coloured by a passion of
loyalty—to an ideal rather than to a person, for with
Montrose, in Plato's words, the quest of truth did not
lack the warmth of desire.

> " My dear and only love, I pray
>   That little world of thee
> Be governed by no other sway
>   Than purest monarchy ;
> For if confusion have a part,
>   Which virtuous souls abhor,
> And hold a Synod in thine heart,
>   I'll never love thee more.
>
> As Alexander I will reign,
>   And I will reign alone ;
> My thoughts did evermore disdain
>   A rival on my throne.
> He either fears his fate too much,
>   Or his deserts are small,
> That dares not put it to the touch,
>   To win or lose it all.
>   .   .   .
> And in the Empire of thine heart
>   Where I should solely be,
> If others do pretend a part
>   Or dare to vie with me,
> Or if Committees thou erect,
>   And go on such a score,
> I'll laugh and sing at thy neglect,
>   And never love thee more.
>
> But if thou wilt prove faithful then,
>   And constant of thy word,
> I'll make thee glorious by my pen,
>   And famous by my sword ;
> I'll serve thee in such noble ways
>   Was never heard before ;
> I'll crown and deck thee all with bays,
>   And love thee more and more." [1]

---

[1] The texts of this famous song vary considerably. There is no copy
extant in Montrose's handwriting. It was first published and attributed to
Montrose in Watson's *Choice Collection of Scots Poems,* 1711, apparently from
an earlier broadside (*Mem. of M.,* II., 467). Its authenticity has never been
questioned, and indeed some of the phrases are to be found in Montrose's

1642 This is the song of a man who has at last found assurance, the confession of a soul which has a vision of a noble purpose, and holds no risk too high in its attainment.

II

Montrose was soon to be called to witness to his faith. Charles returned to London from Scotland in November 1641, to be confronted with the Grand Remonstrance, which demanded a government responsible to Parliament, and the summoning of an assembly of divines to settle the religious problem. On January 4, 1642, he was guilty of a supreme blunder when, on his queen's advice, he attempted to enter the Commons and arrest the Five Members. Six days later he left London, to which he was not destined to return till he returned to die. The last hope of a peaceful settlement had gone, and both sides began the raising of armies—the Parliament by ordinances, and the king by commissions of array. On 23rd April Sir John Hotham shut the gates of Hull in Charles's face, and civil war began. On 22nd August the royal standard was set up at Nottingham, and in that month and from that place the king wrote to Montrose :

"I send Will Murray to Scotland to inform my friends of the state of my affairs, and to require both their advice and assistance. You are one whom I have found most faithful, and in whom I repose greatest trust. Therefore I address him chiefly to you. You may credit him in what he shall say, both in relation to my business and to your own ; and you must be content with words until I be able to act. I will say no more but that I am your loving friend . . ." [1]

correspondence with Prince Rupert (*Mem. of M.*, II., 465). I agree with Mark Napier that the piece is a political and not a love poem, though Lord Stanhope thought otherwise (*Historical Essays*, 172). Lord Stanhope puts the date of its composition as 1648, and Lady Violet Greville as after his wife's death (*Montrose*, 82), but internal evidence seems to suggest 1642, the last season of quiet before the storm broke. A large number of verses, many of them indifferent, are printed by Napier, I. App. *Mem. of M.*, II., 470–475. Montrose's full poetical works will be found in the appendix to the second volume of Napier's *Montrose and the Covenanters*, Lady Violet Greville's *Montrose*, c. 4, Eyre-Todd's *Scottish Poetry of the Seventeenth Century* (Glasgow, 1895), and Professor Rait's edition of *Montrose and Marvell* (London, 1901).

[1] Napier, II., 372.

It would have been well for Charles had he trusted
Montrose in Scots affairs. But Hamilton, as we know
from Clarendon, had given him assurances that " he
would at least keep that people from doing anything
that might seem to countenance the carriage of the
Parliament," and it was to Hamilton that Murray went.
In the previous November the king had appealed to
the Scottish Privy Council for help in dealing with the
Irish rebellion. The Council responded by an energetic
levy of troops, the first batch of which went to Ulster
in February 1642, and sent Lothian and Lindsay to
London to attempt to mediate between king and Parliament. Scotland found herself courted diligently by
both sides, and returned evasive answers. A special
meeting of the Council was held in May 1642, when
Montrose and his friends endeavoured to induce it to
stand to its many pledges and refrain from assisting the
Parliament with arms. The presence of the royalist
nobles in Edinburgh raised the usual cry of a design
against the lives of the Covenanting leaders, the gentry
and clergy of Fife flocked to the capital as a bodyguard for the menaced statesmen, and the Privy Council
was confirmed in its cautious detachment.[1]

But this detachment could not be kept up for ever.
In July the General Assembly met in St. Andrews,
when king and Parliament renewed their solicitations
to the body which especially represented the opinion of
Scotland. The English Puritans did not ask for a definite alliance, but they declared their detestation of
the English episcopacy, and their earnest desire for " an
advancement of the true religion and such a reformation
of the Church as should be made agreeable to God's
Word." This gave the Assembly its cue ; " agreeable
to God's Word " must mean Presbyterianism ; so it
petitioned the king to labour for " blessed unity in
religion, and uniformity of Church government "—in
other words, the establishment of Presbytery in England. Argyll was in command at St. Andrews, and
ruled the Assembly as he ruled the Scottish Parliament.

[1] Baillie, II., 43.

1642 When Murray arrived in the early autumn, he found
Hamilton living in Argyll's company, and negotiating
a marriage between his eldest daughter and Lord Lorn.
The Assembly's appeal brought a reply in September,
for the English Parliament voted unanimously that the
present government of the Church of England must be
abolished, and that the national Church must be reconstructed with the aid of an assembly of divines.
This seemed to grant to the Kirk what it had been seeking—the end of the hated episcopacy, and Presbytery
established from Devon to Caithness. Small wonder
that it leaned to the Parliament's side, and that the
Scottish people, whom it controlled, had the same
bias.

Meantime Edgehill had been fought, and in November
the Parliament applied to Scotland for aid. Charles
replied with a defence of his policy, and Hamilton,
roused out of his dreams by the sudden crisis, and anxious
at least to save his country from naked rebellion, persuaded the Privy Council to publish the royal declaration. But Argyll insisted that the English Parliament's
appeal should also be published, and there was the usual
game of petition and counter-petition, in which Argyll
won. That of Traquair and Hamilton asked no more
than that Scotland should do nothing to commit itself
to the path of disloyalty and civil war.[1] That such
a policy should have been vehemently opposed both
by the Assembly and the Estates shows how Scottish
opinion had hardened against the king.

It was high time that Charles should know the
facts—that from Scotland would come no aid for his
cause, but only augmentation to his enemies—for he
could learn nothing from the vain and obtuse Hamilton.
An effort had been made to draw Montrose again into
the Covenant camp. He had no following among
either nobles or people, but his opponents appreciated
the strength of his character and his talents for war,
and he was offered, if he would join them, the lieutenant-
generalship of the army, and, says Wishart, " quæcunque

[1] Burnet, *Mem. of the Hamiltons,* 206.

alia quæ suæ forent potestatis." [1] The offer must have
come from Argyll, who had the wits to recognize ability,
who desired to have on his side a military genius which
he did not himself possess and which he may well have
believed to be superior to old Leven's, and who must
have noted Montrose's sincere attachment to Presbytery
and the reluctance with which he differed from the Kirk.
If Hamilton was privy to it, it can only have been
because he desired to compromise one whom he hated,
for his shallow mind still held to the belief that he could
keep Scotland out of the war. The incident forced
Montrose to be up and doing. The royal cause at the
moment was not unprosperous in the field. In spite of
the check at Turnham Green, Charles had consolidated
his position in the Oxford district, Newcastle was firm in
Yorkshire, and Hopton had cleared the south-west. The
way to London might soon be open unless the Scots
army took the royalists in flank from the north. The
peril from Scotland must at once be made known to
the king.

In February 1643 Montrose, with Ogilvy and Aboyne,
crossed the Border. The Court was at Oxford, whither
Ogilvy and Aboyne repaired, but Montrose, hearing at
Newcastle that the queen was arriving from Holland,
went to meet her at Bridlington Bay. A year before
she had gone to the Hague to sell the crown jewels for
munitions of war, and had now returned with stores and
money, to be greeted in her bedroom by the round shot
of the Parliament fleet. Montrose urged an immediate
grant of a royal warrant to authorize a loyal rising in
Scotland. He believed that if Charles struck the first
blow the opposition might be overawed, or at any rate
crippled. Henrietta was too sea-sick and flustered to
listen, and told him that she would discuss the matter at
York. But to York had posted Hamilton and Traquair
with their smooth words, and the distracted lady followed
the path of least resistance. Montrose was dismissed
as an alarmist, and Hamilton's optimism prevailed. [2]

He had not long to wait for his vindication. Loudoun,

[1] Wishart, c. 2.   [2] Ibid., c. 3. Burnet, *Mem. of the Hamiltons*, 212.

Henderson, and Wariston had gone as a commission to
the king at Oxford, to mediate for peace on the basis of
Presbyterian uniformity in England, and there Henderson argued the question of episcopacy with no less a
person than Jeremy Taylor.[1] The commission asked
for a Parliament that summer, though under the grant
of triennial parliaments the next did not fall due till
June 1644, and this request Charles refused. But Argyll
had business on hand which could not wait, and on his
own account he arranged for the summoning of a Convention of Estates on June 22, 1643. Here was an act
of rebellion as final as Sir John Hotham's, but Hamilton
persuaded the king to ignore the breach of prerogative
and sanction the meeting, which he himself attended, to
watch, as he said, the royal interests.[2] He had just
been made a duke, to encourage his slack-lipped loyalty.

Montrose did not attend the Convention. For him
and his friends the final parting had come. During
the spring of 1643 Argyll's offer had been renewed. He
would be given high military command, and his debts,
mainly incurred in legal expenses, would be paid if he
would join the dominant party. The story reached the
ears of the queen, and in a letter of 31st May she offered
him arms from Denmark and assured him of her confidence, though she had heard that he had " struck up
an alliance with certain persons that might well create
apprehension in my mind." [3] In the early days of June
Montrose was in the north with Airlie, Huntly, and
Marischal, attempting to form a coalition—an attempt
frustrated by the lightheadedness of the latter two.
This visit seems to have alarmed Argyll, for he made one
last desperate bid for Montrose's support. If others
were blind to the powers of this young man of thirty,
the dictator of Scotland knew capacity when he met it.
He was aware that Montrose had been snubbed by the
queen, and he hoped to catch him on the rebound.
Montrose had not bluntly refused his overtures, but

[1] Orr, *Alexander Henderson*, 294–295.
[2] Rait, *The Parliaments of Scotland*, 156.
[3] Napier, II., 380. *Mem. of M.*, II., 77.

had hinted that certain scruples stood in his way. To
solve them, the Moderator of the Kirk, Alexander
Henderson, was dispatched to interview the doubter.

One day in the middle of June he met Montrose in a
meadow on the banks of the Forth near Stirling. It
was a curious meeting, the embarrassed Sir James
Rollo,[1] brother-in-law of both Montrose and Argyll,
acting as Henderson's second, and Lord Napier, Lord
Ogilvy, and Stirling of Keir being present as witnesses.
The Moderator frankly avowed that the Covenanters
were about to send an army to England in support of
the Parliament, and repeated the old offer. " Nothing
was more earnestly desired than that he should join
with his peers and the other estates of the realm ; it
would bring joy to all, and not only profit, but also
honour to himself. His example would at once bring
over the few, if there were any, who respected the empty
shadow of royalty. As for himself, his most hearty
thanks would be due to God if He would deign to make
him the minister and mediator of so great a work." [2]
Montrose asked Rollo if Henderson had authority to
make the offer. Rollo said he had, but Henderson said
no, but believed that the Convention would substantiate
his promises. This gave Montrose the chance to avoid
a direct refusal. He replied that in these circumstances
he must ask for time to consider, and took a friendly
leave of the man in all Scotland from whom he was most
loth to differ. They never met again. Three years
later, after he had seen Montrose's splendour and decline,
as well as the failure of his own hopes, Henderson died.
His last words were : " I am near the end of my race,
hasting home, and there was never a schoolboy more
desirous to have the play than I am to have leave of
this world."

---

[1] Sir James Rollo, or Rollock, was the eldest son of the laird of Duncrub,
who was made a peer by Charles II. in 1651. He married first Montrose's
sister Dorothea, and secondly Argyll's half-sister Lady Mary Campbell. He
was present at Inverlochy, and fled in Argyll's boat. He was among the
company at Montrose's funeral in 1661. His brother, Sir William, was
Montrose's faithful companion till he was executed at Glasgow after Philiphaugh.

[2] Wishart, c. 2. Baillie, II., 74. Guthry, 130.

1643   Before the Convention in June, Charles, in a declaration to the people of Scotland, had stated his case against the English Parliament, and had solemnly protested his loyalty to the rights recently assured to the Scottish nation. He was not believed. The war in Ireland had ceased, and the Kirk dreaded that an army might thereby be freed for the defence or restoration of episcopacy. Moreover, Lord Antrim, whose incompetence rivalled Hamilton's in every field of action, had got himself captured in Ulster, along with a budget of letters from Nithsdale, Aboyne, and others. There seemed a risk of a popish invasion. Scotland was to be overrun by Irish kerns, Charles was to join hands with Nithsdale on the Solway, Macdonalds and Macleans were to harass the Campbells, and Huntly and Montrose were to fire the north. Montrose's recent visit to Aberdeen seemed to give authority to the tale.[1] Moreover, things were going ill with the English Parliament. In June John Hampden had fallen on Chalgrove Field, and Fairfax had been defeated in Yorkshire at Adwalton Moor ; in the south-west Hopton had cleared Devon, and in July scattered Waller's forces at Landsdown and Roundway Down, while Bristol, the second port of the kingdom, was about to fall to Prince Rupert. To Baillie it seemed that " for the present the Parliament side is running down the brae." But the Covenanters had gone too far to draw back : the triumph of the king meant in their eyes summary vengeance on those who had intrigued with his enemies.

Formerly the English Parliament had asked chiefly for a deputation of divines, but in August commissioners from the English House, among them the younger Vane,[2] arrived to ask for an army. The General Assembly met on 2nd August in a small room in the east kirk of St. Giles, and to Convention and

---

[1] Baillie, II., 74.

[2] " He who contributed most to it, and who in truth was the principal contriver of it, and the man by whom the Committee in Scotland was entirely and stupidly governed, Sir Harry Vane the younger, was not afterwards known to abhor the Covenant and the Presbyterians more than he was at that very time known to do, and laughed at them as much as he ever did afterwards." Clarendon, VII., 266.

Assembly was presented the English demand. The request for 11,000 troops was complied with, Lanark using the royal seal for a warrant which levied war against its owner, and the price of this support, a new bond to bind still closer the two countries, was drafted by Wariston and Henderson. This document, the Solemn League and Covenant, was accepted by the Estates, and ratified at Westminster by what was left of the English House, being thereafter solemnly subscribed in St. Margaret's Church on September 25, 1643. On 13th October it was sworn by the Estates and the Assembly, and later by the Scottish people in the parish kirks. It was signed by English Parliamentarians, because it was the price of the sorely needed Scottish help. It was extensively signed in Scotland, because the authorities saw to it that those who did not sign should suffer in person and estate.[1]

The Kirk had seized the chance to realize its dream of uniformity, but the dream came through the gates of ivory, and was to vanish ere morning. In return Kirk and nobility had involved their land in a course of hypocrisy and dishonour. They wished both to have their cake and eat it; in the Solemn League and Covenant, of which the price was armed rebellion, they vowed also to " preserve and defend the king's majesty's person and authority." They had broken a plain contract with the king; was it any defence to say that they feared lest Charles at some future date might break his contract with them? Montrose, the day before his death, put the point to his inquisitors. " When the king had granted you all your desires, and you were every one sitting under his vine and under his fig-tree, that then you should have taken a party in England by the hand, and entered into a league and covenant with them against the king, was the thing I judged it my duty to oppose to the yondmost." [2] It was not as if the Scots were republicans or shared the advanced constitutional views of certain of the Parliamentarians.

---

[1] The text of the Solemn League is in *A. P. S.*, VI., 42, and Burnet, *Mem. of the Hamiltons*, 238.　　　　[2] See p. 372, *infra*.

1643 They were almost to a man confused and sentimental royalists, and they had been granted every liberty which they had asked for. The verdict of history must be that for the sake of an ecclesiastical whimsy the bulk of the nation chose the path of civic dishonour. The question was not of the relative wisdom of monarchist or Parliamentarian doctrines, but of Scotland forswearing a creed, which she avowedly and sincerely held, for the bribe of a futile dream.

To Montrose the way was clear. To him it seemed that towards Scotland the king had behaved, though tardily, with justice and generosity, and had been rewarded by flagrant bad faith. Apart from the matter of personal honour, he believed that the path which the Covenant had chosen led only to anarchy and an ultimate tyranny. Every article of his political philosophy was at stake. The one hope seemed to lie in Charles's success. He set off at once for the south, and reached Oxford some time in August. The king had gone to the siege of Gloucester, and Montrose found that he could do nothing with the queen. Her trust in Hamilton was unshaken, and on 28th August she wrote to him reaffirming her confidence.[1] He then sought the king at Gloucester, but the courtiers persuaded Charles that the young man was an alarmist, and that the scheme he proposed was moonshine. Meantime the Solemn League and Covenant had been ratified, Leven was mustering his men, and every day the chance of forestalling him grew more slender. In an agony of anxiety Montrose pled and expostulated.

But as the autumn passed and the king returned to Oxford to winter, the letters of Hamilton and Lanark took a new tone. They confessed that the game was up, that they had been deceived, that Leven was on the eve of marching. Charles sent for Montrose at last and listened to his plan, and Antrim, who had escaped from captivity, was at hand to promise support. In December the Hamiltons came to Oxford to brazen it out, and found their conduct the subject of a commission of inquiry.

[1] Burnet, *Mem. of the Hamiltons*, 241.

There could be no question of the verdict. Montrose *1644*
and Aboyne, Nithsdale, Kinnoull,[1] and Ogilvy were there
to testify to a long course of double-dealing, supineness, and folly, which was only saved from being flat
treason by the mental confusion of those who pursued it.
Hamilton was arrested and sent a prisoner to Pendennis
castle in Cornwall; Lanark escaped—first to London,
where he shared the bed and board of Mr. Robert
Baillie, and then to the Covenant army. At long last
the king turned to the only man who could give him
hope.

Montrose abode with the court at Oxford during the
bitter early months of 1644,[2] and elaborated his plans.
It seemed a desperate remedy. The only project he
could offer was to " raise Scotland for the king "; but
it seemed as if Scotland had effectively risen for the
king's opponents. Leven's blue-bonnets were over the
Border, and the whole line of the Marches was controlled
by the Covenanters. They held every city and town in
Scotland; Parliament and General Assembly alike were
their creatures; the revenue of the country was in their
hands; the greater part of the nobles had joined their
standard. A year ago there had been a chance; now
it seemed the wildest of wild ventures. If the Scottish
people were tired of their taskmasters they had given
no sign of it, and the supposed loyalists, with a few
shining exceptions, had proved the most brittle of reeds.
Except for Kinnoull, Ogilvy, and Aboyne, Montrose
seemed to have no following even among the royalists
of his own class. Huntly disliked him, Crawford was
jealous of him, Traquair feared him; the nondescripts,
like Carnwath, Morton, Southesk, Nithsdale, Roxburgh,
and Home, were disinclined to obey a youth.

But in that strange Oxford, where the colleges had
become courts or barracks, and trenches were at the

---

[1] This was the second earl, who died at Whitehall, October 5, 1644. His
son George, the third earl, joined Montrose after Tippermuir, and was a loyal
adherent of his cause till his death in Orkney in the autumn of 1649. For the
fourth earl, see note on p. 357.

[2] When Leven crossed the Tweed, on January 19, 1644, the ice was so
thick that the baggage carts could pass over on it.

1644 back of Wadham and across St. Giles's, and Rupert and his horse swung over Magdalen Bridge of a morning to raid in the Chilterns—an Oxford of junketing and brawling, hymns and drinking songs, fiery hearts and anxious minds,[1] there were men like Endymion Porter and Digby, men in the inner circle of the royal councils, in whom the grave purpose of the young Scottish earl commanded respect. Among so much that was self-seeking and half-hearted, his ardour was like a sea-wind in a stifling room. They had the wit to recognize that a certain kind of spirit may win against any odds. Hyde, too, was probably his friend. The future Lord Clarendon detested Scotland and all things connected with her, but he loved an honest man and a stout heart ; and we know from a letter of Evelyn to Pepys that " the brave Montrosse " was one of the portraits in his private cabinet at Cornbury.[2] In any case it was no season for prudence, for Newcastle was in desperate straits in the north. " I will not," said Montrose, " distrust God's assistance in a righteous cause, and if it shall please your Majesty to lay your commands upon me for this purpose, your affairs will at any rate be in no worse case than they are at present, even if I should not succeed."

He asked for little help. Antrim was to raise troops in Ireland and the Isles, and land them in the west of Scotland to keep Argyll occupied in his own country. A body of horse from Newcastle's army would assist him to cut his way through the Lowlands to the Highland line. The King of Denmark might lend some German cavalry, and by hook or by crook a sufficient store of arms and ammunition must be transported to the north.[3] Charles consented, and Antrim was dispatched to Ulster with instructions to land 2,000 troops in Argyll

[1] For Oxford during the Civil War see the brilliant account in Mallet, *History of the University of Oxford*, II., c. 18.

[2] Vernon Watney, *Cornbury*, 231. Clarendon notes especially his modesty. *History*, XII., 16.

[3] Montrose's proposal to use foreign troops was natural at a time when half the fighting in Europe was done by mercenaries. A far more flagrant case was the employment of Dutch and Hessian troops against the Highlanders in 1745. The use of Catholic Irish was a more doubtful affair, in view of the recent Irish rebellion, but the troops actually used were chiefly expatriated Macdonalds.

by April 1, 1644.[1] Montrose was offered the commission *1644*
of viceroy and captain-general of the royal forces in Scotland, but very wisely he declined ; the title was bestowed
on the king's nephew, Prince Maurice, and Montrose
was content to be known as his lieutenant-general. He
knew something of the jealous temper of the northern
forces, and he had no desire to wreck his expedition on
an empty name.[2]

The six years of waiting were ended. The fates had
cleared the stage, and the waverer had an issue of his
perplexities. Words were to give place to deeds ; the
narrow streets of Edinburgh and the heavy air of conventions and assemblies to the clean winds and the wide
spaces of the hills. He had before him a straight path
of duty, and little it troubled him that it ran into dark
shadows. Once more he had recaptured his boyish
ardour, and there was no happier man in the world
than Montrose when, on that March morning, with the
ash buds black in St. John's gardens, he rode north out
of Oxford to win a kingdom.

---

[1] The agreement between Montrose and Antrim, in Montrose's handwriting,
is still extant in the possession of the Antrim family. In it Antrim is styled
" His Majesty's General of the Isles and Highlands of Scotland," and he
undertakes to raise troops before 1st April from the Isles, as well as from Ireland.
It is dated 28th January, and Montrose is called the king's lieutenant-general,
three days before his commission was issued. The agreement is witnessed by
Digby and Sir Robert Spottiswoode.

[2] The commission as lieutenant-general is dated Feb. 1, 1644. There is a
commission extant, dated Feb. 13, appointing him captain-general, and styling
him marquis (*Hist. MSS. Comm.*, 2nd Report, 172), but this does not seem to
have been acted on, though it is superscribed by the king, for there was a
separate warrant for the marquisate, dated May 6, 1644, and the commission as
captain-general was issued a year later, May 4, 1645.

BOOK II
ACTION

CHAPTER VI

THE CURTAIN RISES

(*March* 1644–*August* 1644)

Worcester. I will unclasp a secret book,
And to your quick-conceiving discontents
I'll read you matter deep and dangerous,
As full of peril and adventurous spirit
As to o'er-walk a current roaring loud
On the unsteadfast footing of a spear.
    Hotspur. If he fall in, good night !—or sink or swim !—
Send danger from the east unto the west,
So honour cross it from the north to south,
And let them grapple.

                    First Part of King Henry IV.

S T. THERESA, when she set out as a child to convert the Moors, was engaged on a mission scarcely less hopeful than that which Montrose had now set himself. It seemed the wildest of gambles against impossible odds. In the true knight-errant fashion Charles had given him a sword engraved with the arms of the flower of his race, Prince Henry,[1] but he could give him little more. Montrose was to raise Scotland for the king, but where was he to find an army ? The best of the semi-professional levies were with Leven in the north of England. The soldiers of fortune from the German wars were already for the most part under Leven's banner. He could get nothing from the towns and villages of the Lowlands, for, whatever the feeling of the people, the Kirk and the Estates had a firm control of the machinery of enlistment. As for the nobles, the most powerful were

---

    [1] It was for long the property of the Gartmore family, till it was purchased by John Ballantyne and presented to Sir Walter Scott, who lent it to his cousin, the knight marshal, to wear at the visit of George IV. to Scotland. It is now in the Abbotsford armoury. See Lockhart, II., 395 ; V. 190.

Covenanters, and even if it had been otherwise, were
far too jealous and self-centred to follow a young man
of no higher rank than their own in a cause which was,
at the best, forlorn. Did he hope that his words of
wisdom, his far-sighted political doctrines, would carry
conviction to a backward peasantry, harassed by temporal want on the one side and the fear of eternal punishment on the other ? Besides, he proposed to bring
Antrim's Irishry to his aid, and Antrim's Irishry, though
most of them were Scots, seemed to the Lowlands so
many emissaries of the Pope and the devil. With such
allies he would not attract a single doubting Presbyterian
to his standard.

As in most great adventures, there was no solid
hope save in the soul of the adventurer. In a desperate
case the man who risks most is usually the wisest, and
Montrose staked everything on the speed and gallantry
of his spirit. It seems impossible that at this period
he can have intended to raise the Highlands. He relied
on his kinsmen in Perth and Angus, and he had some
hope of the Gordons. It was the gentry of the northern
lowlands — Grahams, Drummonds, Erskines, Stirlings,
and Ogilvies—in whom he trusted, if he trusted in any
one besides himself, and not in the clans of the hills.
Probably at the time he knew very little about the
Highlands, and his experience in the Bishops' War cannot
have prepossessed him in favour of the desultory bands
who accompanied Huntly's lowland levies to battle.
Had he known more he would not have been greatly
encouraged. Argyll, poor soldier as he was, had worked
his will with Morvern and Badenoch, Atholl and
Lochaber. Nor were there any of the ordinary politics
in the hills. The chiefs were royalists only in as much
as they were not Covenanters. He might indeed count
on the assistance, could he reach them, of all those who
hated the name of Campbell—Clan Chattan, Clan Donald,
the Macleans, the Stuarts, and the Camerons. But Seaforth and his Mackenzies would never fight on the same
side as a Macdonald, and, if he enlisted the Gordons, he
might look to find the Grants in the other camp.

If Montrose's venture was desperate in purpose, it was no less desperate in the lack of a base. He was to fling himself into the midst of a hostile country to improvise an army. Nothing could be looked for from the king except the royal commission. Even had Charles been that ideal monarch which certain royalists created out of their fancy, he could have done little to help his champion. As it was, he passed from blunder to blunder, enraging by his obtuseness and duplicity both friend and foe. The man who fought for a Stuart must be content to wage war without reserves. His life and his reputation alike must be in his own keeping.

Crawford, Reay, Nithsdale, Ogilvy, and Aboyne accompanied Montrose as he rode out from Oxford, on his way to Newcastle's camp. The two first presently turned off with a squadron of horse towards Shrewsbury. Arrived at York, Montrose found that Newcastle was at Durham, so he sent on Colonel Cochrane to acquaint him with the king's commission and his need of men and money. The reply came that at Durham there was little of either, and the king's lieutenant-general, on March 15th, proceeded thither to reason with the royalist commander. Already the news of his coming north had sent Argyll post-haste into Scotland, whither, Montrose wrote to Sir Robert Spottiswoode at Oxford, " we intend to make all possible dispatch to follow him at his heels, in whatever posture we can." [1] Newcastle, the great potentate of the north-east, now a marquis and after the Restoration to be a duke, was a man of sumptuous and scholarly tastes, a devout loyalist, and brave and scrupulous in all the relations of life. He was the idol of his second wife, but in her praise of his gentility, " which hath something in it of grandeur," [2] we can detect the source of his failure. He was too fine for the rough task before him—the complete dilettante, who, in Clarendon's words, " the articles of action no sooner over, returned to his delightful company, music, and the softer plea-

---

[1] Napier, II., 391. Spottiswoode was an Oxford man, of Exeter College, as was also Hamilton. Mallet, *Hist. of Univ. of Oxford*, I., 253.
[2] *Life of Duke of Newcastle*, 1667.

sures." [1] As a soldier he was neither fortunate nor
skilful, for he had no experience of war.

On 19th January Leven, with 18,000 foot and more
than 3,000 horse, had crossed Tweed. He halted for
three weeks before the town of Newcastle, and then on
28th February the bulk of his army, assisted by the
prayers of Mr. Robert Baillie in far-away London,
forded Tyne. By 2nd March he was across the Wear,
and two days later entered Sunderland. Newcastle,
who had only 5,000 foot and 3,000 horse, was oppor-
tunely strengthened by the arrival of Sir Charles Lucas,
made a feeble demonstration against him, and then fell
back on Durham. Leven followed, but finding his com-
missariat difficult in that devastated country, remained in
the district between Tyne and Wear, and decided to lay
siege to the positions which guarded the mouth of the
former river. The marquis, when Montrose arrived, was
in the worst of spirits. The town of Newcastle still held
out, but Leven was at its gates, and Manchester and
Fairfax were closing up on him from the south. Even
as against the Scots he was outnumbered, and he might
soon be caught between two formidable fires. He was
in no condition to spare a silver piece or a man.

Nevertheless, as a great nobleman, he honoured the
king's commission and did his best. A hundred ill-
mounted troopers and two small brass cannon were the
most the perplexed commander could spare Montrose
for the conquest of Scotland. He called out for him,
however, the militia of Cumberland and Westmoreland,
and sundry local gentlemen were willing to join his
standard. Another disappointment was in store, for
Carnwath, who happened to be in Newcastle's camp,
refused to accept from Montrose's hand the royal
commission as lieutenant of Clydesdale. It was a fore-
taste of the spirit of even the loyal among the Scots
nobles. There was a curious wildness in the Carnwath
family, conspicuous even in a wild age. At the head of a
troop of horse rode a certain Mrs. Pierson, who passed as
Carnwath's daughter, and whose commission was made

[1] *History*, VIII., 85.

out in the name of Captain Francis Dalziel. Her cornet
carried a black banner, which displayed on a sable field
a naked man hanging from a gibbet, under the motto
" I dare." [1]

Montrose's coming stirred the Marquis of Newcastle
to action. Leven, at the mouth of the Tyne, was cut
off from his base and his heavy guns at Sunderland.
Here was a chance for a bold stroke, so on 23rd March
he advanced to Chester-le-street, and next day took
up position at Hilton north of the Wear, a few miles
from Sunderland, with Leven on a hill to the east.
But even Montrose's influence could not put speed into
Newcastle's languid soul. There was an artillery duel
and some fighting between advanced troops, but on the
25th Newcastle suddenly drew off towards Durham,
and Leven was enabled to inflict considerable damage
on his rear. Presently the news of Fairfax's approach
caused the marquis to hasten south to York.

With Newcastle's campaign Montrose had no con-
cern, for his business lay north of the Border. He
marched towards Carlisle with 200 horse, mostly gentlemen who had served in the foreign wars ; Crawford of
the fierce counsels, Nithsdale, Ogilvy, and Aboyne were
with him, and Captain Francis Dalziel with her grisly
banner.[2] The Cumberland and Westmoreland men,
800 foot and three troops of horse, joined him on
the road, and on 13th April he led a force of some
1,300 men across the Border. But he had not forded
Annan before trouble began. Most of the English
militia, worked upon by the emissaries of Sir Richard
Graham,[3] deserted, and the loss was not atoned for by

---

[1] Napier, II., 393. Deposition of Major John Erskine, *Hist. MSS. Comm.*,
2nd Report, 174. Carnwath is best known as the man who seized Charles's
bridle at Naseby when he was about to charge at the head of his Guards, an
incident to which Clarendon attributes the loss of the battle.

[2] Wishart, c. III. Depositions of Major John Erskine and Major James
Leslie. *Hist. MSS. Comm.*, 2nd Report, 174.

[3] Graham had been an attendant of Buckingham, and had accompanied
Buckingham and Charles to Spain on their visit in 1623 to see the Infanta.
Montrose, according to Wishart, had once esteemed him, but he was a noted
trimmer, and did espionage work for the Parliament. Having been raised
" from the dunghill," he founded the families of Esk and Netherby. Wishart,
c. iv. ; M. and S. 51.

the accession of Lord Herries with a small following. With his little force of a few hundreds Montrose reached Dumfries, and occupied the town without opposition. The provost, one John Corsane,[1] welcomed him gladly, and in consequence had five years' trouble with the Estates and the Kirk.

It was at once apparent that nothing could be done in the southern Lowlands. The Maxwells and Johnstones of the Dumfries neighbourhood were in no mood to rise, and their heads—Nithsdale and Hartfell—were jealous of the new commander. Annandale, Morton, Roxburgh, and Traquair, though nominally royalists, refused, like Carnwath, the king's commissions of lieutenancy, by means of which Montrose had hoped to organize a formidable opposition.[2] Farther east Lothian was hot for the Parliament, and the " bauld Buccleuch," a young man of eighteen, was commanding—with no particular credit to himself—a regiment under Leven. The peasantry of Dumfries were under the thumb of the ministers and of fickle noblemen like Glencairn. Montrose issued a declaration, headed by the device which appears on the cover of this volume, explaining that he was now in arms for the king on the same principle as he had once been in arms for the Covenant —" for the defence and maintenance of the true Protestant religion, his Majesty's just and sacred authority, the fundamental laws and privileges of Parliament, the peace and freedom of the oppressed and enthralled subject." " Knew I not perfectly," he added, " his Majesty's intentions to be such, and so real as is already expressed, I should never have embarked myself at all in his service. Nor, did I but see the least appearance of his Majesty's change from these resolutions or any

---

[1] Spalding (II., 391) says that the provost was Sir James Maxwell, and that he was executed for his surrender of the town the following July ; he is followed by Lang and by McDowall (*Hist. of Dumfries,* 410). But it is clear from the town records that Corsane was provost, and his subsequent troubles will be found in the Acts of Parliament and the minutes of the Dumfries Presbytery. See *Mercurius Aulicus,* May 4, 1644, and Mr. James Barbour's paper in the *Proceedings of the Dumfries and Galloway Antiquarian Society.* The Maxwell who was hanged was a Maxwell of Munches.

[2] See Montrose's instructions to Lord Ogilvy. Napier, II., 406–409.

of them, I should never continue longer my faithful endeavour in it." [1] His case was unanswerable; he stood in the direct tradition of the National Covenant and of the spirit of the Glasgow Assembly. But he was speaking a tongue which the burghers of Dumfries, and for that matter the Scottish people, did not understand. " It was not," in Mr. Gardiner's words, " for the restoration of a dead past that he drew the sword. He stood up for that which was, in some sort, the hope of the future." [2] And the language of the future is always strange to contemporary ears.

Montrose lingered on, waiting for news of Antrim's men, from which it would appear that Galloway, as well as Argyll, was their objective. But no news came and his hopes sank, for Antrim had always been uncertain as the wind. He received, however, a message of another kind—from his niece, Lady Stirling of Keir— inviting him, on behalf of the commander, Lord Sinclair, to take possession of the castle of Stirling and the town of Perth. Sinclair and his second in command, Sir James Turner,[3] were probably sincere in their offer, but it was fortunate for Montrose that he did not attempt to accept it. For the Covenant had got wind of the intention of the pair, and, while Montrose was reading his niece's letter, Callander, with Sinclair and Turner in tow, was marching south. Callander, who had once been Almond and a party to the Cumbernauld Bond, presently occupied Dumfries, while Montrose and his handful recrossed the Esk. They barely escaped, and had to leave some of their guns in Annandale.[4] Meanwhile two events had befallen the royalist leader. He had received his patent of marquis from the king, and had been excommunicated by the Kirk in Edinburgh. The latter honour was also conferred at the same time upon Huntly, who had just been conducting an aimless

---

[1] *Mem. of M.*, II., 146–147.   [2] *Civil War*, II., 132.
[3] See Turner, *Memoirs* (1829), 35. Turner was the original of Dugald Dalgetty.
[4] *Papers relating to the Army of the Solemn League and Covenant* (S.H.S.), II., 317. These guns were " yrne," and not Newcastle's brass pieces : they must have been part of the armoury captured by Montrose in Dumfries.

and confused rising in the north, and was now hiding
from Argyll in Strathnaver.[1]

There was no course open to Montrose except to wait
for Scottish news on English soil, while he kept Callander
and his 7,000 levies busy on the western Marches, and
to strike a blow, if occasion offered, on behalf of the
hard-pressed Marquis of Newcastle. He had no illu-
sions about either that general or the royalist troops in
the north of England. He had seen the quality of
the Cumberland and Westmoreland militia, most of the
gentry were watching the omens, and the Percy's spur
was cold in Northumbria. The centre of the war was
shifting into Yorkshire, but Montrose's duty was to
keep close to Scotland, and his task was only desultory
Border fighting. It was sufficient, however, to inspire
acute anxiety in the breast of Mr. Robert Baillie and
the Covenant leaders.

If Newcastle was to be retained and the position of
its marquis improved at York, a blow must be struck
forthwith in the north.   The town of Morpeth was
strongly held by a Covenanting garrison under Somerville of Drum (afterwards the tenth Lord Somerville), and
on 10th May Montrose marched against it, assisted by
Colonel Clavering, and with Crawford as his intractable
colleague. He attempted to carry the place by assault,
was repulsed, and then, after bringing up six guns from
Newcastle, breached its defence and entered it on 29th
May. The air was full of wild rumours, and to a certain Captain John MacCulloch, who parleyed with him,
Montrose gave a romantic account of a great disaster
to Leven at York, and of the success of the royalists in
Scotland.[2] The garrison was disarmed and dismissed,
and after the surrender Montrose entertained the governor to dinner. He then recaptured the fort at South
Shields which Leven had taken on 20th March, and
attacked Sunderland, where he was checked by the
energy of its seamen and the cavalry sent by Leven from

[1] Gordon of Ruthven, 50.
[2] Napier, II., 399–402.   Spalding, II., 379.   *Memorie of the Somervilles*
(1819), II., 306, etc.   Terry, *Alexander Leslie*, 285.

York.[1] The Covenanting general was in difficulties, for so long as he had the Marquis of Newcastle to deal with he could do little against Montrose. His only hope was Callander, who was making his leisurely way from the western Border.[2] Montrose was collecting provisions from the Alnwick neighbourhood and succeeding in getting them into the beleaguered Newcastle, when at the end of June he received a peremptory summons to join Prince Rupert, who was marching through Lancashire to the relief of York.

Rupert did not wait for Montrose. He relieved York indeed, but before he and Montrose met the king's arms had suffered their first crushing disaster. On 2nd July, about five in the afternoon, he engaged the Parliament forces at Marston Moor, and discovered that new thing in England—the shock of Cromwell's horse. The Huntingdonshire grazier, turned parliamentarian, had made himself also a great soldier, and had hammered into being an army to suit his purpose. On that fierce day David Leslie also wrought famously, and disputes as to the true architect of victory did not improve relations between Scots and English.[3] The king's army was scattered, Newcastle fled overseas, and Rupert, lamenting the loss in action of his white dog which Puritans believed to be his familiar spirit,[4] rode with some 6,000 troops into the western hills. Two days after the battle Montrose found him in an inn at Richmond. " Give me a thousand of your horse," he said, " and I will cut my way into the heart of Scotland." But Rupert had nothing to give ; on the contrary, he stood much in need of Montrose's scanty recruits. So with a sad heart the new marquis rode by Brough and Appleby to Carlisle to indite his report to the king. The western Marches were now safer for him, since Callander had gone east to Newcastle.

Four months had passed and nothing had been done. Ogilvy and Sir William Rollo had journeyed secretly into Scotland, and had returned with ill news. The

[1] Whitelocke, I., 270. *Cal. S. P., Dom.* (1644), 242. [3] Baillie, II., 196.
[2] Terry, *Alexander Leslie,* 235 n., 256, etc. [4] Vicars, *God's Ark,* 277.

land lay quiet under the Covenant, and Antrim's levies
seemed to have vanished into the mist. The nobles,
headed by Traquair, were tumbling over each other in
their anxiety to swear fealty to Argyll. There seemed
nothing to be done except to surrender the royal commission, and to wait abroad for a happier time. So
his friends advised, and Montrose made a pretence of
acquiescing. He set out for Oxford with the rest, having
taken Ogilvy (and later Aboyne) into his confidence. A
little way from Carlisle he slipped behind, but as his
servants and baggage went on it was presumed that he
was following. Had he continued, he would have shared
in the capture of the whole party by Fairfax at Ribble
bridge.[1]

He had resolved on the craziest of ventures. He
would break through the Covenant cordon in the
Lowlands, and win to his own country. There, at any
rate, were loyal hearts, and something might be devised
to turn the tide. He chose as his companions the lame
Sir William Rollo and an officer, Colonel Sibbald, who
had fought under him in the Bishops' War. They wore
the dress of Leven's troopers, while Montrose followed
behind as their groom, riding one ill-conditioned beast
and leading another.

It was a dangerous road to travel. The country was
strewn with broken men and patrolled by Covenant
horse, and a gentleman in those days was not easily
disguised. At first all went smoothly. Passing through
the woods of Netherby, they learned that Sir Richard
Graham had joined the Covenant, and in its interests
had constituted himself Warden of the Marches. His
servant, from whom they had the news, spoke freely,
as if to Leven's troopers. A little farther on they fell
in with a Scot, one of Newcastle's soldiers, who disregarded the troopers but paid great attention to their
groom, hailing him by his proper title. Montrose tried

---

[1] The chief prisoners taken were Lord Ogilvy, Sir John Innes, and Montrose's natural brother, Harry Graham. When Newcastle fell in the following October, Lords Crawford, Reay, and Maxwell, and Wishart, Montrose's
biographer, were among the captives.

to deny it, but the man exclaimed, " What, do I not know
my Lord Marquis of Montrose well enough ? But go
your way, and God be with you ! " A gold piece rewarded the untimely well-wisher.

The journey must have grown hourly more anxious
till the Forth was passed. " It may be thought,"
wrote Patrick Gordon, " that God Almighty sent His
good angel to lead the way, for he went, as if a cloud
environed him, through all his enemies." [1] We do not
know the road they travelled—whether by Annandale
and the springs of Tweed and Clyde, or up Eskdale and
thence over the Tweedside range to the Lothians. The
safest route was probably by the belt of bleak moorland
which runs north by Carnwath almost to the Highland
hills. Riding chiefly by night, the party made good
progress. On the fourth day they came to the Montrose
lands in Stirling and Strathearn, but they did not draw
rein till they reached the house of Tullibelton, between
Perth and Dunkeld. Here lived Patrick Graham of
Inchbrakie, he who had seen to the ordering of Montrose's little library at St. Andrews, and here was safe
shelter for the traveller while he spied out the land and
looked about for a following.

It was the hour of portents. Airy armies were seen
to contend on a hill in Banff ; in Buchan the sun shone
clear at midnight, and a kirk was filled with a choir of
unearthly music ; a cannon shot echoed over the whole
kingdom to warn men that an invader was landing in
the west.[2] But the true portent came in humbler form.
The curtain rises, and the first act of the great drama
reveals a forlorn little party late on an August evening knocking at the door of a woodland tower above
the shining reaches of Tay. The king's lieutenant-
general makes a very modest entrance on the scene.
Two followers, four sorry horses, little money and no
baggage seem a slender outfit for the conquest of a
kingdom; but in six months he had Scotland at his feet.

[1] Gordon of Ruthven, 71.
[2] Ibid., 62–63. Forbes Leith, *Memoirs of Scottish Catholics*, I., 288.

CHAPTER VII

TIPPERMUIR

(*September* 1644)

Hotspur. " The purpose you meditate is dangerous ; the friends you have named uncertain ; the time itself unsorted ; and your whole plot too light for the counterpoise of so great an opposition ! "   Say you so, say you so ? . . . By the Lord, our plot is a good plot as ever was laid ; our friends true and constant : a good plot, good friends, and full of expectation ; an excellent plot, very good friends.   What a frosty-spirited rogue is this !
First Part of King Henry IV.

I

FOR six days the king's lieutenant lay close in hiding while his comrades scoured the country for news.   Tullibelton was too near the lowland town of Perth, and its laird too noted a loyalist for his guest to run needless risks, and Montrose spent most of his time among the woods and hills, sleeping at night in hunters' bothies, and soothing his soul with the lights and colours of a Scottish autumn.   The scouts returned with a melancholy tale.   Huntly had failed ruinously in the north, and the Gordons were leaderless and divided, while the influence of their uncle, Argyll, was driving Huntly's sons to the Covenant camp.   Some of the Graham and Drummond kinsmen even, with the alternative of prison and fines before them, were in arms for the Estates.   There were rumours of Covenant levies in Aberdeenshire, and in the west Argyll had his clan in arms.   Montrose in his despondency may well have wondered at this strange activity.   The tide of war had rolled over the Border, and with Scotland in so iron a grip such precautions must have seemed odd to one who knew the economical spirit of his opponents.

He was soon to learn the reason, and at the same time to recognize his opportunity. The incident is best told in the words of Patrick Gordon, who had the story from Montrose's own lips :

"As he was one day in Methven Wood, staying for the night, because there was no safe travelling by day, he became transported with sadness, grief, and pity to see his native country thus brought into miserable bondage and slavery through the turbulent and blind zeal of some preachers, and now persecuted by the unlawful and ambitious ends of some of the nobility ; and so far had they already prevailed that the event was much to be feared, and for good patriots ever to be lamented. And, therefore, in a deep grief and unwonted ravishment, he besought the Divine Majesty, with watery eyes and a sorrowful heart, that His justly kindled indignation might be appeased and His mercy extended, the curse removed, and that it might please Him to make him a humble instrument therein, to His Holy and Divine Majesty's greater glory. . . . While he was in this thought, lifting up his eyes he beheld a man coming the way to St. Johnstoune (Perth), with a fiery cross in his hand, and, hastily stepping towards him, he inquired what the matter meant. The messenger told him that Coll Mac Gillespick—for so was Alexander Macdonald called by the Highlanders—was entered in Atholl with a great army of Irishes, and threatened to burn the whole country if they did not arise with him against the Covenant, and he was sent to advertise St. Johnstoune, that all the country might be raised to resist him." [1]

Antrim's levies had come out of the mist at last.

Presently Montrose received a letter from Alasdair Macdonald himself, directed to the king's lieutenant-general at Carlisle. The messenger who carried it asked directions from Inchbrakie, who took the dispatch and promised to deliver it. In the letter Macdonald announced his arrival and begged for instructions. If Montrose needed help, no less did the Irish commander.

Alasdair Macdonald was of the ancient stock of Dunyveg in Islay, the son of Macdonald of Colonsay, commonly called Coll Keitach, or "Coll who can fight with either hand." The name, corrupted into Colkitto, was transferred by the Lowlanders (like the Gruamach appellation in the case of Argyll) from the father to the son. Sorley Boy Macdonald, the father of the first

---

[1] Gordon of Ruthven, 71–72.

Earl of Antrim, had been his father's great-uncle. The
Macdonnells of Antrim were near blood-relations of
Alasdair's own people of Islay and Kintyre, and the
Campbell oppression of the latter clan had left bitter
memories on both sides of the North Channel. Alasdair
was a man of herculean strength and proven courage;
self-indulgent and somewhat inclined to drunkenness;
obtuse and incapable of framing or understanding any
complex strategy : " no sojer," wrote Sir James Turner,
" though stout enough." [1]   But he was a born leader of
men, and so impressed Leven in Ireland that he did his
best to reconcile him to Argyll, and sent him to Scotland
for the purpose. But the chief of the Campbells treated
the Irish commander with contempt, and Alasdair returned to Ulster with all his hereditary grievances inflamed, and burning for revenge.[2]

Antrim, whom Clarendon thought a man " of excessive pride and vanity, and of a marvellously weak and
narrow understanding," had been conspicuous for his
large promise and meagre performance. The clan of
Macdonnell had a hard life under the fruitless escapades
of their chief; " we are worn spectre-thin," sang their
bard, " by the earl's oft frequenting of the wave." [3]
But now at last he was to influence the course of history.
After many difficulties he raised, by the end of June
1644, 1,600 recruits among the exiled Macdonalds and
Macleans, and he invited Alasdair to lead them against
the ancestral foe. Early in July the invaders landed
in Ardnamurchan, an old territory of the Macdonalds,
and proceeded to exact vengeance on the unfortunate
Campbell settlers. The king's quarrel was forgotten in
a more intimate and personal strife. Alasdair ravaged
the peninsula with fire and sword, and seized as a base
the castle of Mingary on Loch Sunart, and the keep of
Lochaline, which still stands where the little river Aline
enters its sea-loch. He sent messengers throughout the
West Highlands to summon the clans to help him in his
task. But there was no response; Macdonalds and

Macleans, Macleods and Macneils, were alike silent; the hand of Clan Diarmaid lay too heavy on the mainland and the isles.

Soon his position became desperate, for Argyll was raising an army of pursuit; so he swept back to his base, only to find that all his ships had been destroyed. Alasdair, whatever his defects as a general, was a bold fighting man; his only hope was the Gordons, and he resolved to bid for their support though it meant marching across the breadth of Scotland. Accordingly he led his forces through Morvern and round by the head of Loch Eil to the Lochaber glens, the western fringe of Huntly's country. Here he had his second piece of ill tidings. Huntly's revolt was over, and the Gordons had made their peace with the Covenant. There was nothing for it but to try the more northern clans, and his next venture was Kintail. But the Mackenzies, little though they loved the Campbells, had a long memory of Macdonald misdeeds, and their chief, Seaforth, warned off the intruders.

Headed back on all sides, Alasdair decided that the boldest course was the safest. He marched south again to Badenoch and the head waters of Spey, and himself issued a summons, calling upon the clans to rise in the name of the king and Huntly. This brought him some 500 recruits, most of them Gordons; but he could get no nearer to the heart of that powerful clan, for the Grants, Forbeses, and Frasers blocked the road down Spey, and a thousand of Seaforth's Mackenzies lent their aid. Alasdair now seemed in a fair way for destruction. The Campbells intercepted his retreat to the sea, and Argyll was hot-foot on his track. Seaforth cut him off from the north and east; the new Badenoch levies were mutinous and distrustful, and south lay the unfriendly Lowlands, and clans like the Stewarts of Atholl, who would never serve under an alien tartan. He had proved that whoever might band the Highlands into an army, it would not be a man of Highland blood. Hence his despairing letter to the king's lieutenant-general asking for help and instructions. He can scarcely have hoped

for much from his appeal, for Carlisle was far from
Badenoch and he had the enemy on every side.

'Montrose sent back an answer, bidding Alasdair be
of good heart and meet him at Blair. It must have
seemed a hard saying to a man who believed that
his correspondent was still at Carlisle, but he obeyed,
and, guided by a Clanranald man,[1] one Donald the
Fair, who had seen service in the German wars, he
marched into the braes of Atholl. The local clans
resented his intrusion, the fiery cross was sent
round, and there was every likelihood of a desperate
conflict between two forces who alike detested the
Covenant and followed the king. The Irish were stout
fellows in hard condition, but they were uncouthly
dressed, wild-eyed from long travel, and, after their
custom, attended by a mob of half-starved women
and children. The Atholl clans, living on the edge of
the Lowlands, may well have looked askance at such
outlandish warriors. Moreover, Alasdair's men were
Catholics, and the Reformation in some sort had come
to Atholl, as had tales of Irish barbarities in the recent
rebellion. The Earl of Atholl was a minor, and the pressure of Argyll kept the leaderless clan quiet, in spite
of long memories of Campbell reivings and burnings.
Donald Robertson, the Tutor of Struan, seems to have
joined Alasdair at once,[2] but the Robertsons as a clan
held aloof ; and when the Irish had taken the castle of
Blair, they were faced by angry and watchful levies,
waiting for the word to make an end of them.

The situation was saved by a hairbreadth. Montrose, accompanied by Patrick Graham, the younger, of
Inchbrakie—Black Pate, the countryside called him—
set out to walk the twenty miles of hill between Blair
and Tullibelton to keep the tryst. He had acquired
from Inchbrakie a Highland dress—the trews, a short
coat, and a plaid for the shoulders ; he wore a blue
bonnet with a bunch of oats as a badge, and he
carried a broadsword and a Highland buckler. Thus
accoutred, he entered suddenly upon the scene in the

[1] Forbes Leith, I., 291.   [2] Spalding, II., 261.

true manner of romance. Alasdair and his ragged troops were waiting hourly upon battle, when across the moor, between the hostile camps, they saw two figures advancing. Black Pate was known to every Atholl man, and there were many who had seen Montrose. Loud shouts of welcome apprised the Ulsterman that here was no bonnet-laird, but when he heard that it was indeed the king's lieutenant he could scarcely credit the news. He believed him to be still on the road from Carlisle, and he had looked for cavalry, an imposing bodyguard, and a figure more like his own swashbuckling self than this slim young man with the quiet face and the searching grey eyes.

In a moment all quarrels were forgotten. Montrose revealed his commission, and Alasdair gladly took service under him, thankful to be out of a plight which for weeks had looked hopeless. The Atholl clans were carried off their feet by the grace and confidence of their new leader, and the Stewarts and Robertsons brought to his side those broadswords which an hour before had been dedicated to cutting Ulster throats. Montrose slept the night at the house of Lude, and next morning unfurled the royal standard on a green knoll above the Tilt. The king's lieutenant had got him an army.

II

We pause, on the eve of Montrose's campaign, to consider the conditions under which, in that era, battles were fought. Some knowledge of the methods of war in the fifth decade of the seventeenth century is necessary if we are to understand the magnitude of Montrose's achievement and the causes of his success.

It was an age when, in both Scotland and England, relatively to the population, surprisingly large numbers of men were called to arms, but only a small proportion was brought into action.[1] Difficulties of transport,

---

[1] In the summer of 1642 Essex was supposed to have 24,000 foot and 5,000 horse, but at Edgehill he numbered only some 13,000. In April 1643 he started nominally with 16,000 foot and 3,000 horse ; in July he had actually only 6,000 foot and 2,500 horse. Firth, *Cromwell's Army*, 23.

when roads were few and bad ; an imperfect intelligence
system ; the necessity of masking fortresses and protecting communications ; pay chronically in arrears ; the
absence of a strong central authority on either side, and
the dissipation of effort in divergent operations ; the
lack of any adequate provision for recruiting losses—
such were the main reasons why the opposing strengths
were so slow in forcing a decisive issue. Success must
fall to the man who could best overcome or disregard
these handicaps, who could move his troops fast and
far, who had early news of his enemy's plans, who had
no civil problems to perplex him, whose levies had an
inducement to fight other than their pay, and who
could concentrate all his powers on a single purpose.

Infantry were still held in less esteem than cavalry.
A foot regiment consisted of musketeers and pikemen
in the proportion of two of the former to one of the
latter.[1] The pikemen wore iron corselets and head-
pieces, and carried pike and sword, and their chief
business was, as at Marston Moor, to repel a cavalry
charge. They were heavy troops, and for rapid work
the musketeer, who had no body armour, was coming into
favour. The musket of the period was still, for the
most part, the old matchlock, which required an elaborate rest. It fired a bullet which weighed about an
ounce and a quarter, took a long time to load and discharge, and had a range not exceeding 400 yards. It
demanded a great deal of match, and in the enemy's
neighbourhood it was necessary to keep the match
lighted, so that the troops were at the mercy of the
weather.[2] The defects of the matchlock were bringing
the flintlock into fashion, and in the Parliament armies
the latter was employed for cavalry carbines and pistols
and for special companies detailed to guard the artillery.
The flintlock was primarily a sportsman's weapon,
and must have been used by many private citizens
when the regular army weapon was the matchlock.

---

[1] In the Scottish army in 1644 as 3 to 2. *Memorie of the Somervilles*, II., 307.
[2] As at the battle of Preston. Turner, *Memoirs*, 59. *Cf.* also the position
at Kilsyth and Dunbar. Firth, *op. cit.*, 84.

There were certainly flintlocks in the Scottish cavalry
in 1644.[1] An infantry regiment being composed of
musketeers interspersed with pikemen, its efficiency
depended upon an exact discipline which could combine
the movements of both arms. Only then could it hope,
like the regiments of Maitland and Lindsay at Marston
Moor, to beat back a charge of horse.

The infantry formation was conditioned by the time
which a musketeer required to load and fire, for it was
the custom for the first rank to discharge their pieces
and then fall to the rear to reload. The ordinary formation at this time was six deep, but in an emergency the
files might be reduced to three, to prevent outflanking
or to obtain a broader front of fire. At first only one
rank fired at a time, till Gustavus Adolphus introduced
the fashion of three ranks firing simultaneously, the first
kneeling, the second stooping, and the third standing
upright. But armies are conservative things, and, in
spite of the lesson of Leipsic, it was not till Cromwell's
New Model that the method became the accepted practice in Britain. Montrose used it, being in this, as in
other things, a reformer.

Infantry tactics were elaborate. Since distinctive uni-
forms were unknown, it was necessary to have badges,[2]
and watchwords or " field signs." These being settled,
an action usually began by sending out a body of
musketeers, called a " forlorn hope," who fired and fell
back. When the main bodies came into touch the
musketeers delivered a couple of volleys, and then the
pikemen charged. This was for a pitched battle ; in
lesser engagements there might be something like open
order, the troops taking shelter in ditches and behind
hedges, as at Worcester.[3] Such cover was eagerly
sought by the foot, for it was the best preventive of a

---

[1] In Argyll's troop, *A. S. P.*, VI., i., 65 ; see *Army of the Covenant* (S.H.S.),
I., xlvii. In 1668 Lord Atholl complained of his instructions to arm the
Perthshire militia with matchlocks, on the ground that his men were " altogether unacquainted with the use of any other gunnes but fyrelocks, and
wherewith they are weill provydit." *P. C. R.*, June 4, 1668.

[2] The Parliament army had orange scarves at Edgehill, green branches at
Newbury, and white badges in their hats at Marston Moor.

[3] Firth, *op. cit.*, 99.

cavalry charge. The ordinary soldier marched slowly,
for he carried a monstrous weight—at least double the
forty pounds of to-day, and in the case of the pikemen
far more. The longest day's march of the New Model
during 1645–46 seems to have been thirteen miles.[1]

The mounted arm was then at the height of its
fame, and the current view was that in a well-equipped
army the horse should in numbers be not less than half
the foot. In England the old heavy cavalry were
becoming obsolete, and their place taken by harque-
busiers, who carried sword, pistols, and carbine, and
by lightly armed dragoons, who were to all intents
mounted infantry. They wore a light steel casque, a
light cuirass, or often only a padded buff coat. Scotland stood to the old ways, and still armed her horse
with four pistols, a carbine, and a lance.[2] The light
horse did the outpost work of the army, reconnoitred,
seized bridges and passes in an advance, and covered a
retirement. In action a cavalry charge was at first
made slowly, at a trot rather than a gallop, and trusted
largely to the volley from the saddle. The old formation was five deep ; this Gustavus reduced to three, and
his example was beginning to be followed in England,
as also his instructions to cavalry to reserve their fire,
to charge at top speed, and to charge home. Rupert
owed much of his early success to adopting the Swedish
plan, and Montrose followed suit.[3] Rupert also insisted upon cavalry taking the offensive, and both he
and Cromwell anticipated the later shock tactics.[4] The
charge was always made in close order, knee to knee.
The Scottish cavalry had no Rupert to make tactical
experiments, and had to wait for reform till David Leslie
copied the methods of the New Model.

The field gun employed varied from the culverin,
which fired a ball of nearly twenty pounds, had an
extreme range of about 2,000 paces, and needed eight

---

[1] Sprigge, *Anglia Rediviva*, cited by Firth, *op. cit.*, 107–108.
[2] Firth, 114. *Army of the Covenant*, I., xcvii. Baillie, II., 440. *Cal. S. P.,
Dom.* (1640), 616.
[3] *e.g.* at Auldearn. See p. 248, *infra*.   [4] Firth, 134–142.

horses to move it, down to the little three-pounder.[1]
Loading a heavy piece was a cumbrous and perilous
business, since the powder was usually carried loosely
in a barrel. Scotland began by having a powerful
artillery train, for Leven had learned from Gustavus the
scientific use of that arm. His master of ordnance, Sir
Alexander Hamilton (" dear Sandy " to his countrymen),
had an ingenious turn, and in 1644 had invented a new
kind of light twelve-pounder, which a single horse could
carry.[2] Though the New Model siege train was one of
the chief factors in bringing the Civil War in England
to an end, it cannot be said that cannon played a
decisive part in the field, except at Langport in 1645.
In Scotland, after her great effort in equipping Leven,
it would seem that the zest for artillery was relaxed,
and at Preston the Scots had not a single gun of any
kind—" dear Sandy being grown old and doated, and
giving no fitting orders for these things." [3] Yet the
mere possession of field-guns, however antiquated and
badly handled, was a conspicuous asset against a Highland force. The Highlander detested the " musket's
mother " as something outside the decent order of
things, and needed much persuasion before he would
face cannon.[4]

The army's intelligence was in the hands of the
scoutmaster-general, but whatever the energy of this
officer, he had in Lowland and English scouts material
not comparable to that afforded by the Highland clans,
to whom the most daring espionage was the breath of
life. . . . Every regiment dressed as its commander
ordained, but red was coming in fast; in Scotland the
usual wear was probably hodden-grey, except for the
officers and the cavalry.[5] . . . The common soldier's

---

[1] Firth, Appendix H.
[2] Terry, *Alexander Leslie*, 178, etc. *Army of the Covenant*, I., lxxxvii., etc.
Firth, *op. cit.*, 157.
[3] Turner, *Memoirs*, 59.
[4] Especially if " grenadoes " (*i.e.* shells) were fired, as at the siege of Black-
ness in 1651 : " They swear they will never fight more against guns that shoot
twice, meaning in two cracks—the mortar and the shell." Douglas, *Cromwell's
Scotch Campaigns*, 168 n.
[5] *Army of the Covenant*, I., xciii., etc.

1644 food was bread and cheese, except in garrison; the articles of war enjoined payment for all supplies commandeered, but the pay-chest was often empty. . . . Discipline was provided for by elaborate military codes, such as the one which Leven promulgated in 1644, which, in addition to much that was sensible and humane, enjoined the formation of a kirk-session in every regiment.[1] Religion was amply provided for in the armies of both king and Parliament, but Baillie laments that in 1644 it was hard to get enough ministers.[2] The army chaplain of these days was a useful person, and his duties were secular as well as sacred, for he was the historian of a campaign and the seventeenth-century substitute for the war correspondent.[3]

Such is a rough sketch of the constitution of the regular armies of Scotland and England in the year 1644. The pick of the Scottish regulars were with Leven, who in January had taken across the Border twenty-one regiments of foot, nine troops of horse, a regiment of dragoons, and an artillery train.[4] What Montrose had to meet was the Scottish second-line army, the home-defence force, raised and equipped like the first line, but a little ruder, clumsier, less disciplined. His own command was meagre and shabby in the extreme. Alasdair had about 1,100 men divided into three regiments—men who might be called regular soldiers, inured to discipline, and seasoned by hard campaigns. They had firearms, for the most part ancient matchlocks, an occasional claymore, and a variety of pikes and cudgels. The Badenoch men, mainly Gordons and Keppoch Macdonalds,[5] numbered perhaps 300, and the Atholl clans provided another 800; both, at their own request, were commanded by young Inchbrakie. Of this total of 2,200, nearly half—the Highland contingent—were most inadequately armed. Some of the gentry may have carried flintlocks, there were a good

---

[1] *Army of the Covenant*, I., xcviii., etc.   [2] I., 213.
[3] *e.g.* Case and Byfield with Essex; Ashe and Goode with Manchester; Bowles and Hugh Peters with Fairfax and Cromwell; Wishart with Montrose; and Thomas Gumble with Monk.
[4] Rushworth, V., 604.   [5] Spalding, II., 261.

many claymores, but the weapons of most were clubs
and bows and arrows. These Highland warriors presented the same picture as the Highland contingent in
Leven's army of 1641—lean, red-shanked mountaineers,
plaided, armed with sword and bow, such deadly marks-
men that with the latter they could kill a running deer.[1]
Nor was the lack of firearms all ; ammunition was so
scarce that only one round could be provided for such
weapons as they possessed. There was no artillery of
any kind, and not a plack in the treasury. The cavalry
was limited to three horses, perhaps the unfortunate
beasts which had carried Montrose and his friends from
Carlisle—skin and bone, says Wishart, " omnino strigosos
et emaciatos."

Yet, in the then condition of Scotland, there was in
that ragged levy the makings of a most formidable
force. If it could find a leader and loyally follow him,
it might gravely perplex the home-defence army, for it
had none of its faults. The Highlander, accustomed to
full meals of meat from the chase, was physically far
superior to the bannock-fed Lowland peasant or the
apprentice from the foul vennels of the little cities.
He was swift where they were slow, cunning where they
were simple, adroit where they were blundering, daring
when they were supine. A Highland army could pursue
a strict military purpose, for it had no civil preoccupa-
tions to compel the holding of town or fortress.[2] Living
on the country, it could do without pay-chests and
transport wagons. It had no communications to be cut ;
its base could not be taken, for its base was the inviolable hills. Under a general who understood its peculiar
virtues, it might be to the second line of the Covenant
as a rapier to a ploughshare.

[1] Terry, *Alexander Leslie*, 153.
[2] On the fatal lure of fortresses in the Civil War see Sir John Meldrum's
testimony. *Cal. S. P., Dom.* (1644–45), 91.

III

It was the true opening of Montrose's military career, and he seems to have undergone a change of spirit. He was now thirty-two years of age, and, as men went in his era, might be held to have left his youth behind him. Hitherto we have seen him perplexed and tormented, walking delicately and a little sadly in the difficult ways of conscience. He goes steadfastly on the path of duty, but with head bowed. To his contemporaries he must have seemed something of a dreamer and a doctrinaire, with nothing of that large impulsive power which carries men perforce to do its will. He had a good repute as a soldier, but that repute was largely academic. In the Bishops' War he had shown no special gift except speed, and in the Border campaigning, earlier in the year 1644, he had fought with weapons which snapped in his hand. But now some seal is broken in him. Conscious of high talents for command, he sees an army spring up miraculously at his call, and he has the wit to perceive in that motley force the germ of a new kind of war. His spirit is suddenly enlarged, and he recaptures his youth and his humanity. Something goes out from him which kindles the ardour of Ulsterman and Highlander alike, and which makes Alasdair follow obediently a man the processes of whose mind are utterly beyond his ken. He discovers a boyish zest for adventure and the desperate chance. He indulges in a boy's whimsies—the dress which captures the fancy, the proud word that stirs the heart. He strides at the head of his men, daring the wildest cateran to outvie in hardihood this intimate of scholars, this familiar of courts and senates, the king's lieutenant-general.

Apparently he sent formal warning to Argyll, as befitted the holder of the royal commission to the king's principal antagonist.[1] If a blow was to be struck it must be prompt, for the Council was arming fast against

---

[1] *Mem. of M.*, II., 147.

Campaign of

TIPPERMUIR AND ABERDEEN

Montrose's First March ———
Montrose's Second March ---

0 5 10 15 20 25 30
English Miles

Alasdair, though as yet Edinburgh had no news of
Montrose. Lord Elcho was at Perth with a large force
drawn from the burghers of the second city of Scotland,
men from Fife and the Perthshire lowlands, and the
mounted gentry of the neighbourhood. Lord Burleigh
had another army at Aberdeen, with the young Gordons
serving under him; while from the west Argyll was
leading his formidable clan to avenge the smoking home-
steads of Morvern and Ardnamurchan. To wait in
Atholl was to starve, to retreat farther into the hills was
to court disaster. Montrose had no supplies, no ammunition, no means of increasing his force except by victory.

On the 30th day of August he left Blair and marched
west up the Tummel valley in blue autumn weather. He
did not take the shortest road to Perth, for Argyll was
coming from the west, and it would be well by fetching a
circuit to get news of him before engaging Elcho. Also
he had hopes of collecting allies in Strathearn. Round-
ing Loch Tummel, the army crossed the hills by the
eastern side of Schiehallion to Aberfeldy. At Castle
Menzies, whose laird was an ally of Argyll, they encountered a slight opposition, and burned a hut or two
and some corn in sheaf. Late that night they crossed
Tay, and put the river between them and the hostile
Menzieses. Next morning at dawn Black Pate led the
Atholl men forward as an advance guard, and the army
marched with Highland speed across Strathbran, and
by the Sma' Glen to the Almond. There at the Hill of
Buchanty they fell in with an unexpected reinforcement.
Lord Kilpont, the eldest son of the seventh Earl of
Menteith; David Drummond, the Master of Maderty;
and Sir John Drummond, a younger son of the second
Earl of Perth, had raised 500 bowmen at the order of
the Estates to oppose Alasdair's invasion. The leaders
were kin to Montrose—young Maderty was his brother-
in-law—and when they learned who was advancing their
purpose changed. They gladly joined the royal general,
and brought him a welcome accession of stalwart
peasants, who, living on the border-line between Highlands and Lowlands, had some of the virtues of both.

The force crossed the ridge to Strathearn, and spent the night on the moor of Fowlis.

It was now Sunday, the 1st of September. Elcho had something under 7,000 infantry, the levies of Fife and the Scottish midlands ; 700 horse, composed of the local lairds and their following ; and nine pieces of artillery, light pieces firing at the most a five-pound ball.[1] He had ample munitions of war, and his troops were fortified by the Sabbath morning exhortations of an array of ministers. " To give them their due," says Wishart, " they performed their part stoutly at the expense of their lungs, promising them in the name of God Almighty an easy and bloodless victory. Nay, one of them, Frederick Carmichael [2] . . . did not hesitate to declare in his discourse, ' If ever God spoke certain truth out of my mouth, in His name I promise you to-day a certain victory.' " [3] With Elcho were many of the neighbouring Covenanting gentry, including Lord Murray of Gask,[4] and some who were not Covenanters, like Lord Drummond, Perth's eldest son; and he had the assistance of at least one experienced professional soldier, Sir James Scott of Rossie, who had just come from serving under the flag of Venice. Small wonder that the Covenant forces were in good heart. They had seen something of the Highlander in the Bishops' War, and thought little of his prowess. They knew that Alasdair's troops were in rags—as one of the ministers described them, " naked, weaponless, ammunitionless, cannonless men." The view of the leaders was that of Elspeth's ballad in *The Antiquary :*

" My horse shall ride through ranks sae rude
As through the moorland fern ;
Then ne'er let the gentle Norman blude
Grow cauld for Highland kerne."

Besides, they outnumbered the enemy by nearly three

---

[1] Wishart says 6,000 foot, while 8,000 is the figure given by one of Alasdair's Irish officers. Carte, *Ormonde Papers*, I., 73.
[2] Minister of Markinch in Fife.   [3] Wishart, ch. v.
[4] Wishart anticipates and calls him " Earl of Tullibardine." He succeeded his father as fourth earl four days after the battle. *Military History of Perth-shire*, I., 252.

to one. So, very early in the day, Elcho with his army marched three miles westward to Tippermuir, accompanied by a host of Perth citizens who were not unwilling to see a surprising judgment fall upon their ancient foes. He took up a good position in open ground, where his cavalry, his most formidable arm, had room to manœuvre. His battle-cry was " Jesus and no quarter ! " [1]

Montrose had at the most 2,700 men, all of them foot-soldiers, for his cavalry, as we have seen, was confined to the three lean horses from Carlisle. His artillery consisted of Kilpont's bowmen. The most grievous lack was ammunition, for the Irish, who alone had guns, had but one round apiece. On Tippermuir, however, there were plenty of stones, and with these as missile weapons he bade the rest arm themselves. He put the three regiments of Irish under Alasdair in the centre of his little force, and Kilpont with his bowmen on the left, while he himself, carrying targe and pike, took command of the Atholl men on the right flank. Elcho's dispositions were not unskilful. He commanded the right wing, Murray of Gask the centre, and Sir James Scott the left, opposite Montrose. The 700 horse, equally divided between the two wings, were under Lord Drummond.

Montrose, faced with so great a numerical superiority, had at all costs to avoid outflanking. So he abandoned the ordinary six-rank formation, and drew up his men in a long line only three deep. He saw further the danger from Drummond's cavalry unless he scattered the enemy foot out of hand by striking at its heart. He knew something of the temper of the unwilling Lowland levies—men drawn from the counter and the plough-tail to a work for which they had no stomach. To such the wild charge of the clans would be a new experience. Then, true to his duty as a constitutional commander, he sent the Master of Maderty with a flag of truce to inform Elcho that he was acting under the royal commission, that he wished above all

---

[1] *A True Relation of the Happy Successes of His Majesty's Forces in Scotland under the conduct of the Lord James, Marquis of Montrose*, etc., 1644. Copies of this rare pamphlet are in the Bodleian and the National Library of Scotland.

things to avoid shedding Scottish blood, and to summon him to remember his due and lawful allegiance ; in any case, let there be a truce so that the Sabbath should not be profaned. Elcho replied that he had " made choice of the Lord's day for doing the Lord's will " ; he had no mind for a truce which would give the doomed royalists a chance to slip away. Moreover, he made the envoy prisoner and dispatched him to Perth in the custody of two Forfar lairds, who told him genially that he would be hanged when the fight was over. The Covenanters were to show throughout their struggle with Montrose a strange reluctance to accept the etiquette of civilized warfare.

The battle began with a skirmish. As the two forces approached within cannon shot, Drummond sent forward a mounted squadron, in order to entice Montrose into one of those frontal attacks to which an undisciplined army is prone. It was Elcho's one glimmer of tactical wisdom. But Montrose was ready. He had adopted the method used by Gustavus at Leipsic by which all three ranks fired at once, though the weapons of the third rank were only stones ; and the first volley sent Drummond's troopers flying and halted Elcho's advance. Then he gave the order for a general charge. From behind the smoke came the fierce kerns of Ulster and Badenoch, with pike and claymore and Lochaber axe. The nine guns were submerged by the torrent. Elcho's centre crumpled like paper, and in a few minutes was racing back on the road to Perth. The cavalry could do nothing in the face of such fury and speed. On the Covenant left alone was there any serious resistance, where on rising ground stood Scott, the wary professional soldier, with the best of the Fife levies. But Montrose presently won the ridge, and Scott fled with the rest. The plain was strewn with lathered horses and panting foot.[1]

---

[1] The first-hand evidence for Tippermuir will be found in the depositions before the Committee of Estates, *Mem. of M.*, II., 149, etc. ; *Hist. MSS. Comm.*, 2nd Report, 174 ; and in the Irish officer's narrative in Carte, *op. cit.* There are accounts in Wishart, Spalding, and Gordon of Ruthven. See also Gardiner, *Civil War*, II., 139-142, and *Military Hist. of Perthshire*, I., 251-252. There

Then followed a grim business. Scarcely a dozen men fell in the battle, but nearly 2,000, according to Wishart, died in the rout, and the Irish officer, whose story has come down to us, declares that a man might have walked to Perth on the dead.[1] Some perished from the swords of Montrose, some from sheer fatigue —for the pursuit lasted till nine in the evening of a hot autumn day—and we are told that ten of the Perth burgesses succumbed unwounded to their un- usual exertions. Presently the enemy was at the gates of Perth, and the city surrendered without a word. Cannon, arms, supplies, tents, colours, drums, baggage, all became the spoil of the victors. Montrose held his wild forces in a stiff discipline. He refused to allow the captured guns to be turned on the fugitives, and he permitted no violence of any kind within the walls. He contented himself with fining the burghers £50 sterling, which went to Alasdair, who was in desperate straits for money, with compelling the Covenanting sheriff-clerk to copy out a summons to the local lairds, and with levying a large contribution of cloth to amend the " looped and windowed " raggedness of his army.

For three days Montrose tarried in Perth. He took up his quarters in the town, in the house of one Margaret Donaldson, and sent to Kinnaird for his old tutor, William Forrett, to act as his secretary, and for his two elder sons, Lord Graham and Lord James. Like Crom- well, he had the ministers to dinner, and one of them, Mr. George Haliburton, was afterwards taken to task by the Presbytery for saying grace at his table.[2] The

seems to be no warrant for Baillie's charge of treachery against Lord Drum- mond (II., 233). Second-class mounted troops were useless against a Highland charge.

[1] Wishart's figure must be exaggerated. Baillie, who loved horrors, mentions only " some hundreds of the honest burgesses of Fife " as slain in the flight. II., 233.

[2] For Montrose's stay in Perth, see the depositions in *Mem. of M.*, II., 149, etc., *Chronicles of Perth* (Maitland Club), 39, and the *MS. Register of the Pres- bytery of Perth*. For Mr. Haliburton and other perplexed ministers, see *The Diocese and Presbytery of Dunkeld*, I., 84, etc. One of the most perplexed was Montrose's old friend and mentor, Mr. Robert Murray of Methven. The minister of Tippermuir was censured for giving Montrose a cup of water when he called at the manse on the morning of the battle.

news of the victory carried consternation to the Covenant leaders in London, who had written off Montrose
for good, and caused them heart-searching as to whether
the judgment was due to the sins of Assembly, Parliament, army, or people.[1] It drew off some of the Scots
troops from Newcastle,[2] but it did not give Montrose
the recruits he had hoped for, Lord Dupplin being the
only man of note who arrived at his camp.[3] The Atholl
and Badenoch men, according to their custom, made off
to their homes to secrete their booty, and his force was
soon reduced to little more than Alasdair's Irishry.
There were other armies waiting to be met, and one of
them, Argyll's, was approaching rapidly from the west.
Montrose decided that his force was not sufficient to
oppose Argyll, and at that time he was probably not
aware of the existence of Burleigh at Aberdeen. His
immediate aim was to collect recruits in his own county
of Angus, and, if possible, capture Dundee.[4] On the
4th of September he left Perth and, crossing the Tay,
reached the neighbourhood of Coupar-Angus. On the
10th Lothian, with Argyll's vanguard of horse, entered
the city, and the following day at long last came Argyll
himself.

On the night of the 6th the camp was stirred by a
tragedy. Young Lord Kilpont shared a tent with one
of his lieutenants, James Stewart of Ardvoirlich, whose
castle still stands among the birch woods on the south
shore of Loch Earn. A quarrel arose in the small hours,
and Stewart stabbed Kilpont to the heart, killed two
sentries, and with his son and some friends escaped to
the Covenanters. Argyll three months later procured
him a pardon from the Estates,[5] who, on 12th September,
to give further proof of their partiality for assassination,
offered a reward of some £1,600 sterling to any one who
would slay Montrose and exhibit his head to them in

---

[1] Baillie, II., 228.   [2] Ibid., II., 226.
[3] See note on p. 161.
[4] Mr. Gardiner assumes that Montrose left Perth with the intention of engaging Burleigh at Aberdeen ; but Wishart says clearly (ch. vi.) that he did
not get news of Burleigh's army till he was in Angus.
[5] *A. P. S.*, VI., i., 359.

Edinburgh.[1] The murderer was also to have a free
pardon for any crimes he might have been unfortunate
enough to commit in the past. Mr. Gardiner dryly points
out the inconsistency of this course. " The favourable
reception given by Argyll to the supposed murderer was
a sign that all who joined in a Highland rising might be
assassinated with impunity as far as the Covenanting
authorities were concerned. It is seldom indeed that
a civilized community metes out to a less civilized one
the measure by which it judges itself. When Argyll
desolated the Highland glens with fire and sword, he
was but inflicting due punishment upon barbarians.
When Montrose gathered the Highlanders to the
slaughter of the burghers and the farmers of the Lowlands, he placed himself outside the pale of civilized
warfare." [2] The natural presumption from Argyll's
reception of Stewart is that Stewart had been endeavouring to anticipate the wishes of the Estates, and had
tried to persuade Kilpont, who had refused. For such
a view there is no evidence, and it is intrinsically unlikely. Kilpont would have offered barren soil for any
such proposal, and this Stewart must be assumed to
have known. It is more probable that the account given
in Stewart's official pardon is the true one. He had proposed to desert, and Kilpont, divining his intention,
tried to prevent him and was slain. Or, if we like, we
can take the family tradition referred to by Scott in his
Legend of Montrose, that Stewart had challenged Alasdair,
and that afterwards, in their cups, Kilpont and Stewart
had words which ended in the fatal blow. The Estates
have so many deeds of violence on their shoulders that
the historian is glad to relieve them of one.

[1] *Mem. of M.*, II., 163. This barbarous practice was not confined to one
side, for in 1639 Charles set a price upon the heads of Alexander Leslie and
Alexander Hamilton, but only £500 apiece. *Cal. S. P., Dom.* (1639), 81.
[2] *Civil War*, II., 142–143.

CHAPTER VIII

ABERDEEN AND FYVIE

(*September–December* 1644)

> There is dross, alloy, and embasement in all human tempers; and he flieth without wings who thinks to find Ophir or pure metal in any. For perfection is not, like light, centred in any one body ; but, like the dispersed seminalities of vegetables at the creation, scattered through the whole mass of the earth, no place producing all, and almost all some. So that 'tis well if a perfect man may be made out of many men, and, to the perfect eye of God, even out of mankind. . . .
>
> If generous honesty, valour, and plain dealing be the cognizance of thy family, or characteristic of thy country, hold fast such inclination. . . . Fall not into transforming degeneration. . . . Be not an alien in thine own nation : bring not Orontes into Tiber. SIR THOMAS BROWNE.

I

1644
September

DUNDEE proved beyond Montrose's powers. It was too well garrisoned for 1,500 men to take, and the guns captured at Tippermuir were no siege pieces. He moved accordingly to the upper waters of the Esks in the hope of enlisting some of the loyal gentlemen of Angus. Here he had definite word of Burleigh's army at Aberdeen, which determined his next step. The Angus recruits came in slowly. Lord Airlie indeed appeared, the father of Lord Ogilvy who had been captured at Ribble Bridge. No Ogilvy was ever anything but a king's man, and two of his sons, Sir Thomas and Sir David, accompanied their father. With the Gordons Montrose fared no better than had Alasdair Macdonald. Huntly was still lurking among the bogs of Strathnaver ; Aboyne, the second son, was fighting for the king in the garrison at Carlisle ; and Lord Gordon, the heir, and his younger brother, Lord Lewis, were with Burleigh at Aberdeen. The clan,

198

however, was not wholly unrepresented in the royal army. Nathaniel Gordon had been with Huntly in his rising, and now rode joyfully to join the king's lieutenant. He was an intrepid and seasoned soldier, but as rash as any subaltern of Alasdair's. It is a pity that no romancer has made him the subject of a tale, for his career, both early and late, offers rich material. Before he took part in politics, brigandage, kidnapping, piracy, and the baiting of Mr. Andrew Cant had been among the simple diversions of his life.[1] He brought thirty horsemen with him, and Airlie had forty-five, so the little army was no longer without cavalry.

Montrose left his second son, Lord James, in his house of Old Montrose to continue his schooling, and then, keeping to the skirts of the hills, reached the Dee valley by the pass known as the Cryne's Cross Mounth.[2] The river was crossed about midway between Banchory and the Mills of Drum, and Crathes—the stately castle of the Burnets of Leys, which lay on the north bank— was peacefully occupied. Sir Thomas Burnet was that rare combination, a friend of Huntly's and a staunch Covenanter; he hospitably entertained the royal lieutenant and his staff, and offered him a sum of money, which was refused. The following day, the 12th of September, the army advanced down the river to within two miles of the town of Aberdeen, where they found Burleigh awaiting them. Montrose had chosen his route to avoid the strongly fortified bridge of Dee, and in the hope of effecting a surprise; but the Covenanters had had ample warning, and had taken up a good position on the slopes of a hill. A lane, the present Hardgate, ran downwards from their centre, and around the foot of it were houses and gardens, which were strongly held. Burleigh had in all some 2,000 foot and 500 cavalry,[3] and he possessed heavier artillery than the little pieces captured at Tippermuir. His cavalry

---

[1] He was of the Gordons of Ardlogie. For his earlier doings, see Spalding, *passim*.
[2] See Fraser, *Old Deeside Road*, 75.
[3] Wishart, ch. vi. Guthry says 2,500 foot; Gordon of Ruthven gives him 3,000 foot and 600 horse.

seem to have been chiefly the Forbes, Fraser, and Crichton gentry, and eighteen horse under the separate command of Lord Lewis Gordon. His infantry were the usual Covenant levies, including a proportion of Aberdeen townspeople, and the remnants of Elcho's Fife regiment.[1] Montrose had 1,500 foot and some 70 horsemen. It was his business to beat his opponent as soon as possible, for Argyll, with a formidable army, was lumbering in his wake, and Fabian tactics would land him between two fires.

On the morning of the 13th, according to his custom, he sent an envoy to the magistrates of the city summoning them to surrender, advising them at any rate to send the women and children to a place of safety, and warning them that those who stayed could expect no quarter. The magistrates returned an embarrassed answer, summarizing his words as " no quarter except to old persons, women, and children " (which was not what he had written), and subscribing themselves first " your lordship's faithful friends to serve you," and then altering this to " your lordship's as ye love us." [2] Why did Montrose preface this engagement with a threat so foreign to his character and practice ? It would seem that he was in a mood of anger and strain. Kilpont's murder had outraged his feelings ; his force was heavily outnumbered and needed encouragement ; he realized that his affairs stood on a razor edge, and that his failure now would mean destruction. His mood was to be further embittered. The magistrates courteously entertained his messenger and made a drummer-boy who accompanied him the present of a silver piece, but as the two returned under a flag of truce the child was treacherously shot by one of the Fife soldiers. A breach of the laws of war always revolted Montrose, and this breach was especially cruel and wanton. In a sudden fury he vowed to make the enemy pay dearly for the misdeed, and promised Alasdair the sack of the city if the day

[1] The second-line regiment. The first-line Fife regiment, commanded by Dunfermline, was with Leven in England.
[2] See the two letters in Napier, II., 452–453, and facsimiles in Spalding, II., 264.

THE
BATTLE OF ABERDEEN

Covenanting Army ☐
Montrose's Army ◼

Road to Aberdeen Crabstone

How Burn

Burn to Ferry Hill Mills

Hard-gate

Handgate

Service Road to Upper Mills

Flank movements of Covenanters

Marsh Burn

Upper Justice Mills

Lower Justice Mills

Dam

Dam

Dam

Marsh

How Burn

N

was won. Such a promise was as unjust as it was barbarous and unwise. It was not the city which had offended, but levies from the south that were little loved by the townsmen of Aberdeen.

Without further delay he deployed his forces for battle. He bade his men plunder the adjacent corn-fields, and, in order to distinguish themselves from the enemy, stick each a bunch of oats in his bonnet. The Irish as before held the centre, and on the right wing Sir William Rollo and Colonel James Hay commanded, while Nathaniel Gordon had the left. He divided his scanty cavalry into equal portions, and placed one on each wing, following an old custom of the Thirty Years' War by stiffening the score or two of horsemen with musketeers and bowmen interspersed among them—a thing only made possible by the discipline and skill of Alasdair's men. The little force thus marshalled was the nearest approach to a regular army that Montrose had yet commanded, for most were adequately armed, and almost all had some experience of war. Burleigh, who was nothing of a general, was content with his strong position, superior numbers, especially in cavalry, and heavier guns. He had little authority and no plan of battle, and his lieutenants followed their own devices.

The action began with an attack on the houses and gardens which protected the Covenant centre. Alasdair had little difficulty in driving the enemy out of these and advancing up the slope. Lord Lewis Gordon charged with his eighteen horsemen on Montrose's right wing—a mad boy's escapade in the old cavalry style, discharging their pistols and retiring at the cara-cole. He made no impression, and Lord Fraser and Crichton of Frendraught [1] followed vainly in the same manner; they knew nothing of the meaning of shock tactics, and sporadic and half-hearted assaults of this

---

[1] Frendraught was the son of the grim hero of the ballad *The Fire of Fren-draught* (Child., No. 194), and was born about 1620. He was with Montrose in his last campaign, and assisted him to escape after Carbisdale. The story of his suicide after that battle, given by the old peerage writers and accepted by the *Dictionary of National Biography*, is without foundation. He lived till 1664 or 1665. See Napier, II., App. VI., and Balfour Paul, *The Scots Peerage*, IV., 129–130.

kind were easy to repulse. The rest of the cavalry on the Covenant's left wing had apparently no orders, but sat staring at the battle.

Presently, however, the meaning of this manœuvre was plain. It was a diversion against Montrose's right to cover a dangerous attack upon his left. Following a mill road which was out of sight of the combatants, 100 Covenant horse and 400 foot worked their way to a position a little in the rear of Montrose's left flank. A bold attack there might have decided the battle, but the assault was delivered half-heartedly, and Nathaniel Gordon, with his little body of horse and musketeers, was able to hold it until Sir William Rollo's detachment was brought up from the right wing. With this accession of strength Gordon delivered a counter-attack, drove off the Covenant cavalry, and cut to pieces the Covenant foot.

But the denudation of the royalist right did not escape the eye of Sir William Forbes of Craigievar, who commanded on Burleigh's left. There were now no horsemen there to stiffen the defence, and with his cavalry he charged forthwith on that weakened wing— no futile demonstration like Lord Lewis Gordon's, but a charge to be pushed home in the manner of Rupert or Cromwell. Ordinary foot soldiers would have broken, but not Alasdair's Irish. With perfect coolness they opened their ranks and let Forbes's troopers thunder through ; then, facing round, they pursued them with volleys. Saddles emptied fast, and the cavalry became a flying rout. Rollo returned from the now secure left wing, and completed Forbes's destruction.

It was the turning-point of the fight, which had now lasted for several hours. Montrose, who had darted from place to place, reinforcing and heartening his men, called for a general advance. The Irish responded with enthusiasm, the whole army swept forward, and the Covenant centre broke and fled. The ground between the battlefield and the city walls became a shambles, and Alasdair's men, mindful of Montrose's promise before the fight, broke into the streets in pursuit.

Patrick Gordon says that the victors lost but seven
men and the vanquished a thousand, which is manifestly
absurd ; but beyond doubt the flying Covenanters were
cut down without quarter, and stripped before the fatal
blow, that their clothes might not be soiled with their
blood.   In the streets unarmed citizens were butchered,
women were violated and slain or carried into captivity,
and death did not spare the very old and the very
young.   For three terrible days the orgy lasted.   Montrose had returned to his camp, and the miserable business
continued unchecked, though Donald Farquharson, true
to his character for gentleness and mercy, endeavoured
to plead for the unhappy city.[1]   The mischief was done,
and Montrose's record had received its darkest stain.[2]

What is the truth about the sack of Aberdeen ?   On
the nature and magnitude of the atrocities it is hard
to dogmatize.   The damning evidence is that of the
royalist Spalding,[3] and it is explicit not only as to the
giving of no quarter to men, but as to the slaughter of
women.   Alexander Jaffray, who served with the Covenant cavalry and fled as fast as his horse would carry
him, says that " about seven or eight score men, besides
women and children, were killed."[4]   He may have
spoken from hearsay, but the burgh records of Aberdeen record the slaughter of all found on the streets,
" old and young," and it is fair to assume that both
sexes are included.   There can be no ground for dis-
belief in the melancholy fact.   As to the extent of the
killing, one may be more sceptical ; looting there was
on a colossal scale, and no quarter was given to Covenanters in arms, but the slaughter of citizens was probably less than 200.   Spalding, though his list does not
profess to be exhaustive, enumerates only 118.   Baillie,
not likely to minimize the misdeeds of his opponents,
puts the number of slain at seven score,[5] and in another passage his words are : " A great many Aberdeen

[1] Gordon of Ruthven, 111.
[2] The evidence for the battle is chiefly in Gordon of Ruthven, 81–84.
Wishart's account (ch. vi.) is unintelligible.
[3] II., 265, etc.
[4] *Diary* (Aberdeen, 1856), 50.   [5] II., 234.

men were killed, and the town ill plundered." [1]   This
evidence scarcely suggests a general massacre.   Moreover, the Cromwellian Richard Franck, visiting Aberdeen
in 1657, had heard of a great battle there, but clearly
of no atrocities, for he seizes the occasion for a panegyric on Montrose's "incomparable conduct." [2]

But on Spalding's evidence we must regard the main
charge as proven : Montrose, faithlessly faithful to his
rash promise to Alasdair, permitted the plunder of the
city, the killing of men in cold blood to the number of over
a hundred, and of some women, and the carrying off of
other women as spoil by the Ulstermen.   Among the
female prisoners in Selkirk gaol after Philiphaugh are
found names like Dunbar, Anderson, Forbes, Lamond,
Young, Simson, Tait, Watson, Walker, Park, and
Stuart [3]—it may be, some of the unfortunates who were
now compelled to follow Alasdair's drum.   On Saturday
the 14th Montrose entered the city with Airlie, Dupplin,
and others, and slept the night there, busied with trying
to call his troops to order.   But they had got out of
hand, and when the march sounded on Monday morning
many of the Irish were still at their evil work.   When
he saw the wretched townsfolk fruitlessly mounting his
own whimsy of oats in their bonnets to save their lives,
his heart may well have misgiven him. [4]   On that day he
learned his lesson, and for the remainder of his campaigns he held his men in a grip of iron.   Henceforth
when he captured a town there might be looting, but
there was no murder or outrage.

The sack of Aberdeen was not only a crime, it was
a fatal error.   This was no Covenanting city, and the
majority of those who perished inside its walls had been
forced into the fight—as Spalding says, " harllit out sore
against their wills to fight against the king's lieutenant."
Montrose had spoiled his chance of getting recruits for
the king among the burghers of Deeside.   All over
Scotland, too, the tale, zealously disseminated by the

---

[1] II., 262.   [2] *Northern Memoirs* (ed. 1821), 226.   [3] *A. P. S.*, VI., i., 492.
[4] Spalding, II., 265–267.   This seems to be the occasion referred to in the
pamphlet, *A True Declaration*, etc.   Bodleian, 40, L., 73.

Covenanters, and no doubt wildly embroidered, must have deterred moderate men from casting in their lot with one whose methods seemed more like a Tilly or a Wallenstein than a kindly Scot.

II

On Monday, the 16th of September, Montrose left the city and marched to Kintore on the Don. From there he sent a dispatch [1] to the king by the hand of Sir William Rollo. On the 19th the heavy-footed Argyll entered Aberdeen and proceeded to exact contributions from the surviving citizens. Soon the news of the battle reached Edinburgh, and the Estates were gravely disquieted. Argyll might be a pillar of the Kirk, but he was very slow in bringing malefactors to book ; he complained that his army was too small, so requisitions were promptly sent to Leven. Yet Argyll had at least 2,500 foot from the western levies, and Lothian, his master of horse, had 1,500 cavalry.[2] Montrose continued up Strathdon to Kildrummie, whence he sent Nathaniel Gordon to Strathbogie (Huntly castle) and the Bog of Gight (Gordon castle) in a desperate appeal to the Gordons. But the clan was dumb. It would not stir without Huntly's word, and Huntly, jealous of a royal commission which interfered with his own lieutenancy of the north, and not forgetful of his treatment by Montrose in the first Bishops' War, refused to give it.

The place was growing unhealthy for a loyalist with Argyll a day's march off, so Montrose withdrew by way of Strathavon and Tomintoul to the vicinity

---

[1] This dispatch, dated 14th September, is referred to in the dispatch sent after Inverlochy. Rollo, on his return, fell into the hands of the Covenanters, and, according to Wishart (ch. xviii.), was released by Argyll on the understanding that he would assassinate Montrose. There is no evidence to verify or disprove the story.

[2] Spalding (II., 270) says that Argyll had Lawers's regiment of foot and Dalhousie's regiment of horse, but he seems to be anticipating. Lawers's regiment, which was part of Callander's force in England, does not seem to have been against Montrose till Auldearn, or Dalhousie's till Philiphaugh. See *Army of the Covenant*, I., Introd.

of Rothiemurchus, that ancient pile on Loch-an-Eilean, of which Shaws and Mackintoshes and Grants have been successive masters. Somewhere on the road he buried the cannon which he had captured at Aberdeen.[1] The Grants and the other Speyside families showed some inclination to dispute the way, so Montrose turned down the river to Abernethy, which brought him within twenty miles of Argyll, now at the Bog of Gight, and his 4,000 men. Presently he turned south again and made for the head of Spey and the Badenoch country, for he had been compelled to change his plans. Alasdair insisted on departing for the west on an expedition of his own, to raise recruits among the Clan Donald and to see to the security of his castles of Mingary and Lochaline. This left Montrose with no more than 500 men, and compelled a revision of his strategy. For the present he must content himself with troubling the soul of his enemies.

In Badenoch he fell seriously ill; it was rumoured in the south that he was dead, and from a hundred pulpits the Almighty was publicly thanked for espousing the Covenanters' quarrel. The illness lasted for several days, and seems to have been a fever caused by excessive fatigue.[2] By the 4th of October he was on the move again and heading for Atholl. Now began what Baillie calls a " strange coursing," Montrose leading the dance, and Argyll, some seven or eight days behind, footing it heavily from Spey to Tay and from Tay to Don. Alasdair with his female following had left him, and the king's lieutenant travelled light. He passed into Angus, and, clinging as before to the flanks of the hills, crossed the Dee at his old ford on the 17th of October. Now he sanctioned for the first time the burning of the lands of Covenanting lairds, like the Frasers and the Crichtons,

---

[1] Mr. Gardiner says that the guns were buried at Rothiemurchus (*Civil War*, II., 149); Wishart says simply *in palustri quodam* (ch. vi., 374); Gordon of Ruthven gives the locality as between Strathdon and Strathavon. According to Wishart, Huntly dug them up and appropriated them after Philiphaugh, so the *cache* was probably nearer the Gordon centre than Rothiemurchus.

[2] Monteith, 176. This remarkable author, who became secretary to Cardinal de Retz and a canon of Nôtre Dame, must have met Montrose later in Paris, and often records details which he probably had from him in conversation.

in retaliation for the fire and sword which Argyll had carried to every one suspected of loyalism. By the 21st he was in Strathbogie, busy once more with fruitless appeals to the Gordons. Here he had word of Argyll's approach, reinforced by fourteen troops of horse under Marischal, the result of the appeal of the Estates to Leven. Accordingly he turned east into the bleak uplands of Buchan, and on the 24th was at Fyvie on the Ythan. He thought that Argyll was scarcely yet across the Grampians, when in reality he was almost within musket-shot. For once his intelligence failed him, and the king's lieutenant was caught napping.

Fyvie, an old seat of the Earls of Dunfermline, had by this date become more of a seventeenth-century dwelling-house than a baronial keep. On three sides lay bogs with a few strips of hard ground too narrow for the approach of an army. On the eastern side was a low ridge of hills, which—a rare thing in that countryside—was thickly wooded on one flank. Montrose cannot have had more than 800 foot,[1] and at the moment of the surprise 150 mounted Gordons whom he had recruited in Strathbogie deserted his standard, leaving him with only 50 horse. Argyll outnumbered him by at least five to one, and he dared not meet him on the level; to defend Fyvie was to be caught in a trap; his only hope lay in the strong defensive position afforded by the hill-face broken with ditches and drystone walls, and the good cover in the adjacent scrub. He was desperately short of ammunition, and melted down the pewter vessels of the castle to make bullets; for powder he could only look to the pouches of the enemy.

Argyll, believing that at last he had driven his nimble foe into a blind alley, and strong in the consciousness of a force many times as large, attacked the position with—for him—considerable spirit. At last the omens were propitious, for he had heard of the

---

[1] Wishart says 1,500, apparently forgetting that Alasdair and his Irish were absent. Montrose had scarcely increased his non-Irish infantry since Aberdeen

Gordon desertions. A regiment of foot advanced up the little hill and carried some of the dykes and trenches, difficult places from which to eject well-armed men. Montrose saw that the only hope lay in cold steel. He called to a young Ulsterman, Magnus O'Cahan,[1] whom Alasdair had left behind him, and bade him drive the enemy from the slopes. A gallant handful of Irish charged with pikes and broadswords, drove back the Covenanters and made prize of many bags of powder for their famished muskets. It is recorded that one of them, looking at the booty, cried : " We must have at them again ; these stingy hucksters have left us no bullets." Then came a charge of Lothian's horse on the flank. Montrose had his men well in cover, and, had the enemy been drawn in sufficiently deep, there might have been an end of Lothian's 500. But the excitement of the Atholl men brought about a premature volley, the battle was joined too soon, and the Covenant cavalry were easily routed by the charge of Montrose's 50 mounted men supported by his musketeers. After that followed some half-hearted skirmishing, in which Lord Marischal's brother was slain on the Covenant side, and then Argyll withdrew and put the Ythan between himself and his enemy.[2]

But Fyvie was no place to tarry in, since 800 men cannot for ever defy an army. Under cover of darkness Montrose slipped away, and was presently heard of in Strathbogie. Here he hoped for news of Alasdair and his western men, but no news came. His aim is clear ; he had still expectations from the Gordons, and was loth to leave their country. This Argyll knew well,

---

[1] His name is also spelt O'Kean, O'Cathan, O'Kyan, and MacGahan. The *Clanranald MSS.* calls him " Magnus, son of the Giolla Dubh MacCathan." He was Antrim's foster-brother, and commanded one of Alasdair's three Irish regiments. The O'Cahans were one of the native Irish septs who became attached to the Macdonnells. He was captured at Philiphaugh, and hanged in Edinburgh without a trial. See p. 295. I have followed Wishart's account, but Gordon of Ruthven (91) gives the exploit to Donald Farquharson, who was Huntly's bailiff of Strathavon.

[2] I have followed Gordon of Ruthven's story rather than Wishart's : Patrick Gordon describes the country as if he knew it, and he gives only one day to the fighting ; more likely than Wishart's " plures dies," for Montrose could not afford to make too long a business of it.

and he, too, followed to Strathbogie, keeping up a show
of attacks which were easily repulsed. But the Campbell
chief was engaged on work more suited to his genius
than fighting, and busied himself with making overtures to Montrose's Lowland officers.[1] Since Alasdair
went, Montrose had more officers than rank and file, and
these Angus and Perthshire and Aberdeen gentry, half-
hearted about the campaign and timid about their estates,
appeared to be fruitful soil. He did not ask them to
betray their cause; he only offered, of his generosity,
free passes to any who wished to go home, asking no
payment in return. It was a subtle plan, and it largely
succeeded. Sibbald, a companion on the ride from
Carlisle, left, and the seeds were sown of further dis-
content.[2] A council of war was called, and it was
resolved to retreat into the hills. The royalists marched
by moorland roads to Speyside, and at Balveny, on the
west bank of the Fiddich, out of reach of Argyll's
horse, took stock of their position. Argyll, avoiding
the mountains, went south by an easier road, and lay
with his army in the neighbourhood of Dunkeld.

At Balveny matters came to a crisis. The Lowland
gentlemen had no love for a campaign in midwinter,
conducted at Montrose's incredible speed, and offering
little hope of finality. They feared for their lands and
families, now at the mercy of the Covenant. Moreover,
Highland and Lowland are ill to mix, and they may well
have disliked their associates. Montrose accordingly
proposed a descent on the Lowlands, the plan which
he had always had in view, for his aim was to relieve
the king by drawing back Leven's army from England.
So far his victories had availed nothing to that purpose,
for Newcastle had fallen on 19th October, and Tyne-
mouth on the 27th. Leven was now in Scotland, his
army was in winter quarters, and a descent upon the

---

[1] He seems also to have attempted O'Cahan's Irish. Forbes Leith, I., 298.
[2] Forbes of Craigievar appears to have broken parole and fled to Argyll.
He was accompanied by Nathaniel Gordon. Spalding, II., 286. There is
here a wild story of intrigue and adventure lost to us, for Nathaniel Gordon
was always loyal. He may have bluffed his way into the Covenant favour, as
Bishop Guthry suggests, in order to get in touch with Lord Gordon.

Border would gravely embarrass the Parliament plan
of campaign. But the scheme found little favour.
The Lowlanders argued that success in hill warfare was
no warrant for victory against regulars in a settled and
hostile country, and the Highlanders had grievances of
their own to avenge, which they thought of far greater
moment than any royal necessities. Men like Dupplin
(now Earl of Kinnoull), Colonel Hay, and Sir James
Drummond, slipped away to make a temporary peace
with the Covenant. Almost alone of the gentry old
Airlie and his gallant sons refused to leave. They, like
Montrose, fought not for safety or revenge, but for an
ideal of statesmanship.

III

It was now far on in November. In the levels the
heavy rains told of the beginning of winter, the high
tops were whitening with snow, the bogs were morasses,
the streams were red with flood, and the days were
short and dark. Argyll was at Dunkeld, busy with
attempts on the loyalty of Atholl, and he must have
believed that no general in his senses would continue
the war in such inclement weather. Indeed he had
already sent his cavalry, his chief arm, into winter
quarters. Montrose resolved to disappoint his expectations, and led his handful of troops through the Badenoch passes for a descent on Dunkeld. His route was
by Dalnaspidal and Dalwhinnie to Blair, and in a single
night he covered twenty-four miles. But long ere he
could reach the Tay Argyll had news of him, and wisely
decided that he could not face him with foot alone,
even though the odds were four to one, and that he at
any rate would end the campaign. He fell back on
Perth, dismissed his Campbells to their homes, and himself posted with Lothian to Edinburgh, where he surrendered his commission as general-in-chief into the
hands of the Estates. He complained that he had not
been supported—" whether through envy or emulation,

or negligence or inability " ; [1] but it is hard to see what more he could have needed in the way of foot, horse, or guns ; neither Kirk nor Council could give him a genius for war. His reception was a little chilly ; [2] his services were formally approved, but it was dryly observed that the approbation was the greater because he had shed so little blood. The question was who should succeed him. Lothian and Callander brusquely declined the thankless post, and the Estates fell back upon a professional soldier, William Baillie of Letham, one of the best of Leven's generals in England.

At Blair Montrose met Alasdair returning out of the western mists. The meeting changed his plans. He may have thought of winter quarters, like his opponents, but that would be a difficult business, since they must be in the desert and hungry hills, and at the best a fruitless one, since precious months would be lost. But now he had the Ulstermen again under his command, and with them a formidable levy of the western clans. Alasdair had been no laggard. Clan Donald had not forgotten Argyll's commission of fire and sword in 1640, and Clan Gillian had long scores to settle with the secular enemy of their name. Five hundred Macdonalds —of Glengarry, Keppoch, Clanranald, and the Isles— had flocked to his standard. None of the resounding names which, forty-five years later, were to muster under another Graham, were lacking. There were Macleans from Morvern and Mull, Stewarts from Appin, Farquharsons from Braemar, and the eastern Camerons of Lochaber. John of Moidart, the Captain of Clanranald, brought his fierce spirit and devoted following to Montrose's side. There was young Æneas of Glengarry, with his three uncles, and Donald Glas of Keppoch, and the chiefs of the fierce septs of Glen Nevis and Glencoe.[3] The middle Highlands, for the first time since Harlaw, were united, but it was not in the king's cause. The hatred of every clansman was directed not at the Covenant, but at the house of Diarmaid. Now

[1] Baillie, II., 262.   [2] Spalding, II., 287.
[3] See for this gathering of the clans the *Clanranald MSS.*

was the time to avenge ancient wrongs, and to break
the pride of a chief who had boasted that no mortal
foe could enter his borders. The hour had come when
the fray must be carried to Lorn.

Montrose had that supreme virtue in a commander
which recognizes facts. He could not maintain his
army without war, and to Lowland war they would not
listen. If he looked for their help in the future he must
steel their valour and rivet their loyalty by fresh successes. In return for their assistance in the king's
quarrel they must have the help of the king's lieutenant
in their own. Again, a blow at the Campbells in their
own country would put fear into the heart of the Covenant, and shatter Argyll's not too robust nerve. It was
a wild venture, an unheard-of thing to scour the hills
when decent soldiers were warm in camp, and even the
shepherds and the hunters lay snug in their bothies ;
but in its audacity lay its merit, for wild ventures have
their psychological value in war. In a sense, too, it
had always been Montrose's second line of strategy, for
we have seen him writing to Sir Robert Spottiswoode
from York : " We intend to make all possible dispatch
to follow him (Argyll) at his heels in whatever posture
we can." [1]   He had the wit to see that a deadly thrust
might be delivered in a region far from the main front
of the campaign. There may have been a further
reason. The Estates had confiscated his lands and
taken captive his friends. Wishart, his chaplain to be,
and Lord Ogilvy, his dearest comrade, were in the
Edinburgh Tolbooth ; his kinsfolk, when hands could
be laid on them, had been consigned to squalid prisons.
A blow at the arch-enemy would be some little solace to
a heart which was only too prone to the human affections.

[1] See p. 169.

CHAPTER IX

INVERLOCHY

(*December* 1644–*February* 1645)

Through the land of my fathers the Campbells have come,
The flames of their foray enveloped my home ;
Broad Keppoch in ruin is left to deplore,
And my country is waste from the hill to the shore.
Be it so ! By St. Mary, there's comfort in store !

Though the braes of Lochaber a desert be made,
And Glen Roy may be lost to the plough and the spade,
Though the bones of my kindred, unhonoured, unurned,
Mark the desolate path where the Campbells have burned—
Be it so ! From that foray they never returned.

IAN LOM MACDONALD.
(*Mark Napier's translation.*)

IN seventeenth-century Scotland Clan Campbell stood
by itself as a separate race, almost a separate state,
whose politics were determined by the whim of its ruling
prince. Built upon the ruins of many little septs, it
excelled in numbers and wealth every other Highland
clan ; indeed, if we except the Gordons, it surpassed in
importance all the rest put together. It was near enough
to the Lowlands to have shared in such civilization as
was going, including the new theology. Craftsmen had
been brought to Inveraray from the Ayr and Renfrew
burghs, schools had been established, and of a Sunday
the townsfolk could listen to notable preachers of the
Word. On the other hand, its territory was a compact
block, well guarded on all sides from its neighbours,
so that it enjoyed the peace and confidence of a separate
people. With its immense sea-coast its doors were open
to the wider world, and the Campbell gentry acquired
at foreign universities and in foreign wars a training
which few landward gentlemen could boast ; while

Flemish velvets and the silks and wines of France came
more readily and cheaply to its little towns than to the
burghers of Perth or Edinburgh. The country, though
less fertile than the Lowlands, was a champaign compared to Lochaber or Kintail. Thousands of black
cattle flourished on its juicy hill pastures, and farms
and shielings were thick along the pleasant glens that
sloped to Loch Fyne and Loch Awe. In the town of
Inveraray the clan had its natural capital, and from
Inveraray ran the Lowland road through Cowal and
Dumbarton for such as preferred a land journey. Compared with other clans, the Campbells were prosperous
and civilized; they did not live from hand to mouth
like the rest, nor did each winter find them at the brink
of starvation; yet they still retained the martial spirit
of the Gael, and could put into the field the most formidable of Highland levies. Accordingly, by their neighbours they were both detested and feared. They had
eaten up the little peoples of Benderloch and Morvern,
and their long arm was stretching north and east into
Lochaber and Strathtay. Every Maclean and Stewart
who could see the hills of Lorn from his doorstep had
uneasy thoughts about his own barren acres. The
Campbells had a knack of winning by bow and spear,
and then holding for all time by seal and parchment.

Not without reason Argyll boasted that his land was
impregnable, for strategically it had every advantage.
On the eastern side, where it looked to the Lowlands,
there were the castles of Roseneath and Dunoon to keep
ward, and deep sea-lochs to check the invader. Besides,
the Lowlands and Argyll were always at peace. South
and west lay the sea, and the Campbells had what little
navy existed at the time in Scotland. The Macleans in
Mull were too small and broken to take the offensive,
and in any case it was a long way from the coast at
Knapdale to the heart at Inveraray. North and east
lay a land of high mountains and difficult passes, where
no man could travel save by permission of the sovereign
lord. Moreover, the Campbells of Lochow and Glenorchy had flung their tentacles over Breadalbane, and

held the marches around the headwaters of Tay. There might be a raid of Macgregors or Maclarens on the east, or a foray from Appin on Loch Etive side, but not even the king and his army could get much beyond the gates. " It is a far cry to Lochow," so ran the Campbell ower-come, and it was a farther cry to Inveraray.

Montrose, when he assented to Alasdair's wishes, resolved to strike straight at the enemy's heart. He would wage war not in the outskirts, but in the citadel. From Blair there was little choice of roads. To go due west by Rannoch and the springs of Etive would mean a march among friendly clans, but a few score Campbells could hold the narrows of Loch Etive or the Pass of Brander against the strongest army. The Lowland road by Dumbarton and Loch Lomond was out of the ques-tion, for it meant a dangerous proximity to the Covenant-ing westlands and the difficult pass of Glencroe. But midway through Breadalbane ran a possible route, among wild glens and trackless bogs, which at this winter season would be deep in snow. This was the old raiding road out of Lorn, and Argyll flattered himself that his clan alone had the keys of it.[1] But with Montrose were men who had made many a midnight foray into the Camp-bell domain, and who knew every corrie and moss as well as any son of Diarmaid. A Glencoe man, Angus MacAlain Dubh, was the chief guide, and he promised Montrose that his army should live well on the country, " if tight houses, fat cattle, and clear water will suffice." [2] Accordingly, with Airlie and the Ogilvys and his eldest boy, Lord Graham, as his Lowland staff, the king's lieutenant ordered the march to the west. The army travelled in three divisions : the Ulstermen under Alasdair in three regiments, commanded respectively by James Macdonnell, Ranald Og Macdonnell, and Magnus O'Cahan ; the western clans, Macdonalds, Camerons, Stewarts, and Macleans, under John of Moidart, Captain of Clanranald ; the Atholl, Badenoch,

---

[1] The difficulty of the road lay not in precipitous gullies, such as Montrose found later in Lochaber, but in its bogs, which in the then undrained condition of the valleys were a most serious obstacle.   [2] *Clanranald MSS.*

and Aberdeenshire contingents, and the small Lowland force under the king's lieutenant himself. Montrose had now some 3,000 troops,[1] drawn from every corner of Scotland. There were men from Orkney, from Uist, and from Skye; from the whole Highland mainland between Knoydart and Braemar; from Kintyre; from Angus and Moray and Buchan; from the villages of Forth, Earn, and Tay; even from Lothian, Galloway, and the distant Borders.

Montrose left Blair on or about the 11th day of December. The road was at first the same as that taken in the march to Tippermuir. The lands of the small and uncertain clan of Menzies were traversed, and the laird of Weem taken prisoner. Then westward by both shores of Loch Tay swept the advance, where the Macdougal settlers from Lorn suffered, till the confines of Breadalbane were reached and a country that owned Campbell sway.[2] Up Glen Dochart [3] they went, following much the same road as the present railway line to Oban, past Crianlarich and Tyndrum, and into the glens of Orchy. John of Moidart, with the western men, was sent on in advance, and did not rejoin the army till Kilmartin Glassary, far down in Argyll; his business was to collect food, and he brought in a thousand head of cattle. In Glen Dochart Montrose was joined by the local septs, the Macnabs and the Macgregors, and it was by a ruse of the former wily and resourceful clan that the difficult narrows of Loch Dochart were passed, and the island castle was surrendered. [4]   A Catholic priest was the meteorologist of the army, and he had promised them that the weather would hold, since the wind blew from the east; he proved right, for there was neither rain nor snow to hinder their speed.[5]

[1] Gordon of Ruthven, 94.

[2] Father Macbreck's letter in Forbes Leith, I., 302. The laird was Sir Robert Campbell of Glenorchy, a strong Covenanter, but his brother Patrick, of Edinample, was with Montrose.

[3] On this point Mr. Gardiner's map (*Civil War*, II., 151) is wrong. He makes Montrose go up Glen Lochay from Loch Tay, which is against the authorities, and in any case would have meant a considerable circuit and the crossing of a high and difficult pass.

[4] Forbes Leith, I., 308–309. Gordon of Ruthven, 97.

[5] Forbes Leith, I., 308.

It was partly a raid of vengeance, and behind them
rose the flames of burning roof-trees. Presently Loch
Awe lay before them under the leaden winter sky, and
soon the little fortalices of the lochside lairds smoked to
heaven. All fighting men who resisted were slain or
driven to the high hills, every cot and clachan was set
alight, and droves of maddened cattle attested the rich-
ness of the land and the profit of the invaders. It was
Highland warfare of the old barbarous type, no worse
and no better than that which Argyll had already carried
to Lochaber and Badenoch and the braes of Angus.[1]

Argyll was well served by his scouts, and to him at
Edinburgh word was soon brought of Montrose's march
to Breadalbane. He must have thought it a crazy
venture. Now at last was his enemy delivered into his
hands. No mortal army could cross the winter passes,
even if it had the key, and the men of Glenorchy would
wipe out the starving remnants at their leisure. Full
of confidence he posted across Scotland to Inveraray.
There he found that all was quiet. Rumours of a foray
in Lorn were indeed rife, but the burghers of Inveraray,
strong in their generations of peace, had no fear for
themselves. Argyll saw to the defences of his castle,
and called a great gathering of his clansmen to provide
reinforcements, if such should be needed, for the Glenorchy and Breadalbane men, who by that time had
assuredly made an end of Montrose.

Suddenly came the thunderbolt. Wild-eyed shepherds
rushed into the streets with the cry that the Macdonalds
were upon them. Quickly the tale grew. Montrose
was not in Breadalbane or on the fringes of Lorn ; he
was at Loch Awe—nay, he was in the heart of Argyll

---

[1] There is no record of any violence done to women and children. Gordon
of Ruthven (98) says that " although, out of a generous and merciful disposition
he (Montrose) would have spared the people, yet the Clan Donald, wheresoever
they found any that was able to carry arms, did without mercy dispatch them."
But, as there was little resistance, I doubt if there was much slaying (see Forbes
Leith, I., 309), and I do not believe in the story that John of Moidart in his fury
killed 895 men " without battle or skirmish." The only witness for this is the
Clanranald MSS., and the Clanranald chronicler tells his tale in the high
heroic manner of an Irish saga, and is always carpeting the ground with dead.
Father Macbreck says that the business was chiefly house burning " in just
reprisals of war," and that even in this the humbler folk were spared.

itself. The chief waited no longer. He found a fishing-
boat and, the wind being right, fled down Loch Fyne
to the shelter of his castle of Roseneath. The same
breeze that filled his sails brought the sound of Alasdair's
pipes, and he was scarcely under way ere the van of
the invaders came down Glen Shira. The miracle had
happened, and the impregnable fortress had fallen.
" We see," commented Mr. Robert Baillie piously, but
obscurely, " there is no strength or refuge on earth
against the Lord." [1]

Then began the harrying of Clan Campbell. Leaderless and unprepared, they made small resistance to
Montrose's lean and battle-worn warriors. Macleans
and Macdonalds, Stewarts and Camerons, satiated their
ancient grudges with the plunder of Inveraray. The
kerns thawed their frozen limbs at the warmth of
blazing steadings, and appeased their hunger at the
expense of the bakers and vintners and fleshers of the
burgh. Never had the broken men of Lochaber and
the Isles fared so nobly. For some happy weeks they
ran riot in what for them was a land of milk and honey ;
while the townsmen, crouching in cellars and thickets,
or safe behind the castle gates, wondered how long it
would be before their chief returned to avenge them.
There seems to have been no special barbarity about the
treatment of Inveraray. Here and there a refractory
Campbell may have been dirked, but Alasdair's men
sought victuals and cattle rather than blood.

Meantime word had gone from the exile at Roseneath to the Estates in Edinburgh. William Baillie of
Letham, the new commander-in-chief, was a natural
son of Sir William Baillie of Lamington ; an old soldier
of Gustavus, he had done good service at Marston Moor
and at the siege of Newcastle, and he brought to Scotland some of the best of Leven's infantry, which he
increased by local levies. He took up the task un-
willingly, and his distaste was not lessened by the
behaviour of Argyll, who required that he should take
instructions from him. Baillie refused, and, says he in

[1] II., 263.

L.Clunie
(Ft.Augustus)
Killcummin
L.Luing
Loch Ness
R.Findhorn
Dulnain W.
Mts
Mon a dliath
L.Garry
R.Lochy
L.Arkaig
Cairn
Balloch
L.Lochy
Lochaber
R.Spey
Glen Roy
GRAMPIAN
L.Eil
L.Laggan
Ben
Alder
L.Treig
MOUNTAINS
Inverlochy
Ben
Nevis
Loch Ericht
Glen Garry
Blair
Athol
Loch Eil
L.Tummel
Weem
L.Leven
L.Rannoch
Glencoe
Loch Lydoch
R.Lyon
Loch Tay
L.Erve
Glen Lochay
Glen Orchy
Glen Dochart
R.Earn
Loch Awe
L.Earn
Loch
Lubnaig
N
Inverary
Loch Fyne
L.Lomond
Katrine
Ben
Lomond

0 5 10 20 30
English Miles

CAMPAIGN OF
INVERLOCHY Montrose's March

his "Vindication," "My lord seemed to be displeased, and expressed himself so unto some, that if he lived he should remember it, wherein his lordship indeed hath superabundantly been as good as his word." [1]   He was instructed by the Estates to repair to Roseneath and consult with Argyll on the best way of crushing Montrose.   But at Roseneath he found the exile in a difficult humour.   There must be no stranger general in the Campbell fastness.   It was for the chief, and for the chief alone, to avenge the wrongs of his clan.   Accordingly, the Estates ordered Baillie to transfer to Argyll sixteen companies of foot, representing the flower of the Scottish militia.   Baillie himself was sent to Perth, and was presently given Sir John Hurry (who had been a royalist a year before and was to be a royalist again) as his second in command and master of horse.[2] He was bidden keep in touch with the Covenanting garrison that had been left in Aberdeen and with Seaforth's northern army in Inverness.   Argyll, at Roseneath, had had a fall from his horse which incapacitated him from leading his troops in person, so he sent hastily to the army in Ireland to summon back his kinsman, Sir Duncan Campbell of Auchinbreck, the best soldier that the clan could boast.[3]   It looked as if the king's lieutenant had walked into a final trap.   He would be caught between Argyll and Seaforth, and if he tried to escape to the right Baillie and Hurry would await him. It seemed the certainty on which Argyll loved to stake. His view was that of the general's ministerial cousin, Mr. Robert Baillie : " If we get not the life of these worms chirted out of them, the reproach will stick on us for ever."

Midwinter that year was open and mild ; the sun shone brightly on Christmas Day.   Had it been otherwise, Clan Campbell, driven out of house and home, must have been all but annihilated, and Montrose would never have led his men safely out of Argyll.   About the

---

[1] The "Vindication" is printed in Robert Baillie's *Letters and Journals*, II., 416–419.   [2] *A. P. S.*, V., 182.

[3] " A stout sojer," says Robert Baillie, " but a very vitious man."   II., 263.

middle of January he gave the order for the march.[1] He had as yet no news of Argyll's preparations, but he must have realized that the avenger would not be slow on his track. His immediate intention was to come to an account with Seaforth, who not only barred him from the Gordon country, but was chiefly responsible for the opposition of the Moray and Speyside gentry, and the powerful clan of Mackenzie. He had guides who promised to show him an easy way out of Lorn into Lochaber, whence the road ran straight by the Great Glen to Inverness. Laden with miscellaneous plunder, and cumbered no doubt with *spreaghs* of cattle, the army passed the north end of Loch Awe, where Alasdair is said to have rescued certain kinsmen from the dungeons of " a strong castle." [2] In the Pass of Brander legend says that an old woman with a scythe opposed the advance and killed a soldier, and that Montrose intervened to save her life.[3] Arrived at the shore of Loch Etive, the bulk of the army turned west towards the narrows at Connel. The shorter road by Glen Etive, King's House, and the Moor of Rannoch, was no route for a heavily-laden force in midwinter, but a detachment may, as tradition avers, have followed the steep brink of the loch to Glen Etive, and there crossed the *beallach* by the old drove road to Appin.

The march from Loch Awe had been in the teeth of a violent south-west gale, but at Connel a windless calm fell upon the sea. It was the weather for crossing, but there were no boats, the land behind them was a provisionless desert, and the great Campbell keep of Dunstaffnage lay menacingly on their flank. The situation was saved by Campbell of Ardchattan—a Macdonald on

[1] Wishart (ch. viii.) says that Montrose left Lorn on the 28th or 29th of January. But he was at Kilcumin, on Loch Ness, on 31st January ; and, as a bond was signed there, he must have arrived by at least the 30th. From Lorn to Kilcumin was four or five days' march even for Montrose. Further, we know from Balfour (*Annales*, III., 256) that the Estates heard by 18th January that Montrose had left Lorn and was in Glen Urquhart. This may have been a false report, but it is probable that the royalists began to leave about the middle of the month, and that the rearguard had gone by the 26th at latest.

[2] Innischonain or Kilchurn. Father Macbreck says "his father and two brothers." Forbes Leith, I., 323.

[3] A legend told me by the late Captain T. A. Nelson of Achnacloich.

his mother's side—who undertook to supply ferry-boats
on condition that his lands were unmolested. By means of these, in two days of bright sunshine, the army crossed Loch Etive, the horses swimming alongside. The first camp in Benderloch was made memorable by the shipwreck of an armed sloop sent by Argyll to harass the flank of the march ; it and its brass guns became the prize of the royalists. Also 150 young men of the Appin Stewarts arrived as recruits. Montrose hurried north through Appin, and was welcomed by the MacIans of Glencoe. Once again the weather broke, this time in a thunderstorm and a deluge of rain, and the roaring Cona seemed to offer an impassable barrier. But boats were somehow found, the river was crossed at its mouth, the sky cleared, and the advance continued—either by Glencoe, Loch Treig and Glen Spean, or by Loch Leven and Mamore. The king's lieutenant was safe in Lochaber.[1]

Montrose halted one night at Inverlochy, but no more. He had Seaforth in front of him, and Argyll behind, and dared not tarry. By the evening of Wednesday the 29th of January, he was at Kilcumin, at the head of Loch Ness, in a none too friendly country. The weather continued to be mild and dry for the season of the year. Most of the Atholl men and the bulk of Clanranald had left him, after their custom, to deposit their booty. No more than 1,500 remained—Alasdair's Irish, a few hundred Macdonalds, Stewarts, Macleans, and Camerons, and sufficient horse to mount the Lowland gentry and provide an escort for the standard.

At Kilcumin Montrose had definite news of Seaforth. He was thirty miles off at Inverness with 5,000 men— Frasers, Mackenzies, and regulars from the Inverness garrison ; a disorderly multitude, says Wishart, for, apart from the old soldiers of the garrison, it was " a mere rabble of new levies, peasants, drovers, shopmen, servants, and camp-followers." [2] Montrose was pre-

---

[1] The details are mostly taken from Father Macbreck, who, since the Irish were of his own communion, had special sources of information. Forbes Leith, I., 308–319.   [2] Ch. viii.

paring to make short work of Seaforth, when he received
graver tidings. Ian Lom Macdonald,[1] the bard of
Keppoch, arrived by the hill-road from Glen Roy to tell
of Argyll at his heels. The Campbells were less than
thirty miles behind at Inverlochy, 3,000 men-at-arms
eager to avenge the shame of Lorn. They were burning
and harrying Glen Spean and Glen Roy and the Lochaber
braes, and their object was to take Montrose in rear
what time Seaforth should hold him in front.

At Kilcumin Montrose had prepared a bond to which
all the chiefs set their names. Such bonds and mani-
festos were favourite devices of the king's lieutenant.
They were his Covenants, the only means by which he
could advertise to the world the principles for which he
fought. The signatories swore to fight to the death for
their sovereign and his legitimate authority against the
" present perverse and infamous faction of desperate
rebels now in fury against him," and never to swerve
from their oath as they " would be reputed famous
men." [2] The little army had need of all the heartening
it could get, for its plight seemed hopeless. Fifteen
hundred very weary men were caught between two
forces of 5,000 and 3,000. There was no way of escape
to west or east, for the one would lead them to a bare
sea-coast, and the other into the arms of Baillie's foot.
Of the two hostile forces Seaforth's burghers were the
less formidable. Montrose knew well that the fighting
spirit of Clan Diarmaid was equal to any in the Highlands, and, now that they were commanded by a skilled
soldier and infuriated by the burning of their homes,
he could not hope to fight them at long odds. But it is

---

[1] Napier, II., 480. Guthry (178) gives the name of the messenger as Alan
Macildowie of Lochaber, as does the MS. history of Gordon of Buthlaw. Alan
Macildowie is also the second-sighted man (" ane old fox ") who warned Argyll
before Inverlochy that " there would be a battle lost there by them that came
first to such battle." (Gordon of Ruthven, 100.) To Father Macbreck he is
the aged " Lord of Lochaber," who brought in the western Camerons to
Montrose after Inverlochy. Forbes Leith, I., 323. The sixteenth chief of
Lochiel, Alein MacDhonh'uill Dubh (whose grandson Ewen was then in Argyll's
charge), was a very old man who had been protected by Argyll, and his
politics were undecided. He may have sent Ian Lom to Montrose. He is
called Alan MacCoilduy in the *Memoirs of Lochiell.*

[2] The original is in the Montrose charter-chest. See *Hist. MSS. Comm.,*
2nd Report, 176. *Mem. of M.,* II., 172.

the duty of a good general, when he is confronted by two urgent perils, to meet the greater first. Montrose resolved to fight the Campbells, but to fight them in his own way.

Early on the morning of Friday, the 31st of January, began that flank march which is one of the great exploits in the history of British arms.[1] The little river Tarff flows north from the Monadliath mountains to Loch Ness. Up its rocky course went Montrose, and the royal army disappeared into the hills. Scouts of Argyll or Seaforth who traversed the Great Glen on that day must have reported no enemy. From Tarff Montrose crossed the pass to Glen Turritt, and following it downward reached Glen Roy. Pushing on through the night, he came to the bridge of Roy, where that stream enters the Spean, on the morning of Saturday the 1st of February.

The weather on the high hills was deathly cold, and the march had been through a hyperborean hell. The upper glens were choked with snowdrifts, ravines had to be threaded where avalanches and cornices of ice overhung the adventurers, the rocks were glazed, and impassable save for Highland brogues. Passes were crossed so narrow and steep that a dozen men could have held an army at bay. But there were no patrols of Argyll among those inhospitable wastes; the only enemies were cold and hunger and the uttermost fatigue. The army had neither food nor fire. Now and then in a patch of wood a hind or roedeer may have been found, and its blood lapped and its uncooked flesh devoured by the fortunate discoverers. The rations for gentle and simple alike were oatmeal and water. As they struggled along at the pace of a deerstalker, Montrose

---

[1] The ordinary route, given by Napier and others, is by the pass of Corrieyairack, down the sources of the Spey, and thence into Glen Roy. But such a route would have taken Montrose too far to the east and over unnecessarily high ground. Dr. Morland Simpson, basing his view on the *Clanranald MSS.*, has suggested a much more probable way—namely, up the Tarff, crossing above Cullachy; then parallel to the canal till the Calder burn was reached above Aberchalder Lodge; then ascending the burn and turning due south up the Alt-nan-Larach till the headwaters of the Turritt were reached; then south-west into Glen Roy along the " Parallel Roads." Pryce, *The Great Marquis of Montrose*, 240 *n.*

walked by his men, shaming them to endurance by the spectacle of his own courage.

From Roy Bridge to Inverlochy is some thirteen miles. But to take Argyll by surprise a circuit was necessary, and Montrose followed the northern slopes of the wild tangle of mountains, the highest in Britain, that surround Ben Nevis.[1] He crossed the Spean at a ford below the present house of Corriechoille, and seems to have met a foraying party of Argyll's and stopped their mouths for ever.[2] Hugging the skirts of the hills, he went by Kilchonate and Leanachan, and before darkness fell was at the base of Meall-an-t'suidhe. In the ruddy gloaming of the February day the vanguard saw beneath and before them the tower of Inverlochy scowling by the sea waves, and not a mile off the men of Clan Diarmaid making ready their evening meal. They had been within sight during the day of that spot, Mucomir, on the north bank of the Spean, where another Graham was to review the assembled clans on the eve of Killiecrankie.[3]

Shots were exchanged with the enemy pickets, but no effort was made to advance. The surprise had been achieved; it need not be prematurely disclosed. Montrose waited quietly in the gathering dusk till, by eight o'clock, the rest of his famished column had arrived. There, supperless and cold, they passed the night, lighting no fires, and keeping up a desultory skirmishing with the Campbell outposts. The moon was full, and the dark masses of both armies were visible to each other. Argyll thought the force he saw only a contingent of Highland raiders under Keppoch or some

---

[1] Highland tradition in general credits Montrose with descending on Argyll by way of Glen Nevis. To do this it would be necessary to march to the head of Loch Treig, and then up Glen Treig and so into Glen Nevis, or, alternately, by way of the Learg-nan-Leacan. This would mean a very long journey for very tired men, accompanied by horses; an unnecessary toil, for Argyll would expect Montrose by the main road which descended the Lochy, and would be equally taken by surprise by a flank march along the northern skirts of Ben Nevis. Montrose had excellent guides in the Camerons and Macdonalds. This would seem to be also the view of Gardiner, Lang, and Morland Simpson. See also Dr. Cameron Miller's paper, "Montrose in Lochaber, 1645" (Fort William, 1910).

[2] *Clanranald MSS.*

[3] *Grameid* (S.H.S.), 120. *Memoirs of Locheill*, 234.

petty chief. As Montrose watched the strip of moonlit
loch between him and the dark hills of Loch Eil, he saw
lights moving towards a little vessel which swung at
anchor. Argyll had been persuaded by the Campbell
chiefs to retire to his lymphad and take no part in the
coming battle. There was little reason why he should,
and charges of cowardice are foolish. Auchinbreck, not
he, was in command ; he was not by physique a useful
fighting man, and he was still suffering from a damaged
shoulder ; he was the chief pillar of the Covenant in
Scotland, and the head of a great clan ; for him to risk
his life, sword in hand, against desperate men was
against every counsel of prudence and common sense.
Alan McIldowie's prophecy, too, may have influenced
his clan in their determination to keep him out of action.
His companions on the galley were Sir James Rollo,
Wauchope of Niddrie, an Edinburgh bailie, and a
minister, Mr. Mungo Law, whom we may take to have
been the travelling committee which the Estates were
accustomed to send out to fortify their generals.[1]

At dawn on Candlemas Day, the 2nd of February, his
ears were greeted by an unwelcome note. It was no
bagpipes such as Keppoch might use, but trumpets of
war, and the salute they sounded was that reserved for
the royal standard. Then came the fierce Cameron
pibroch, " Sons of dogs, come and I will give you flesh."
The king's lieutenant, who two days before was for
certain at Loch Ness, had by some craft of darkness
taken wings and flown his army over the winter hills.
There was no alternative but to fight. Till Montrose
was beaten the Campbells could neither march forward
to join Seaforth nor backward to their own land.

Auchinbreck drew up his forces with the fighting men
of Clan Campbell in the centre, and the Lowland regiments borrowed from Baillie on each wing. A stiffening
of Highlanders was added to the flanks, and behind the
main battle was a strong Highland reserve with two
field-pieces. Montrose placed the Irish on his wings—

---

[1] Guthry, 178. Baillie, II., 263. Gordon of Ruthven, 100. Baillie and
Gordon take the charitable view of Argyll's action.

the right under Alasdair, and the left under O'Cahan;
he himself led the centre, which was composed of the
Atholl, Appin, and Glencoe men and the Camerons;
Clanranald and Glengarry had the second line, and there
was a mixed Highland and Ulster reserve. Sir Thomas
Ogilvy commanded the little troop of horse which had
managed to make its way with the infantry over the
terrible hills. This was the one advantage Montrose
possessed; otherwise he had an army inferior in numbers
by at least a thousand, weary with travel and on the
brink of starvation, having had scarcely a mouthful
for forty-eight hours. He himself and Lord Airlie had
no breakfast except a little raw oatmeal mixed with
cold water, which they ate with their dirks.[1]

Before battle the Catholics in his ranks knelt in
prayer, while their priests signed their arms with the
cross.[2] The action began with the charge of Alasdair and
O'Cahan against the enemy wings; they reserved their
fire till, in Patrick Gordon's words, " they gave it in
their breath." The firing of famished men with ancient
muskets may have been wild, but in a second they were
come, as Montrose wrote, " to push of pike and dint of
sword." The Lowlanders made no stand; in spite of
the experience of many of them with Leven, a Highland
charge was a new and awful thing to them, and they
speedily broke and fled. This left the centre with naked
flanks, and down upon it came Montrose. It was forced
back on its second line, which, instead of opening ranks
to receive it and so constituting a new battle-front, itself
wavered and cracked. Inverlochy was won by strategy.
Of tactics there was little, and that little was as rudimentary as at Tippermuir. The Campbell clansmen,
outflanked and unsupported, did indeed make a valiant
stand; " stout and gallant men," says Wishart, " worthy
of a better chief and a juster cause." They knew that
they could expect no mercy from their hereditary foes,
to whom they had shown none, and they were not forgetful of the honourable traditions of their name.

But in time they also broke. Some rushed into the

---

[1] Gordon of Ruthven, 100.   [2] Forbes Leith, I., 321.

loch and tried in vain to reach the galley of their chief,
now fleeing to safety ; some fled to the tower of Inverlochy, where they presently surrendered. Most scattered along the shore, and on that blue February noon
there was a fierce slaughter from the mouth of Nevis
down to the narrows of Loch Leven. The Lowlanders
were given quarter, but, in spite of all his efforts, Montrose could win no mercy for the luckless Campbells.
The green Diarmaid tartan was a badge of death that
day. The western Camerons, hitherto dubious allies of
Argyll, now came over to the royal cause and joined in
the pursuit.[1] On the royalist side only four perished,[2]
but one of them was Sir Thomas Ogilvy, who died shortly
after the battle. On the Covenant side the slain almost
equalled the whole of Montrose's army. At least fifteen
hundred fell in the flight, and among them were the
veteran Auchinbreck, and forty of the Campbell barons.[3]
Well might Keppoch's bard exult fiercely over the issue :

" Though the bones of my kindred, unhonoured, unurned,
    Mark the desolate path where the Campbells have burned—
    Be it so ! From that foray they never returned." [4]

Inverlochy was in one respect a decisive victory, for
it destroyed the clan power of Argyll. From its terrible
toll the Campbells as a fighting force never recovered.
Alasdair's policy was justified, and the Macdonalds were
amply avenged ; the heather, as the phrase went, was
above the gale at last.[5] To Montrose at the moment
it seemed even more. He thought that with the galley
of Lorn fell also the blue flag of the Covenant. He

---

[1] Forbes Leith, I., 323. Mackenzie, *History of the Camerons*, 92, etc.
[2] So say Montrose and Wishart. The *Clanranald MSS.* says eight.
[3] Fifteen hundred is Montrose's figure in his dispatch to the king ; so also
Guthry ; Patrick Gordon gives 1,700. The *Clanranald MSS.* says that every
Campbell was killed or made prisoner. Balmerino, at the next meeting of the
General Assembly, had the audacity to claim that Argyll had only lost 30 men.
Guthry, 180. The authorities for the battle are : Montrose's dispatch (*Mem. of
M.*, II., 175) ; Gordon of Ruthven, 100–102 ; Guthry, 178–179 ; Wishart,
ch. viii. ; Carte, *Ormonde Papers*, I., 76 ; Forbes Leith, I., 320–323 ; Baillie,
II., 263.
[4] The whole poem is in Napier, II., 483.
[5] The heather is the Macdonald badge ; the gale, or bog myrtle, the
Campbell.

wrote straightway to the king, giving him a full account of the fight, and ending on a high note of confidence :

" The more your Majesty grants, the more will be asked ; and I have too much reason to know that they will not rest satisfied with less than making your Majesty a King of straw. . . . Forgive me, sacred sovereign, to tell your Majesty that, in my poor opinion it is unworthy of a King to treat with rebel subjects while they have a sword in their hands. And though God forbid I should stint your Majesty's mercy, yet I must declare the horror I am in when I think of a treaty, while your Majesty and they are in the field with two armies, unless they disband, and submit themselves entirely to your Majesty's goodness and pardon.

" As to the state of affairs in this kingdom, the bearer will fully inform your Majesty that, through God's blessing, I am in the fairest hopes of reducing this kingdom to your Majesty's obedience. And if the measures I have concocted with your other loyal subjects fail me not, which they hardly can, I doubt not before the end of this summer I shall be able to come to your Majesty's assistance with a brave army, which, backed with the justice of your Majesty's cause, will make the rebels in England, as well as in Scotland, feel the just rewards of rebellion. Only give me leave, after I have reduced this country to your Majesty's obedience, and conquered from Dan to Beersheba, to say to your Majesty then, as David's general said to his master, ' Come thou thyself, lest this country be called by my name.' " [1]

---

[1] Napier, II., 484, etc. *Mem. of M.*, II., 175, etc. This famous dispatch was first printed as an appendix to Welwood's *Memoirs*, 1699, and was said to be derived from a MS. copy in the handwriting of the Duke of Richmond. It is referred to in Wodrow, *Analecta*, IV., 301.

CHAPTER X

THE RETREAT FROM DUNDEE

(*February–April*, 1645)

I mean to proceed bridle in hand ; for if the bubble bursts, and Madrid falls, we shall have a run for it.

SIR JOHN MOORE,
Dec. 6, 1808.

IT was not till March that Charles received tidings of Inverlochy. By that time he had already rejected the proposals of the Treaty of Uxbridge, one of which was that Montrose should be exempted from the act of oblivion, and the news of Argyll's disaster gave him hopes of a diversion in the north. He wrote to Montrose telling him that he was sending him 500 horse under Sir Philip Musgrave, and announcing that he himself with his army would make his way to Scotland with all possible dispatch. It was a scheme of Digby's which Cromwell was soon to frustrate. Steadily since Marston Moor antagonism had been growing between the new great English soldier and the older generals of the Parliament. In especial Cromwell hated the Scots and the Presbyterians, and all who had art or part in the Solemn League and Covenant. " Against these " (the Scots), wrote Manchester in November 1644, "his animosity was such, as he told me, in the way they now carried themselves, pressing for their discipline, he could as soon draw his sword against them as against any in the king's army." [1] Robert Baillie now christened him the " darling of the sectaries," and had hopes of getting the firebrand removed from the army.[2] But the firebrand prevailed.

*1645
February*

---

[1] Terry, *Alexander Leslie*, 344.   [2] II., 245.

On February 15, 1644, his New Model was constituted—twelve regiments of foot, eleven regiments of horse, 1,000 dragoons—a total of 22,000 picked men under a new training, who were destined to be the undoing both of the Covenant and the king.

Inverlochy had an important effect on Leven at Carlisle, since it increased his reluctance to move south, as Parliament demanded, while Montrose was at large north of the Border. To the Estates in Edinburgh it brought disappointment and panic. Argyll arrived ten days after the battle, with his arm in a sling, to be publicly thanked for his services. Baillie and Hurry were exhorted to fresh efforts, and further calls were made upon Leven. On the 11th of February James Graham, sometime Earl of Montrose, was declared a traitor and his life and estates forfeited.[1] The Kirk, not to be outdone in martial zeal, renewed the excommunication of the preceding spring, and proposed, since it was so hard to lay hold of the chief malefactor, to make a beginning with those in its power. Did not Crawford and Ogilvy and Wishart lie fast in the Tolbooth? Mr. David Dickson, Mr. Robert Blair, Mr. Andrew Cant, Mr. James Guthrie, and Mr. Patrick Gillespie attended as a deputation from the General Assembly to urge their immediate execution. Parliament commended the " zeal and piety " of the clergy, but hinted that, with Montrose victorious in the field, it would be as well to wait a little before making an end of his hostages. It contented itself with, for no apparent reason, outlawing Carnwath, and declaring " whosoever shall kill him to have done good service to his country." [2]

After resting a few days at Inverlochy, Montrose marched northward again. The right course, had it been possible, would have been an immediate descent upon the capital. But for Lowland warfare he needed cavalry, and cavalry could not be manufactured in Lochaber. To get them he must go where alone in the north they could be had—among the Gordon gentry.

---

[1] *A. P. S.*, VI., i. 313, etc.
[2] Guthry, 180–181. Balfour, III., 268, 270, 282.

He found that the opposition had melted away. Having no war-chest, he was compelled to provide for his forces by fines and requisitions from the Covenanting lairds, and when these were not forthcoming there was burning and pillage.[1]   Inverness was too strongly garrisoned to take, so Montrose passed it by, having no nervousness about fortresses in his rear.   On Friday, the 19th, he entered Elgin without sign of Seaforth or any other opponent.   The Mackenzies had disappeared into the fastnesses of Kintail.   At Elgin, to his joy, he found that recruits began to come in.   The first was the laird of Grant with 300 men, and at a plundering of the houses of certain Covenanting absentees the new convert showed himself highly assiduous.[2]

Presently came a far more welcome ally.   Nathaniel Gordon's politic desertion had been fruitful; he rode over from the Bog of Gight, bringing with him no less a person than Huntly's heir, now weary of the ways of his uncle Argyll.[3]   Lord Gordon was accompanied by his brother, Lord Lewis, whom we have already seen twice arrayed against Montrose at Aberdeen, first with Aboyne and then with Burleigh.   He was still in his teens, a fiery and perverse young man, of undoubted gallantry, but of an excitable and fantastic mind.   With the Gordons, as an earnest of Gordon support, came 200 well-mounted troopers, a sight to gladden Montrose's eyes, for cavalry could alone make possible that Lowland campaign on which he had set his heart.   Lord Gordon was more than a comrade in arms; he was to prove, for the short span of life that remained to him, Montrose's tenderest and truest friend. Last of all came Seaforth to make his peace; he had never been much of a Covenanter, but Mackenzie and Macdonald could not easily mix.   Montrose received

---

[1] He issued a recruiting proclamation under his commission of royal lieutenant, requiring all between the ages of sixteen and sixty " to repair to his standard under the pain of burning and slaying." Napier, II., 491.

[2] Spalding, II., 300.   The laird of Grant had a royalist wife, a niece of Huntly's, who " as a sweet, charming nightingale, did never cease powerfully to agent the justice of the king's cause with her husband." Gordon of Ruthven, 85.

[3] Spalding, II., 298.

him joyfully, and dispatched him to hold his own
countryside for the king. At Elgin, and at the Bog of
Gight, which was the next halting-place of the royal
army, the bond prepared at Kilcumin received further
signatures. It is odd to read in the document, which
is still preserved in the Montrose charter-chest, the
names of Grant and Seaforth beside the scrawls of
Alasdair and Clanranald, and to remember that, when
the latter signed, the former were the foes against whom
the bond was aimed.

Montrose had now a compact force of 2,000 foot and
about 200 horse. The backbone of his infantry was still
Alasdair's Irish, who may have numbered a thousand
men. The Lochaber and Badenoch clans had gone home
with their booty after Inverlochy, and the rest were
Stewarts and Robertsons, the remnant of the Atholl
levies, the 300 Grants, and small contingents from
Moray, Nairn, and the Gordons. The cavalry, with the
exception of the few who had been with Ogilvy, were
wholly Gordon. Montrose may well have believed
himself strong enough, what with the hope of further
Gordon aid and the certainty of more recruits from
Atholl, to meet Baillie on equal terms south of the Tay.

At Gight he suffered a sore bereavement. His eldest
boy, Lord Graham, now in his fifteenth year, had been
his father's companion ever since William Forrett had
brought him to Perth after Tippermuir. The swift
marches over the winter hills had worn him out, and
his life was part of the price paid for that miraculous
descent on Inverlochy. He died in the early days of
March, and was buried in the neighbouring kirk of Bellie.
Shortly after, old Lord Airlie fell dangerously sick, and
was sent to Huntly's castle of Strathbogie, with a guard
of several hundred men, which the royal army could ill
afford. Montrose had to lock up his grief in his heart,
for there was no time to spare for sorrowing. He marched
east, and by the 9th of March was close upon Aberdeen.
There had been much plundering of the little towns
and the lands of Covenanting lairds, but no shedding
of blood. Aberdeen had been evacuated by Covenant

troops; a deputation of its burgesses met him at Turriff, and, remembering with regret his last visit, he undertook that his Irish should not come within eight miles of the city.

There, however, grave misfortune befell the royal army. Nathaniel Gordon, with eighty cavaliers, rode into Aberdeen from the camp at Kintore on a friendly errand of amusement. Word was sent by certain local Covenanters to Sir John Hurry, who was in the Mearns with his Covenant cavalry. This soldier of fortune, who at Oxford had given Rupert that warning of the Parliamentary convoy at Thame, which led to the battle of Chalgrove Field and John Hampden's death, had the military virtue of speed. With a detachment of Balcarres's horse, Hurry made a dash on the city in the evening. Such royalists as he found in the street were promptly cut down, most of the horses were driven off, and among the dead was Donald Farquharson, the bailie of Strathavon and the chief member of the great family of Braemar. It was an irreparable loss, for he had been one of the best of Montrose's lieutenants. " One of the noblest captains among all the Highlandmen of Scotland," wrote Spalding,[1] and Patrick Gordon is eloquent on his virtues. " He was beloved of all sorts of people, and could not be otherwise, for he was of such a harmless and innocent carriage that there was none alive whom he could hate; he was never seen to be angry, nor knew he what that unruly passion meant, and yet he gave proof of as much true courage as any man could have; he was so far from pride and vainglory that he was all men's companion, not out of silly simplicity, but out of a gentle and mild freedom, in a nature which did always dispose him to a joyful alacrity, for his conversation, even in the saddest and most desperate times, was ever jocund and cheerful." [2] Hurry made off as fast as he had come, and on his way back took prisoner the new Lord Graham, who was with his tutor at Montrose, and sent him to Edinburgh. The king's lieutenant waited in Aberdeen to bury the dead

[1] II., 304.   [2] Gordon of Ruthven, 110.

Farquharson, at whose funeral Alasdair behaved with
almost complete propriety;[1] and then on Monday,
the 18th of March, began his southward journey.

There was burning in the Mearns and the braes of
Angus, now a laird's house, now a manse, and, as the
parish records show, there was a general upsetting of
life and a fleeing of Covenanters to strong places. It
was done under strict discipline, and unauthorized
practitioners were hanged.[2] On 21st March the town
of Stonehaven was burned, and the outbuildings of
Dunnottar castle. Marischal, who, like so many Scots
nobles, blew hot and cold in turn, was for the present
by way of being a Covenanter, and in the company of
sixteen ministers watched from its impregnable keep
the destruction of his lands, finding what comfort he
could in the consolation of Mr. Andrew Cant that the
smoke of his barns was " a sweet-smelling incense in the
nostrils of the Lord." By the end of March Montrose
was at Fettercairn, with Hurry and his 600 horse only
six miles off. There he all but made an end of Hurry.
That general, confident in his cavalry, came out to
battle near Halkerton castle, and, believing from his
scouts' reports that only 200 horse were opposed to him,
charged them gaily. But behind the horse Montrose
had concealed his best musketeers in a glen of a burn,
and Hurry was received with a fire which emptied his
saddles and put his cavalry in confusion. Then the
royalist horse turned and charged, and Hurry fled in-
continent across the South Esk, never drawing rein till
he had covered the twenty-four miles between him and
Dundee. Next day the royalists occupied Brechin,
which was plundered, and the town of Montrose, which
was spared by the general for the sake of old times.

Here he heard of the advance of a more considerable opponent than Hurry. Baillie, with 3,000 seasoned
infantry, was blocking the road to the south. Veteran
troops had been recalled from Ireland, and Leven had

---

[1] " He was much respected and well entertained for his love and favour which
he showed in not doing wrong, nor suffering much wrong to be done, except
one or two remarkable Covenanters which was plundered." Spalding, II., 305.
[2] *Fraser Papers* (S.H.S.), 61.

given up some of his best regulars.[1]   Montrose hastened
to meet him, and found him in the neighbourhood of
Coupar-Angus.   But Baillie was a cautious commander,
and he respected his enemy.   He was determined to
fight only on the most favourable ground, and he knew
that Fabian tactics were the likeliest to wear out an
army which had no base, no reserves, and no coherence
save in the personal influence of its leader.   The river
Isla ran between the two forces, and Montrose dared not
try to wrest the passage in the face of superior strength.
So in the true cavalier fashion he sent Baillie a challenge,
offering to cross and fight him, if the passage were
permitted, or to let him cross unhindered if he preferred
the other bank.   Baillie wisely replied that he would
fight at his own pleasure, and not to suit his adversary's
convenience.

Seeing that it was hopeless to wait longer, Montrose
devised a new plan.   He struck camp and marched west
to Dunkeld, with the intention of descending on the
Lowlands by another road.   At Dunkeld he could cross
the Tay in safety, and after that he had a straight path
to the Forth.   Baillie could not keep up with him, and
retired south—on his way to Fife, it was reported.   Now
was the chance for that avalanche from the hills which
would sweep the Covenanting Lowlands, and gather up
with it all the disaffected and anti-Covenant elements
which Montrose believed to be plentiful in the south of
Scotland.   Baillie had obviously gone off to hold the
bridges and fords of Forth, and it would be strange if
Highlanders, with less ground to cover, could not get
there before him.

But at Dunkeld Montrose was to be reminded of the
nature of the Highland army which he led.   Once more
his forces began to melt away.   The Atholl men slipped
back to their homes, and so did the recent levies from
the north of the Grampians.   The Gordon cavalry, led

---

[1] It is not clear what regiments Baillie had drawn from Leven, but it is
probable that there had already come north, or from Ireland, the foot regiments
of Cassilis (Kyle and Carrick), Crawford-Lindsay (Fife), Loudoun, Lanark,
Lawers, Glencairn, Lauderdale (Midlothian), and Balcarres's regiment of horse.
The units are hard to trace in the *A. P. S.*, and Balfour.

by Lord Lewis, began to grumble, and, though they did
not desert yet awhile, he knew that he could not long
count on their assistance.[1] Presently his strength had
shrunk so gravely that any attempt on the Lowlands
was out of the question.

Something must be done if only to keep his remnant together. Twenty-four miles off lay the town of
Dundee, the chief base of the Covenant in Angus. To
read Dundee a lesson might be a profitable employment,
till he saw his way more clearly. Moreover, his soldiers
were short of every kind of supply. Their clothes
scarcely held together, and they were shod for the most
part with sandals made of the raw hides of looted cattle.[2]
He had now no infantry but Alasdair's Irish. Of them
he sent the weaker half on to Brechin with the baggage,
and with 600 foot and 150 horse left Dunkeld at midnight on the 3rd of April. By ten o'clock next morning
he was under the walls of Dundee.[3]

Dundee in the year 1645 was a little town with a
big kirk and a market-place in the centre, from which
radiated the four main streets. It had a volunteer
garrison and substantial walls, and inside the walled
area at the north-west corner was a mound called the
Corbie Hill, long since levelled, on which guns had been
mounted. Montrose sent a trumpeter, one John Gordon,
a servant of the laird of Rothiemay, to summon the
magistrates to surrender, but the reply tarried, and the
assault was begun before it could be written, so the
envoy was committed to the Tolbooth.[4] Dundee was
a strong place, but the walls were being mended in the

---

[1] Wishart (ch. ix.) implies that Lord Lewis Gordon deserted before Dundee.
Gordon of Ruthven (115) denies this, and in W. Gordon's *History of the Illustrious
Family of Gordon* (II., 453), Lord Lewis's presence at Dundee is asserted on the
authority of an eye-witness. This seems the better view, for the Gordons would
take the easiest road home, which lay through Angus, and would not miss the
chance of a sack. See Gardiner, *Civil War*, II., 218 n.   [2] Forbes Leith, I., 325.
[3] Wishart makes it clear that Montrose left Dunkeld shortly *before midnight*
on 3rd April. Gardiner (*Civil War*, II., 219) says he left *before dawn* on the
3rd. The march was twenty-four miles, and the speed was evidently considered remarkable, but, on Gardiner's account, there would be nothing remarkable in doing twenty-four miles in thirty hours.
[4] He was tried and found guilty, but Napier (II., 496 n.) concludes too
hastily that he was put to death. The *Register of the Committee of Estates* shows
that he was alive in Edinburgh on 13th June.

north-west angle, and there the royalists soon made a breach.   The guns on the Corbie Hill were captured and turned against the town, the defenders of the West Port and the Nethergait Port were taken in the rear, and presently the church and the market-place were in the invaders' hands.   Several houses were set on fire, but pillage rather than burning was the order of the day. The booths of the merchants were turned inside out, and the plenishing of many a well-doing citizen took to the streets on Highland backs.[1]   Stores of ale and wine were discovered, and soon many of the assailants, who had marched all night without a halt, were in that state of bodily and mental ease which Wishart describes as " vino paululum incalescentes." [2]

It was now late afternoon, and, as Montrose stood on the Corbie Hill watching the ongoings in the town, his scouts brought him startling news.   Baillie and Hurry had not crossed the Tay on their way to Fife. With 3,000 foot and 800 horse they were now within a mile of the West Port of Dundee.   It was as parlous a position as any commander ever stood in, and his colonels gave counsels of despair.   Some urged him to leave his half-drunken troops to their fate and save himself, on the plea that another army could be found, but not a second Montrose.   Others, of a more heroic temper, cried out that all was lost but honour, and were for dying in a desperate charge.   Only Montrose kept his head.   He was resolved to escape, not alone, but with his army—a decision which shows the flawless courage of the man.   Somehow or other—how, Heaven only knows—he beat off his men from their plunder : a feat, says Mr. Gardiner, " beyond the power of any other commander in Europe."   Four hundred of his foot he sent on in front, and behind them he kept 200 of his best musketeers, as a support to the horse in case of a stand.   Last, as rearguard, went his 150 cavalry. As the royalists rode out of the Seagait and the East Port, Baillie entered at the West Port, and Hurry's van was within a gunshot of Montrose's rear.

[1] *A. P. S.*, VI., i., 519.   [2] Ch. ix., 385.

Night had now fallen, the clear night of a northern April, but the Covenanters were confident of their prey. Hurry followed hard on Montrose as he marched east along the sea-coast. A few miles from Dundee he tried to charge, but the picked musketeers among the royalist horse were too much for him, and their fire beat off his 800 troopers. He fell back, while the king's lieutenant pushed on in the direction of Arbroath. The shock of peril had sobered the Irish, and they marched like heroes. Meanwhile Baillie had conceived a better plan. He knew that Montrose must break westward for the hills as soon as possible, not only for safety, but to pick up the men he had sent on to await him at Brechin. He observed, too, that his enemy was marching along the arc of a circle, and he resolved himself to take the chord. He had made arrangements for guarding the nearest hill passes, and he hurried north-east towards Arbroath to hem his enemy between his troops and the sea.

It was precisely the strategy that Montrose had anticipated. At midnight he turned sharp in his tracks, marched south-west to Panbride, and then north by Carmyllie, Guthrie, and Melgund, and so quietly slipped round Baillie in the dark. By daybreak he was at Careston castle, a Carnegie house on the South Esk, with the friendly hills in sight and at hand. Here he had news from Brechin that the men who were to meet him there had already been given the alarm, and had betaken themselves to the mountains. He halted for a little to give his weary troops a breathing-space. In the past thirty-six hours they had marched fifty or sixty miles, fought several engagements, drunk quantities of liquor, and sacked a town. When the halt was sounded nearly every man dropped to the ground and slept like the dead.

Meanwhile Baillie at the first light of dawn had discovered his mistake. Hurry had rejoined him, and Hurry's cavalry were soon hot on the trail of the man who had so befooled them. Montrose got the alarm in time, but his sleepy soldiers would not stir. It looked

Campaign of

DUNDEE ᴀɴᴅ **AULDEARN**

March of Montrose before
the taking of Dundee ——

March of Montrose after
the taking of Dundee - - -

0   5   10   15   20

English Miles

as if the three miles which still intervened before the
hills were won might be three miles too many, and the
labours of that marvellous night rendered vain. But
the officers, at the point of the sword, managed to
beat up sufficient troops to make some sort of stand,
and Hurry's horse were checked.[1] Then, with a last
desperate effort, the exhausted royalists managed to
struggle the last miles into a country of heath and
bog, where cavalry could not follow them. Hurry
fell back, and by midday Montrose was safe among
the wilds of the North Esk.

The retreat from Dundee, however we look at it,
remains an astonishing feat of arms. Hurry's cavalry
were the troops which had done brilliant service under
Leven, and Baillie's foot contained some of the best
first-line regiments that Scotland could show. Man
for man the Gordon horse, sulky and mutinous as they
already were, could not compare with them. The Irish
were, of course, tried veterans, and superior to any of the
Covenant infantry. But Montrose's men were at the
best bone-weary, and at the worst half-drunk and laden
with their precious plunder. The general who could
stop the sack of a town in a few minutes was a superb
leader of men, and he who could execute such a flight
was a consummate strategist.   " Which," wrote Wishart,
" whether foreign nations or after times will believe I
cannot tell, but I am sure I deliver nothing but what is
most certain of my own knowledge.   And truly, among
expert soldiers and those of eminent note, both in
England, Germany, and France, I have not seldom heard
this expedition of his preferred before Montrose's greatest
victories." [2]

---

[1] Baillie, in his " Vindication," complains bitterly of Hurry's jealousy and
treachery, " which did appear clear enough by his not charging the rebels with
our whole horse at their retreat from Dundee ; nor yet would bring them up to
me, from whence the rebels might have been charged in flank, notwithstanding
I did require him to it several times by the laird of Brodie and Mr. Patrick
Pitcairne, as they witnessed thereafter unto the Parliament at Stirling."
Robert Baillie, *Letters and Journals*, II., 418.

[2] Ch. ix. The translation is from the first English edition of 1647. In
Gardiner's map (*Civil War*, II., 217), the position of Careston castle is not quite
accurate, and the route up Glen Esk is wrongly given.

CHAPTER XI

AULDEARN AND ALFORD

(*April–July*, 1645)

> *King.* And is this not an honourable spoil ?
> A gallant prize ? ha, cousin, is it not ?
> *Westmoreland.* In faith
> It is a conquest for a prince to boast of.
> > *First Part of King Henry IV.*

I

1645
April

THE letter written by the king in March, promising a body of horse and holding out hope of his own coming to Scotland, was carried by a gentleman of the name of Small, and found Montrose somewhere among the Grampians. On his way back to the royal head-quarters the messenger, disguised as a common beggar, was seized by the Covenanters on the south shore of the Firth of Forth, taken to Edinburgh on 28th April, tried and condemned, and hanged on 1st May. Small had been captured by the Estates the year before, and banished the kingdom under pain of death, so his fate was strictly in accordance with law.[1] From the documents in his possession his captors had their first news of the king's intention, and it deeply disquieted them. They disseminated wild reports of the flight from Dundee, declaring, in order to allay popular fears, that only a few royalists had escaped to the mountains. But Argyll could not deceive himself, and he knew that the coming north of the king, with Montrose unbeaten in the field, meant that he and his ambitions would be caught between two fires. He communicated his anxiety to the generals, and Covenanting strategy

---

[1] *Register of the Committee of Estates*, Sept. 20, 1644. Guthry, 186.

acquired a new vigour. The credit probably belongs to Hurry, for Baillie, though a competent soldier, never displayed any strategic ability. The Covenant army was divided. Instead of pursuing the elusive enemy in one cumbrous whole, it was resolved to try to hold him between two separate forces operating from different bases. The Estates ordered a levy of 8,800 infantry and 485 cavalry from the counties south of the Tay, and many cadets of Lothian and Border houses joined the Covenant standard. It was believed that north of the Grampians large forces could be raised, so Hurry, borrowing from Baillie 1,200 foot—the regiments of Loudoun and Lothian [1]—and keeping 160 of his horse, hastened north to pick up these levies and to form the upper millstone for the projected grinding of Montrose. Baillie, with 2,000 foot and 500 horse, settled himself in the neighbourhood of Perth.

For Montrose there was once more the weary task of finding an army. Lord Gordon was dispatched to Strathbogie to try to raise Gordon troopers in place of those who had gone off with his petulant brother. Alasdair went west into the Macdonald country to whip up those of his clan who had departed after Inverlochy.[2] Black Pate of Inchbrakie went into Atholl to organize the Robertsons and Stewarts. Montrose himself had to await the result of these missions before he could again take the field. But for him waiting was never inaction. He resolved to investigate the state of affairs on the Highland Line, and to keep Baillie out of mischief. He also wished to gather to his standard one or two gentlemen of his kin who had been hiding in Menteith, and he may have had hopes of pushing south to get some news from the royalists across the Border. He wrote to the king from Doune on 20th April ; [3] in that letter he spoke no longer of leading an army into England, for he had no army to lead. The most he could do was to keep the Covenant busy in Scotland.

---

[1] Spalding, II., 311.
[2] The Irish were terrible stragglers, and Montrose had to issue severe orders for dealing with them. See his letter to the Captain of Blair, Napier, II., 520.
[3] *Mercurius Aulicus*, May 10, 1645.

Already with 500 foot and 50 horse he had swept down upon the Perthshire lowlands, halting for the night at the village of Crieff, twelve miles from Baillie's camp. The Covenant general, as soon as he got the news, set off in the night to surprise him, and at dawn on the 17th found the little army drawn up for battle. A glance convinced Montrose that the odds were too great even for him, so, with his horse fighting a rear-guard action, he retreated up the Earn past Comrie, and by the evening was safe from pursuit at the head of Loch Earn. Next day he turned south by Balquhidder, into the heart of the Trossachs. Here he fell in with a welcome ally—no less than Aboyne, Huntly's second son, who had escaped with sixteen horsemen from be-leaguered Carlisle, and had a dislocated shoulder, which did not affect him as did Argyll's at Inverlochy. He found other friends, too, for by Loch Katrine side he met his nephew the Master of Napier, and a son of the Earl of Stirling, who had eluded the Covenant's vigilance.[1] Montrose had more than his share of family affection, and the kinsmen, says Spalding, " were all joyful of each other."

Here he had news which put an end to his southern wanderings. Baillie was busy burning in Atholl, and Hurry, now north of the Grampians, was bidding fair to destroy Lord Gordon and his slender forces. Hurry had failed to raise dragoons on Deeside, had had trouble with a mutiny in Lothian's regiment, and the day before had marched out of Aberdeen for the west. Montrose retraced his steps by one of those lightning marches which were the despair of his opponents and a confusion to the chroniclers of his day. He could not fight Baillie as he was, and to meet Hurry he must first find his Gordons. Some time on the 20th he was at Doune ; by Strathyre he reached Lochearnhead, and thence sped by Glen Ogle to Loch Tay, and across the shoulder of Schiehallion into Atholl. Then by one of the

---

[1] Spalding, who is followed by Napier, makes a younger Stirling of Keir join Montrose in Menteith, but there does not appear to have been any such person, since Sir George Stirling of Keir had no family.

Angus glens he reached Glen Muick, forded Dee, and by
the last day of April was at Skene on lower Deeside.[1]
Somewhere on the road Alasdair joined him, and at
Skene he found Lord Gordon with 1,000 foot and 200
horse.[2] His army was badly off for ammunition, so
Aboyne undertook an expedition to Aberdeen for the
purpose of supplies. With eighty troopers the young
soldier seized the town, found twenty barrels of gun-
powder in two vessels lying in the harbour, and brought
back the loot to headquarters the same evening. Whatever the faults of the Gordon blood, it had no lack of
fire and speed.

Montrose's force was now a little over 2,000 foot and
some 250 horse. Hurry meantime had not been idle.
The Covenanters of Moray and Elgin had risen at his
call. Seaforth had recanted his lately professed loyalty
and brought the Mackenzies to his side. Sutherland
was hastening to his support with his clansmen, Lovat
rallied the glens of Beauly, and Findlater was bringing
the men of Easter Ross. The local gentry, who hated
the Gordon name—Frasers, Forbeses, Roses, Inneses,
Crichtons—carried their swords to his standard. He
had under him four regular regiments, all first-line, and
two of them among the best in the kingdom.[3] Altogether he had in being and in immediate expectation a
force of perhaps 4,000 foot and not less than 400 horse.[4]
While Montrose lay on the Dee, Hurry was on Speyside
with the road to Strathbogie open before him. It was
a vital matter for Montrose to keep the Gordons in good
humour, and for this purpose their lands must be pro-

---

[1] There is some difference of opinion as to the details of Montrose's march
after crossing the Dee at Ballater. Gardiner's map sends him to Speyside; he may have misunderstood Wishart. Napier, following Spalding,
takes him to Skene, about ten miles from Aberdeen. Aboyne's raid on Aberdeen (Spalding, II., 315) would have been possible only from such a base as
Skene.

[2] The figures are from Wishart (ch. x.). I suspect the numbers given for
the infantry, for Montrose at Auldearn only allows himself 1,400 horse *and* foot.

[3] Montrose's dispatch of 17th May (*Mercurius Aulicus*, June 2, 1645) gives
the four as Buchanan, Lawers, Loudoun, and Lothian.

[4] The figures, as usual, differ in the contemporary accounts. Spalding gives
Hurry 4,000 foot and 500 horse, and Montrose 3,000 foot and horse; Gordon of
Ruthven gives Hurry 3,000 foot and 700 horse; Montrose estimated the enemy
at between 4,000 and 5,000, and his own force at about 1,400.

tected. So he hastened from Skene, by way of the
upper Don, the Avon, and the Spey, to give battle with
all speed to the enemy.

Hurry was something of a strategist, and retired for
two reasons. First, he wanted to draw Montrose out
of the friendly hills and the Gordon country; and
secondly, he had still to receive some of the promised
forces of Seaforth and Sutherland. From Elgin to
Forres he drew the royalists on, keeping only a little
way ahead, but far enough to prevent Montrose doing
him harm. The ruse succeeded. By the evening of
the 8th of May Montrose had reached the little village
of Auldearn, on the ridge of high treeless ground between
the valleys of the Findhorn and the Nairn. He believed
Hurry to be retreating on Inverness, and meant to follow
him thither the next day. It was a drizzling evening,
and the neighbourhood was Covenanting to a man,
loving not the Gordons nor the Highlanders, and least of
all Alasdair's Irish, whom it remembered after Inverlochy. No news of the enemy was likely to be got from
the country-folk. Montrose pitched his camp, posted
his pickets carefully, as was his custom, and settled
down for the night.

The position needs exact understanding if we are
to appreciate the events that followed. The hamlet of
straggling cottages ran south from the parish kirk of
St. Colm on the line of the present Boath road. East
of the village curved a low ridge of upland. Below the
houses to the west were the gardens and pig-styes of
the villagers, and beyond them lay a flattish piece of
ground covered with wildwood and sloping gently to
the bog of a sluggish burn. North of this bog was the
eminence of the Castle Hill, and beyond the burn the
ground was hard. South of it, and nearly west of the
hamlet of Auldearn, stood a bare hillock, now called
Deadman's Wood and planted with trees. The burn,
which caused the bog, bent round to the south in a
ravine, and so protected the south part of the ridge
which curved behind the village. The position was
therefore in the shape of a horse-shoe, if we take the

firmer and higher ground to the east as the rim.   In the
middle lay the village, and enclosed between the points
were the bog and the rough land which sloped from the
gardens and pig-styes.   The wet weather had swollen
the stream and filled the marshes, and made even the
higher ground heavy going.[1]

II

Some time before midnight on the 8th Hurry turned
to strike.   It was a moonless night with drenching rain,
and the royalist patrols were not inclined to go too
far into the darkness.   But Hurry gave notice of his
approach, for his men, finding the powder in their
muskets damp, fired them off to clear them.   They were
then five or six miles distant, but the quick ear of
Alasdair's sentinels caught the sound, and Montrose
guessed at once what was afoot.   A wet, misty dawn
was breaking when he drew up his line of battle.   He
placed Alasdair with a portion of the Irish and some of
the Gordon foot at the north end of the ridge, between
the village and the Castle Hill, and into his keeping he
gave the royal standard, in order that Hurry might
believe the king's lieutenant to be there in person and
deliver there his chief attack.   He boldly denied himself a centre, and instead scattered a few men in front
of the cottages, with instructions to keep up a con-
tinuous firing so that the enemy might think the village strongly held.   This—and the Castle Hill—was the
place for his cannon if he had had any, but during the
rapid marches of the past eight months he had not had
time to recover the guns which he had buried after
Aberdeen.   The rest of his infantry he kept to the south
of the village, concealed behind the crown of the ridge,
with the cavalry under Lord Gordon in a hollow on his
left wing.   It was a brilliant disposition, made at the
shortest notice in the half-light of morning.   If Hurry
attacked Alasdair under the impression that he was
Montrose, he would have difficulty with his cavalry

[1] See Bain, *History of Auldearn*, 14.

among the village gardens, while Montrose, at the right
moment, would be free to swing round his horse from
their cover and take him unprepared on his right flank.

Three-quarters of a mile off, at Kinnudie, Hurry
put his column into line of battle. The front of advance,
between the Castle Hill and the bog, was narrow, so a
single regiment, that of Lawers, formed the van, with
the three other regular regiments in support. On his
left wing, a little withdrawn, were the northern levies,
while his right wing was composed of a detachment of
Moray horse under Major Drummond. The main body
of cavalry, under his personal command, he held in reserve. His problem was more difficult than he realized.
On that narrow front he could not properly deploy his
men and reap the advantage of his superior strength.
Montrose had calculated right.

But there was one mistake in his calculations.
Alasdair was undermanned. He had no more than 500
men, all infantry, to oppose the attack of at least six
times their number, aided by a strong cavalry contingent.
If we remember that the musketeer of those days was
held to be unable to face cavalry unless drawn up
behind hedges or palisades, we get some notion of the
desperate odds. They were increased by Alasdair's
own impetuous conduct. He was never the man to
await an onset, and while Hurry's army was struggling
through the marshy burn he sacrificed the advantages
of his higher and drier ground and rushed to meet them.
Eight to one is odds reserved to the champions of fairy
tales. "Why, how the devil," asks Major Bellenden in
Old Mortality, "can you believe that Artamines, or
what d'ye call him, fought single-handed with a whole
battalion? One to three is as great odds as ever fought
and won, and I never knew any one who cared to take
that, except old Corporal Raddlebanes." But Alasdair's
deeds were worthy of the Fianna, and it is not hard to
understand how in Gaelic legend his fame is made to
outshine Montrose's. He and his Irish conducted themselves like the fierce warriors of the sagas. They were
forced back, fighting desperately, into the nest of en-

THE
BATTLE OF AULDEARN
Montrose..... ▨
Hurry........... ▭
Scattered Troops ····
Hill marked A now covered with wood
and known as Deadman's Wood

0   ⅛   ¼   ½
Scale of Half a Mile

closures in front of the village. Like Ajax by the ships, he himself was the last to retreat. His targe was full of pikes, but he swung his great broadsword round and cut off their heads like cabbage-stalks. He broke his blade, but got another from a dying comrade. Again and again he rushed out to help the stragglers to enter. One of his men, Ranald Mackinnon of Mull, fought swordless against a dozen pikemen, with an arrow through both cheeks and no weapon but his shield. So raged the Thermopylæ among the pig-styes, and every moment Alasdair's case grew more desperate.[1]

Montrose, on the crest of the hill, learned from a galloper what was happening, and decided that the moment had come for that stroke on which the success of his tactics depended. The Gordon horse, in the hollow on his left flank, could see nothing of the fight in the village. They were not seasoned troops, and it was essential that they should go into action in high heart. So Montrose cried to Lord Gordon, their leader : " Macdonald drives all before him. Is his clan to have all the honours this day ? Are there to be no laurels for the house of Huntly ? " It was the word to fire their spirit. Moreover, they had a grim wrong to avenge. They had not forgotten the death of Donald Farquharson in Aberdeen at Hurry's hands ; and a few days before, young Gordon of Rynie, a mere boy, who had been wounded and left behind in a cottage, had been brutally murdered by two of Hurry's lieutenants. With the cry on their lips, " Remember Donald Far- quharson and James of Rynie ! " the chivalry of Strath- bogie wheeled to the charge.

It was the first time that Montrose had used shock tactics. Hitherto his horse had been so few that he had been compelled to employ them after the old fashion of the Thirty Years' War, more like mounted infantry, trusting largely to their pistol fire. But he had not forgotten the new tactics which Rupert had introduced

---

[1] The *Clanranald MSS.* give a Homeric account of this part of the battle. Its author is not disposed to allow much merit to the Gordon foot with Alasdair. Auldearn is to him a clan battle, Macdonalds against the Lawers Campbells.

at Edgehill, and which in Cromwell's hands had given
the Ironsides the victory at Marston Moor.[1] Now was
the time for the *arme blanche*—for cold steel and the
weight of thundering horses. Montrose had that high
gift in war which can adapt its methods not only to its
ends but to its material. He could make his cavalry
play a defensive part, with musketeers interspersed, when
he was too weak to do otherwise ; but when the chance
came he could use it as cavalry should be used, with all
the dash and fury of a Murat ; and he could inspire
bonnet-lairds on cart-horses with the spirit of the Maison
du Roi.

Hurry, happy in his belief that he was driving Montrose to his death in the village, was suddenly assailed
by the cry of " Strathbogie ! " as the Gordons, skirting
Deadman's Wood, came down on his right flank. His
flank guard, Drummond's horse, having had a difficult
time crossing the bog, were in no case to withstand
that assault of fresh cavalry with the impetus of the
slope in their favour. Moreover, in this crisis Drummond
gave the wrong word of command, and wheeled his horse
to the left instead of to the right, so that he overrode
some of his own infantry, and offered a naked rear to the
Gordon assault.[2] Presently his troopers were flying, and
many a saddle was empty. Lord Gordon, with half his
force, followed in pursuit, and Aboyne, with the rest,
attacked the now defenceless flank of Hurry's regular
infantry. At the same time Montrose unleashed his
reserves, hitherto concealed behind the eastern ridge,
and the whole line swept down upon the doomed four
regiments. Meanwhile, among the pig-styes, Alasdair
collected his men for a last effort. He had lost seventeen
of his best officers, but the royal standard was safe, and
with his bloodstained remnant he charged Hurry's reeling
centre. It was the last straw needed to turn the balance.

---

[1] The tactics were those of Gustavus Adolphus, and their first use in Britain
has been generally ascribed to Cromwell. See, however, as to Rupert's claims,
Bulstrode, *Memoirs*, 81 ; Fortescue, *History of the British Army*, I., 200 ; and
Firth, *Cromwell's Army*, 133.

[2] I see no reason to assume treachery, for this kind of mistake has often
been made in the history of war. Drummond was court-martialled and shot in
Inverness.

The Covenant army became a mob, and the mob a shambles. The four regiments died gallantly, but the northern levies on their left rear, and the cavalry in reserve, fled without striking a blow. The blood of Ulster and the Isles that day had recovered its ancient berserk fury, and the Gordons were in no mood to spare their foes. Donald Farquharson and James of Rynie did not go unattended to the shades.

For fourteen miles the pursuit continued. Of the Ulstermen who had held the village many must have fallen, and almost all the rest were wounded, but otherwise the royalists had suffered little. It was very different with the Covenanters. The estimates of their dead vary, but the number cannot have been less than 2,000. Sir Mungo Campbell of Lawers, who fought in the centre against Alasdair, perished with most of his fine regiment.[1] There fell, too, the flower of the Lowland officers with Lothian's Border regiment—a Murray of Philiphaugh,[2] two Gledstanes of Whitelaw, nine nephews of Douglas of Cavers.[3] It was on the four regular regiments and a portion of the cavalry that the brunt fell. The northern earls, with their dishonoured levies, fled to Inverness, and Seaforth, in the wilds of Kintail, had leisure to reflect on the rewards of the forsworn. Hurry himself, with a remnant of 100 horse, escaped to Baillie. He was no coward, and was one of the last to quit the field.[4]

Auldearn is the most interesting, as it is tactically the most brilliant, of Montrose's battles. It was the first time that he had commanded a reasonable force of cavalry, and the first time that he had been the attacked

[1] It was reckoned one of the two "stoutest regiments in the Scots army." *Memorie of the Somervilles*, II., 315. The regiment cannot have been entirely destroyed, for it was present at Alford. *A. P. S.*, VI., i., 469.

[2] Wishart mentions also a Sir Gideon Murray, who cannot have been of the Elibank family, though he bore their favourite Christian name, for the Elibanks of the time were staunch loyalists. *Cf.* J. W. Buchan, *History of Peeblesshire*, II., 483.

[3] Entry in Gledstanes Bible in Hawick Museum.

[4] The battle of Auldearn has been brilliantly reconstructed by Mr. Gardiner (*Civil War*, II., 223–227). The contemporary accounts in Wishart (ch. x.), Gordon of Ruthven (123, etc.), the *Clanranald MSS.*, Spalding (II., 319), and the *Wardlaw MS.* (S.H.S.), 295, are far from clear.

instead of the attacker. Hurry had shown considerable strategic ability, and had attempted with no little art to meet him with his own methods of surprise. It is rare in the history of war that a man who can devise lightning raids shows an equal coolness and skill when he stands on the defence. But the dispositions made within a few minutes on that wet May morning could not have been bettered though they had been the result of days of preparation. Genius for war, working as it does within certain inexorable limits, repeats with variations the same methods in every age. The reserving of fire till close quarters was followed by Dundee at Killiecrankie,[1] and became a famous usage in the British army, as witness Fontenoy. The device of a weak right, dedicated to a desperate holding battle, and forming the hinge on which the rest of the army swings to break the enemy's centre, was used on a majestic scale amid the snow of Austerlitz.

III

The news of Auldearn had its influence on the war in England. Leven, already aware of the king's plan of coming north to join Montrose, was summoned by Fairfax to support Brereton at Manchester, who had been driven out of Cheshire by Charles's advance from Droitwich. He announced his coming, but added that he meant to travel by way of Westmoreland, as that route was easiest for his guns. His reasons for this circuit are plain. He wished his army to cover the road to Scotland, for he feared that at any moment the king might come north and Montrose come south, and he knew that their meeting in the Lowlands would mean the end of his Covenanting masters. The same fear kept him long in Westmoreland when he was urgently needed in Yorkshire. He was beginning, like most of the Scots, to be very weary of his Parliamentary colleagues, and had already told an English colonel that, if he did

[1] *Memoirs of Locheill*, 267.

not do his will about a certain fort at Carlisle, he " desired
no better occasion to cut them all in pieces." [1] The
Estates in Edinburgh were no less concerned, and their
first step was revenge. Lord Napier, now a man of
seventy, whose only offence was that he was Montrose's
brother-in-law, was heavily fined and kept in close confinement. The young Master had escaped and was with
his uncle; but his wife, his sisters, and his brother-in-law,
Stirling of Keir, shared the old lord's fate. Montrose
succeeded in making an exchange of certain lesser prisoners with Argyll, and he used the fact that he held a
Campbell of Crinan at Blair to prevent further reprisals
upon the Napier family. But Lord Graham was also
imprisoned, and his younger brother, Lord Robert, a boy
of seven, by an order of the Estates, was committed to
the charge of Montrose's wife. It is one of the few
glimpses we get of this lady. Apparently she had made
her peace with the Covenant through her own family,
for Southesk and his son Carnegie were of the type that
value property and a quiet life above scruples of honour
and a barren renown.

Montrose had now won four notable battles, but it
was still as difficult as ever, in Bishop Burnet's phrase,
to " fix his conquests." Hurry's army was gone, but
Baillie's remained, and Baillie blocked the way to the
Lowlands. He had 2,000 foot and several hundred horse,
and, burning his way through Atholl, had by the beginning of May crossed the Dee and entered Strathbogie.
As a reserve to this force, Montrose's college friend,
Lord Lindsay of the Byres, who had been granted by
the Parliament the forfeited earldom of Crawford, was
commanding a newly raised army on the borders of
Perth and Angus. Lindsay fancied himself a military
genius, and, having trenchantly criticized the per-
formances of Argyll and Baillie, had persuaded the
Committee to try him in high command. He seems
to have had the ear of Parliament, for on their
order Baillie, as we shall see, was soon compelled to
lend him more than a thousand of his veterans, and

[1] *Cal. S. P., Dom.* (1644–45), 558.

accept in exchange 400 of Lindsay's raw Lowland
levies.[1]

After Auldearn Montrose went first to Elgin, where
he halted for a time to rest his weary troops and look
after his wounded. As usual, many of the Highlanders
went home, and Aboyne departed on sick leave, but he
still kept his Irish and the Gordon horse. He marched
into Strathbogie to draw Baillie, and proceeded to out-
manœuvre him up and down the valley of the Spey.
He had no desire to fight until he had recruited his
strength, for after such a battle as Auldearn there was
need of a breathing-space. From Strathbogie he moved
to Balveny and thence to Glenlivat, where Baillie lost all
trace of his quarry. He found him again at Abernethy-
on-Spey, and presently Montrose was on the outskirts
of Badenoch—" a very strait county," says Baillie, and
one by no means pleasant to campaign in. Here the two
opponents halted and looked at each other. Montrose
with his Highlanders could draw supplies from the
countryside, but Baillie could only starve. The thing
was soon past bearing, so the Covenanters withdrew to
Inverness to lay in provisions.

The road was now open to deal with Lindsay, who
was waiting in Atholl to prove his boasted generalship.
The news of Montrose's coming sent him back in hot
haste to Newtyle, in Angus, to be nearer his base.
Montrose sped down the upper glens of Dee, through
Glen Muick, and down the headwaters of the South Esk.
But when he was on the Isla, within seven miles of
Lindsay, and that general was already repenting his bold
words, a message arrived from the north to spoil all his
plans. Huntly had summoned his clan back to Strathbogie. The reason of his conduct we do not know. The
natural explanation is that the chief of the Gordons took
this opportunity of showing his jealousy of Montrose and
of paying back old scores. So Lord Gordon interpreted

---

[1] Wishart (ch. xi., 393) says that Baillie gave up 1,000 men and got only
" tirones et rudes."   Baillie, the general, says he gave up 1,500 and got 400.
Robert Baillie, *Letters and Journals*, II., 419.   He got from Lindsay Cassilis'
regiment (Kyle and Carrick), and gave him the regiments of Hume (which had
come from Ireland), Lindsay (Fife), and Lauderdale (Midlothian).

CAMPAIGN OF ALFORD   Montrose's March

it, and was with difficulty restrained from dealing sum-   *1645*
marily with those of his clan who proposed to obey his   *June*
father's commands.   But it is at least as probable that
Huntly, with Baillie in the neighbourhood, was merely
anxious for the safety of his own possessions.   Montrose
had no other course but to turn back and begin recruiting
again.   He might have fought Lindsay without cavalry
and with a much inferior force—he had taken risks as
great before ; but on this occasion there was a strong
reason for retiring.   To defeat Lindsay would not advance
by one step the main strategy of his campaign.   He
would still have to go back and settle with Baillie, and
he would still have to collect an army for the Lowland
war.   It seemed wiser to do these necessary things first,
and to leave Lindsay to be dealt with later—or, more
likely, to fall a victim to the endless Covenanting
bickerings.

Montrose went back the road he had come, crossed
the Dee, and settled himself at Corgarff castle, at the
head of Strathdon.   Here he was in a strong position,
whether to retreat, if necessary, to the high hills, or
to sweep down upon the Aberdeenshire lowlands.
Once more he sent off Alasdair to collect the Clan
Donald, while Lord Gordon and Nathaniel Gordon
departed to recruit the men of their name.   In this
way the time passed till the last days of June.   Baillie
was thoroughly sick of the business, and begged in vain
to be allowed to resign his command.   Some of his
veteran regiments showed ugly symptoms of mutiny.[1]
He was in receipt of the daily and most vexatious instructions of the warlike Committee of Estates, which,
with tried warriors like Argyll, Elcho, and Burleigh
among its members, was resolved to confide nothing to
Baillie's unaided judgment.   They were represented at
the front by a branch committee, who interpreted their
resolutions, and must have driven the unfortunate commander to the verge of madness.   One of their per-
formances, as we have seen, was the transfer of the
flower of Baillie's foot, first to Argyll, who refused the

[1] Gordon of Ruthven, 128.

command, and then to Lindsay, who employed them in
futile raidings in Atholl.[1] The Providence which does
not suffer fools gladly was preparing for them their
reward.

In the last days of June, Baillie, having ravaged the
Gordon lands, prepared to lay siege to Huntly's castle
of Bog of Gight. The great keep, well defended by
Gordon of Buckie, was in no real danger, but the position seemed to call for Montrose's intervention, especially as Lord Gordon had now returned with some 250
troopers. As he advanced he heard of the transfer which
Baillie had been compelled to make to Lindsay, and he
may have guessed at the tyranny of the peripatetic
committee. He found the Covenanters at Keith, on the
Deveron, drawn up on high ground, with a gap in front
of them strongly held by horse and commanded by
artillery. The royalists skirmished before the gap, and
endeavoured to draw the enemy, but Baillie was too wise
to move. Next morning Montrose sent him a challenge
by a trumpeter, inviting the honour of an encounter in
the levels, but Baillie replied that he was not in the habit
of taking his marching orders from the enemy. Montrose accordingly broke up his camp and retired southward to Strathdon. He argued that Baillie might be
induced to follow if he saw his enemy marching away
from the Gordon country in the direction of the Lowlands.

He was right in his guess, for Baillie had heard
further news which cheered his spirit. Alasdair and
most of the Irish were absent from the royal standard.
Auldearn had put the fear of Ulster into the hearts of
the Lowland foot, and, as the word sped through the
ranks that the terrible Alasdair had gone, the courage
of the Covenanters rose. With all speed they hastened
south after the enemy, and early on the morning of the
2nd of July came up with him at Alford on the Don.

---

[1] " Vindication," Robert Baillie, *Letters and Journals*, II., 418–419. It is
possible that Hume's regiment from Ireland (the Redcoats) may have been
transferred because they were mutinous and half-hearted. See Gordon of
Ruthven, *loc. cit.*

IV

Montrose had marched from Deveronside by the
ancient Suie Road, which forded the Don at the village
of Forbes, and was continued to Deeside by a path which,
after the " Forty-five," became one of the specially
constructed military highways. It was the straight
route to Angus and the Lowlands, and Baillie believed
that his enemy was in full retreat. South-west of the
ford lay the Muir of Alford, with the kirk and smithy
and ale-house which then constituted the hamlet of that
name, two miles west of the present village.[1] Directly
south of the ford stood an eminence called the Gallows
Hill, sloping gently towards the north. On this hill
Montrose stationed his army, concealing, as at Auldearn,
the greater number behind the crest, so that to an
enemy beyond the river it seemed an inconsiderable
force. It was a strong position, for it was protected on
the left rear by the marshy ravine of the Leochel burn.
The upper Don, which in these days of surface draining
is a shallow and easily crossed stream in the month of
July, was then a far more formidable river, with long
stretches of bog along its banks. The only good ford
was the Boat of Forbes, and it was Montrose's intention
that Baillie should cross there. His own position on
Gallows Hill was a little to the south-west, and he
calculated that Baillie, believing him to be weak in
numbers, but not caring to face the direct ascent of the
hill, would try to outflank him on the right. If he did,
he had some marshy levels to traverse before he reached
the *glacis* of Montrose's position, and a defeat would put
his army in grave jeopardy, with a bog and a river
behind it.

Baillie walked into the trap. But as soon as he
crossed the Don he observed that his adversary had
altered his alignment, and was now facing not north
but north-east, which would prevent the turning movement he had designed. It is not easy to be certain of

---

[1] This dates only from 1859, when the railway was constructed.

the numbers on both sides. Lindsay's drafts had reduced Baillie to 1,200 foot, but that number must have
been increased by levies among the northern counties.
We know that of first-line material he had what remained
of the regiments of Cassilis, Lanark, and Glencairn.[1]
Montrose's infantry after Alasdair's departure must have
fallen well below 2,000, so it is probable that in foot the
two forces were nearly equal. The Gordon cavalry
numbered about 250, and Baillie cannot have had less
than from 400 to 500. One advantage Montrose possessed ; he had early notice of the enemy's coming, and
was able to make his dispositions at his leisure. They
were very different from Auldearn. The horse were
placed on each wing and strengthened by Irish musketeers. On the right Lord Gordon commanded, with
Nathaniel Gordon in charge of the foot. Aboyne had
the cavalry on the left, with a small Irish contingent under
O'Cahan. The centre, drawn up in files of six deep,
was composed of Badenoch Highlanders, the Farquharsons, and some of Huntly's lowland tenants, and was
under the charge of Drummond of Balloch and Angus
Macdonald of Glengarry. The reserve of foot, concealed behind the ridge of the Gallows Hill, was commanded by the Master of Napier.

When Baillie saw Montrose's change of front he
halted irresolutely in the bog. He would probably have
declined battle had he not been overruled by his precious
committee, and by Balcarres, his master of horse, who
trusted to the superiority of his cavalry. The latter was
about to charge under the committee's instructions,
when Montrose anticipated him. Baillie had brought
along with him herds of cattle looted from Huntly's
lands, and the sight of his father's beasts penned up
in an enclosure behind the Covenanters' camp infuriated
the young Lord Gordon. He swore to drag Baillie by
the throat from the midst of his bodyguard. Accordingly he led his horse to the charge on the royalist right
with the same fury that at Auldearn had avenged James
of Rynie. The Covenant left broke under the onset,

[1] *A. P. S.*, VI., i., 469.

Montgarrie

Suie Rd

Baillie's March

Forbes

To Strathdon

R. Don

Bridge
of Alford

Woodend

R. Leochel

Kirk of
Alford

Gallows
Hill

Gordon Stane

Feight
Faulds

ALFORD

To
Aberdeen

Suie Rd

Baillies intended March
to cut off Montrose's rear

Muir
of
Alford

N

THE BATTLE OF ALFORD

Montrose's Army

Baillie's Army

0   ¼   ½   1

Scale of Miles

but Balcarres was a stout soldier who did not easily yield. He managed to rally his three squadrons of horse, and for a little a fierce and well-matched cavalry battle raged on the edge of the bog. It would appear that during this struggle the remainder of both armies stood still and watched.

It was Nathaniel Gordon who turned the tide. He led the foot on the right wing to the support of the horse, and he conceived a better way of support than by firing into the mass, where they were in great danger of wounding their own side. He cried to his men to fling down their muskets, draw their swords, and stab and hough Balcarres's horses. The cruel device succeeded. The Covenant troopers broke and fled, and the Gordons turned their swords, as at Auldearn, against the unprotected left flank of Baillie's infantry. Meanwhile Aboyne, with his horse, had at length charged on Montrose's left, and O'Cahan's Irish followed. The two royalist wings closed in on the Covenant centre, and against it also Glengarry led the Gordon foot. The turn of the battle had arrived. Baillie's veteran regiments, having reduced their files to three to prevent outflanking, were utterly overborne. It needed only the advance of the Master of Napier with his reserve to turn the defeat of the Covenant into a rout. The very camp-boys in the royalist army mounted the baggage ponies and took their share in the confusion. Baillie and Balcarres, with their surviving cavalry, escaped by the skin of their teeth. Argyll, on his third horse, just evaded Glengarry's sword.[1] The Lowland foot remained to die on the field. All day the pursuit continued through the Howe of Alford and far down the Don.[2]

On the Covenant side the slaughter fell little short

---

[1] *Clanranald MSS.*

[2] The contemporary authorities for the battle are Wishart (ch. xi.), Gordon of Ruthven (128, etc.), and the *Clanranald MSS.* Mr. Gardiner's ingenious reconstruction (*Civil War*, II. 280–283) is vitiated by his assumption that the village of Alford was the modern village, which puts all his topography awry. The account of Wishart, which he rejects, seems to be literally accurate. I am greatly indebted to a convincing article on the subject by the librarian of Aberdeen University, Dr. W. Douglas Simpson, in the *Aberdeen University Review* for June 1919.

of Auldearn. The royalists, considering how desperate was the cavalry battle, lost curiously few officers and men, but they sustained one loss which made the victory little better than a defeat. Lord Gordon, determined to avenge the theft of his father's cattle, charged the retreating horse once too often. His aim was to capture Baillie, and he was actually seizing that general by the sword-belt when he was shot dead from behind— whether by accident or design will never be known. His death threw the royalist army, more especially Montrose and the Gordons, into the uttermost grief. He had been the young Marcellus of the cause, the one hope of the North. Aboyne stopped his pursuit of Balcarres, and—in Wishart's words—" forgetting their victory and the spoil, they fixed their eyes upon the lifeless body, kissed his face and hands, commended the singular beauty of the corpse, compared the nobility of his descent and the plentifulness of his fortune with the hopefulness of his parts, and counted that an unfortunate victory that had stood them in so much." It was a sorrowful band that, led by Montrose, took its way slowly to Aberdeen, where the young lord was laid in the Gordon aisle of the old church of St. Machar. He was only twenty-eight years of age, and had spent his short span of life cleanly and chivalrously in the service of his country. To Montrose the loss was irreparable, for Lord Gordon was the one man who in temper and attainments was fitted to be his companion. Patrick of Ruthven, a clansman, has described that noble friendship in arms :

" Never two of so slight acquaintance did ever love more dearly. There seemed to be a harmonious sympathy in their natural dispositions, so much were they delighted in a mutual conversation. And in this the Lord Gordon seemed to go beyond the limits which Nature had allowed for his carriage in civil conversation. So real was his affection, and so great the estimation he had of the other that, when they fell into any familiar discourse, it was often remarked that the ordinary air of his countenance was changed from a serious listening to a certain ravishment or admiration of the other's witty expressions. And he was often heard in public to speak sincerely, and confirm it with oaths, that if the fortune of the present war should prove at any time so dismal that Montrose, for safety, should be forced to fly into the mountains without any army or any one to assist him, he would live with him as an outlaw, and would prove as faithful a consort to drive away his malour, as he was then a helper to the advancement of his fortunes." [1]

V

The armies of Baillie and Hurry had ceased to exist. To be sure there was still Lindsay, but he was hardly to be taken seriously. The news of Alford, when it reached the south-west of England, roused the drooping spirits of Charles. " It is certain," Digby wrote, " that the king's enemies have not any man in the field now in Scotland." [2]   Charles had need of heartening, for his cause, whether he realized it or not, had received its deathblow. Shortly after Alford, Montrose had news— perhaps from his friend Thomas Saintserf, who, disguised as a packman, travelled between his camp and the Border [3]—of a cataclysmic disaster in the English midlands. On the 14th of June, at Naseby, Cromwell's " company of poor ignorant men " [4] had scattered Rupert's chivalry and annihilated the royal foot. The battle had two vital consequences for Scotland. It was Cromwell's first clear personal triumph, and it enabled him to press on with his policy of religious toleration which must sooner or later destroy the tyranny of the Covenant. [5]   On the other hand, it put an end to the danger of Charles's advance to the north, and Leven was able to withdraw his army from Westmoreland and march south in his leisurely way to the siege of Hereford, very anxious lest the slaughter of the Irish women after Naseby should be made a precedent by malignants for reprisals on the immense female concourse which accom-

[1] Gordon of Ruthven, 138. The character of the dead boy on pp. 131–132 is one of the great passages of seventeenth-century prose.

[2] Digby to Rupert, July 28, 1645, cited by Gardiner, *Civil War*, II., 283.

[3] Saintserf seems to have travelled as a theological colporteur. See *The Covent Garden Drollery*, 1672 :

" When to the great Montrose under pretence
Of godly books thou broughtst intelligence."

[4] *Letters and Speeches* (ed. Lomas), III., 247.

[5] Cromwell to Lenthall. *Ibid.*, I., 206.

1645
July panied the Scots.[1] Moreover, on the 28th of June Carlisle, after a heroic defence, capitulated to David Leslie, and thereby released for service elsewhere a veteran force of horse and foot, and a general who had none of Leven's timidity. If the royal standard was still to fly in Britain, it was high time that Montrose crossed the Border.

[1] He was said to have had a following of 4,000 women and children. Nicholas to Rupert, July 11, 1645, cited by Gardiner, *Civil War*, II., 264 *n*.

CHAPTER XII

KILSYTH

(*July–August* 1645)

When we look back upon the great things which God hath done for us, and our former deliverances out of dangers and difficulties, which to us appeared insurmountable, experience breeds hope ; and when we consider how, in the midst of all our sorrows and troubles, the Lord our God hath lightened our eyes with the desirable and beautiful sight of His own glory in His temple, we take it for an argument that He hath yet thoughts of peace and a purpose of mercy towards us. Though for a small moment He hath forsaken us, yet with great mercies He will gather us. He hath lifted up our enemies that their fall may be the greater, and that He may cast them down into desolation for ever. Arise ! and let us be doing. The Lord of Hosts is with us, the God of Jacob is our refuge !

Proclamation of the General Assembly, 1645.

THE Covenant made one last effort to ride the storm. The plague had broken out in Edinburgh, so Parliament was compelled to move to Stirling on the 8th of July. Stirling, however, proved no refuge, and the seat of government was transferred to Perth.[1] Fresh orders were sent to the nobles and gentry of the Lowlands, and an Act was passed to levy a new army of 10,000 foot and 500 horse, a considerable part of which was appointed to assemble at Perth on the 24th of July. Baillie had brought back no infantry from his last campaign, but he had saved a respectable cavalry contingent, probably at least 400 strong. He had returned in a sullen temper, and had resigned his office ; but Parliament passed a vote of thanks to him for his services, and insisted on his taking command of the new levies. For his comfort it appointed the usual committee " to advise," a phrase which, as Baillie well knew, meant to dictate. Among the sixteen members

1645
July

[1] The plague soon reached Perth, as it did nearly every Lowland town. The beautiful ballad of *Bessie Bell and Mary Gray* refers to this summer.

were Argyll, Tullibardine, and Burleigh—experts in
their way, for all had already suffered at Montrose's
hands.[1]

Alford was fought on the royalist side lacking
Alasdair and most of his Irish, the western clans, and
the Atholl men. For the final assault on the Lowlands
it was necessary to collect all available forces. This
meant some weeks of waiting at the shortest, and Aboyne
was dispatched to Strathbogie to enlist troopers. He
made little speed, either because the Gordons were disinclined to fight south of the Highland Line, or because
he was a poor recruiting sergeant, and Montrose had to
send him back to try again. Aboyne is a difficult figure
to decipher on the page of history. He was devoutly
loyal to the king's service; his gallantry was beyond
question; but he had much of the intractable and suspicious temper of his brother Lewis and his father
Huntly. The fine flower of the Gordon race had gone
with the young lord. Montrose waited for a few days
at Craigton,[2] on the south side of the Hill of Fare (where
is a spot still called Montrose's Trench), till the news of
the muster and the session at Perth decided him to go
south. It was a sovran chance to strike at the heart of
the opposition.

He forded Dee, and marched through the hills to
Fordoun in the Mearns, where he waited to receive his
expected allies. They arrived in good force. Alasdair
brought the rest of his Irish, and a body of Highlanders
some 1,500 strong. Among them came the ever-faithful
Macdonalds of Clanranald and Glengarry, and not less
than 700 Macleans from Mull, under their chiefs Lachlan
of Duart and Murdoch of Lochbuie. This warrior clan
as a fighting force was second only to the Ulstermen.[3]

---

[1] Balfour, III., 294.

[2] Wishart (ch. xii.) gives "Craigston," and Napier, who is followed by
Mr. Gardiner, assumes that he marched north to Craigston castle in Buchan, a
detour of thirty miles, which would have been impossible in the time. Montrose,
in his letter of 6th July, calls it "Craigtoune." *Mem. of M.*, II., 214. Murdoch
and Simpson identify the place with Craigton on Dee, seven miles from Aberdeen, but the Hill of Fare site is confirmed by the kirk session records of the
neighbouring parish of Echt. See Mr. George Duncan's paper in *Scottish Notes
and Queries* for March 1903.

[3] They were said to be able to put 2,000 men in the field. Napier, II., 654 *n.*

Moray Firth

R.Spey

Elgin
Bog of Gicht
Gordon Cas.
Fochabers
Fraserburgh

Peterhead

Strathbogie
Huntly Cas.
INVERNESS
Balveny
Huntly

R.Findhorn
R.Spey
Abernethy
Alford
Monymusk
Kintore

Kildrummie
Cluny
Cas.
ABERDEEN

Rothiemurchus
R.Don
Hill
of Fare
Drum
Mills

R.Dee
Banchory
Stonehaven
Dunnottar Cas.

L.Ericht
Fordoun
Fettercairn

Nth.Esk
NORTH

Blair
Athol
Brechin
Sth.Esk
SEA

L.Rannoch
Weem
Kirriemuir

Aberfeldy
Dunkeld
Forfar

Loch Tay
Cupar Angus
Arbroath

Earn
Buchanty
Dundee

Tippermuir
Perth
Firth of Tay

R.Eden
N

Kinross
L.Leven

R.Forth
Stirling
Firth of Forth

Kilsyth
EDINBURGH

GLASGOW
R.Clyde
Pentland Hills

CAMPAIGN OF KILSYTH

Montrose's March ⌣

0 5 10 15 20 25 30 35 40

English Miles

There were Macphersons from Badenoch, Camerons from
Lochaber, Stewarts from Appin, Farquharsons from
Braemar, and Macnabs and Macgregors from the southern
Highlands. Young Inchbrakie arrived later with a con-
tingent of the Atholl men. Save for his lack of cavalry,
Montrose had now the strongest force he had yet
commanded. He marched by his old route down
the Isla to Dunkeld, to watch the movements of the
Covenanters in Perth, and to wait for Aboyne and
the Gordons.

Parliament met on the 24th of July under the guard
of a large body of infantry and 400 horse. If Montrose
was to upset their peace of mind and have leisure for his
own business, it was necessary to make a show of cavalry
to keep the 400 at home. Accordingly he mounted some
of his foot on baggage horses, and as the Perth citizens
cast their eyes to the north they were amazed to see a
cloud of royalist cavalry on the horizon. It was sufficient to make them shut their gates and keep close
within their walls. For a few days, from their camp at
Methven eight miles off, the royalists held the ancient
city in terror. At any moment the assault might come,
and Parliament debated with the fear of sudden death
in each debater's heart.

But the bluff could not be long sustained. Presently
it was discovered that the cavalry were a sham, being
no more than eighty troopers and some amateurs on
pack-horses. The courage of the Covenant horse revived,
and a sally was ordered. Montrose had no wish to fight
a battle till the time was ripe, so he fell back on his camp
at Methven. But Methven was too near the plains to
be any permanent refuge, and as the Covenanters advanced he was compelled to retire, till he had reached
the skirts of the hills. The Covenant horse harried his
rear, but his Highland sharpshooters lay in wait for
them, and, stalking them through the undergrowth,
emptied a saddle with every shot. The retreat, however, had been too hurried to be without disaster. Some
of the Irish women among Alasdair's camp-followers had
straggled too far behind in Methven wood, and were

seized and butchered by the Covenanters.[1] " As at
Naseby," says Mr. Gardiner, " the notion of avenging
injured morality probably covered from the eyes of the
murderers the inherent brutality of their act." [2] But
these poor creatures were no painted madams of the
court, but the womenfolk of humble soldiers, who followed their fathers, husbands, and lovers for the same
motive that had attracted Scotswomen in hundreds to
the tail of Leven's army in England.

For a week Montrose waited at Dunkeld till Aboyne
arrived with 200 Gordon cavalry and 120 musketeers
mounted on baggage ponies. These latter were the
equivalent of the dragoons of the New Model Army, and
acted both as light cavalry and as mounted infantry.[3]
Not the least welcome was old Lord Airlie, now recovered
from his sickness, who rode in with 80 of his Ogilvys,
including his son, Sir David Ogilvy of Baldovie, and
young Alexander of Inverquharity. Montrose now
commanded a force of at least 4,400 foot and 500 cavalry,[4]
a seasoned force, for all were tough fighting men, and
the thousand Irish were probably the best infantry at
the time in Britain. Most of the troops had, under his
leadership, been present at more than one victory, and
all had wrongs to avenge on some section or another of
the Covenanters. It was the first time, with the exception of Alford, that he had commanded an army comparable in the strength of all arms to its opponents.

Meanwhile Baillie at Perth was in a sombre and distrustful mood. He thought little of his new levies, and
he was distracted by his committee of advice. He con-

---

[1] Wishart (ch. xii.) is the only authority for the massacre, but, except
when he tries to expound a battle which he does not quite understand, he is
an accurate chronicler. He may well have had the account of it from the
Irish after Kilsyth, and, as Murdoch and Simpson point out, the latter showed
great exasperation afterwards in their march past the Ochils.

[2] *Civil War*, II., 292–293.

[3] Fortescue, *Hist. of the British Army*, I., 216.

[4] Wishart makes the Gordon contingent 200 horse and 120 mounted
musketeers. Gordon of Ruthven, who generally overstates the Gordon
strength, gives them 400 horse. Montrose had nearly 100 horse before they
joined (Wishart), and Ogilvy brought 80. Gordon probably included the
musketeers among the Gordon cavalry. Five hundred seems a reasonable
estimate for the total mounted strength of the royalists. Hope, the Lord
Advocate, gives them 3,500 foot and 600 horse. *Miscellany* (S.H.S.), I., 128.

sidered that he could have cut off Montrose from the
hills in his sally from Perth but for the negligence of
Hurry and his cavalry. Once again he resigned, and
once again he was induced to withdraw his resignation.
Montrose marched by way of Logiealmond to have a
look at the enemy, and the Covenanters promptly retired
to their fortified camp of Kilgraston on the Earn. As
Montrose followed at his leisure by way of the field of
Tippermuir, he had news which determined his strategy.
The Covenant was making a desperate bid for success.
Cassilis, nicknamed the " Solemn," a zealot of the old
rock ; Eglinton, called " Grey Steel," one of the chief
promoters of the Solemn League ; Glencairn, the eternal
Laodicean whose actions no man could forecast—were
raising the Covenanting westlands. Lanark had collected the Hamilton tenantry, and with 1,000 foot and
500 horse was hastening from Clydesdale. Baillie's
army was already superior in numbers to his own, and
Montrose did not wish the odds to be too great, for he
realized as well as did the Covenant that on the coming
fight must depend the future of the king's cause in
Scotland. He resolved, therefore, to fling himself between Baillie and Lanark. Baillie was lying at Kilgraston waiting on the Fife regiments. If he fought
him now, he would still have the men of Fife to deal
with, not to speak of Lanark. If he cut off the Fife
men, he would still have Baillie, and during these
manœuvres Lanark would have arrived. The wiser
plan was to let Baillie get his Fife recruits, and then
cut him off from the west. Besides, the farther he
could draw the Fife levies from their own country, the
less stomach would those home-keeping souls have for
fighting.[1] Lanark he knew of old, and he may well
have argued that, if he routed Baillie, he could have
little to fear from the Hamiltons.

---

[1] The poor fighting quality of the Fife levies was a byword at the time.
Some of them had already given Baillie trouble in the advance to Methven.
Robert Baillie, *Letters and Journals*, II., 419. Wishart calls them " minus
bellicosi." If we are to trust the *Clanranald MSS.*, Baillie had a number of
sailors in his command, "who never fought on land before that time," and
these could only have come from Fife.

On or about the 10th of August Montrose, having crossed the Earn between Dupplin and Forteviot, swept down Glenfarg to the neighbourhood of Kinross. Baillie must have guessed that he had gone to cut off the Fife recruits, but the arrival of these levies presently in his camp convinced him that this was not Montrose's aim. Then came the news that the grim tower of Castle Campbell, above Dollar, an Argyll possession, had been sacked and burned.[1] While the Covenanters lay at the north-east end of the Ochils, Montrose was turning the southern flank. He could only have one object—to get to the west of Baillie and frustrate his junction with Lanark. Further tidings of him came from the lands of Lord Mar, who was the father-in-law of the Master of Napier. In so large a force Montrose could not exercise the personal supervision which is possible in a small army, and the Irish seem to have got out of hand, for they plundered the little town of Alloa and some of the Mar holdings. Mar, however, bore no grudge, for, while Alasdair led on the foot in advance, he invited Montrose and his staff to dine with him at Alloa House.

By this time Baillie had made up his mind. As Montrose was at dinner he received the intelligence that the Covenanters were marching with all speed along the north side of the Ochils to cut him off. It was vital to his strategy that he should keep ahead of them, so, hastily catching up his foot, he led his army that night across the Forth by the Fords of Frew, a few miles above Stirling. Next day he continued his march in the direction of Glasgow, passing over the field of Bannockburn, and by the evening of the 14th of August was encamped in an upland meadow on the Colzium burn, one of the affluents of the river Kelvin, about a mile north-east of the town of Kilsyth. He argued that it was now Baillie's business to find him and fight him, for the Covenanters must pass beneath him before they could join Lanark, who was marching from Glasgow.

---

[1] Young Ewen Cameron of Lochiel was in the castle at the time.

Baillie, making the best possible speed past Dunblane and down the Allan Water, was compelled by Argyll to waste time in burning Lord Stirling's castle of Menstrie, and the Graham house of Airth.[1] He found, as he expected, that the presence of the committee made discipline almost impossible. That band of heroes was now enlarged, and included Argyll, Lindsay, Burleigh, Tullibardine, Balcarres, and Elcho; Montrose had beaten them all except Lindsay, whom as yet he had only scared. The Fife levies, too, grew more out of humour and spirit with every mile that increased the distance from their homes. On the evening of the 14th he was encamped at Hollinbush, on the road from Stirling, only two and a half miles from where Montrose lay. His scouts—for he was in a friendly country—had kept him well informed of the enemy's whereabouts, and a great dispute arose in the committee. Baillie, realizing the gravity of the coming engagement, was for taking no risks, and waiting till Lanark, now only twelve miles distant, brought up his reinforcements. But Argyll and his colleagues would brook no delay. They had 6,000 foot and 800 horse. They were in the Lowlands at last ; Lanark, at the latest, would be with them in a few hours ; Montrose had the Forth behind him to cut off his retreat to the Highlands ; he lay in a hollow, and had left the higher ground unoccupied. Let them strike home at once, and Lanark, when he arrived, would help to take order with the fugitives.

It had been a hot summer, the weather that breeds pestilence, and the bent on the hills was as yellow as grain. The dawn of the 15th was windless and cloudless, giving promise of a scorching August day. With the first light the Covenanters were on the move. They left the road and made straight across country in the direction of Montrose's camp, wading through fields of ripen-

---

[1] Argyll denied this at his trial in 1661, but he also denied the similar case of Forthar, which is proved from his own letter of instructions. See p. 117, *supra*. Baillie seems to confirm the story. " Did they (the Committee of Advice) not in that capacity sometimes commend . . . such acts of hostility as I, without a special warrant from the Estates (though I had been in charge by commission), could not now have answered but at the rate of my head ? " Robert Baillie, II., 424.

ing bear and oats, and scrambling up the slopes of the
Campsie Hills. Soon they reached the rim of the basin
where the royalists lay, and Baillie, believing his men
to be tired by the rough journey, would have preferred
to halt in what seemed an impregnable position. He
held the high ground, and below him the hill fell steeply
to the little burn, beyond which lay Montrose. But the
military genius of the committee conceived a plan. A
quarter of a mile to the right the glen closed in, and the
burn descended through a narrow ravine. They believed that Montrose was doomed to defeat, and their
only fear was lest he should escape to the north, for there
was still a way open to the Highlands through Menteith.
If they could outflank him and take up a position on the
ridge due north from his left, he would be pinned inex-
orably between them and the Lowlands.

As Montrose watched the enemy's doings he was
content with the ground he had chosen. He had left
the higher ridge unoccupied as a bait to draw his opponents into action. He did not believe that Baillie
would charge down the steep ; if he did, the use of horse
on such ground was impossible, and he could guess the
condition in which the heavily accoutred Lowland infantry would arrive at the bottom. He believed that
the Covenanters would simply wait for Lanark, and he
had made up his mind to charge their position, since the
slopes of the Campsies were nothing to men who knew
Glencoe and the Rough Bounds. He asked his army
whether they were for retreat or fight, and the fierce
cry for battle assured him of their spirit. Foreseeing
the heat of the day, he bade his Highlanders cast their
plaids and fight in their coarse saffron shirts, knotting
up the long tails of the latter between their legs to give
them freedom of action.[1] His horse he ordered to wear
their shirts above their buff jerkins in order that they
might be easily distinguishable from the enemy. It was
a necessary precaution in an army of many different
levies, where the separate parts were scarcely known to

---

[1] *Clanranald MSS.* For the Highland costume in battle, see Gardiner, II.,
296, and M. and S., 213.

1645
August

each other. Alasdair's men in the heat of battle must
have some clear mark to distinguish friend from foe, or
regrettable incidents might occur. Near the head of the
glen, and on the hill where the Covenanters stood, were
several cottages and little gardens walled with dry-stone
dykes.[1] It was a sort of Hougoumont, a place which
any prudent commander must seize, so he ordered its
occupation by an advance guard of Alasdair's centre,
which happened to be a body of a hundred Macleans,
under Ewen of Treshnish.

But as Montrose watched the crest of the hill he
observed the Covenanters in motion. He could scarcely
believe his eyes when he perceived that they were about
to attempt a flank march across his front. It is never a
safe or an easy manœuvre, more especially when the foe
is almost within musket shot, and in mobility and speed
is the superior of the side attempting it. Baillie bitterly
protested, and he was supported by Balcarres, but the
committee would have their way, and for the rest of the
day he was carrying out orders not his own. To reach
the hill directly above Montrose's left it was necessary
to make the circuit of the glen and cross the ravine of the
burn. The movement was led by Balcarres and the
horse, and Baillie, accompanied by Lindsay and Burleigh, followed close behind with the foot. His three
field-pieces, which might have been of incalculable
value in covering the movement, were apparently
forgotten.

On one condition alone might such a course have
succeeded. If the Covenanters had kept behind the
ridge in their march, leaving a small force to occupy
their old position on the crest of the hill, they might
have safely reached their goal; and once there, with a
gradual slope before them on which horse could be
used, they would have seriously embarrassed Montrose.
But such tactics needed a speed and a precision which
the Covenanters did not possess. Almost at once they
were visible to the royalists below, owing to a grave
breach of discipline. A certain Major Haldane, observ-

---

[1] On the present farms of Auchinrivoch and Auchinvally.

ing the cottages which Treshnish had occupied, decided, on his own authority, that he must attack the position. Accordingly, with a handful of musketeers, he broke off from the main march and started down the hill. He was soon driven back, but it was never the Highland way to repel without a counterstroke. Alasdair launched the whole body of Macleans against the assailants, and they were at once followed by their old rivals, the Macdonalds of Clanranald, who vied with them in the race for the ridge. Young Donald of Moidart won, but Lachlan of Duart was little behind. On surged the billow of Celtic war till it struck the Covenant line in the middle. Colonel Hume, who commanded there, drew four foot regiments—his own, Argyll's, Cassilis', and Glencairn's—behind some dykes on the hill-top, and attempted a stand. But the Highlanders leapt the walls with their targes high and their heads down, and in a few minutes the Covenant centre was in flight. Alasdair's breach of orders had succeeded beyond its deserts, and Baillie's army was cut in two.

Meanwhile the Covenant van had crossed the burn and rounded the head of the glen. Montrose, who at first can only have guessed at the aim of the flank movement, now saw clearly its motive. It was impossible to let the enemy occupy the height on his left, so he dispatched a body of Gordon foot, under their adjutant, to forestall them. The bulk of Balcarres's horse must have been still behind the ridge, for if Montrose had seen their full force he would have attempted to hold the hill in greater strength. The Gordons found the task beyond their power. They were driven back, and to the eyes of Aboyne—whom Montrose, remembering Lord Gordon's fate at Alford, had kept at the rear with a strong bodyguard—seemed to be caught in a death-trap. He broke away with the Gordon horse to the assistance of his kinsmen.[1] But he, too, was surrounded, so Montrose called upon Airlie and his Ogilvys to redeem the day. The gallant old man, for

---

[1] Wishart seems to imply some hesitation in the Gordon cavalry, but he is not an unprejudiced witness.

THE BATTLE OF KILSYTH

R. Dullator

R. Kelvin

C

D

B

A

Slaughter
Howe

Kilsyth

A. Attack of the Highlanders   C. First Position of the Covenanting Army
B. Attack of the Gordons   D. Flank March of the Covenanting Army

English Miles

0   ¼   ½   1   1½   2

all his sixty years, led his troopers to the charge, and
the tide of battle on the hill began to turn. Then Montrose dispatched Nathaniel Gordon with the remainder of the cavalry, seeing that Alasdair was having his own way in the rest of the field. Balcarres's cuirassiers were driven off the ridge, the advance foot were routed, and the Covenant van shared the fate of the Covenant centre.

Baillie was soon aware that the day was lost. Haldane's escapade brought him racing back from Balcarres's side, but the mischief had been done. He endeavoured in vain to rally the foot at the ravine of the burn, and then in despair galloped to the rear for the Fife reserves. But the men of Fife had early despaired of the issue, and were in full flight for their homes. About the same time Montrose's trumpets sounded the general advance. The whole royalist army swept up the hill, but no foe awaited them on the crest. The semicircle of the little amphitheatre was empty, and the outside rim was strewn with fleeing horse and foot. Of the 6,000 men who had set out that morning to fight under the Covenant's banner only a few hundreds escaped. The murder of their women in Methven wood had not disposed Ulsterman or Highlander to a mercy which they knew would never be extended to themselves. Many of the horse, too, perished, caught in the mires of Dullatur. The leaders escaped, as commonly happened in the Covenant's battles. The lairds and nobles had better horses, and they had no scruple of honour in saving their own necks and leaving the plain folk, who had trusted them, to die on the field. Well for themselves that the western Covenanters were too late for the fight and had ample time to escape. Lanark fled to Berwick, Glencairn and Cassilis to Ireland. Baillie and Holbourn sought sanctuary in Stirling castle, where they were joined by Balcarres, Burleigh, and Tullibardine. Loudoun and Lindsay posted to England. Argyll galloped twenty miles to Queensferry on the Forth, where he found a boat which landed him in Berwick in the safe keeping of the Scots garrison. As at Inveraray and at Inverlochy, he escaped by water from Montrose's swords.[1]

The decisive battle had at last been fought. So far as Scotland was concerned, the forces of the Covenant were annihilated, and its leaders were in exile. Scarcely a year had passed since that August evening when, with two companions, Montrose had alighted at the door of Tullibelton—without men, money, or prospects, and with no resources for his wild mission save the gallantry of his heart. Since then he had scourged the Covenant from Lorn to Buchan, and from Lochaber to Angus. With halting allies and few troops, with poor weapons and scanty ammunition, amid broken promises and private sorrows and endless disappointments, he had sought out his enemies and had beaten them wherever he found them. He had excelled them in strategy and in tactics, in cavalry and in infantry movements, in the offensive and the defensive. He had shown himself able to adapt his slender resources to any emergency, and to rise superior to any misfortune. His reward had come. For the moment he was the undisputed master of all Scotland.

[1] The contemporary authorities for the battle are Wishart (ch. xiii.), Gordon of Ruthven (137, etc.), the *Clanranald MSS.*, and Baillie's own account (*Letters and Journals*, II., 420, etc.). Mr. Gardiner, from a careful inspection of the ground, has produced what must be taken as the final account of the tactics (*Civil War*, II., 295–300).

CHAPTER XIII

THE WAR ON THE BORDER

(*August–September* 1645)

> Had one seen him returning from a victory, he would by his silence have suspected that he had lost the day; and had he beheld him in retreat, he would have collected him a conqueror by the cheerfulness of his spirit.
>
> THOMAS FULLER.

I

"I PROFESS to you," wrote Digby to Jermyn on the 21st of September, a month after Kilsyth, "I never did look upon our business with that assurance that I do now, of God's carrying us through with His own immediate hand, for all this work of Montrose is above what can be attributed to mankind." [1]   To Charles, uneasily moving about the Welsh marches, the star that had arisen in the north seemed to herald a better dawn.   Even at that late hour it is clear that, if there had been any other royalist leader with a tithe of Montrose's genius, the king's crown need not have fallen.   But from England he received only empty praise.   What had become of Sir Philip Musgrave's 500 horse, what of the 1,500 men whom Digby had promised?   Montrose had been true to his word; he had scattered the Covenant in Scotland, and deprived Leven and Leslie of a base.   But to "fix his conquests" was beyond the power of mortal man unless help came from the south.   He himself thought otherwise.   He hoped still to lead a great army across the Border, and redress the sinking balance in Charles's favour.   He had no fear of his antagonists; "though God should rain

---

[1] Digby to Jermyn, *Bankes MSS.*, cit. by Gardiner, *Civil War*, II., 344 *n.*

Leslies from Heaven, he would fight them." [1]   But his
courage outran the possibilities.   Scotland was subdued,
not converted, and, unless the king came north as a
conqueror, Montrose would have to wrestle daily and
desperately to hold her to her unwilling allegiance.
Never in history have Highlands dominated Lowlands
for long.

But at first the prospect had a delusive brightness.
After waiting two days at Kilsyth, during which he
sent a message of assurance to the city of Glasgow, the
victorious general entered the capital of the west.   Here,
seven years before, had been held the General Assembly
at which episcopacy in Scotland had been abolished, and
Montrose, in his Presbyterian zeal, had shown himself
the foremost in the baiting of Hamilton.   The place
had never evinced the fanatic virulence of Edinburgh.
Pride in their great church, happily saved from the
iconoclasts, had kept its citizens on the side of decency
and temperance in religious affairs.   A deputation from
the town council met the king's lieutenant outside the
walls, offering the value of £500 in English money as a
largesse to the soldiers, and praying that the city might
be left unmolested.   To this request Montrose readily
agreed.   He issued stringent orders against theft and
violence, and his entry was welcomed with a popular
enthusiasm hardly to be looked for in the Lowlands.
Zachary Boyd, that erratic singer of Israel, wrote Latin
verses in his honour.   Unfortunately the sight of the
well-stocked booths and the prosperous dwellings of the
Saltmarket and the Gallowgate was too much for some
of his followers, who had not believed that so much
wealth existed in the world, and could not readily forget
their Highland creed that spoil should follow victory.
Looting began, and Montrose, true to his word, promptly
hanged several of the malefactors.   But he saw that
Glasgow would prove too severe a trial to his army, so
two days after his arrival, about the 20th of August, he
marched six miles up the river to Bothwell.

Here he took measures for the government of Scot-

---

[1] Row, *Life of Blair*, 176.

James Marquesse of Montrose, Earle of Kingcairne, Lord Græme, Baron of Mont dieu, etc. Lieutenant Governour and Capt. General For His Matie in the Kingdome of Scotland.

A. Matham fe.

MONTROSE
FROM AN ENGRAVING BY A. MATHAM.
FORMING THE FRONTISPIECE
TO THE 1647 HAGUE TRANSLATION OF WISHART

land, which the fortunes of war had entrusted to his
hands. The first business was to stamp out the embers
of disaffection. Some of Eglinton's levies were still
threatening in the west, and Alasdair was dispatched
to bring them to reason. He met with no opposition,
and to his surprise was welcomed cordially at Loudoun
castle by the wife of the Covenanting chancellor. The
shires and burghs of Renfrew and Ayr sent in their
submission and petitioned for favour.[1] Other towns
and counties followed suit, and presently arrived the
nobles and gentry to greet the rising sun. The midlands
of Scotland were naturally foremost. Loyalists like
Seton [2] and Fleming and Erskine, cautious men like
Linlithgow and Carnegie and Maderty, declared opponents like Drummond, who had commanded the Covenant horse at Tippermuir, hastened to Bothwell. More
important were the recruits from the south, the nobles
whom Montrose had solicited in vain at Dumfries the
year before. Annandale and Hartfell swore allegiance,
as did powerful lairds like Charteris of Amisfield, and
those Border earls, Roxburgh and Home, who for the
past four years had coquetted with both king and Covenant. Traquair, another waverer, sent his son, Lord
Linton, with the promise of a troop of horse. Carnwath's
brother, Sir John Dalziel, brought the wildest blood in
the Lowlands to the standard. And to crown all came
the Marquis of Douglas, who, as Lord Angus, had been
the travelling companion of Montrose's youth. The
prestige of the Bloody Heart had not wholly died even
in an age which had tried to bolt the door on the past,
and the vast Douglas lands in Clydesdale and Dumfries
promised a rich recruiting ground.

There were other allies to be gathered. At the
earliest opportunity the Master of Napier and Nathaniel
Gordon were dispatched Edinburghwards on a gaol de-
livery. From the prison of Linlithgow they released
Lord Napier and Stirling of Keir, and the ladies of the

---

[1] Guthry, 195. Metcalfe, *History of Renfrew* (1905).
[2] The house of Winton was always loyal and always on the losing side, and
came to final disaster in 1715. The Eglintons (paternally Setons) were more
worldly-wise.

Napier and Stirling families. Arrived within four miles of Edinburgh, they summoned the city in the king's name, and received the humble submission of a deputation from the town council. A money fine was offered, and it was explained that the city had been driven into rebellion against its will by the craft of a few seditious men. The plague, which was still raging, had sapped all civic valour, and Edinburgh was ready to promise anything for peace. The Tolbooth was full of royalists, and during the year death and sickness had raged in that noisome place. Crawford, Ogilvy, Reay, Irvine of Drum, Ogilvy of Powrie, and Wishart the chaplain were among those set free, and the released captives, white and gaunt as a bone, stumbled out into the sunlight. Wishart never forgot the experience. It made him, as he said, " a friend of prisoners for ever " ; in later years he could not enjoy a good meal at his episcopal table till he had sent part of it to the Tolbooth ; and he bore the marks of the rats' teeth to his grave. One captive they did not recover. The young Lord Graham was in the castle, and the castle was still in Covenant hands. The gallant boy refused an exchange, declaring that it would ill become one so young and useless to deprive his father of a single prisoner.[1]

Napier and Gordon had another mission to execute in the east. They carried a letter from Montrose to Drummond of Hawthornden, begging for a copy of his *Irene*, the pamphlet written in 1638 during Montrose's Covenanting days, that it might be printed and published " to the contentment of all His Majesty's good subjects." [2] He had already granted him a special protection for his house and property. The old poet promised to transcribe and send the paper, " since, by the mercy of God on your Excellency's victorious arms, the Golden Age is returned " ; but before it arrived Scotland was back in the age of iron.[3]

---

[1] Thomas Saintserf, in his dedication to the second marquis of his translation of the *Entertainments of the Course* (London, 1658). See Napier, II., 563.
[2] It was not published till it appeared in the folio edition of Drummond's works in 1711.
[3] Masson, *Drummond of Hawthornden*, 405.

By the 1st of September Napier and Gordon, with their released prisoners, were in the camp at Bothwell. On that day Sir Robert Spottiswoode, the king's secretary for Scotland, arrived with letters from Charles. He brought with him a patent, dated at Hereford on the 25th of June, creating Montrose lieutenant-governor and captain-general of Scotland.[1] The royal instructions were to join the Border earls and march with all haste to Tweed. As these had been issued before Alford and Kilsyth, they seemed to Montrose to have redoubled force, now that he was master of all Scotland. Besides, Home and Roxburgh had written pleading with him to come to Tweedside and add their spears to his standard. Every prospect seemed rosy, and Montrose dispatched a post to the king, announcing that he hoped speedily to cross the Border with 20,000 men. On the 3rd of September he held a great review of his troops in Bothwell haugh, when the royal commission was presented to the viceroy and handed for proclamation to Sir Archibald Primrose, the founder of the family of Rosebery. Montrose's first act under his new patent was to confer upon Alasdair the honour of knighthood. He had nobly earned it. The next four months of blundering in Argyll were to show how little of a general the Ulsterman was on his own account. Two years later he was to disappear from history, stabbed in the back in an obscure Irish fray. But as Montrose's chief brigadier he was worth an army, and his stand at Auldearn will live as long as feats of valour can stir the hearts of men.

As soon as the king's commission was received, Montrose, as viceroy of Scotland, took steps for the administration of the government. He had already in the king's name assured loyalists in the possession of lands which Argyll or the Estates had threatened.[2] He now issued proclamation to the chief towns, summoning a Parliament to be held in Glasgow on the 20th of October following, " for settling religion and peace, and

---

[1] *Hist. MSS. Comm.*, 2nd Report, 173.
[2] *e.g.*, he issued letters of assurance to Alan Maclean of Ardgour. *Highland Papers* (S.H.S.), I., 333–334.

freeing the oppressed subjects of those insupportable burdens they have groaned under this time bygone." He prepared also a statement which he probably intended to present to Parliament when it assembled.[1] It is on the lines of his Dumfries manifesto, but a fuller and clearer confession of faith. He repeats the justification of the National Covenant—the evils of an unnatural and enforced prelacy, under which ecclesiastics intermeddled with civil government, and " the life of the Gospel was stolen away by enforcing on the Kirk a dead service book." To every line of that Covenant he still adhered, but long ago its mission was accomplished. First at Berwick and then at Ripon the king had granted all their demands. Further no true Covenanter could go, for the cause of the Covenant was also the cause of king and country. All that had been done since had been alien to the true Covenant spirit, and every honest man must needs part company with its perverters. " We were constrained to suffer them to deviate without us, with the multitude misled by them, whose eyes they seal in what concerns religion, and whose hearts they steal away in what concerns loyalty." He expounds his own difficulties—" wrestling betwixt extremities "—till facts decided for him. The nobles had tasted the " sweetness of government," and they would not be content till they had destroyed " lawful authority and the liberty of the subject." The Kirk had coerced men into a blind obedience, a tyranny worse than papacy. He took up arms, he says, first, for national religion, " the restoration of that which our first reformers had " ; second, for the maintenance of the central authority, the king's ; and, third, for the " vindication of our nation from the base servitude of subjects who, like the Israelites, have their burdens doubled, but are not sensible of them." He answers his critics, especially those timorous souls who are " so stuffed with infidelity that they can believe nothing but what they see, and can commit nothing to

---

[1] The document is printed in *Mem. of M.*, I., 215, and Napier, I., App. III. It is in the elder Lord Napier's handwriting, but the context makes it clear that Montrose is speaking. Mr. Gardiner agrees with Mark Napier in assigning it to this period.

God." If he had used the services of Alasdair Macdonald, a "professed Papist," had not his opponents employed in Ireland, under Monro, the selfsame people? He repudiated the charge of blood-guiltiness. He had never "shed the blood of any but of such as were sent forth by them to shed our blood and take our lives," adding with a touch of the Covenanters' own idiom, "and what is done in the land it may sensibly seem to be the Lord's doing, in making a handful to overthrow multitudes." Freedom and toleration in religion, a strong central government, and a lighter taxation for the burdened people of Scotland—for these he had drawn the sword.

It was the appeal to his countrymen on which he hoped to build a civil authority to correspond to that which he had won in war. As an ideal of statescraft it was profound; as tactics, as a step in the political game, it was bound to fail. The appeal was unintelligible to all save a few, and the defence did not convince. The people of the Lowlands had lost friends and kinsmen in the Highland wars, their ears had been horrified with endless tales of pillage and violence, and at the back of every Lowland heart lay a jealousy and dislike of the Celt, whether Ulster or Scottish, as of a race they did not understand. To say that Monro had used similar troops in Ireland was no more convincing to most people than to urge that the clans had once fought bravely at Bannockburn for Scottish independence. To point to Argyll's barbarities in the Highlands as worse than any of Alasdair's doings was to miss the point of the grievance. To a Lowlander the victims in the first case were savages and aliens, and in the latter they were "kindly Scots." As for the king, there was still some loyal sentiment for him in Scotland, a clannish feeling, for had she not given to England the royal house? But the feeling was only sentimental, while Montrose's royalism was a reasoned appeal for a central authority, whatever name it might be given—an appeal which nobody, except perhaps Napier, understood. As for the Kirk, no doubt its encroachments were becoming a burden, but it had the terrible mastery over its people which is given by the

possession of the keys of heaven and hell. Before that
tyranny could be broken there were to be long years of
struggle and much shedding of innocent blood. Besides,
the Lowlands had no other voice or ear than the ministers. They were the sole interpreters, teachers, and
guides. No mere proclamation could break through
that plate-armour of defence to the starved and puzzled
souls behind it. The one argument of practical value
was the promise to reduce the grievous weight of taxation. But a Lowland burgher or peasant might well
have been pardoned for doubting whether Montrose,
with an army of hungry kerns to keep, would prove an
easier tax-collector. The remonstrance, while of the
highest value as a clue to Montrose's philosophy, shows
that he wholly misread the immediate political situation.
He could look for recruits only to those who were tired
of the domineering Kirk and jealous of the Covenant
leaders. Such were to be found among the nobles and
gentry alone,[1] and these, and the tenantry they could
command, were all that appeared in his camp at Bothwell.

Meanwhile that army which had fought under him
in so many battles was beginning to melt away. The
Highlanders wanted to get back to their homes. It was
their duty, for the families left behind had rarely food
for more than a week or two, and would starve if the
husbands and fathers did not return often to replenish
the pot. Miserably poor, war was a business to them,
and they had to deposit their winnings. They had
stayed on after Kilsyth, in the hope of the plunder of
Glasgow, but Glasgow was inviolate, and one or two of
them, who had tried to use the rich town as they considered it should be used, were now swinging from
Glasgow gibbets for their pains. Further, the £500
which the citizens had offered was not to be paid. The
town council, fearing lest the meeting of Parliament

---

[1] Here and there a minister may have been covertly or overtly on his side.
In the *Assembly Commission Records,* and in presbytery and burgh records, we
meet cases of ministers suspended or deposed for alleged sympathy with
Montrose. Most of them were no doubt unlucky time-servers, but there may
have been one or two sincere disciples.

would cost the city large sums, had begged to be let off
the contribution, and Montrose had consented. The
clans were disgusted, and began to trickle away. There
were other reasons. The Macleans must look after their
homes in Mull, or the Campbells would be avenging
Kilsyth. Clan Donald had still grudges to avenge on
Clan Diarmaid, which not even Inverlochy had satisfied.
There is no reason to blame the Highlanders unduly.
Organized Lowland warfare, such as Montrose now proposed, was a thing which they did not understand, and
which upset the whole system and tradition of their lives.
Alasdair alone deserves censure. He was an experienced
soldier, and knew something of the difficulties that lay
before his chief. But his knighthood and his new post
of captain-general of the clans under Montrose seem to
have turned his head. He proposed to himself a campaign in Argyll which should root the Campbells out of
the peninsula.[1] He promised to return, and no doubt
honestly meant it, but from the moment when he
marched off with half his Irishry and all the Highlanders, Montrose never saw his old lieutenant again.
Five hundred Ulstermen, under the gallant O'Cahan,
refused, to their eternal honour, to leave the royal
standard.

Douglas and Ogilvy had been already dispatched to
the Border to recruit, and on the 4th of September
Montrose broke up his camp at Bothwell and began his
advance towards Tweed. His plan was to march through
the Lothians, and then descend by one of the passes of
the Lammermoors to the country of Home and Roxburgh. But at the end of the first day he had to face a
defection more serious than Alasdair's. Aboyne had
been rapidly getting out of humour, and his ill-temper
was zealously fomented by Huntly, his father. He was
insulted because Crawford, instead of himself, had been
given the command of the cavalry. The return of Lord
Ogilvy had restored to Montrose his oldest comrade,
and to the Gordon it seemed that an Ogilvy was preferred before him. A narrative of the campaign by

---

[1] The Macdonnells of Antrim had always laid claim to Kintyre.

Sir William Rollo, which he had seen, was, in his view, insufficiently laudatory of his own doings, and Montrose refused to suppress it. Last and most important there was old Huntly, whose every letter upbraided his heir for alliance with an enemy of his house. The untamable perverseness of the Gordon blood triumphed over his loyalty to his king and his duty to his general. In spite of Ogilvy's appeals he marched off with all the Gordon horse and foot. Nathaniel Gordon alone remained; for him the comradeship in arms begun after Tippermuir was to end only with death.

II

Montrose traversed the moorland country of the Lothians, avoiding plague-stricken Edinburgh, to Cranstoun, south-east of Dalkeith. It was now Saturday, the 6th of September, and on the following day it was intended that Wishart should preach to the army. But news was received from Lord Erskine which changed the situation. David Leslie,[1] the future Lord Newark, and a soldier far abler than either Leven or Baillie, had, after the fall of Carlisle, taken his horse to the assistance of Leven at Hereford. He was then sent into the midlands in pursuit of the king, but the news of Kilsyth altered his plans. His men refused to continue the war in England while Scotland was defenceless, and, though his first intention was to take only half his force, he was soon compelled to take the whole 4,000. On 1st September the siege of Hereford was raised—it was the one direct result of Kilsyth in the king's favour—while Leslie was hastening with all speed to the north. Had the king's army been better handled he would never have reached the Border. There was one moment at Rotherham, as he himself admitted, when, if the adjacent royal forces had struck, he would have been destroyed.[2] But

---

[1] He was not, as some historians have stated, a relative of Leven, but a Fife man, the son of Leslie of Pitcairly.

[2] Clarendon, IX., 86.

CAMPAIGN OF PHILIPHAUGH

Montrose's March ———
Leslie's March ......- - -

0   5   10   15 20 25 30
English Miles

he passed unchallenged, and, collecting reinforcements
of foot from the garrisons of Newcastle and Berwick,
he crossed Tweed on the 6th of September. John
Middleton of Caldhame commanded his advance guard ;
he had served under Montrose at Aberdeen in the Bishops'
War, and was to live to receive an earldom and mis-
govern Scotland after the Restoration. Leslie followed
the coast road to the Lothians, his aim being to cut off
Montrose from the Highlands, and his plan to take
up position somewhere on the neck of land between
Forth and Clyde.

He had under him not less than 6,000 men. Of these
more than 5,000 were mounted troops—his own regiment, the regiments of Dalhousie, Eglinton, Middleton,
and Leven, Fraser's Dragoons,[1] Kirkcudbright's Dragoons, and Sir David Barclay's independent troop of
horse. He had picked up 800 foot on the way from the
regiments of Clydesdale, Tweeddale, Galloway, Montgomery, Strathearn, and Kenmure.[2] He had also acquired at Berwick a more doubtful increment, no less
than ten members of the Committee of Estates, most of
them fugitives after Kilsyth, like Argyll, Lindsay, and
Lanark.[3] But he did not suffer the committee to interfere with the conduct of his operations as it had done at
Kilsyth and was to do later at Dunbar. The crisis was
too sharp for a peripatetic debating society.

Lord Erskine advised a retreat beyond the Highland
Line while yet there was time, but Montrose refused. He
was bound by his duty to the king to carry relief to
England, and that at once. His problem was the old
one of how to raise an army, but to go north among
the clans again would mean an intolerable delay, and
he believed that he could achieve the same result on
the Border. Cavalry was his first need, for Aboyne's

---

[1] " Known, with Lawers' regiment of foot, to be the stoutest regiment in
the Scots army." *Memorie of the Somervilles*, II., 315.

[2] *A. P. S.*, Balfour's *Annales, The Army of the Covenant* (S.H.S.), I., Introd.
Sir Walter Scott's great-great-grandfather, Sir William Scott of Harden, was
lieutenant-colonel of the Tweeddale regiment. *Letters*, I., 391. Rushworth
(VI., 231) gives Leslie nine regiments of horse and two of dragoons.

[3] *Account of the Routing of the Scottish Rebels at Philiphauch*, etc. London,
Sept. 18, 1645.

defection had left him with scarcely a hundred troopers, most of them Lord Airlie's Ogilvys. He hoped for large levies as a consequence of Douglas's recruiting, and still more from Home and Roxburgh. His further plans we do not know—whether he intended to seek out and test the quality of David Leslie or to march boldly southward to the king. His immediate business was to get an army, so on the Saturday afternoon the royalists turned to their right and marched down Gala Water towards Tweedside. Next day, at Torwoodlee, Douglas and Ogilvy joined them with a large body of horse from Nithsdale and upper Clydesdale. The recruits were all lairds or lairds' sons, and their immediate retainers—a half-hearted and unstable crew, who had none of the old moss-trooping fire. Somewhere, too, on Gala Water, Linton arrived with his Peeblesshire troop, and his father, Traquair, rode over to visit the viceroy. He came in all likelihood to spy out the nakedness of the land, with results which we shall see.

Marching slowly down Tweed, Montrose reached Kelso on the 8th or 9th. It was the appointed rendezvous, but he found no sign of Home or Roxburgh. He waited for a day, and then he heard ominous news. The Border earls were with Leslie—prisoners, so ran their own story, captured by Middleton and his advance guard. It was a tale which common opinion scouted, and indeed it is inconceivable that two powerful nobles, in their own countryside, twenty miles from Leslie's line of march, and with complete knowledge of his coming, should not have been able to escape if they had wished it. It is far more probable that, knowing Leslie's strength and Montrose's predicament, they sought security by putting themselves in the enemy's power.[1]

To tarry at Kelso was mere folly, so Montrose turned wearily up Tweed. The spring he had most counted on was dry. Douglas held out hopes of raising the westlands—vain hopes, for in no quarter of Scotland was the power of the ministers so great; he rated the pres-

---

[1] Wishart, ch. xv. See Gardiner, *Civil War*, II., 352.

tige of the Douglas name higher than was warranted by facts. Montrose accepted the plan, for in any case it would lead him back to the hills to which he had always turned his eyes for help. He marched to Jedburgh, but there was nothing to be looked for from the Kerrs, whose chief, Lothian, was a Covenanting general. Then he entered the Scott country, but Buccleuch was with Leslie, and the old raiding spirit was dying in the glens. The successors of Wat of Harden and Dickie of Dryhope were a peaceable folk, and brawls at a fair or a clipping were their only form of war. He would have fared better among the Armstrongs and Elliots farther south, who, as Cromwell was to discover, were still good men of their hands.[1] There was another reason for his failure in the presence of his Irish contingent, for Border memories are long, and a hundred years before Hertford, in his invasion of Scotland, had used Irish in his work of destruction, and these Irish had taken no prisoners.[2]

During the march Sir Robert Spottiswoode wrote a letter [3]—never posted—to Digby, who was still nursing his vain dreams. He told him of Montrose's desperate plight, and upbraided him for not detaining Leslie in England. He asked what had become of the promised cavalry. " You little imagine the difficulties my lord marquis hath here to wrestle with. The overcoming of the enemy is the least of them ; he hath more to do with his seeming friends. . . . All these were great disheartenings to any other but to him, whom nothing of this kind can amaze. With the small forces he hath presently with him he is resolved to pursue David Leslie, and not suffer him to grow stronger." Digby at the moment, and for a fortnight later, was full of hope and confidence, which even the disaster of Rowton Heath could not shake. Stories were reaching him of a mysteri-

---

[1] *Scotland and the Commonwealth* (S.H.S.), xix. *Scotland and the Protectorate* (S.H.S.), xxxiv., etc.

[2] Hertford wrote to Henry VIII. : " For the better execution thereof I sent with them 100 Irishmen, for the Borderers will not now willingly burn their neighbours." *Hamilton Papers*, II., 406 ; *Cal. S. P., Dom.* (Henry VIII.), V., 523 ; *The Border Elliots*, 67.

[3] The letter is in Napier, II., 572–573, and *Mem. of M.*, II., 233–234.

ous fight in Westmoreland, in which Crawford and Ogilvy were said to have annihilated Leslie. Soon he was to hear from Byron that the soldiers in Poyntz's army were celebrating a great victory which had shattered Montrose's power.[1] The first tale was false, the second only too true.

On the afternoon of the 12th of September Montrose arrived at the gate of the hill country, the flat of Philiphaugh, under the little burgh of Selkirk, where the two glens of Yarrow and Ettrick meet. Just below the junction of the streams, on the left bank of Ettrick, is a level meadow a quarter of a mile wide, with the water on one side and a rugged hill on the other. Here he fixed his camp, and placed the few guns which had been part of the booty of Kilsyth. It was protected on the south and east by the Ettrick, on the north by the hills, and on the west by Yarrow and the steep wood called the Hareheadshaw. The position was a strong one, but as the army did not expect a battle it was very loosely held. There was no premonition of immediate danger. Leslie was believed to be far away on the Forth, and, in Sir Robert Spottiswoode's letter to Digby, Montrose was said to be resolute to chase him. He did not know that the pursued had become the pursuer.

At Gladsmuir, in East Lothian, late on the 11th of September, Leslie had received a letter revealing the whereabouts and the weakness of the royalist force. Popular tradition made Traquair the sender, and there is no reason to disbelieve a tale so consistent with the character of a family which, during the Covenant, as during the later Jacobite wars, was uniformly treacherous. Traquair had also shown his hand by sending a message to his son, Lord Linton, to withdraw him and his troops from Montrose's camp.[2] Leslie, when he got the news, at once changed his plans. He marched straight down Gala Water, crossed the ridge at Rink

---

[1] Gardiner, *Civil War*, II., 347.

[2] For the conduct of the Jacobite Traquair, see *Memoirs of John Murray of Broughton* (S.H.S., 1898). Patrick Gordon says that Traquair recalled his son four days before the battle; Wishart, with whom Guthry agrees, says " on the very night."

by the old Edinburgh-Selkirk road, and forded Tweed
below the Rae Weil.[1]   Late on the night of the 12th he
reached the hamlet of Sunderland, which stood on the
peninsula formed by the junction of Tweed and Ettrick.
There to his relief he had news of the enemy.   Some
pickets, under Charteris of Amisfield, were in the village,
and these were driven out with a few casualties.   Leslie
was now less than three miles from the royalist camp.
He had caught his quarry, but only by the skin of his
teeth, for another day would have seen Montrose safe
in the hills.

A little trenching was done on the eastern and
western flanks before Montrose's small army settled
down for the night.   A mounted patrol was sent out
under Ogilvy of Powrie, and returned to report that all
was quiet; they were probably impressed local men,

---

[1] Sir Walter Scott, in his *Minstrelsy of the Scottish Border* (II., 21), apparently
following local tradition, makes Leslie encamp on the night of the 12th at
Melrose, and he is followed by Mr. Mowbray Morris (*Montrose*, 1892).   For
several reasons I find it difficult to accept this view.   (1) Leslie was at Gladsmuir when he received the news from Traquair, or whoever sent it.   He knew
his enemy, and his object was to cut off his retreat into the hills; therefore he
must have chosen the shortest route to the opening of the hills at Selkirk.   He
left Gladsmuir the day that Montrose left Jedburgh, so he had no time to lose.
If he had crossed by Soutra, and marched down Leader Water, he would have
passed Melrose; but we know that he came by Gala (Wishart, ch. xvi.).   To
follow Gala to its foot below Galashiels, and then ford Tweed and encamp at
Melrose, would have been a perfectly aimless detour.   Further, it seems certain
that Montrose arrived at Selkirk early on the afternoon of the 12th, and his
presence there would be known in Galashiels, and communicated to Leslie on
his arrival.   The easiest way from Galashiels was over the Rink hill to Sunderland.   (2) Gordon of Ruthven says definitely that Leslie was at Sunderland
on the night of the 12th, and if so he could not have been at Melrose unless he
had left Melrose early in the afternoon and forded Ettrick.   But in that case
Montrose would have got word of him.   Wishart does not mention Sunderland;
he says that the Covenanters spent the night five miles from Selkirk, which
is not decisive.   But, in describing the turning movement executed by
Leslie's 2,000, he writes "quos adversa amnis ripa hostes transmiserant."
Now they would not have crossed Ettrick, if they had been coming from
Melrose, till just at the battlefield, and Wishart's words indicate a crossing
at the beginning of the morning's march.   One Covenant account (*A More
Perfect and Particular Relation*, etc., Haddington, Sept. 16, 1645, cited by
Lang) says that Leslie encamped within three miles of the enemy.   (3) Local
tradition seems also to point to the Galashiels-Sunderland route.   In the
preposterous ballad of the "Battle of Philiphaugh" (Scott's *Minstrelsy*, II.,
26–30), Leslie is said to have sent his right wing round Linglie Hill, the height
between Ettrick and Yair on Tweed.   Such a movement, absurd as it is, would
have been impossible to a force coming from Melrose, and shows the popular
notion of the Covenant march.   The subject has been fully discussed by Lieut.-
Colonel the Hon. Fitzwilliam Elliot in his *The Trustworthiness of Border Ballads*
(1906), where the conclusion arrived at is that of my text.

maybe Traquair's tenants, and they may have taken their commander where nothing could be seen or heard. The king's captain-general left the posting of the pickets to his officers, and retired himself with his cavalry leaders to a lodging in the West Port of Selkirk.[1] Here for most of the night he busied himself with dispatches to the king. He had many heavy matters on his mind, and was suffering from one of those fits of bodily and mental languor which come at times upon the greatest commanders. No doubt he had given instructions that, except for the most urgent business, he was not to be disturbed. The night had fallen moonless and dark as pitch. Some time before midnight Charteris of Amisfield arrived with his story of having been driven out of Sunderland village. His account must have been confused, and the incident was apparently regarded by the headquarters staff as a drunken brawl among Charteris' troopers or a brush with hostile country-folk [2]—at any rate not of sufficient moment to break in upon the privacy of the captain-general.

The morning of the 13th dawned with one of those thick autumnal fogs, which in the valley bottoms in the early hours prevent a man seeing three yards before him. Scouts were sent out again at the first light, and reported that the country was clear. So it was to north, south, and west, on all sides except the east, the direction of Sunderland, and Amisfield's report from that quarter had already been discounted. The army in the haugh cooked a leisurely meal, and Montrose, in his Selkirk lodging, with only an hour or two of sleep behind him, sat down to breakfast.

Meantime Leslie had launched his thunderbolt. He had divided his forces into two parts, and with one marched swiftly up the left bank of Ettrick. The other, 2,000 strong, which included Kirkcudbright's Dragoons,

[1] Craig Brown, *Hist. of Selkirkshire*, I., 185, etc. As a proof of the attitude of the local peasantry towards Montrose, it is said that the woman of the house was busy putting a sheep's head into a pot when the general passed the kitchen door, and was heard to exclaim that she wished it was Montrose's head, for in that case she would be careful to hold down the lid.

[2] Selkirk was notoriously hostile to Montrose, Pringle of Blindlee being almost the only recorded royalist in the shire.

under the command of James Agnew of Lochnaw,[1] had crossed that water, and by way of Will's Nick had reached the Selkirk road.   The royalists, having finished their meal, were assembling for parade, when through the thinning mist came the rush of Leslie's horse.

To Montrose in the West Port arrived his scout-master, Captain Blackadder, with the shattering news. He flung himself on his horse, and with Airlie, Crawford, and Napier, galloped to his army.   He found the field in confusion.   Douglas's bonnet-lairds, in spite of their gallant leader, had fled at the first shot.   The 500 Ulster-men, however, were fighting a desperate fight in their shallow trenches.   Montrose collected a hundred troopers, and charged Leslie so madly that for a moment he drove back the whole Covenant horse.   But 600 men taken by surprise, and with no advantage of position, cannot for long do battle with 6,000.   Leslie's other division harassed the royalist right flank with musketry fire from beyond the stream, and presently had forded Ettrick and were attacking it from behind.   The Irish were beaten out of their trenches into a second position, the folds of Philip-haugh farm.[2]   Again and again the Covenant troopers charged, only to be driven back by the heroic Ulstermen ; again and again Montrose's hundred cut their way deep into the enemy's ranks.   Philiphaugh was less a battle than a surprise and a massacre.   Soon only fifty horse were left, and of the Irish more than 400 were dead. The remnant under their adjutant, Stewart, were in-duced to surrender on a promise of quarter.[3]

[1] *Hereditary Sheriffs of Galloway*, II., 26.

[2] Guthrie, 203.   Leslie to Leven in *The Great Victories*, London (1645) (Bodleian).

[3] The authorities for Philiphaugh are Wishart (ch. xvi.), who was probably an eyewitness, Gordon of Ruthven (156, etc.), and Guthry (201, etc.).   The various Covenanting newsletters (*A More Perfect and Particular Relation*, etc., *Montrose Routed in Tividale*, *The Great Victories*, etc.), exaggerate the numbers on the royalist side ; these were probably as stated in the text, except that it is difficult to believe that Douglas had the 1,200 with which Gordon of Ruthven credits him.   Leslie's own account to Leven puts the royalist force at 2,000, and adds : " I never fought with better horsemen and against more resolute foot."   He referred, after Dunbar, to Philiphaugh as an easy victory (*Ancrum and Lothian Correspondence*, II., 297).   For some of the country stories about it see Russell, *Reminiscences of Yarrow*, and Craig Brown, *History of Selkirkshire.* The ballad on the subject is probably an eighteenth-century production, and of no use as evidence.   The ancient father who guided Leslie must have been

Montrose fought with a gallantry and a desperation worthy of Alasdair, and but for his friends would have died on the field. Lord Douglas and Sir John Dalziel pled with him to take the chance of flight, urging that so long as he lived the king's cause need not go down. He allowed himself to be constrained. With about thirty others, including the two Napiers, Lord Erskine, and Lord Fleming, as well as Dalziel and Douglas, he cut a road to the west and repulsed a feeble attempt at pursuit. The little party galloped up Yarrow vale, and at Broadmeadows took the drove-road across Minchmoor to Tweeddale. As they disappeared into the green hills, with them disappeared the dream of a new and happier Scotland. Montrose's cycle of victories had proved like the fairy gold which vanishes in a man's hand. The year of miracles was ended.

at least 116 at the time, for he boasted of having been at Solway Moss, which was fought a century before. He was a prophet as well as an ancient, for he added that he had been at " curst Dunbar," which was not fought till five years later. The ballad was written to glorify Buccleuch's regiment—" The Scotts out o'er the Graemes they ran "—which they certainly did not, for very few of Leslie's foot can have come into action.

CHAPTER XIV

AFTER PHILIPHAUGH

(*September 1645–September 1646*)

> O truth of Christ,
> O most dear rarity,
> O most rare Charity,
> Where dwell'st thou now ?
> In the Valley of Vision ?
> On Pharaoh's throne ?
> On high with Nero ?
> With Timon alone ?
>
> CARMINA BURANA
> (*Miss Helen Waddell's translation*).

I

MONTROSE did not draw rein till he reached the old house of Traquair, whose grey and haunted walls still stand among the meadows where the Quair burn flows to Tweed. Its lord shut his door on the fugitive ; his welcome was reserved for the conquering Leslie, when, with Argyll and Lothian, he arrived later in pursuit. He did not cross Tweed at the bridge of Peebles, but rode up the right bank by the Sware to Manor, and thus to Stobo by the Glack.[1] Thence the company pushed on to Biggar in Clydesdale, where they spent the night, and long before the next daybreak were in the saddle and heading for the north, guided by

1645 September

---

[1] Wishart makes him halt for the night at Peebles, but as that ancient burgh is only sixteen miles from the battlefield, and as the fighting was over by twelve o'clock, it is difficult to believe that the fugitives stayed more than a short space to rest. They probably rode on fifteen miles to Biggar before halting for the night. *Cf.* J. W. Buchan, *History of Peeblesshire*, III., 472. Tweeddale as a shire was far more royalist than Selkirk. Peebles had some of its burgesses serving with Montrose, and many of the gentry, like Tait of the Pirn, Porteous of Hawkshaw, Veitch of Dawyck, and Murray of Elibank were on his side. The county furnished the prototype of Sir William Worthy in Allan Ramsay's *Gentle Shepherd*. Pennecuik, *Tweeddale*, 99.

Dalziel, who was now in his own countryside. Fugitives were picked up by the way, including an Ulsterman, who had wrapped the colours of the foot round his breast, and, having found a horse, caught up Montrose and restored to him one of the standards. The other, the cavalry colours, was carried by Kinnoull's brother, William Hay, into England, and months afterwards was brought to Montrose in the north. At a ford of Clyde they met, to their joy, old Airlie and Crawford, who had probably taken the route by Megget and upper Tweed, and had collected on the road some of Douglas's fleeing troopers. Somehow the party made their way through the midlands, and by the 19th were safe in the Perthshire hills.

The Scots troops in Newcastle entertained the mayor and aldermen to a dinner to celebrate the victory of Philiphaugh.[1] Elsewhere the celebrations were of a grimmer kind, for now came the harvest of the triumphant Covenant. It began on the day of the battle, when 300 Irishwomen, with their children, were butchered on the field. Those who wish to sup deep on horrors can find the details in Patrick Gordon. The cooks and horseboys also perished to the number of some 200. The remnant of the Irish under Stewart had surrendered on terms, but the ministers who accompanied Leslie remonstrated against the Lord's work being hindered by a foolish clemency. They argued that quarter had been granted to Stewart alone, and not to his men; Leslie professed being himself convinced by this shameless quibble, and the unarmed Irish were cut down as they stood, or shot next morning in the courtyard of Newark castle.[2] O'Cahan and another officer, Lachlan, were

---

[1] *Army of the Covenant* (S.H.S.), I., 285.

[2] The authorities for the slaughter of the Irish are Wishart (ch. xvi.), Gordon of Ruthven (160), and Guthry (203). These are, of course, hostile sources, but Leslie in his letter to Leven says that " all Montrose's forces that were Irish or Highlanders (were) killed upon the place (*The Great Victories*, etc., 1645). The reader will find the little that can be said in extenuation in Dr. Mitchell's introduction to the *Commission of the General Assembly Records* (S.H.S.), I. Leslie does not appear to have been a man of scrupulous honour. A similar case at the surrender of Dunavertie, in Kintyre (Guthry, 243), is denied by Sir James Turner, who was present (*Memoirs*, 238). Turner was naturally anxious to defend his general, but on the other side there is the

spared for the moment, only to be hanged later in Edinburgh without a trial. Stewart was also destined for death, but was fortunate enough to escape to Montrose.

The zeal of the Covenant against the daughters of Heth was not satiated by the butchery of Philiphaugh. Many had escaped, and were slaughtered singly as they wandered among the moors of Tweed and Clyde. In most county histories the slaying is ascribed to the infuriated country people, but for this there is no evidence. The Lowland peasantry have never had a taste for such brutalities, and the murders were probably the work of the soldiers of the Covenant, who beat the hills for royalists, as Lag's dragoons were to beat them forty years later for Covenanters.[1] One large party of the poor creatures was brought to Leslie's camp at Linlithgow. They were flung over the bridge of Avon, and were either drowned in the river or stabbed with the pikes of the soldiers who lined the banks.[2] The records of the Irish rebellion hold no more horrid cruelties. The inspiration was not Leslie's; it came from the fierce bigots who accompanied him. Sometimes the soldiers sickened of the work, and asked their clerical advisers, as Leslie asked Nevoy at Dunavertie, "Mr. John, have you not once gotten your fill of blood?"[3]

evidence in the action raised after the Restoration against Argyll by the Macdougals of Dunolly (*A. P. S.*, VII., 337), and Turner himself records an instance of Leslie's bad faith towards Alasdair's father at the siege of Dunyveg in Islay (*Memoirs*, 48). *Cf.* also Montereul (Montreuil), *Correspondence* (S.H.S.), II., 103. The dishonouring of paroles and promises of quarter seems to have been the official creed of the Covenant. In the " Interloquitur of Parliament " of January 10, 1646, occurs this startling sentence : " If this defence of quarter be sustained, then the whole nation, especially the Estates of Parliament, does violate the oath of the Covenant, and the oath of the Parliament anent the prosecuting and censuring of malignants, opposers of the Covenant " (*A. P. S.*, VI., i., 249).

[1] The Deid Wife, a hill near Stobo, in Tweeddale, commemorates one such slaying.

[2] Gordon of Ruthven, 160. Sir George Mackenzie, *Vindication of the Government in Scotland* (1691), 20. Wishart, ch. xvii. (he gives the story without mentioning the place).

[3] Guthry, 243. Nevoy, a nephew of Mr. Andrew Cant, was the minister of Newmilns, and Loudoun's chaplain. He was in the affair at Mauchline in June 1648, and after the Restoration was banished to Holland. He had a part in revising the Scots metrical version of the Psalms, and turned the Song of Solomon into Latin verse.

For these barbarities, sanctioned and inspired by the
Kirk, there can be no defence. It is hard to understand
the view taken by some apologists that the Irish were
nameless savages, who by their crimes had forfeited all
consideration from mankind. It is a royalist historian
who has left the most hostile account of them. " The
Irish in particular were too cruel ; for it was everywhere
observed they did ordinarily kill all they could be master
of, without any motion of pity, or any consideration of
humanity. Nay, it seemed to them there were no dis-
tinctions between a man and a beast, for they killed
men ordinarily with no more feeling of compassion, and
with the same careless neglect that they kill a hare or
capon for their supper. And they were also without all
shame, most brutally given to uncleanness and filthy
lust ; as for excessive drinking, when they came where
it might be had there were no limits to their beastly
appetites, as for godless avarice and merciless oppression
and plundering of the poor labourer. Of these two
crying sins the Scots were as guilty as they." [1] It is a
grave indictment, but it could be written of most armies
of the time, and Patrick Gordon, who, as a decent Aber-
donian, disliked the rude western clans, was a stern
critic. No doubt it was brutal warfare, and in an army
of volunteers discipline must have been hard to enforce.
The Irish, who were mainly Scottish Macdonalds, slew
fiercely in battle, but so did the Covenant troops at
Philiphaugh and Carbisdale, so did the Campbells when
Argyll carried fire and sword through the north, and so
would have the Covenanters in the first Bishops' War if
Montrose had not restrained them. On at least two
occasions, Aberdeen and Inverlochy, they gave little or
no quarter, but there is no evidence that they murdered
in cold blood prisoners who surrendered after an action.
Nor is there any record, except for the sack of Aberdeen,
of the slaughter of women which stains the fair fame of
their opponents, both Covenanters and Cromwellians.
Our evidence shows that they were cheerful ruffians, who
loved fighting for fighting's sake, and cracked jokes in

[1] Gordon of Ruthven, 161.

the thick of a battle. As for the women, no doubt they were often concubines rather than wives, and no doubt they stole; but marriage lines were not universal in the Covenant's armies, and Leven's female followers thieved like daws.[1] Nor can we place the two sets of outrages in different moral categories, because the Covenanters were inspired by a religious creed. It makes small difference in the guilt of murder whether the murderer slays because his blood is hot in battle and he likes it, or whether he massacres at leisure because he is playing at being an early Israelite. The motive of both clergy and laity—and their only defence—was naked fear, and there is no such begetter of cruelty. Legends, born partly of the Irish rebellion and partly of rumours from the north, had magnified the Irish into monsters of terror; the same rumours were to be rife later about Cromwell's English soldiers [2]—with more reason, perhaps, for some of them had been at Wexford and Drogheda. Also the theocracy knew that it was fighting for its life.

The roll of captives was long. Some of Montrose's closest friends, like Lord Ogilvy, Sir Robert Spottiswoode, Sir William Rollo, and Nathaniel Gordon, were in enemy hands, having surrendered on promise of quarter. Leslie marched slowly through the Lothians towards Glasgow, where a provisional committee dealt with the prisoners. Meantime the two Irish officers, O'Cahan and Lachlan, had been hanged on the castle hill of Edinburgh—the last we shall hear of two very gallant gentlemen. The royalist leaders were all reserved for death, though the lay members of the court were disposed to be merciful. On the 20th of October, on the date and in the place which Montrose had appointed for the Parliament, the Committee of the Estates sat in judgment. The first to be dealt with was Sir William Rollo, whose brother had married Argyll's sister. For all his lameness he had never left Montrose's side, and

---

[1] Nicholas to Rupert, July 11, 1645, cited by Gardiner, *Civil War*, II., 263 *n.*
[2] Douglas, *Cromwell's Scotch Campaigns*, 33. Whitelocke, *Memorials*, III., 224, etc.

he had been one of his most trusted brigadiers. He was beheaded at the Mercat Cross on the 28th. On the following day there died Sir Philip Nisbet, who had fought with Rupert and with Montrose on the English Borders, and young Ogilvy of Inverquharity, a boy in his teens, a " lovely young youth," said the Glasgow bailie who presided at his execution.[1] The lay Covenanters had their scruples over these executions, and Mr. Robert Baillie remembered with disquiet that " to this day no man in England has been executed for bearing arms against the Parliament." [2] But the ministers were inexorable. " The work gangs bonnily on," was their comment.[3] Only by blood could the wrath of the strange deity they worshipped be appeased.

Owing to a raid threatened by Montrose the rest of the executions were postponed. They began again in St. Andrews after Christmas. The Kirk was in terror lest Parliament should be too merciful, and appeals flowed in from synods and presbyteries. Galloway prayed that the " sword of justice may be impartially drawn against those persons now in bonds who have lifted up their hands against the Lord, the sworn Covenant, and this afflicted Kirk." " We need not lay before your honours," said the voice of Dumfries, " what the Lord calls for at your hands in the point of justice, nor what you owe unto the many thousands of His people." " We are confident," wrote the gentle ministers of the Merse, " that your hearts will not faint nor your hands fail until you have cut off the horns of the wicked." Wariston excelled himself, for he proved to his own satisfaction that past lukewarmness in bringing malefactors to justice " had provoked God's two great servants against them, the sword and the pestilence, which has ploughed up the land with deep furrows." [4]

---

[1] Wishart, ch. xviii. Gordon of Ruthven, 167. Guthry, 208. Napier, II., 589.   [2] *Letters and Journals*, II., 322.

[3] Guthry attributes the saying to Mr. David Dickson, but one would fain believe him mistaken. The minister of Irvine, philosopher and poet, and professor of divinity first at Glasgow and then at Edinburgh, was not of Nevoy's school. His politics were more of the stamp of Mr. Robert Baillie's.

[4] Balfour, III., 324, etc. *Mem. of M.*, 245, etc. *Hist. MSS. Comm.*, 2nd Report, 175.

The delay, according to the Commission of the General
Assembly, was " displeasing unto the supreme judge of
the world, and grievous unto the hearts of the Lord's
people."

The Lord's people were soon to be comforted, for
the Estates set to work in earnest. But meantime
one of their chief victims escaped. Lord Ogilvy could
look for no mercy, for his family were the pet aversion
of Argyll, and during his short three weeks of liberty
he had been the right hand of the king's captain-general.
But he was a cousin of Lindsay and akin, on the maternal
side, to the Hamiltons, so he was permitted the last
consolation of a visit from his mother, his wife, and his
sister. He was sick in bed when the ladies were admitted in the dusk of a December evening. Adopting
Lady Nithsdale's device of a later day, his sister put
on his nightcap and got into his bed, while he dressed
himself in her clothes. When the guards entered, they
found three tearful women taking farewell of the doomed
prisoner, and conducted them to the prison gate. Horses
were waiting close at hand, and Ogilvy galloped across
Fife to join Inchbrakie in Menteith. Argyll would have
visited his wrath on the heroic lady, but the Hamilton
influence was strong enough to save her from punishment.

There was no hope for the others. They were tried,
not as the law enjoined by their peers or by the whole
Parliament, but by a self-appointed committee. Some
of the judges voted with qualifications, but the verdict
was certain. Hartfell indeed was pardoned. He was
disliked by the Hamiltons, and Argyll owed them a tit-
for-tat for their clemency towards the Ogilvys. On
January 20, 1646, the " Maiden," which had been
brought from Dundee, was set up at the cross of St.
Andrews, and the ancient city saw again " the auld rusty
lass linking at a bluidy hairst." [1] That day Nathaniel
Gordon, Andrew Guthrie—a son of the Bishop of Moray
—and Sir Robert Spottiswoode paid the last penalty.
Three days later died William Murray, a boy of nineteen,

[1] *Rob Roy*, ch. xxix.

whom the half-hearted pleas of his Covenanting brother,
Tullibardine, could not save.[1] Mr. Andrew Cant and
Mr. Robert Blair attended the prisoners in their last
hours, and found a penitent in Nathaniel Gordon, who
was accordingly released on the scaffold from an old
sentence of excommunication; for that stout adventurer had a good many dark patches in his career.[2] But
with the others the ministers did not succeed. Andrew
Guthrie declared that he could not conceive a greater
honour than to meet an honourable death in so just a
cause. The boy, William Murray, confessed his private
sins, but denied that he was a traitor; his death, he
said, was a new distinction for the house of Tullibardine.

The case of Sir Robert Spottiswoode had given qualms
to many of his judges. He was an old man; he was a
learned lawyer and a ripe scholar; he had been Lord
President of the Court of Session; he was a non-com-
batant, and had surrendered on a promise of quarter to
Lanark, whom he had succeeded as the king's secretary
for Scotland. There was nothing in his life which his
enemies could cavil at. While the Covenant still kept
up a pretence of royalism and legality, his execution was
plain murder. He was not permitted to read an address
from the scaffold,[3] and replied to the importunities of
Mr. Robert Blair that his blasphemous outpourings were
abominable to God. His last words were: " Merciful
Jesus, gather my soul unto Thy saints and martyrs, who
have run before me in this race."

The night before his death Sir Robert wrote a letter

---

[1] Murray was charged, among other things, with the murder of the minister
of Kirkton, near Hawick, after Philiphaugh (*A. P. S.*, VI., i., 526). How he
found time, while a fugitive from the battlefield, to kill a minister is one of the
minor mysteries of the period.

[2] A pamphlet, *Treason and Rebellion*, etc. (London: Bostock, 1646), gives,
in two letters from St. Andrews, an account of Nathaniel Gordon's edifying
end and the impenitence of the others. It makes Gordon repent of his politics,
but Wishart (ch. xix.) says that, in signing his confession, he declared that
" if there was anything in that document derogatory to the king and his
authority, he utterly disowned it." On a matter like this Wishart could
scarcely be mistaken; if the truth had been otherwise he would not have
dared to suppress it. The process against Gordon is in *Hist. MSS. Comm.*,
2nd Report, 174.

[3] The address is printed in his grandson's edition of his *Practicks of the Laws
of Scotland*, and as an appendix to the 1819 edition of Wishart.

of farewell to Montrose,[1] which breathes a spirit of
Christian forbearance unhappily lacking in those who
had the name of religion always on their lips. He commends to the viceroy's care his orphan children and
nephews, and hopes to do more for the king's cause by his
death than by his life. " One thing I most humbly recom-
mend to your Excellence that, as you have always done
hitherto, so you will continue by fair and gentle carriage
to win the people's affection for their prince, rather than to
imitate the barbarous inhumanity of your adversaries."
The advice was nobly followed. There were no reprisals
on the Covenant prisoners confined in the castle of Blair.
" Never," ran Montrose's address to his troops, " shall
they induce us to rival their crimes, or seek to outdo
them except in valour and renown." In a great civil
struggle neither side has a monopoly of the virtues.
There were many in the Covenant ranks in whom the
fire of religious faith had burned up all human fears,
and who were to give honourable proof of the manhood which was in them. It was a time of darkness
and suffering, when men's minds were turning from the
bleak world of sense to the dream of a better world
beyond the grave, and in such seasons the homely virtues
on which depends the conduct of our mortal life are apt
to be forgotten. This forgetfulness was most marked in
those who lived most constantly in the contemplation
of a promised immortality ; and in the matter of human
charity and mercy there can be little comparison for the
unbiased historian between the two parties. Montrose's army was guilty of acts of cruelty in hot blood,
but never at its worst did it approach the consistent,
deadly barbarity of the Kirk and the Estates. Twenty
years later, when the Covenant was the losing side, and
the fanatics who now ruled in Scotland had been driven
to the mosses, there must have been many quiet, old-
fashioned folk in the land, who, casting back their
memories to the days after Philiphaugh, saw in the

---

[1] The letter, from the *Spottiswoode Papers*, is reprinted in *Mem. of M.*, II.,
254. Ewen Cameron of Lochiel visited Spottiswoode in prison, and that visit
was the turning-point of his life (*Memoirs of Locheill*, 76–82).

change the slow grinding of the mills of God. In one
respect the later persecution, bad and indefensible as it
was, fell short in grossness of the earlier, for its per-
petrators in their evil work did not profane the name of
the meek gospel of Christ.

II

For Montrose defeat was only a spur to fresh effort.
The flexible steel of his courage could not be bent or
broken. From his refuge in Atholl he sent Erskine to
recruit in Mar, and Douglas and Airlie to raise the
royalists of Angus. He made a further effort to get
into touch with Alasdair, and wrote again to Digby,
begging for horse. In Atholl the country-folk were
busy with the late harvest, but the name of the viceroy
was a spell, and 400 followed him. But his principal
aim, as ever, was the Gordon cavalry. He hastened
over the Grampians, and early in October was at Drumminor castle, near Strathbogie, where Aboyne, his late
grievances apparently forgotten, joined him with 1,500
foot and 300 horse. A less welcome recruit appeared in
the person of the mischievous Lord Lewis. There followed news of the father. After Kilsyth Huntly had
removed himself from the Strathnaver bogs, and was
now at his castle of Gight. He sent Montrose a tepid
message of good wishes, and spoke nobly of what he and
his clan would still do for the king. For the moment
it looked as if the chief of the Gordons had learned
wisdom in exile.

Meanwhile Middleton, with 800 of Leslie's horse, had
marched north to the Aberdeenshire lowlands, and was
now lying at Turriff. Montrose had two alternatives
before him. He could attack Middleton with his new
army and settle with him before turning to Leslie.
Such a course would protect the Gordon lands, and
might keep Huntly in good humour. On the other hand,
his friends were prisoners in Glasgow, and unless he
rescued them forthwith they would perish. Leslie,
too, was the more formidable foe, and it was always

Montrose's habit to take the greater danger first. Besides, Leslie lay between him and the Border, and on the Border he still cherished vain dreams of meeting the king. Accordingly he gave marching orders for the south.

Lewis Gordon, with such of his clan as he could induce to follow him, deserted on the second morning. Aboyne remained for another day's march, but peremptory letters arrived from his father to recall him. Huntly's insane jealousy had revived, and he would neither fight himself nor permit his men to fight under another leader. Montrose sent Lord Reay and young Irvine of Drum to reason with him, but they were unable to shake his purpose. The precious days were slipping past in this barren diplomacy, and on the 22nd of October Montrose, then at the Castleton of Braemar, decided to advance without the Gordons. That night he lay in Glenshee, and on the 23rd was on Lochearnside, where he may have heard that the first executions of his friends had taken place. He was momentarily cheered by a message from Aboyne that he hoped soon to join him, and, as he waited for the Gordons, Ogilvy of Powrie appeared with other news. The king had at last made a desperate effort to fulfil his promise, and on the 14th of October Digby and Langdale had set out from Welbeck with 1,500 horse. Montrose was summoned to join hands with them on the Border, and he at once sent off word to Huntly and Aboyne. But, as he waited, there presently arrived melancholy tidings. On the 15th Digby and Langdale had scattered Poyntz's infantry at Sherburn, but were in turn surprised and driven north in confusion to Skipton. Digby himself, with Nithsdale and Carnwath, resolved to make a wild dash for the Border, and, in spite of a defeat at Carlisle, pushed on across Esk with a small party of horse. On the 22nd or 23rd he was as far north as Dumfries, but he could not stay. He had no news of Montrose, and far too much news of Leslie ; he began his retreat, his men deserted into the Cumberland hills, and he himself was compelled to flee to the Isle of Man. On the day that

Montrose left Braemar, Digby's raid had come to an inglorious end.

Montrose's one object was now to prevent further executions, so he marched south into the Lennox, where lay his own lands of Mugdock, now transferred by Parliament to Argyll. He had a force of some 1,500, mostly Atholl men and Farquharsons, including 300 horse raised by Erskine and Ogilvy, and his appearance so near Glasgow did indeed procure a postponement of the bloody work at the Mercat Cross. He took up his quarters at Buchanan on Lochlomondside—then the seat of the Covenanting Sir George Buchanan,[1] but now the home of Montrose's descendants—and for a week or so threatened Glasgow. Leslie had 3,000 troops in or about the city, and Montrose, with his raw levies, did not dare to meet that veteran horse in open battle. It was a hopeless form of war, as he soon realized, and early in November he passed into Menteith. Presently he made a journey into Angus, from which he was hunted back by Middleton's dragoons. Historians have assumed that he went to attend his wife's funeral, but, since Lady Montrose lived till 1648, that explanation must be abandoned.[2]

He returned to Atholl to find that his brother-in-law and most trusted adviser, the old Lord Napier, had died at Fincastle in his absence. Napier was over seventy years of age, and had spent his long and blameless life in the pursuit of the liberal arts and the service of his fellow-men. He was the wisest head in the Scotland of his day, a staunch Presbyterian, an upholder of popular liberties, an exponent of the unpopular doctrine of toleration—the type of what the Covenanters might have been in happier circumstances. About the same time Montrose received a letter from Charles, written from Newark on 3rd November, which

[1] The *A. P. S.* calls him George ; Wishart calls him John.
[2] Napier took the story from Burns's diary in Maidment's *Historical Fragments*, and it has been generally accepted. But in the disposition of the Montrose lands by the Committee of Estates to Sir William Graham of Claverhouse on February 21, 1648, provision is made for her liferent. She seems to have died shortly afterwards. See Balfour Paul, *The Scots Peerage*, VI., 253. Her life was so retired that a story like Burns's passed without contradiction.

may have done something to sweeten his memory of
Digby's failure. " As it hath been none of my least
afflictions and misfortunes," the king wrote, " that you
have had hitherto no assistance from me, so I conjure
you to believe that nothing but impossibility hath been
the cause of it. . . . Be assured that your less prosperous
fortune is so far from lowering my estimation of you,
that it will rather cause my affection to kythe (show)
the clearlier to you. . . . Upon all occasions, and in
all fortunes, you shall ever find me your most assured,
faithful, constant friend." [1]

From his old friend's grave Montrose turned again
to the weary business of chaffering with Huntly. He
sent Sir John Dalziel to him to ask for a conference ;
but Huntly, as shy as he was vain, seemed to fear to
meet his rival and declined. Montrose resolved to see
him at all costs, and early in December set off again
from Atholl across the hills. It was now midwinter—
a worse cold, says Wishart, than his generation had ever
known. [2] A bitter frost coated everything with ice, but
did not make the streams the easier to cross, and that
December passage of the barrier mountains of Esk and
Dee lived in the memory of men who were no strangers
to hardships. The feet of the infantry were clogged with
snow, the horses floundered in half-frozen bogs, or
crashed through the ice of mountain pools. Christmas
that year, which saw the death sentences of his friends
at St. Andrews, found Montrose pursuing the evasive
Huntly from one refuge to another. He looked for him
in Strathbogie, but Huntly fled to the Bog of Gight.
Thither Montrose followed, and the Gordon, at bay, was
obliged to receive him. Under the spell of the viceroy's
grace and courtesy the cloud of suspicion seemed to lift.
Huntly was roused to interest. He had 1,400 foot and
600 horse. These, combined with Montrose's 800 foot
and 200 horse, would make a formidable army. He
promised his support in the northern war, and offered
to lead his men through the lowlands of Moray to

---

[1] Napier, II., 613–614.
[2] It was as bad in England. See Turner, *Memoirs*, 41.

the siege of Inverness, while Montrose marched down
Strathspey. The capture of that town might fix Seaforth's loyalty, which once more was up for auction.
Aboyne and Lord Lewis wished, in Wishart's phrase,
" damnation to themselves " if they failed the king in
the future. They were to do their best to earn it.

.. The operations of the year 1646 began, therefore,
with good promise of success. The promise was not
fulfilled. The next few months must have been among
the most wretched in Montrose's life. With a heart
aching from the loss of his comrades, with a drenched
and starving following, and with no news save the
gloomiest from the south, he conducted an ineffective
guerilla war up and down Speyside. Huntly had nearly
twice his number of foot and thrice his number of horse,
but he refused to co-operate. The splendid fighting
force of the Gordons was frittered away, and their chief
declined to undertake any operation of war except the
siege of some little castles in Moray to gratify private
animosities. Montrose's patient letters to him are the
only clues we have as to the movements of the royal
army.[1] It was at Advie and Castle Grant in the end of
December 1645, moving about Strathspey in January
1646, at Kylochy on the Findhorn in February, and at
Petty on the coast in March.[2]

Elsewhere there were bold deeds to record. Twelve
hundred of Argyll's clan, under Campbell of Ardkinglass,
finding commons short in Lorn, had come raiding to the
Menteith lands of Napier and other royalists, where
they were joined by oddments of various clans, like the
Menzieses and the Stewarts of Balquhidder. Inchbrakie
and young Drummond of Balloch, having been sent to
recruit in Atholl, heard of these doings, and, with some
700 of the Atholl men, came up with the raiders on the
13th of February, near Callander, and thoroughly routed

---

[1] See the letters in *Mem. of M.*, II., 260, etc., and the itinerary in M. and S.,
164 *n.*

[2] Boswell found at Coll two letters from Montrose to Maclean of Coll, one
written from his camp at Petty, urging him to make efforts with "those slack
people that are about you" (*Tour to the Hebrides*, ch. xi.). Much of Montrose's
time was always spent in the work of a recruiting sergeant.

them. The remnant was found by Argyll huddling under the walls of Stirling; he dispatched them into Renfrewshire, where the local Covenanters would have none of these strange allies of the Covenant, and finally —Inchbrakie and his men having gone north—sent them back into the Lennox to live on the country.[1] Another fine performance was the defence of Kincardine castle by the young Lord Napier. With fifty men he held the place against Middleton for fourteen days, and then, when capitulation was imminent, escaped by night with Drummond of Balloch to Montrose. Middleton, on the 16th of March, burned the house where Montrose had spent his youth, and left the viceroy landless and homeless.[2]

There were no such exploits to redeem the futile campaign in the north. The vital objective was Inverness, the capture of which would not only give control of a large piece of territory and important communications, but would recruit trimmers like Seaforth and the Mackenzies, the Grants, Macleod of Skye, and Macdonald of Sleat. Accordingly, early in April Montrose sat down before Inverness, and on the 29th of that month drew his lines close and fixed his guns on the top of the old Castle Hill. The Ness was unusually low, and the invading army lived largely on the Fraser country to the west of it.[3] The garrison was strong and well-supplied, and it ruthlessly destroyed all outlying buildings of the town which might give shelter to the enemy; but Montrose, strengthened by some of Seaforth's Mackenzies and by Macdonalds from the west, would beyond doubt have captured it had it not been for Huntly. Middleton had come north again, Leslie having departed for England to look after arrears of pay, and the 1,400 men he brought with him, joined to the Aberdeen garrison he had left behind, made a formidable army on the royalist flank. The Gordons lay between Middleton and Mon-

---

[1] Wishart, ch. xix. Guthry, 213–214. Willcock, *The Great Marquess*, 188–189.   [2] Guthry, 215.

[3] "Betwixt the bridge end of Inverness and Guisachan, twenty-six miles, there was not left in my country a sheep to bleat, or a cock to crow day, nor a house unruffled." *Wardlaw MS.*, 315.

trose, and it was their business to watch the former and
prevent him from crossing the Spey. But Huntly was
busy with private vendettas, and sent only insulting
replies to his colleague's appeals. Montrose was, therefore, compelled to detach three troops of horse, which
he could ill spare, to watch the Spey crossings. Lord
Lewis, who held the castle of Rothes, whether out of
treachery or a misplaced sense of humour, sent a false
message to the troops, decoyed them to Rothes, and
detained them there till Middleton was across the
river.[1]

The first news Montrose had of Middleton was the
sounding of his trumpets on the 5th of May, two miles
from Inverness. He had nothing to withstand so strong
a cavalry force, so he was compelled to raise the siege.
With Crawford commanding his rearguard, he crossed
the Ness above the town, marched north-west by way
of the Caiplich, and put the Beauly between him and
his pursuer. In the hurry of his retreat he was compelled to leave behind him all his stores and ammunition and his two brass field-pieces. Middleton followed
at his leisure, but on 8th May Montrose gave him the
slip, doubled back by Strathglass and Stratherrick, and
presently was again on Speyside.[2]

Matters had now reached a crisis. Huntly was not
only no friend, but was becoming an active enemy, and
Montrose resolved to treat him as such. He had just,
with considerable losses, taken and plundered Aberdeen,
and was clearly determined to play for his own hand.
But first Montrose made one final effort to see him and
bring him to reason. On the 27th of May he rode twenty
miles to the Bog of Gight, but Huntly saw him coming
and fled. It was the last straw. The viceroy decided
to write off the Gordons from the royal strength in

---

[1] This is Wishart's account (ch. xx.). Gordon of Ruthven (184, etc.)
loyally attempts to defend Lord Lewis, but his apology does not convince, and
he has no real excuse to offer for Huntly's supineness.

[2] For the siege of Inverness see Wishart, ch. xx. ; Gordon of Ruthven,
177–187; the *Wardlaw MS.*, 314–316. The town of Inverness had a heavy
bill of damages to present to the Estates, largely for destruction caused by
its own garrison. See the details in *More Culloden Papers* (ed. Warrand,
1923), I., 31, etc.

Scotland, and to let Middleton make of them what he pleased. He would form a light flying squadron and ride through the northern Highlands to beat up recruits for the king. If Alasdair was gone beyond reach, he had some hopes of Seaforth and Sleat, he had Reay on his side, and he was certain of the Macleans, of Clanranald, and of Glengarry. It was a course which his wisest counsellors advised, and, with such allies, it would be strange if he could not bring to the field as stout a force as that which had scattered the Covenant in a year of battles.

III

But on the 31st of May a fateful message arrived from the king. This is not the place to describe the alternations of hope and despondency through which Charles passed, between Digby's fiasco in the north and that day in April when he slipped out of beleaguered Oxford to cast himself upon the mercy of the Scots. Negotiations had been for long in progress with Montreuil, the French ambassador, as intermediary, but Leven and his friends, while hinting at much, would commit nothing to writing. The Scots had lost all love for their English allies. The ministers had begun to realize that their conception of Presbytery was very different from that held by the English Parliament and the City of London. "The Pope and the King," wrote Baillie, "were never more earnest for the headship of the Church than the plurality of this Parliament;" and again, "The leaders of the people seemed to be inclined to have no shadow of a king; to have liberty for all religions; to have but a lame Erastian Presbytery; to be so injurious to us as to chase us home by the sword." [1] The Scottish laity were now less high-flying in their demands. They wished to see Presbyterianism entrenched in England as a protection to their own liberties, for they realized the growing military power of Independency; they wished the neighbouring

[1] II., 360, 362.

government to be in the hands of their friends; and
they could not mistake the meaning of the clause in the
capitulation of Exeter which exempted the besieged
from taking the Covenant.[1]   The Independents were
rapidly becoming the national English party, hostile
alike to the French, the Irish, and the Scots.   Argyll
saw this clearly, and his speech in the House of Lords
on 25th June is perhaps his chief claim to statesmanship, for he proposed an elastic and tolerant form of
Presbytery and combined it with some admirable good
sense on the subject of a constitutional kingship.[2]

But the time was past for such moderation.   Antagonisms and suspicions had been created which must battle
together till they destroyed each other.   The mood of
the nation was too feverish to permit of compromise.
The future lay with Hyde and men like him, who would
make no concession to what they regarded as sectional
tyrannies.   " He represented . . . the only living force
with which Cromwell had seriously to count.   The
English Presbyterian members of Parliament, the Scottish Presbyterian lords—nay, even the king himself—
were but the weavers of one vast intrigue with many
faces.   Hyde stood firmly upon the ground of a sentiment which would one day, through the errors of his
antagonists, gain a hold upon the nation, and he knew
how to bide his time till the nation had declared in his
favour.   It was not Puritanism, but the very opposite
of Puritanism—the expansion of the reasoning intelligence—which held the main current of the thought of
the seventeenth century.   Cromwell, mighty as he was,
could but dam back the current for a time, and when
he had done his utmost he would have toiled only that
Hyde might step into his place." [3]

Even had there been a chance of agreement, it would
have been wrecked on the personality of the king.   He
could not realize that the establishment of Presbytery
in England was a bed-rock claim for the Scots; they
could not realize that their sovereign could be blind to

---

[1] By this clause Thomas Fuller was enabled to continue preaching.
[2] *Lords' Journals*, VIII., 392.   [3] Gardiner, *Civil War*, III., 119–120.

this constant article of their faith. Hence all talk about
the king being secured in conscience and honour if he
entrusted himself to them was idle; by these words
the two parties did not mean the same thing. Charles
did not realize that, though the breach between the
Scots and the Independents was widening, there remained
between him and them an impassable gulf. No doubt
there was on the Scottish side a grave lack of candour
and honesty, but there was an equal disingenuousness
on the part of the man who could write, as Charles did
from Oxford in March, that he was " not without hope
that I shall be able so to draw either the Presbyterians
or the Independents to side with me for extirpating one
another, that I shall really be a king again." [1] It is
not safe to take refuge with an army if it is your settled
purpose to betray it; the deceiver is apt in turn to
become the deceived.

On 25th April Charles, disguised as a servant, rode
out of Oxford over Magdalen bridge, and about
seven in the morning of 5th May he arrived in the
Scots camp at Southwell. For what happened in
Montreuil's lodgings at the Saracen's Head we have the
evidence of an eyewitness, Sir James Turner.[2] Before
the king had eaten or drunk, Lothian hurried to his
presence and formulated his demands. The royalist
garrison must surrender Newark, the king must sign the
Covenant, and establish Presbytery in England and
Wales, and must order " James Graham " to lay down
his arms. To this imperious speech Charles replied with
the dignity that never failed him : " He that made thee
an earl made James Graham a marquis."

Then began a pathetic correspondence between the
king who had done so little and his captain-general who
had done so much. The esteem of Charles for his great
servant had ripened into a warm affection. " From
henceforth," he had said a few months earlier, " I place
Montrose among my children, and mean to live with
him as a friend, and not as a king." [3] On 18th April he

---

[1] Charles to Digby, March 26, 1646. Carte, *Ormonde Papers*, III., 452.
[2] *Memoirs*, 41.   [3] Gardiner, *Civil War*, III., 23.

wrote to him from Oxford, telling him of his intention
to go to the Scots army, and suggesting that Montrose,
if he found that Leven had declared for the king, should
join forces with him ; the letter was sent in cypher
through Nicholas to Montreuil to be delivered at the
latter's discretion, and naturally was not forwarded.[1]
On the 19th of May he wrote to Montrose from Newcastle :

" I am in such a condition as is much fitter for relation than for
writing. Wherefore, I refer you to this trusty bearer, Robin Ker,
for the reasons and manner of my coming to this army ; as also,
what my treatment hath been since I came, and my resolutions
upon my whole business. This shall therefore only give you positive
commands, and tell you real truths, leaving the why of all to this
bearer. You must disband your forces and go into France, where
you shall receive my further direction. This at first may justly
startle you ; but I assure you that, if for the present I should offer
to do more for you, I could not do so much."

Montrose received this letter on Speyside on the last
day of May. He called a council of his officers and laid
it before them ; he invited Huntly, who replied haughtily
that he knew all about the matter, having himself had
letters from the king. In his reply on 2nd June Montrose declared himself at his Majesty's commands, but
asked that some protection should be secured for those
who had risked all in the royal cause.

" For, when all is done that we can, I am much afraid that it
shall trouble both those with your Majesty, and all your servants
here, to quit these parts. And as for my own leaving this kingdom,
I shall in all humility and obedience endeavour to perform your
Majesty's command, wishing (rather nor any one should make pretext of me) never to see it again with mine eyes ; willing, as well
by passion as action, to witness myself your Majesty's most humble
and most faithful subject and servant."

He also wrote privately to the king, asking if his surrender to the Scots had been by his own will or by
compulsion ; if the latter, he would keep his army in

---

[1] It is printed in *Mem. of M.*, II., 274, and *Clarendon State Papers*, II.,
224.

being.[1] Then he broke up his camp and marched to Glenshee to await the king's answer.

Charles replied on the 15th of June, repeating his commands, and promising protection for Montrose's followers.

" I assure you that I no less esteem your willingness to lay down arms at my command for a gallant and real expression of your zeal and affection to my service than any of your former actions. But I hope that you cannot have so mean an opinion of me that, for any particular or worldly respects, I could suffer you to be ruined. No. I avow that it is one of the greatest and truest marks of my present miseries that I cannot recompense you according to your deserts, but, on the contrary, must yet suffer a cloud of the misfortunes of the times to hang over you. . . . For there is no man, who ever heard me speak of you, that is ignorant that the reason that makes me at this time send you out of the country is that you may return home with the greater glory; and in the meantime to have as honourable employment as I can put upon you. This trusty bearer, Robin Ker, will tell you the care I have had of all your friends and mine; to whom, albeit I cannot furnish such conditions as I would, yet they will be such as, all things considered, are most fit for them to accept. Wherefore, I renew my former directions of laying down arms unto you, desiring you to let Huntly, Crawford, Airlie, Seaforth, and Ogilvy know that want of time hath made me now omit to reiterate my former command to them, intending that this shall serve for all, assuring them and all the rest of my friends that, whensoever God shall enable me, they shall reap the fruits of their loyalty and affection to my service."

On the 16th of July the king wrote again :

" The most sensible part of my many misfortunes is to see my friends in distress and not to be able to help them, and of this kind you are the chief. Wherefore, according to that real freedom and friendship which is between us, as I cannot absolutely command you to accept of unhandsome conditions, so I must tell you that I believe your refusal will put you in a far worse estate than your compliance will. This is the reason that I have told this bearer, Robin Ker, and the Commissioners here, that I have commanded you to accept of Middleton's conditions, which really I judge to be your best course according to this present time; for, if this opportunity be let slip, you must not expect any more treaties; in which case you must either conquer all Scotland or be inevitably ruined. . . . Wherefore if you find it fit to accept, you may justly say I

[1] Guthry, 219. Montrose must have received a private assurance on this point.

1646   have commanded you, and if you take another course you cannot
July   expect that I can publicly avow you in it until I shall be able (which
       God knows how soon that will be) to stand upon my own feet; but,
       on the contrary, seem to be not well satisfied with your refusal,
       which I find clearly will bring all this army upon you—and then I
       shall be in a very sad condition, such as I shall rather leave to your
       judgment than seek to express." [1]

The command admitted of no refusal. Seaforth and
Huntly were making their own terms; moreover, the
futile Antrim had arrived in Scotland to assist Alasdair
in a private war in Argyll, and was summoning the
Highlanders to follow his own standard.[2] Accordingly,
towards the end of July Montrose met Middleton on the
banks of the Isla to arrange terms. Middleton was to
stain his later record with many crimes, but he had
some of the instincts of a soldier. He granted better
conditions than might have been looked for. A free
pardon was given to all the royalists except the viceroy,
Crawford, and Sir John Hurry, who, since Kilsyth, had
been with Montrose. These three were to leave the
country before the first day of September, the Estates
providing a vessel. All forfeited lands were to be restored, except in the case of the three excepted, and of
Graham of Gorthie, whose estate was already in the
hands of Balcarres. Montrose accepted the conditions,
and, assembling his army on 30th July at Rattray, near
Blairgowrie, bade his men farewell. He told them that
what he did was for the king's sake and by the king's
command. It was a melancholy parting with those
Highlanders of Atholl who had never failed him, and
with comrades such as Airlie and Ogilvy and the young
Napier, who, in good and evil report, had been true
to their salt. For such men "passion" was a harder
service than "action." [3]

---

[1] The correspondence will be found in *Mem. of M.*, II., 277–284, and *Hist.
MSS. Comm.*, 2nd Report, 170.
[2] He claimed to be the king's general of the Isles and the Highlands. See
note on p. 163.
[3] Wishart, ch. xxi. Gordon of Ruthven, 194, etc. Guthry, 219, etc.
Burnet (*Mem. of the Hamiltons*, 280) has a story that the mildness of the terms
was due to the intervention of Hamilton, now released from prison; but the
terms to be offered by Middleton were settled before Hamilton reached New-

The Committee of Estates did not accept with any graciousness the terms which Middleton had agreed. They dared not repudiate their general, for Middleton was not a man to brook insults, and his forces, added to Montrose's, might soon be hammering at the Edinburgh gates. But they did their best to defeat the bargain by delay. Montrose had received a private letter from the king at Newcastle, dated the 21st of August, of which the postscript bade him defer his going beyond seas " as long as you may, without breaking your word." [1] It was a dangerous instruction, but Montrose accepted it. As the last days of the month approached he grew suspicious of the Covenant's good faith. There was no sign of the promised vessel till, on the 31st, a ship put into Montrose harbour with a sullen master and a more sullen crew. English men-of-war, too, had appeared off the coast. When Montrose proposed to embark at once, the skipper declared that he must have time to caulk his vessel and attend to the rigging.[2] This meant that the days of grace would be exceeded, and the viceroy left stranded, an outlaw at the mercy of his enemies.

Happily a small Norwegian sloop was in the harbour of Stonehaven, and its master, one Jens Gunnersen, agreed to sail with the exiles. Hurry, Wishart, and Drummond of Balloch; Harry Graham, Montrose's half-brother; John Spottiswoode, one of the nephews whom old Sir Robert had entrusted to the viceroy's charge; three soldiers, John Lisle or Lillie, whom we shall meet later at Carbisdale, Patrick Melvin, and David Guthrie; a Frenchman Lasound, who had been Lord Gordon's valet; and a young German called Rudolf made up the little party. The sloop sailed down to Montrose roads

castle. *Cf.* Napier, II., 638–639. Hamilton and Lanark may, however, have helped, as Burnet alleges, in the ratification of the terms by the Estates. It was to their interest to get Montrose out of Scotland.

[1] *Mem. of M.*, II., 284. This letter may have been in reply to a private letter from Montrose telling him that Seaforth, who had now declared for the king, could raise 8,000 men, and that there was an offer of 7,000 from the Irish royalists. So Gardiner (III., 152) reads an undated message in the *Archives des Affaires Étrangères*, LIII., 517.

[2] Wishart, ch. xxi. Monteith, 245.

on the 3rd of September,[1] and that evening Mr. James Wood, a minister, and his servant put off in a wherry from the shore, and were taken aboard. The servant was Montrose. " This," says Wishart, " was in the year of our Lord, 1646, and the thirty-fourth of his age."

[1] So Wishart ; Monteith says the 5th. "His friends put out to sea on the 5th of September, having run the risk of being murdered by the country people, who cut the cable while the ship was at anchor, and put them in danger of splitting upon the rocks." *Op. cit.*, 245.

BOOK III

PASSION

CHAPTER XV

THE YEARS OF EXILE

(*September* 1646–*March* 1650)

Byrhtwold spoke and grasped his shield—he was an old companion—he
shook his ashen spear, and taught courage to them that fought : "Thought
shall be the harder, heart the keener, mood shall be the more, as our might
lessens. Here our prince lies low, they have hewn him to death ! Grief and
sorrow for ever on the man that leaves this war-play ! "

Song of Maldon
(W. P. Ker's translation).

I

FOR over two years Montrose had been living the
life of the camp, his mind concentrated upon
the immediate purpose of winning battles.[1] His main
strategical plan of joining hands with the king on the
Border and severing the alliance of the Scots and the
English Parliament had failed through no fault of his,
and the lack of this larger co-operation had nullified his
local victories. But he had not given up hope, even
though Charles was a prisoner. Before he left Scotland
he had sent Crawford to the queen in Paris with a
proposal to raise the clans and rescue the king from his
captors.[2] He regarded himself as still a serving soldier,
and his survey was narrowed to the field of arms. No
more for him those speculations on the theory of the
State, which had been his earlier interest. The time
had gone by for reason and philosophy ; unreason,

*1646
September*

---

[1] It was a life of the sternest kind. "During a winter of exceptional
severity he lived for the most part in the open air, without quarters, without
even tents. He endured all war's hardships, with nothing to appease his thirst
and hunger but icy water or melted snow, without bread and salt, and with
only a scanty supply of lean and starveling cattle " (Wishart, *Dedication*).
[2] *Clarendon Papers*, cited by Napier, II., 653. With Irish and Lowland
support Crawford estimated that he could raise over 23,000 men. He included
Macleods (1,000), Grants (1,000), and Mackenzies (2,000).

armed and mailed, had seized the reins of power, and
the philosopher must now be the warrior and appeal to
a harsher arbitrament than dialectic. Some such nar-
rowing of vision was inevitable. The king was no longer
the king of his discourse on "Sovereign Power," but the
master who commanded his sword, and the kaleido-
scopic changes of events and parties in England he
regarded with an eye only to their military reaction.
His life and thought were restricted to a single purpose.

After a week's tossing in the North Sea Montrose
reached the Norwegian port of Bergen, where he found
a Scot, one Thomas Gray, in command of the castle.
His immediate purpose was to visit Denmark to meet
Christian IV., with whom, as the uncle of Charles, he
might confer on the next step. He had talked for
months with none but rough-handed Scots nobles, and
he needed some one with a wider survey to advise him
on the complications of his task. He had sheathed his
sword at his master's bidding, but his life was dedicated
to the cause, and from that devotion there could be no
release but death. So on 15th September the exiles
started on the overland route to Christiania, probably
sailing up the Sognefiord to Leardalsören, and then
traversing the backbone of mountains by the Leardal
valley and Valders. From the little port of Marstrand
they crossed into Denmark, only to find that King
Christian was in Germany. Montrose passed on to
Hamburg, where he spent the winter waiting for instructions.

But no instructions came—not even his credentials
as ambassador-extraordinary to France which Charles
had promised him. One letter he had from the king,
dated from Newcastle on January 21, 1647, in which he
was referred for orders to the queen; and one from
Henrietta Maria, written from Paris on 5th February,
promising further dispatches, and subscribing herself
his "very good and affectionate cousin and friend." [1]
The parasites and adventurers who surrounded the
queen were resolute that Montrose should not break

[1] *Mem. of M.*, II., 299–302. *Hist. MSS. Comm.*, 2nd Report, 170.

in upon their follies with his untimely zeal. When, *1647* tired of waiting on orders that did not arrive, he left Hamburg in March, he was met in Flanders by John Ashburnham with a second letter from Henrietta, and a suggestion from Jermyn that he should return to Scotland and renew the war. As no reference was made to his own proposals sent through Crawford, Montrose naturally refused to engage in an enterprise for which he had no resources and no warrant from his master. Ashburnham then hinted that he might make his peace with the Covenanters, following the royal precedent. The proposal was indignantly rejected. "Not even the king," he said, "should command his obedience in what was dishonourable, unjust, and destructive to his Majesty himself."[1]

In Paris the queen received him graciously, but, when he preached the immediate necessity of armed intervention in her husband's behalf, she made it very clear that his counsels were not those most grateful to the royal ears. Jermyn and the rest gave him tepid smiles and the cold shoulder. To one of his temper the mingled silliness and vice of Henrietta's court must have been in the extreme repulsive. The king was a captive, the flower of English and Scottish chivalry had died for his sake, and these mountebanks were turning life into a thing of backstairs gossip and idle laughter. There appears to have been a suggestion that his niece, Lilias Napier, a spirited girl in her teens, should become a maid of honour, but Montrose sternly forbade it. "There is neither Scots man nor Scots woman welcome that way ; neither would any of honour and virtue, chiefly a woman, suffer themselves to live in so lewd and worthless a place."[2]

But if the tawdry court-in-exile had little to say to him, Paris made amends. His fame had gone abroad throughout Europe, and the most distinguished men in France came to pay him their respects. He was given

---

[1] Wishart, Part II., ch. i.
[2] Napier, II., 661. I agree with Napier's interpretation of this letter. *Cf.* the letter from Lilias, ibid., 647.

1647 precedence before the regular ambassadors. De Retz,
who had followed his campaigns with admiration, welcomed him as a Roman hero reborn in a degenerate
world. The great Mazarin offered him the command
of the Scots in France, and a lieutenant-generalship
in the French army; then the captaincy of the Gens
d'Armes, with a large pension; and, last, the captaincy
of the king's own guard and the rank of Marshal of
France. The young Napier, who had now joined him,
was eager that he should accept. A dazzling career
opened before him, for with his talents in the field he
might look to be a second Condé, rich, idolized, the
head of a great army, and not the impoverished captain
of a few ragged exiles. But to enter the French service
meant, in common decency, to give up thoughts of any
other, and his sword had been dedicated and was not
his own to sell.[1]

Meanwhile strange things were happening in the
country which he had left. On January 30, 1647, the
Scots army, as Montrose had always anticipated, had
handed over the king to the English Parliament. The
carts, laden with the deferred pay of Leven's soldiers,
were soon rumbling over the Border, while the women
of Newcastle were with difficulty prevented from ston-
ing the retiring troops, and ribald songs were beginning
to be sung everywhere in England and France.[2] It is
difficult to read the dispatches of Montreuil and Bellièvre,
and not believe that the Scots had guaranteed to Charles
personal security; their very Covenants bound them to
this, and beyond doubt, when Charles committed himself to their charge, he believed that with them, even
if he did not find support for his doctrine of government,
he would at any rate be assured of safety. He believed
it, and they knew that he believed it; they seem to have
believed it themselves, for there is on record a declara-

---

[1] Lord Napier to his wife, June 14, 1647. Napier, II., 665, etc.

[2] " Traitor Scot,
        Sold his king for a groat."

" L'Ecosse, parjure à sa foi,
   Pour un denier vendit son roi."

tion of a Commission of the General Assembly that the Scots did not deliver up the king " until sufficient surety was given by both Houses of Parliament ensuring the safety and the preservation of his Majesty's person." Such a guarantee, implied and explicit, was broken by his transference to other hands. But it is no less certain that the consideration for the bargain was not the money. Had Charles complied with their conditions about Presbytery, they would gladly have forfeited the arrears of the English payments and defied English Parliament and English army. They sold their king indeed, but it was for a different price, and one which was never paid—the enforcement, urged by some on prudential and by others on mystical grounds, of an alien church polity which was rapidly becoming anathema to the English nation.

The transference of the king was the defeat of Presbyterianism south of the Border ; thenceforth the struggle was of Royalist and Independent. The division between Scotland and England became sharper ; monarchy and intolerance were arrayed against republicanism and toleration. In June Charles passed from the Parliament into the charge of Cromwell's army, and on his way south he wrote to Montrose from Newmarket, bidding him again take instructions from Henrietta, and thanking him for the present of a sword.[1] It was a strange gift to one whose career in the field was closed for ever. But the doings of Cornet Joyce had alarmed the more moderate of the Covenanters, and that party began to reveal the characteristic of all factions, and split in two. There had been much divided opinion about the transactions of the preceding January ; there was now no dominant party in England to which the Covenanters as a body could adhere ; English dislike of them was returned with interest ; they regarded the sectaries and their gospel of toleration with scarcely more love than they regarded episcopacy and royalism. Hamilton was back in Scotland, and was busy making a party of those who favoured the Covenant but did

[1] *Mem. of M.*, II., 303.

1648 not favour Cromwell, and professed devotion to the principle of monarchy. In November Charles escaped to Carisbrooke castle, in the Isle of Wight—a mere change of prison; and there, on 27th December, he entered into a secret engagement, with Lanark, Loudoun, and Lauderdale as signatories. The scheme was doomed from the start, both by its terms and the character of its promoters. They combined these incompatibles, the king and the Solemn League; their royalism offended the Independents, their Covenant alienated the royalists, and they had nothing wherewith to attract any substantial English following. They had not even a creed to unite Scotland. They strove for nothing which had any real meaning. There was no half-way house between Montrose and Argyll.

Nevertheless, the Estates, when they assembled in March 1648, gave the Engagers a large majority, and sanctioned the raising of an army to rescue the king from that captivity into which a year before they had sold him. Argyll went into opposition, as well he might. Apart from his dislike of the Hamiltons, who sponsored the Engagement, a man of his acumen realized that out of such a medley of half-hearted blunderers there could only come disaster. Robert Baillie, who was against the Engagement, yet deplored the intransigence of the leaders of the Kirk and his own party, was moved to write almost in Montrose's words : " I am more and more in the mind that it were for the good of the world that churchmen did meddle with ecclesiastical affairs only ; that, were they never so able otherwise, they are unhappy statesmen ; that, as Erastian Cæsaro-Papism is hurtful to the Church, so an Episcopal Papa-Cæsarism is unfortunate for the State. If no man were wiser than I am, we should not make so many scruples to settle the throne and pull down the sectaries." [1]

One of the first steps which the Engagers took was to communicate with Henrietta and the Prince of Wales in Paris. The queen did not inform Montrose of their

[1] III., 38–39.

proposals till she had made up her mind to accept them **1648** and had already committed herself. He knew too much of Hamilton to look for great things in that quarter, but he offered to do all in his power to save the situation by enlisting under his own banner those royalists who would enlist under no other, and by supporting the Engagers in the field. Hamilton's envoys, however, had warned the queen that Montrose must have no share in the business, and his offer was coldly declined. In despair he looked elsewhere for a sphere of action where he could further his master's interests and raise troops for his service. Mazarin and his colleagues were half-hearted in Charles's cause, and too cordial in their treatment of the English Parliament. So at the end of March 1648 he slipped away from Paris with some of his friends, and travelled by Geneva and Tyrol to the Emperor's court at Vienna.[1]

Wishart's account in Latin of the *annus mirabilis* of 1644-45 had been published in Holland towards the close of 1647, and had leaped at once into a wide popularity.[2] The doings of the Scottish soldier were

---

[1] Clarendon's explanation of his departure is wounded vanity (XII., 15). Burnet's gossip, given on the authority of Hamilton's daughter, that Montrose left Paris in disgrace with the queen because " he had talked very indecently of her favours to him," is sufficiently refuted by Montrose's character. See Napier, II., 698.

[2] The Latin text of Part I., *De Rebus Auspiciis Serenissimi et Potentissimi Caroli, etc., sub imperio illustrissimi Jacobi Montisrosarum marchionis, etc., Commentarius interprete, A. S.* (Agricola Sophocardius, *i.e.* George Wishart), was issued in 1647 at the Hague or Amsterdam. A second edition, superbly printed, appeared in Paris in 1648, a third at Amsterdam in the same year, and (if we are to believe the preface to the 1756 translation) a fourth in 1649. The first English translation was published by Samuel Browne at the Hague, probably in 1647 (I have in my collection the copy of this edition specially bound for presentation to Prince Charles). It was reprinted in 1648 in a beautiful small quarto, and in 1649 in a barbarous duodecimo, with various passages differently rendered. In 1652 the same translation, with additions consisting of a continuation of Wishart's Part I. by a different hand, and an account of Montrose's trial and death, was issued in London under the title of *Montrose Redivivus.* Another edition, with additional matter, appeared in 1660. A new translation, with various letters and additional notes, was published in 1720 and reprinted in 1724, and a revised version was issued by Ruddiman in Edinburgh in 1756. This was reprinted, with some further notes, by Constable in 1819. Meantime there had appeared in Paris in 1767 a French translation in two volumes. In 1893 Canon Murdoch and Dr. Morland Simpson issued, under the title *Deeds of Montrose,* a complete edition of both parts of Wishart's Latin narrative, with a new English version, and three chapters on Montrose's last expedition, largely based on the Danish and Swedish archives. This must rank as the definitive edition, and the editors' learned and ample notes cannot be overpraised For

1648 the talk of every camp and city in Europe, and at the imperial court Montrose found himself welcomed as a hero. The Emperor Ferdinand IV., whom he found at Prague, gave him the crimson baton of a Marshal of the Empire, and empowered him to raise troops in any quarter of his dominions. The Emperor's brother and successor, the Archduke Leopold, was Governor of the Spanish Netherlands, and Montrose was advised that the western border of the empire was the place for his purpose. It had the further merit of being nearer Britain in case of a summons from home. Germany was too much harassed by war to make easy travelling, so Montrose returned by Cracow and Dantzig to Denmark, and thence by way of Groningen to Brussels. He found the archduke at Tournai, but it was his fate to look for help from those who at the moment had none to give. As he had met Rupert on the morrow of Marston Moor, so he found Leopold on the morrow of Lens, where, on the 20th of August, the genius of Condé had scattered the imperial troops.

He accordingly returned to Brussels, where he received startling news from Scotland. To the bulk of the English royalists the Engagement made no appeal, since it contained " so many monstrous concessions that, except the whole Kingdom of England had been likewise imprisoned in Carisbrooke Castle with the king, it could not be imagined that it was possible to be performed." [1] Scotland was wildly divided. The great bulk of the ministers were opposed to it, for though they liked the English sectaries little they liked the king less ; the pulpits rang with denunciations, and in May there was an armed rising at Mauchline, in Ayrshire, which was with difficulty suppressed by Middleton and Callander.

the bibliography of Wishart see their Critical Introduction. Wishart prefaces his text with a long dedication to the Prince of Wales. This was printed in the Latin edition, and in the first English translation of 1647, but omitted in the subsequent translations. The reason appears in Burnet, *Mem. of the Hamiltons,* 344 : " To oblige the Duke (of Hamilton) the more, a book being dedicated to his Highness containing some passages much to the Duke's dishonour. he refused to accept of it, and ordered it to be called in." The letter on the subject from the prince to Montrose is in Bodleian MSS., 895. This may account for the rarity of the first English edition.

[1] Clarendon, *Hist.,* X., 167.

Argyll, Eglinton, Balmerino, Elcho, Cassilis, and Balcarres, the leaders of the opposition, were joined by Loudoun the Chancellor, who suddenly turned his coat. The Engagers were in desperate straits for money, and in still more desperate straits for leaders, for David Leslie belonged to the other faction. Hamilton, who had not a vestige of military talent, was their commander-in-chief, with Callander, who was no more than a disciplinarian, as his second-in-command; Middleton, his master of horse, was the only able soldier.

Leaving their enemies mustering behind them, the Engagers crossed the Border on 8th July, with Sir Marmaduke Langdale as their solitary English ally, and their only appeal to the English people their proposals to free the king, disband the Parliament army, and restore the Covenant. Lanark would have liked to take order with Argyll and the ministers before leaving Scotland [1]—the wiser plan; but indeed the wisdom of any plan signified little under such generalship as Hamilton's. He had 10,500 men, Langdale had nearly 3,000, and Sir George Monro joined him at Kendal with part of the Scots army from Ireland. The history of the disastrous march may be read in Clarendon and Burnet and the memoirs of Sir James Turner. The Scottish forces were under no central command, and their division was their undoing. Lambert was waiting for them in Yorkshire, and Cromwell joined him on 13th August. On the 17th Callander and Middleton, with the cavalry, were as far south as Wigan; Hamilton was at Preston, about to cross the Ribble, with Langdale behind him, while Monro was far behind with Musgrave in the north. Cromwell, having made, in Montrose's fashion, a swift flank march over the Lancashire hills, fell upon the centre at Preston —it was " St. Covenant's Day," the anniversary of the signing of the Solemn League—routed it and cut the army in two. The dismembered van dribbled south, Baillie with 4,000 foot surrendering at Warrington bridge, and Hamilton with the cavalry at Uttoxeter. During the next weeks Scotland was in dire con-

[1] Burnet, *Mem. of the Hamiltons*, 351.

1648 fusion. Eglinton and Loudoun organized the Whigamore Raid of west-country peasants, which occupied Edinburgh. Monro almost captured Argyll at Stirling, and Lanark, with Monro's aid, could no doubt have destroyed the Whigamores, had not his colleagues overruled him. The Estates capitulated on shameful terms to the Kirk. On 21st September Cromwell crossed the Tweed and met Argyll, and on 4th October was in Edinburgh. He stayed in Lord Moray's house in the Canongate, dined with Argyll and Wariston, and met the leading ministers like Blair, Dickson, and Guthrie. Of the nobles he wrote that " he found nothing in them other than what became Christians and men of honour." [1] Mr. Blair thought him " an egregious dissembler, a great liar . . . and a greeting deevil." [2] Argyll, as usual, was right in his diagnosis. With his keen eye for political values he had attached himself to the strongest force of the day. But he cannot have thought hopefully of the future, for the extremists of the Kirk, to whom both by conviction and policy he was bound, held no single article of Cromwell's creed except his distrust of the king, and they had rejected the only help which could enable them to stand against him. He must have felt the foundations cracking under his feet. He had begun that half-hearted alliance with Oliver which was to bring him to the scaffold.

The news from home revived in Montrose the old eagerness to strike another blow for the king. He had appealed in vain to the queen and her circle ; he was excluded from the dreary and futile schemes of the Engagers ; he had failed with middle age, and during the winter of 1648, in Brussels, he tried an appeal to youth. He wrote to the Prince of Wales, to the Duke of York, and to Prince Rupert—repeatedly to the last, whose temper resembled his own in so far as its besetting sin was not supineness. Rupert was now at Helvoetsluys in charge of the small royalist fleet, much beset by the Parliamentary ships of war under Lord

---

[1] Carlyle, *Cromwell's Letters* (ed. Lomas), I., 369.
[2] Row, *Life of Blair*, 210.

Warwick, and in constant difficulty from mutinous crews
and short supplies.[1] On 7th September Montrose wrote
to him :

" When your Highness shall be pleased to know that I was ever
a silent admirer of you, and a passionate affecter of your person
and all your ways, you will be pleased to allow me recourse to your
goodness and generosity. And the rather that your Highness sees
I am for the present at such distance with all interests, as no end
but naked respect can now prompt me to it ; which, if your Highness
shall do me the honour to take in good part, and command me to
continue, I shall hope it will not wrong the king your uncle's service,
nor what may touch your Highness both in relation to those and
these parts, in either of which I should presume to be able to do you
some small services."

Rupert replied affectionately, and the stately and
involved correspondence continued till January 1649.
A meeting was constantly discussed, but Rupert could
not leave the fleet and come to Brussels, and Montrose
could hardly venture to that nest of spies, the Hague.
The latter's purpose is clear. He wanted Rupert to
take the fleet to Scotland, and he did not want him to
involve himself in Lauderdale's toils.

" Since there be so handsome and probable grounds for a clear
and gallant design if the measures be rightly taken, I should be
infinitely sorry that your Highness should be induced to hazard
your own person, or these little rests (remnants) upon any desperate
thrust."

It does not appear that a meeting ever took place, and
in January 1649, after refitting by the sale of his sister's
jewels, Rupert took the fleet to join Ormonde in Ireland.[2]
Hitherto there had been no word from the Prince of
Wales ; he and his mother had still hopes of the Engagers, and feared to offend them by any intercourse
with their deadly enemy. Presently, however, the
young Charles emancipated himself from the queen and

[1] Scott, *Rupert, Prince Palatine*, ch. xiii.
[2] The correspondence between Rupert and Montrose is printed in *Mem. of M.*,
II., 353-363. *Hist. MSS. Comm.*, 2nd Report, 173. Among the Montrose
papers is preserved the key to the cypher used by Montrose at this time.
Montrose himself is " Venture Fair " ; Hamilton, " Captain Luckless " ; Argyll,
" Ruling Elder " ; Callander, " Almanach " ; Lindsay, " Judas " ; the General
Assembly " the Goodwife that wears the breeches."

her set, and took up his residence with Hyde at the
Hague. Montrose had friends who had the prince's ear,
and in January 1649 he received a message from him,
bidding him arrange with Hyde for a secret interview.
The prince had entered upon the policy of keeping two
strings to his bow. While holding the Engagers in play,
he wished to have Montrose as a last resort ; but, as the
insistence upon secrecy shows, he was anxious to make
the former believe that he looked only to them. Montrose replied that he would joyfully obey the summons,
but implored the prince to distinguish true loyalty from
false. " If your Highness shall but vouchsafe a little
faith unto your loyal servants, and stand at guard with
others, your affairs can soon be whole." [1]

He wrote also : " I never had passion upon earth
so strong as to do the king, your father, service."
This was on the 28th of January. Two days later, on a
snowy afternoon, on a scaffold in Whitehall, that king
" not cowardly " put off his armour.

II

From the day when he heard from Hyde the news
of the tragedy, almost to the close of his life, a strange
oppression settled upon Montrose. A sense of dark and
menacing fate hung like a cloud about him. He had
been no sentimental cavalier ; he did not believe in
Divine Right ; to him the Lord's Anointed had never
had the sanctity which he possessed for many royalists.
But out of his inner soul he had created the image of
an ideal monarch, wise with a wisdom to which no
earthly king has attained, a personification of the dreams
which had always haunted him. He had, too, the
devotion of a loyal soldier to the master for whom he
had risked so much. But, more than all, he saw in the
tragedy the darkening of the skies over his own unhappy land. The savage and stupid barbarism of the
Covenant, which had revelled in blood in the Lord's

[1] *Mem. of M.*, II., 364-365.

name, now seemed at last to have reached omnipotence, for it had destroyed the centre of all civil order. Henceforth there could be no compromise. He knew nothing of the folly and duplicity which preceded Charles's ultimate heroism; his rejection of compromises which would have secured to him all that was worthy in his cause; his futile search for allies who were alike perjured and impotent, and his double-dealing towards those who had on their side both honesty and power. He saw only the shedding of innocent blood, which must make a breach for all time between those who loved righteousness and those who pursued iniquity. When he heard the news he fainted among his friends. For two days he kept his chamber, and when Wishart entered he found on the table these lines :

> " Great, good, and just, could I but rate
> My grief, and thy too rigid fate,
> I'd weep the world in such a strain
> As it should deluge once again.
> But since thy loud-tongued blood demands supplies
> More from Briareus' hands than Argus' eyes,
> I'll sing thine obsequies with trumpet sounds,
> And write thine epitaph in blood and wounds."

From this moment there is an uncanniness about him, as of one who lives half his time in another world. He has himself painted in coal-black armour; his eyes have a fire which changes their cool greyness into something wilder and fiercer; all youthful weaknesses seem purged away—his pride, his intolerance, his condescension—for his patience becomes unearthly, and his gentleness unhuman. He has the air of a " fey " man, for whom the barriers between the seen and the unseen are breaking down.

In the middle of February he met Hyde at Sevenbergen. Hyde never liked him as Nicholas and Hopton and Digby did, and in the writings of the future Lord Clarendon admiration is always tinged with acid. But he was a loyal servant of the new king, and he recognized capacity when he saw it; to him Montrose was the man of the " clearest spirit and honour " among the

king's advisers, and to be preferred " before any other
of that nation." [1] Montrose proposed an immediate
expedition to Scotland, but Hyde urged delay, and
begged him not to show himself as yet publicly at the
king's court. But when the former heard that the
commissioners from Scotland were at the Hague, he
insisted on presenting himself at once to the king.[2] He
found the young Charles already in the thick of Scottish
intrigues, for the immediate result of the king's death
had been to send a wave of loyalty over that distracted
land. On the 4th of February Charles the Second was
proclaimed at the market-cross of Edinburgh by Loudoun
the Chancellor. As we have seen, there had always
been an odd royalism flickering through the nation, often
in the most unlikely places ; the king was a poor thing,
but their own, like the misguided Covenant ; it might
be well for his own people, the Scots, to take order with
him, but it was high treason in those who hated Scotland as much as they hated Charles. The feeling was
of a piece with the later Jacobitism, an assertion of
nationality on the part of a small, proud, bitterly
poor country, jealous of her rich neighbour, not yet confident in herself. It was sentimental, not reasoned, and
was found even among the extreme Covenanters. Mr.
Robert Blair of St. Andrews was anxious to attend
Charles on the scaffold. " He made his account to die
with the king, and would as willingly have laid down
his head to the hatchet as ever he laid his head to a
pillow." [3] In November 1650 we find Mr. Robert
Baillie writing to Mr. David Dickson : " If my lord
Argyll at this strait should desert the king . . . I think,
and many more with me of the best I speak with, that
it would be a fearful sin in him, which God will revenge." [4]
No doubt in ministerial breasts loyalty was intertwined
with the Covenant, but it was loyalty of a kind. Hamil-

---

[1] *Hist.*, XII., 15.
[2] His arrival scared away that whimsical worthy, Thomas Cunningham, the
Scottish Conservator at Campvere, and the fabricator of the " Thrissels-Banner."
See Cunningham, *Journal* (S.H.S.), 188–189.
[3] Row, *Life of Blair*, 215.
[4] Baillie, III., 109. For other examples of clerical royalists see *ibid.* III., 34,
and *Commission of the General Assembly Records*, I., 427.

ton's death on the scaffold in March [1] intensified the feeling of national resentment which Preston had kindled. The luckless duke was not a brilliant figure. His epitaph has been spoken by Alison Wilson in *Old Mortality* : " That was him that lost his head at London. Folks said that it wasna a very guid ane, but it was aye a sair loss to him, puir gentleman." It had been prophesied— and the prophecy had hag-ridden his mind—that he would succeed the king ; but he fell heir not to a throne, but to a scaffold.

Montrose, watching Scotland from a distance, may well have believed that the aspect of affairs was more promising than ever before. There were, indeed, no Gordons to appeal to. Huntly had at last fallen into his enemy's hands, and his " bustling in the north," as Sir James Turner called his vagrant activity, was over for ever. On 23rd March he was beheaded in Edinburgh, lamenting pathetically that he had done so little for the cause he died for, and stoutly refusing to be released from the excommunication of the Kirk, which could not affect him where he was going.[2] Aboyne was in exile, dying of a broken heart, and the Gordon lands were in the power of Lord Lewis, who was soon to make his peace with his uncle. But the great northern clan of Mackenzie was hopeful. Its chief, Seaforth, had arrived at the exiled court, and his brother, Mackenzie of Pluscardine, had raised his clan in March, and along with Reay and Ogilvy had taken Inverness and given much trouble to David Leslie. They were soon to be scattered, but the hope of the Mackenzies remained. Moreover, the Covenanters could not long maintain peace with the English Parliament, or Argyll continue his pact with Cromwell, since they stood for monarchy and the Covenant, while Cromwell would have none of either. In such a quarrel honesty might come by its own.

[1] Burnet gives a long account of his last hours, and prints his beautiful letter to his children. *Mem. of the Hamiltons*, 397. His speech on the scaffold, as well as those of Lord Holland and Lord Capel, was published in a pamphlet by Peter Cole, London, 1649. For the English royalists' view of Hamilton see the pamphlet, *Digitus Dei—God's Justice upon Treachery*. London, 1649.

[2] Balfour, III., 393.

During the next few months the Hague was the battlefield of contending factions. There were three parties in Scottish politics : the rigid Covenanters with Argyll at their head, who were prepared to accept Charles if he would accept the Solemn League and Covenant and agree to the imposition of Presbytery on England ; the Engagers, whose emissaries in Holland were Lanark and Lauderdale, and who had similar principles, but proposed to apply them more laxly;[1] and the royalists *sans phrase*, like Montrose, Kinnoull, Sinclair, and Napier, who were wholly against a Covenant which would make co-operation with the English loyalists impossible. In March the envoys of the Estates arrived, among them Cassilis and Mr. Robert Baillie, who, with many protestations of loyalty, demanded as the price of kingship the Covenant in all its rigidity and the repudiation of all excommunicated persons, " especially James Graham, a man most justly . . . cast out of the Church of God . . . upon whose head lies more innocent blood than for many years hath done on the head of any one, the most bloody murtherer in our nation." [2]

It is not easy to see exactly what Argyll would have been at. He was a realist in politics, and not a dreamer, but it would appear that he was losing his sense of reality. The king's execution had broken his alliance with Cromwell ; his desire was for the establishment of Presbytery in both nations, but his speech in the House of Lords on June 25, 1646,[3] showed that he was prepared to advocate an elastic Presbytery with toleration for other sects ; on such a programme he might have secured most of the Engagers, and considerable English support. But to return to the extreme Presbyterian claims, to demand a subscription from the king which must involve the sin of perjury, to refuse all alliance except with those of the same narrow creed, was to make Cromwell's triumph as certain as the rising of the sun. He was opposed to a great soldier with a powerful army, and he

---

[1] Montrose suspected some collusion between Lanark and Argyll. See Lang, III., 200 *n*.   [2] Baillie, III., 512.   [3] See page 308, *supra*.

began by depriving himself of the best natural fighting
material in Scotland—the clans—and the only generalship of the first order—Montrose's. Moreover, a united
England and Scotland had always been one of his
worthiest policies, and this intransigence was to make
the fissure a gulf. The conditions which he would impose on the king brought on him the hostility of most
loyalists ; his fidelity to monarchy set him in opposition to Cromwell and the Independents ; his insistence
upon the most intolerant Scots type of Presbytery
marshalled against him the whole of England. It is
impossible to resist the conclusion that from henceforth
this adroit politician is losing his grip. He ceased to be
a realist, and fell back upon the deepest strain in his
nature—the religious enthusiasm which he had acquired
long before at the Glasgow Assembly ; and this, shot
with flickering lights of irrelevant worldly wisdom,
remained his mood till his death. " My thought," he
wrote of this period to his son, " became distracted, and
myself encountered so many difficulties in the way, that
all remedies that were applied had the quite contrary
operation. Whatever, therefore, hath been said by me
or others in this matter, you must refute and accept
them as from a distracted man of a distracted subject
in the distracted time wherein I lived." [1]

The Engagers were more politic, and pressed their
demands more modestly, but in substance they asked
for the same thing. Lanark, indeed, in his first zeal
after Preston, was prepared to " join with the lord
Marquis of Montrose and all the king's party," and was
" so far from contesting about command, that he would
be a serjeant under Montrose." [2] But as Duke of
Hamilton in his brother's stead, he fell into timider
courses ; if Charles was to become king it was necessary
to unite Scotland, and Montrose was a perilous bone of
contention. As for Lauderdale, his pure soul had been
shocked (so he said) by Montrose's barbarities, though,
on cross-examination by Hyde, he was unable to give

---

[1] " Instructions to a Son," cited by Willcock, *The Great Marquess*, 223.
[2] *Clarendon State Papers*, II., 460.

an instance of any slaughter " but what was done in the field." The man whose foul table-talk was the byword of the Restoration court, and sickened even the king, was an odd censor of morals. There is a picture by Cornelius Janssen in which Hamilton and Lauderdale are portrayed side by side, a scroll passing between them, and in the dark, uncertain features of the one and the gross, gobbling mouth and cunning eyes of the other may be read all the weakness of the Engagement.

It was Montrose who was now the realist. He desired a policy which would attract the maximum support in the two kingdoms—the restoration of monarchy on constitutional lines, with freedom secured to each country for the kind of church it favoured. Charles demanded an opinion from both the royalists and the Engagers as to the conditions of the Estates. Montrose's reply is still extant, and differs from the other remonstrances and declarations through which he had already published his faith to the world only in that it is directed to a narrower issue.[1] It traced the history of the Covenant movement from its justifiable beginnings to its impossible end; it pointed out that the Covenanters required from the king a renunciation of his own private form of worship, " and yet they made it a ground of rebellion against your royal father that they but imagined he intended to meddle with them after the like kind." The document was read in Charles's council on the 21st of May, the terms of the Estates were refused, and Montrose was confirmed in his viceroyalty and appointed admiral of the Scottish seas.

Apparently the king had made up his mind. He had rejected Argyll and, having accepted Montrose, had also rejected the Engagers. He stood committed now to some such bold attempt as his captain-general had always urged. He wrote to Montrose from Breda on 22nd June that he would come to no decision touching the affairs of Scotland without consulting him, and the Duke of York a month later wrote to congratulate him on his new " occasion of employment." [2] At that time

---

[1] *Mem. of M.*, II., 376, etc.   [2] Napier, II., 206.

the plan was for the king to go to Ireland and establish there his principal base, but Cromwell's expedition in August caused its relinquishment.[1] Scotland remained, and in Cromwell's absence in Ireland during the whole of the winter 1649–50 there lay a sovran chance of organizing the former country for the king. Montrose had wished the king to join him there, but he had acquiesced in the Irish alternative, for his one fear was that Charles should go to Scotland in bond to the Covenant. But already Charles had begun to regard the Scottish expedition with uncertain eyes. He favoured it chiefly that he might have another asset in bargaining with the Estates. In the wars of the Middle Ages both sides on the eve of peace endeavoured to take as many fortresses as possible in order to have something to give up when the day of renunciation came ; and so it was with Charles now. The intrigues with Covenanters and Engagers still went on, though the scene was moved to Paris and the court of Henrietta. Jermyn seems to have patched up a friendship with the new Hamilton, and attempted to get Montrose's commission as viceroy annulled in his favour. " They are all mad, or worse," was the judgment of Elizabeth of Bohemia on that nest of futile and selfish schemers.

III

Montrose, at the Hague, made a new friend, and while following Charles that summer to Breda and Brussels, and when, later in the autumn, he was recruiting among the countries of northern Europe, he had a correspondent who kept a jealous eye on his interests. In his youth sentimental girls had written him love-letters ; his marriage had been a love-match ; but since he had been compelled to serve a new mistress, " the first foe in the field," no woman had played a part in his life. The lady who now entered it was the most celebrated in Europe. Elizabeth of the Palatine, for

[1] M. and S., 233, *n.* 13.

some brief winter months Queen of Bohemia, had the strange compelling power of her grandmother, Mary of Scots, over the hearts of men. As a girl she had been the idol of her country, for she had the fire and brilliance and endearing simplicity of her brother Henry. Her wedding to the Prince Palatine had set all England junketing for weeks. Then came the disastrous episode of the Bohemian throne, the beginning of the Thirty Years' War, the loss of both Bohemia and the Palatine, her husband's death, and the squalor of a court in exile, dependent upon foreign bounty. But misfortune, no more than age, could dim her charm. When Montrose first met her she was in her early fifties, as we see her in the portraits by Honthorst and Miereveldt— a woman who had left youth behind her, one who had known the whole range of mortal joys and sorrows, with a mouth a little narrowed by pain and disappointment, but with great brown eyes still full of the hunger of life. Few crossed her path but were beguiled, and either became her devotees and the sharers in her broken fortunes, or to their dying day cherished the memory of her as if in a shrine. Zachary Boyd, in far-off Glasgow, came under a spell which is patent even in his halting verses. Donne sent her his sermons and his prayers. To the staid Sir Henry Wotton she was " the eclipse and glory of her kind," and he wrote in anguish, " Shall I die without seeing again my royal mistress ? "

> " You meaner beauties of the night,
>   That poorly satisfy our eyes
> More by your number than your light,
>   You common people of the skies,
> What are you when the moon shall rise ? "

Was ever woman praised more nobly ? But the glamour fell on others than the poets. " I see it is not good to be my friend," she once wrote, and indeed a following so loyal could not but suffer in a cause so calamitous. But for Elizabeth's sake men forgot worldly wisdom, and were back in the high days of chivalry. There were the young gentlemen of the Middle Temple, who

kissed a sword and swore a solemn oath to live and die
in her service.   There was Sir Ralph Hopton, who, fresh
from Oxford, accompanied her in the flight from Prague ;
and Conway, and Lord Carlisle, and Sir Dudley Carleton,
and Lord Cromwell, and Sir Thomas Roe, and Christian
of Brunswick.   Soldiers, courtiers, ambassadors, bravos,
each subscribed himself, like Christian, " your most
humblest, most constant, most faithful, most affectionate,
and most obedient slave, who loves you and will love you,
infinitely and incessantly to death."   And there was
Lord Craven, who laid his great fortune at her feet, and
lived only to serve her.

What was there in Elizabeth to draw forth this
wealth of love ?   Reckless, extravagant, exacting, perhaps a little heartless, there was about her a kind of
stellar greatness, a spirit that could not be soiled or
subdued by fate.   Like Constance, she had " instructed
her sorrows to be proud," but it was a laughing pride
which endeared as well as awed.   " Though I have
cause enough to be sad," she wrote to Sir Thomas Roe,
" yet I am still of my wild humour to be as merry as I
can in spite of fortune."   She was a better friend than
a mother, for her daughter Sophia declared that her
monkeys and her dogs came before her children.   The
buffets of the world had a little calloused her.   But her
flawless courage remained, her winning humour, her
subtlety, her abounding zest for life.

Montrose was a soldier after her own heart, and to
him the mother of Rupert and Maurice was a joy in
that rabble of half-hearted casuists.   Her little sheaf of
letters to him during these months shows how gracious
an interlude their friendship was.   She rallies the grave
cavalier, and gives him the news of the court from the
point of view of an ardent well-wisher.   The Prince of
Orange is against him, the Princess for him.   " For
God's sake leave not the king so long as he is at Breda,
for without question there is nothing that will be omitted
to ruin you and your friends."   It was at her request
that he sat for the splendid Honthorst portrait, which
she hung in her cabinet that it might " frighten away

the Brethren." She is full of nicknames : Seaforth is
" my Highlander," Montrose himself, " Jamie Graham."
She commends recruits for his service, she invites him to
Rhenen, her country house, to shoot at the butts with
Kinnoull and exhibit his old undergraduate prowess ;
she sends him gossip to amuse him, and wild rumours
from England. She tells him that " old Brainford "
(Lord Brentford, who had once been Patrick Ruthven)
was constant to him—" he says he is now too old to be
a knave, having been honest ever " ; no doubt he was
honest, but he was rarely sober. And in every letter
she sends fervent prayers for his success, and in the
last for his " safety in Scotland." [1]

The bankrupt Palatines, men and women, were for a
while the most dazzling things in Europe. Of the four
daughters, Elizabeth, the handsome bluestocking and
friend of Leibniz, died a spinster ; the pink and
white Henrietta married the Prince of Transylvania ;
Sophia espoused the Elector of Hanover, and became
the ancestress of the royal house of Britain ; Louise,
charming, kind, ill-dressed, artistic, turned Catholic
and died in extreme old age as abbess of Maubuisson.
In the lively pages of Sophia's memoirs there is a story
of a projected marriage between Montrose and the last
princess, but it may be dismissed as an idle tale.[2] That
chapter in his life had long ago been closed.

IV

The preparations for the Scottish campaign began
in June. Charles had promised that he would do
nothing in any of his negotiations to prejudice Montrose's
commission as viceroy, and he had further nominated
him his ambassador to the northern courts. Recruits
there were in plenty, so far as officers were concerned—
Scots mercenaries who had fought in the German wars
and were only too anxious to find new employment ;
Scots patriots, such as Gustavus's old colonel, John

---

[1] The letters are in *Mem. of M.*, II., 384, etc.
[2] *Memoirs of Sophia, Electress of Hanover* (Eng. trans., 1888), 22.

Gordon, who were eager to strike a blow for their country.[1] Some of the said Scots were compromising allies, and the murder of the Commonwealth envoy, Dr. Dorislaus, at the Hague on 3rd May, did not lessen the difficulties of the king and his captain-general.[2] But foreign troops and foreign money were also necessary, and to secure these Montrose sent his emissaries far and wide. His half-brother, Harry Graham, was dispatched to the Elector of Brandenburg, and got the promise of a large sum, which was never paid. In August Kinnoull, with 80 officers and 100 Danish recruits, set sail for the Orkneys in an ancient patched-up vessel, and after much trouble with tempests and Parliamentary frigates, arrived at Kirkwall in September.[3] The reason for the choice of such a base is clear. The islanders were strangers to the religious strife of the mainland, and Lord Morton, their feudal superior, was Kinnoull's uncle, and well disposed to the royalist cause. The Commonwealth navy, occupied with preventing Rupert's escape from Ireland, was less likely to interfere with the transports if their route lay so far to the north. Further, the parts of Scotland adjoining were close to the Mackay and Mackenzie country, and Montrose looked for support from both clans. If he could command the northern apex of Scotland, then Leslie, to meet him, would have to march through the hostile hill country, and in the event of a royalist victory the central Highlands would rise to a man.

Montrose himself arrived at Hamburg early in September. Here he negotiated for supplies with the Duke of Courland, and presently set off to Schleswig to meet Frederick, the new King of Denmark. He lingered for some time at Copenhagen, for this diplomacy was a slow business, and thence he dispatched letters to Rupert

---

[1] See Gordon's letter in M. and S., 283.

[2] Clarendon (XII., 24) ascribes the murder to Scotsmen, "servants or dependents upon the Marquis of Montrose." A certain Colonel Whiteford, taken at Dunbeath after Carbisdale, was pardoned by the Estates because of his share in this murder. Clarendon, XII., 141. Balfour, IV., 60. *A. P. S.*, VI., 594. The Covenanters seem to have considered it a justifiable vengeance upon a regicide.

[3] See the account of the voyage in Gwynne, *Military Memoirs*, 83–85.

and Ormonde in Ireland, and to his friends in Scotland, which latter epistles were captured by the Estates. There, too, he had news of Kinnoull's successful landing. Morton had welcomed him with open arms, and all was going well for the cause. The common people of Scotland, so Kinnoull reported, were on the eve of revolt against their masters. "Your lordship is gaped after with that expectation that the Jews had for their Messiah, and certainly your presence will restore your groaning country to its liberties and the king to his rights."[1] But he had other news less pleasing. Charles wrote from St. Germains on 19th September :

> "I entreat you to go on vigorously, and with your wonted courage and care, in the preservation of those trusts I have committed to you, and not to be startled with any reports you may hear, as if I were otherwise inclined to the Presbyterians than when I left you. I assure you I am upon the same principles I was, and depend as much as ever upon your undertakings and endeavours for my service, being fully resolved to assist and support you therein to the uttermost of my power."[2]

This was ominous. Henrietta was at St. Germains, and Montrose knew too well her notion of policy.

Early in November, finding it impossible to do much with Frederick, he passed over to Gothenburg in Sweden. The port was full of long-settled Scots merchants, and one, John Maclear, put his house and his wealth at his disposal. Montrose's chief fear was that the reports of a treaty with the Covenant, at which Charles had hinted in his letter, would utterly dishearten the Scottish loyalists, and to counteract such a danger he issued what he had prepared some months before, the last and most famous of his declarations.[3] The document is

---

[1] M. and S., 256. The original is in the *Wodrow MSS.*, in the National Library of Scotland.

[2] M. and S., 263.

[3] The copy in "Civil War Tracts" in the British Museum is dated Copenhagen, July 9, 1649, but the copy in my collection has the imprint of "Gothenberge." I possess another declaration, also dated July 9, 1649, from "Hassuia in the Kingdom of Denmark," and apparently published in London, to which I can find no reference elsewhere. In it Montrose defends himself against "that harsh and uncharitable censure which the Parliament and Kirk of Scotland are pleased to pass against me," and undertakes to do nothing prejudicial to "the well-being and present government of that Kirk and kingdom." He undertakes

inspired by his old unhesitating courage. Montrose is as confident of the sacredness of his mission as any Covenant minister. He begins with a pertinent quotation from Tacitus ; he indicts the Covenanters alike on their past and present policy ; he offers in the king's name pardon to all except proven regicides, and in a noble ending he summons all true Scottish hearts to make a last effort for freedom :

> " Resolving, with Joab, to play the man for their people and the cities of their God, and let the Lord do whatever seemeth Him good ; wherein, whatsomever shall behappen, they may at least be assured of Crastinus's recompense that, dead or alive, the world will give them thanks."

The declaration was circulated in Edinburgh in December, and, on the second day of the new year, Wariston issued the reply of the Estates, in which it was ordered to be burned by the hangman and its author denounced as " that viperous brood of Satan, whom the Estates of Parliament have long since declared traitor, the Church hath delivered into the hands of the devil, and the nation doth generally abhor."

Christina of Sweden, Gustavus's daughter and

---

also to " leave the continuance or alteration of government either in Church or State in his Majesty's other dominions to the judgment and discretion of his Majesty and the Parliaments thereof." He then enumerates the crimes of his opponents, culminating in Charles's death. All this is in Montrose's authentic manner. But the declaration concludes with the astonishing announcement that he is coming presently to Scotland, an invitation to loyalists to meet him at Inverness, and a summons to all rebels to lay down their arms before 1st November, otherwise they will receive no mercy. " I will with all violence and fury pursue and kill them as vagabond rogues and regicides, not sparing one that had any hand in that horrible and barbarous murder, committed upon the sacred person of our late dread sovereign, but utterly extirpate and eradicate them, their wives, children, and families, and leaving none of their cursed race (if possible) breathing upon the face of the earth." This peroration is such manifest folly as a preliminary to the kind of campaign which Montrose projected, and so out of keeping with his general attitude, that one must consider the declaration an unauthorized publication by some hot-headed royalist who perhaps had got hold of one of Montrose's drafts. Though it bears a London imprint the style of printing is not English. Montrose is referred to as captain-general of his Majesty's forces in " Great Britain," not in Scotland only.

The Gothenburg declaration was printed in London in 1650 by Matthew Simmons, together with the reply of the General Assembly and extracts from the reply of the Estates, and a cynical postscript by some Englishman who did not love the Scots. The replies of the Estates and the Assembly were printed at Edinburgh by Evan Tyler in 1650 in English and Latin. They will be found also in an appendix to the 1819 edition of Wishart.

Descartes's erratic disciple, was no more inclined than
her neighbour of Denmark to support publicly the
royalist cause. She could not afford to risk the displeasure of a great sea-power like England. It was
from northern Europe that the Commonwealth looked
for the expected invasion, and every port was full of
its spies.[1] The most she could do was to wink at his
presence in Gothenburg and permit him to buy war
stores. This was his chief task during December, and
it is one of history's ironies that certain supplies of
powder and shot, which he did not take with him to
Scotland, were afterwards used by the Covenanters
against Cromwell.[2] Early in that month a ship arrived
from the Orkneys with melancholy news. David Leslie
had marched north to Caithness in the end of October,
and had written to Kinnoull advising him to depart
while there was yet time. The letter was ordered to
be burned by the hangman, and Leslie went south
without crossing the Pentland Firth.[3] But on the
12th of November the loyal Morton died, and a few
days later Kinnoull fell sick of pleurisy and followed him
to the grave. The loss of his friend and " passionate
servant " was a heavy blow to Montrose. But Sir
James Douglas, Morton's brother, who arrived in the
Orkney sloop, brought good news of the general feeling
in Scotland. He implored the viceroy to sail at once,
for "his own presence was able to do the business, and
would undoubtedly bring 20,000 men together for the
king's service, all men being weary and impatient to
live any longer under that bondage, pressing down their
estates, their persons, and their consciences." [4] Montrose may well have believed a report so consonant with
his desires. His ardour was always prone to make
light of difficulties, and he had no wise old Napier to
remind him that the feelings of Sir James Douglas and

---

[1] In a pamphlet, *The Great Plot Discovered, etc.* (London, G. Cotter), Montrose
was believed to be about to descend upon Norfolk from Denmark as early as
February 8, 1647.
[2] Douglas, *Cromwell's Scotch Campaigns*, 237 *n.*
[3] Gwynne, 86–87.
[4] Nicholas to Ormonde ; Carte, *Ormonde Papers*, I., 345, etc.

his friends were scarcely an index to the temper of
burgesses and peasants, wearied out with poverty and
the terrors of an Old Testament God.

In December he made an effort to leave. Transports
were indeed dispatched with Danish troops and Scottish
officers, as well as ammunition and stands of arms, and
the wild weather they encountered gave rise to tales
of shipwreck which gladdened the heart of the Estates.
He wrote to Seaforth on the 15th of December saying
that he meant to sail for Scotland next day. But the
winds were contrary, and floating ice blocked the harbour, and it was not till January 10, 1650, that he
actually embarked in the *Herderinnen* (" Shepherdess "),
a frigate which Maclear had bought for him from the
Swedish Admiralty. Still he did not start, and on the
18th we find him living in Maclear's house on shore.
We know now the reason of that delay which so puzzled
the Swedish statesmen and the spies of the Commonwealth. He had received word that a dispatch was
coming to him from the king in Jersey. For such a
message he could not choose but wait.

But at that season of the year, in those northern
waters, communications were uncertain, and Montrose
had to leave Gothenburg without the royal letter.
The *Herderinnen*, with stores and guns, sailed at the
beginning of March, and he crossed the snowy backbone
of mountain that separates Sweden from Norway, and
joined her at Bergen. The Commonwealth agents reported him there on 14th March, waiting to collect
various officers, who were immobilized by lack of
passage money at Hamburg or Bremen.[1] Harry May,
the king's messenger, had to follow the viceroy to
Kirkwall in the Orkneys, where he delivered the king's
letter on the 23rd of March. It was dated from Jersey
on 12th January, and with it came the George and the
blue riband of the Garter. There were two letters, one
to be shown to his friends, and the other a private note
for Montrose's own eye, and enclosed in the packet were
copies of the recent correspondence with the commis-

[1] *A Brief Relation* (April 9–16, 1650), 472–473.

sioners of the Estates. In the first letter the king informed his viceroy of the negotiations with the Scots
Parliament and the chance of a treaty. Montrose,
however, is assured that " we will not, before or during
the treaty, do anything contrary to that power and
authority which we have given you by our commission,
nor consent to anything that may bring the least degree
of diminution to it; and if the said treaty should
produce an agreement, we will, with our uttermost
care, so provide for the honour and interest of yourself,
and of all that shall engage with you, as shall let the
whole world see the high esteem we have for you."
It ends with an exhortation to " proceed vigorously
and effectively in your undertaking "; and then, with
an excess of candour, makes clear the reason. " We
doubt not but all our loyal and well-affected subjects of
Scotland will cordially and effectually join with you,
and by that addition of strength either dispose those
who are otherwise minded to make reasonable demands
to us in a treaty, or be able to force them to it by arms,
in case of their obstinate refusal." He desires an asset
to bargain with, a second string to his bow. The
private note merely assured the recipient that Charles
would never consent to anything to his prejudice, and
bade him " not to take alarm at any reports or messages
from others." [1]

It was a clear instruction to proceed with the invasion of Scotland, but it had an ugly air of double-
dealing. The warning against reports argued that
something had been done or said to give good cause for
reports. Montrose, regardless of self, thought only of the
danger to the king—the risk that by trusting his enemies
he might walk into the same trap as his father. In his
reply, on the 26th of March, he repeats that " it is not
your fortune in you, but your Majesty in whatsomever
fortune, that I make sacred to serve "; but he beseeches
his master " to have a serious eye (now at last) upon the
too open crafts are used against you, chiefly in this
conjunction, and that it would please your Majesty to be

[1] *Mem. of M.*, II., 410, etc.

so just to yourself as, ere you make a resolve upon your affairs or your person, your Majesty may be wisely pleased to hear the zealous opinions of your faithful servants, who have nothing in their hearts, nor before their eyes, but the joy of your Majesty's prosperity and greatness, which shall be ever the only passion and study of your most sacred Majesty's most humble, faithful, and most passionate subject and servant ! " [1]

1650
March

There can be no doubt that when he wrote the letters of January Charles was loyal to Montrose, and that he counted more on Montrose's success in the field than on the prospect of a treaty. This was the opinion of the shrewd Commonwealth agent, with an admirable gift of phrase, who contributed to the official gazette of the Council of State, *A Brief Relation.* It was proved by the royal warrants, dated as late as 29th March, appointing the veteran Lord Eythin to be Montrose's second-in-command. The king was no doubt determined to secure honourable terms for his captain-general in any treaty. But he hankered after a union of all Scotland on his side, which would be linked to a royalist rising in England, and he believed that incompatibles might be harmonized by an adroit negotiator, the more if there were a triumphant army in the background. The plan was an idle dream; Montrose was the true realist when he held that Charles's only chance lay in a policy of Scottish ways for Scotland, English ways for England, and the king for both—a policy which meant good-bye to Argyll and the theocrats of the Solemn League. Charles had no intention of bringing Montrose to catastrophe, but he made it certain by the treaty which he pursued, nay, by the very fact of negotiating at all at such a juncture. Moreover, when Montrose received the king's message that had happened which, had he known it, might have added another protest to his reply. As early as 19th January the first letter had been published in Paris, and a précis was in the hands of the Commonwealth Government. It may

---

[1] This tragic letter was printed for the first time by Mr. Gardiner in his *Charles II. and Scotland in 1650* (S.H.S.), 43.

have got out by a clerical blunder, for the royal secretariat was not over-competent.[1] It may have been published by the Montrose faction in Paris to defeat the projected treaty, or the issue may have been authorized by Charles to help the treaty's fortunes. There is evidence for each of the three explanations.[2] But, whether we account for the publicity given to it by accident, maladroit diplomacy, or blundering psychology, the result was disastrous. Already the letter had been broadcast over Scotland. Had Montrose been accompanied by a large and well-equipped foreign army no harm would have been done, but he had still his army to find, and it was in Scotland that he sought it. It is one thing to fight in a crusade ; it is another to share in a campaign whose avowed purpose is no more than to create an object to bargain with. On such mercantile terms you cannot conjure the spirit that wins battles. The half-hearted would wait upon the result of the chaffering. Well might Mr. Secretary Nicholas write to Ormonde : " Some (not without reason) apprehend that the report of the now approaching treaty will make those of a better sort forbear to appear for him, until they shall see the issue of this treaty." [3] The dice had been loaded against the venture before it was begun. The king had sent Montrose to his death.

[1] Long to Ormonde, March 2, 1650. *Ormonde Papers*, I., 367.
[2] See *A Brief Relation* (Feb. 12–19, 1650), 337, (March 12–19) 411, 416 ; and the letter of Abraham Cowley to Ormonde, March 3, 1650, quoted by Gardiner, *Charles II. and Scotland in 1650*, xix.
[3] *Ormonde Papers*, I., 363.

CHAPTER XVI

THE LAST CAMPAIGN

(*March–May*, 1650)

When my affaires goe wrong, I remember that saying of Loucan, *Tam mala Pompeii quam prospera mundus adoret.*

Claverhouse to Menteith, July 1680.

IT has been the fashion among historians to describe the last campaign as doomed from the start. So in a sense it was, but its hopelessness did not lie in the actual military and political situation in Scotland at the moment. That had never been more favourable. Montrose was, indeed, as far off as ever from commending himself and his faith to that Covenanting *bourgeoisie* which he never lost the hope of converting. But the arm of the Covenant was shortened. The disaster at Preston had depleted the fighting strength of the Lowlands, and had driven a wedge into the Estates. Many of the nobles who had once obeyed Argyll were now prepared to follow him only in so far as he allied himself with the king. A real bitterness against England had surged up in the nation, and this meant popularity for Charles, and a fall in esteem for those who had dallied with Charles's enemies. The Estates had no war-chest ; every burgh had been bled white by taxation, and all sections of the people were out of humour with the Edinburgh junta. The government of the Covenanters, now an undisguised theocracy, was as incompetent as it was oppressive. In January of the preceding year the famous Act of Classes had been passed,[1] which excluded from every office—from a ministry of state to a burgh deaconate of crafts—all who were not of one

---

[1] *A. P. S.*, VI., ii., 143-147.

narrow type in political and religious opinions and conduct, and which gave the Kirk an absolute veto on all
public appointments. It was as if the theocracy had
set out to caricature itself, and it was fast disillusion-
ing every sympathizer who had the smallest share of
practical wisdom.

The military situation was not less promising. Of
the former Covenant generals, Leven was too old,
Baillie had been an Engager, and Hurry was now one
of Montrose's companions. Middleton was waiting to
be persuaded.[1] Only David Leslie remained, with his
lieutenants Holbourn and Strachan; of these, Holbourn
had been handsomely beaten at Kilsyth, and Strachan,
an extreme sectary, was not trusted by his commanding
officers. At the most they had 3,000 foot and 1,500
horse, strung out over a wide front in the northern
Highlands. The estimate of what forces might be
raised for the king in Scotland, which Montrose had
sent to Henrietta by Crawford in the autumn of 1646,
had exceeded 20,000.[2] There were uncertain items,
like the 1,000 who had been credited to Lord Nithsdale,
the 2,000 to Macdonald of Sleat, the 1,500 to Huntly,
and the 2,000 to Seaforth; but, putting all doubtful
elements aside, it looked as if in the Highlands alone he
could count on 10,000 men. Things had improved since
the date of that estimate. The clan of Mackenzie had
risen with Pluscardine, and might rise again, for their
chief, the Queen of Bohemia's " Highlander," was
apparently at last on the royalist side. There is no
equivocal figure of that time but has found its defender
—Huntly in Patrick Gordon, Hamilton in Burnet—and
we have Seaforth's defence in the simple pages of his
clansman, Mackenzie of Applecross; but the best that
the author can say is that Seaforth " in the beginning
of the king's troubles had not the light that was afterwards given him." [3] It might reasonably be assumed
that now that light had been vouchsafed. The En-

---

[1] May to Nicholas, *Charles II. and Scotland in 1650*, 49.   Ogilvy of Powrie
to Montrose, M. and S., 286.   [2] See p. 317, *supra.*
[3] *Highland Papers* (S.H.S.), II., 65.

gagers, at least the fighting element in them, were losing
some of their hostility to Montrose.   The new Hamilton
was again declaring his willingness " to trail a pike or
ride a private trooper under him." [1]   The new Huntly,
too, whom we have known as Lord Lewis Gordon, was
reported to be waiting obediently on the king's commands,[2] though a little annoyed at not receiving the
Garter.   Again, if Montrose got one-half of the levies
and supplies promised from the Continent, if he got
one-quarter of the help hinted at from Ireland, he
would be able to put into the field from 4,000 to 5,000
regular troops as well.

Leslie was in a poor position both for attack and
defence, and defeat to him would mean annihilation.
For Montrose to succeed, all that seemed essential was
that he should have sufficient troops in the far north
to win the first round.   If that happened, he might
count on the Macleods and the Mackenzies ; probably,
too, on the Gordons ; and then the safety of his route
to the south would be assured.   Once in Badenoch, he
had all the loyal levies of the west and of Atholl to draw
upon, and with the Lowlands divided it was hard to see
what could prevent him from dominating Scotland.
Then he could cross the Border and appeal to the
royalists and the English moderates, not like the luckless Hamilton with an insolent dogma of Presbyterian
ascendancy, but with a wise recognition of national
rights, a generous policy of toleration, and that constitutional creed of his which John Hampden would not
have scrupled to subscribe.   We know to-day how little
hold the army of the Commonwealth had upon the
affection of the English people.   Of the two leaders,
Montrose was not the inferior in military genius, and if,
with 20,000 Highland and foreign foot and Lowland
horse, and with England's goodwill, he had met Cromwell on his return from Ireland somewhere south of
Trent, the odds are that the Restoration would have
been antedated by ten years.

[1] *A Brief Relation* (March 12–19, 1650), 401.
[2] *Charles II. and Scotland in 1650*, 49.

Dis aliter visum ; rightly, perhaps, for Cromwell had still much to give to the world. As it chanced, every condition of success was to fail. Montrose had far too few foreign troops. The local clans did not rise in his support, and there was no sign of movement in the Lowlands. The king's letter, and the news that negotiations were on foot between him and the Estates, had done their work. Men were weary of fighting, and half-hearted in any cause. The satiety which attended the Restoration was beginning. Let them be shown a way of peace and they would acclaim it, but meantime it was the duty of wise folk to stay at home. The Covenanting régime was becoming so intolerable to every class that, had there been no alternative, many might have grasped at Montrose's way of deliverance ; but, since an alternative was openly held before the nation by the king his master, the cautious man let his sword sleep in the thatch and hoped for a quiet life.

The king might handicap him and stultify his mission, but Montrose was true to himself. For him there could be no turning back on this side the grave, for he had been to the edge of the world and looked over the other side. The " waft of death " had gone out against him, and all his doings have a touch of the unearthly. He devised strange standards, like those which, in Bunyan's *Holy War,* Emmanuel and Diabolus used in their battle for Mansoul. His foot bore on a black ground the bleeding head of the dead king, with the words *Deo et Victricibus Armis.* The cavalry colours, too, were black, with three pairs of clasped hands holding three drawn swords, and the legend *Quos Pietas Virtus et Honor fecit Amicos.* His own flag was of white damask, with two steep rocks and a river between, and a lion about to leap from one to the other. His motto was *Nil Medium.*[1] He was putting it to the touch, as

[1] *A Brief Relation* (Feb. 19-26, 1650), 360 ; Balfour, III., 439. Fantastic standards were the fashion of the age, on both royalist and Parliament side. One of the former had a lion couchant with a cur biting its tail, and the motto *Pym, Pym, Pym ! Quousque tandem abutere patientia nostra ?*—one of the latter, an armed soldier, threatening a kneeling bishop, and the words *Visne episcopari ? Nolo, Nolo.* Firth, 45.

he had sung, " to win or lose it all." There is an air of
doom and desperation in everything, as of some dark saga of the north.

The early days of April were spent at Kirkwall in marshalling his little forces. There were four or five hundred Danish troops already there.[1] The Orcadians, then very far from being a warlike people, were strong on the king's side, and raised 1,000 men. With Montrose were a number of cavaliers and soldiers of fortune : Lord Frendraught, Sutherland's nephew and his old opponent at Aberdeen ; veterans of the German wars like Sir William Johnston and Colonel Thomas Gray ; [2] his half-brother, Harry Graham ; Sir John Hurry, now twice a turncoat ; Sir James Douglas, a brother of Morton ; William Hay, the new Kinnoull ; Sir Francis Hay of Dalgetty, Drummond of Balloch, Ogilvy of Powrie, and Menzies of Pitfoddels ; and one or two English royalists, like that Major Lisle who had left Scotland with him in September 1646. These gentlemen were mounted and made up the whole cavalry of the force, probably some 40 or 50 in all. Hurry was dispatched in advance with a picked band of 500 men, to look into the chances of a landing on the mainland. He found no difficulty, and, hastening on past Wick and Dunbeath, secured the Ord of Caithness — the narrow pass on the shore through which ran the road to the south.

Montrose, with the rest of his army, crossed the Pentland Firth in fishing-boats about the 12th of April. There was little chance of recruiting in Caithness, but some of the gentry, who were partisans of the Reay interest, joined his standard. It was his business, seeing that his forces were so inadequate, to push on with the greatest possible speed, so as to pass the low coastlands and reach the shelter of the hills, where the Covenant horse could do him no harm and reinforcements could be awaited. Leslie held the castles of Brahan, Chanonry,

---

[1] Almost our only authority for the Orkney part of the campaign is Gwynne. He was left stranded in those parts, and finally escaped in a fishing-smack to Amsterdam, where he was found fainting in the streets from starvation.

[2] Was this the ex-governor of Bergen ? See page 318, *supra.*

Eilandonan, and Cromarty ; and the Earl of Sutherland, who was hot for the Covenant, garrisoned Dunrobin, Skibo, and Dornoch—all key-points on the coast road. But Montrose had not hitherto been wont to trouble about fortresses in his rear. If he marched with his old speed, another week should find him in Badenoch.

At first his movements were swift enough. Landing near John o' Groats, he dashed upon Thurso, and the local lairds, except the Sinclairs, took the oath of allegiance.[1] Leaving Harry Graham with 200 men to keep them to their word, he marched south over the Caithness moors to Sir John Sinclair's castle of Dunbeath, took it after a few days' siege, and left a garrison. He had something less than 800 men when he joined Hurry at the Ord of Caithness. Two days later he reached Sutherland's castle of Dunrobin, which he summoned ; admission was denied, and the place was too strong to take, but another day was wasted, and some of his men, who had incautiously ventured between the castle and the sea, were made prisoners.[2]

Now began the fatal delay. There was no need to diminish his tiny army by leaving garrisons behind him. Orkney was not a base the communications with which it was necessary to guard ; he had still to reach his true base, which was the central Highlands. His business was not to waste an hour in getting to Badenoch. But he may have felt himself too weak to face the garrisons of the Dornoch lowlands, and he was in strong hopes of reinforcements from the north-west. So he turned inland up the glen of the Fleet—the route taken to-day by the railway—and moved past Rhaoine to Lairg, at the foot of Loch Shin. It was now the 23rd of April. To reach the south he must cross or turn the long inlet known as the Kyle of Sutherland ; the shortest

---

[1] So, apparently, did the ministers. One, Mr. William Smith, refused ; and Wodrow (*Analecta*, I., 268) has a story that Montrose had him dragged a mile behind a boat, whereupon Mr. Smith prophesied of his tormentor's coming death. This legend has been exploded by Mark Napier in his *Graham of Claverhouse*, I., 98–102. Gordon of Sallagh, a witness hostile to Montrose, mentions the case of the recalcitrant Mr. Smith, but merely says that " he was sent to the ships to be put in irons," but was " afterwards released " (*Earldom of Sutherland*, 552).　　　　　[2] Gordon of Sallagh, 552–553.

CAMPAIGN OF CARBISDALE

Montrose's March ....
Strachan's March .. _ _ _

English Miles
0 5 10 15 20 25 30

N

NORTH
SEA

Duncansbay Hd
Dunnet
Thurso
Keiss
Wick
Strathy
W. Halladale
E. Halladale
Strath More
Lybster
Dunbeath Cas.
Ord of Caithness
Helmsdale
Strath Ullie
Strath Brora
Strath Fleet
Brora
Dunrobin Cas.
Golspie
Bonar Bridge
Dornoch
Kyle of Sutherland
Carbisdale
Dornoch Firth
Tain
Glen More
Glen Debi
Moray Firth
Findhorn
Cullen
Banff
R. Deveron
Cromarty
Elgin
Fochabers
Keith
Ben Wyvis
Dingwall
Rothes
Fortrose
Fort George
R. Nairn
Glen Orrin
Beauly
INVERNESS
R. Findhorn
Strath Dearn
Huntly
Strath Bogie
Glen Strath Farrar
Mullardoch
Glen Cannich
Strath Affric
Mealfourvoume
Glen Moriston
Oulnain W.
Strath Spey
R. Spey
R. Don
Fort Augustus
Loch Lochy
Glen Roy
Kingussie
Cairngorm
Ben Avon
R. Avon
Strath Avon
Strath Don
Aboyne
R. Dee
Castleton
GRAMPIAN MOUNTAINS
MONADLIATH MTS
Loch Ness
L. Eireboll
Ben Hope
Loyal
Ben Hee
L. Naver
Strath Naver
L. More
Ben More
Loch Shin
Glen Cassley
R. Oykell
Lairg
Ben Dearg
R. Carron

way was down the Shin, but the winter had been severe
and the fords were bad, so he preferred to cross the hills
to Rosehall in Strath Oykell. Thence he moved down
the right bank of the Oykell, reaching the Kyle early on
the 25th.[1] He was expecting hourly a great accession
of Mackenzies from the west, and he hoped for recruits
from the Monroes and Rosses [2] south of the Dornoch
Firth. He believed that he need fear no immediate
opposition, and that there was in all Ross but one troop
of enemy horse.[3]

Meantime Leslie was hurrying north to a rendezvous
at Brechin, which he had appointed for the 25th of April.
He had instructed Strachan and Halket, who commanded the Covenant troops in Moray, to do their best
to delay Montrose's advance; so Strachan, with the
garrisons of Brahan and Chanonry, went north to Tain,
where he was joined by other Covenant posts. He had
five troops of horse—220 men in all ; [4] 36 musketeers of
Lawers's regiment, and a reserve of 400 Monroes and
Rosses whom Montrose had vainly hoped to attach to
his standard. Lord Sutherland was sent north of the
Kyle to oppose Harry Graham, and cut off the way of
retreat in that direction.

On Saturday, the 27th of April, Strachan marched
west from Tain to a place called Wester Fearn, on the
southern shore of the Kyle, a few miles south-east of
Bonar Bridge and the mouth of the river Carron.
Leslie only left Brechin the same day. Montrose had
meantime encamped at a spot about five miles off near
the head of the Kyle, under the lee of the steep hill of
Craigcoinichean. It was covered with a light undergrowth, and in front was a piece of more or less level
ground, with the tarn of Carbisdale at the north end,
and to the south-east the deep-cut channel of the Culvain
burn. He had the hill to guard his rear, the Culvain
burn on one flank and the Kyle on the other, and to

---

[1] I have followed throughout this book the old style of chronology, which
was eleven days behind the sun. It was now the first week of a bleak northern May.
[2] Monteith, 511. Both Ross of Balnagowan and Monro of Lemlair had been
in Pluscardine's rising.   [3] Gordon of Sallagh, 553.   [4] Balfour, IV., 9.

defend his front towards the Carron mouth a line of
trenches and breastworks had been erected. Already
Montrose had occupied the position for two days,
waiting for the local clans, notably the Mackenzies.
Had he pushed on, he might have crossed by the hill
road to Alness, and have easily given Strachan the slip.
After that, in another two days he could have passed
Beauly and been on his old secret road to the Spey.
As it was, he had found a strong position, if he chose to
stay by it, for no cavalry could force the pass of Craigcoinichean, and he commanded the shore road down
the Kyle by which his own scouts could bring him early
intelligence of any enemy advance. He had found
that, but nothing more, and meantime the precious
hours were flying.

Strachan reached Wester Fearn about three in the
afternoon of the 27th. He knew from his scouts where
the royalists lay, and he knew their weakness in numbers.
It was his business to draw them down from the hill to
the flat ground, where his cavalry could act. Accordingly he concealed most of his horse among the long
broom which covered the slopes about Wester Fearn.
The contingent of Monroes and Rosses made a circuit
up Strath Carron to a point on the heights above Carbisdale, where they awaited the issue. Like Rob Roy at
Sheriffmuir, their heart was not in the fight, and they
waited to see how the day went before sharing in it.
Strachan then advanced a single troop up the coast till
he had passed the Carron.

Major Lisle, who commanded Montrose's 40 horse,
was sent to reconnoitre, and returned with information
of the single troop. One of the gentleman volunteers,
Monro of Achnes, repeated the assurance which Montrose had already received—that there was but one troop
of horse in all the shire, and that he saw it before him.
Montrose ordered Lisle to halt, and gave the word to
the foot to advance. Meantime Strachan was bringing
up the rest of his force from Wester Fearn. As soon as
the royalists were on the low ground they could see
nothing of his movements, and in the cover of the

broom and the wildwood the whole Covenant cavalry
crossed the Carron.

Suddenly upon Lisle's 40 horse Strachan dashed with
100 of his dragoons. Instantly there appeared a second
troop under Halket, and then the reserves and the
musketeers. Lisle was driven backward upon the foot,
who were not deployed for battle and were easily cast
into confusion. They cannot have been more than
1,200 in all—400 Danes and Germans, and the rest the
raw Orkney levies. The foreigners were not accustomed
to receive a cavalry charge unsupported, and the Orcadians had probably never seen a dragoon in their
lives. They fell back in disorder, and Montrose saw
that his one chance was to regain the safety of the
Craigcoinichean entrenchments. At Dundee, once before, he had done the same thing under greater difficulties; but then his force had been of a different
quality. Had he had his 500 gallant Irish the day would
have been saved, but they had long been below the turf
of Slain-Man's-Lee. The mercenaries retreated in some
order, but the hapless islanders, farm-boys and fisher-
folk unused to war, fled without a blow. Upon the
fugitives came Strachan's reserves, and Lisle's handful
of cavalry, in attempting to cover their retreat, was
cut to pieces. There fell Lisle himself, Menzies of
Pitfoddels, who bore the royal standard, Douglas and
Guthrie and Ogilvy of Powrie. Soon the broken
remnant of the royalists, a few hundreds at the most,
was making its last stand on the wooded slopes of
Craigcoinichean.

Down from the hills came the Monroes and the
Rosses, convinced at last, to take their share of the
victory. The Orkney men were drowned in hundreds
trying to cross the Kyle, or were cut down in the haugh.
Not a family in the islands but lost a son or a brother.
Presently the fire from the woods slackened, and the
royalists, making for the higher slopes across the open,
were shot or stabbed by the horse. Hurry was captured, and with him 58 officers and nearly 400 men.
Montrose had his horse shot under him. It was

Philiphaugh repeated, and once more he was prevented from finding the death which he desired in battle. Frendraught, himself spent with wounds, forced him upon his own horse, and bade him remember his duty to the king's cause. In the late spring gloaming the viceroy of Scotland, accompanied by two of the Sinclair gentry, turned his face from the lost field toward the trackless wildernesses of the west.[1]

He flung away his sword-belt and coat with the star of the Garter that he might escape recognition, and on Frendraught's horse swam the tidal waters of the Oykell. Then he discarded the horse and managed to buy or borrow some rough Highland clothes. Strath Oykell was no place for a mounted man. There were two courses before him: to get into Strathnaver, and so reach Harry Graham at Thurso, and finally pass into Orkney; or to make for the friendly Reay country in the north-west. For the first he must reach Loch Shin and travel by Glen Tirry; for the second his route lay by Loch Shin or by Glen Cassley, and then by Loch More and the Laxford. But he had no knowledge of the country, nor had either of the Sinclairs, one of whom was an Orcadian and the other of Brims in Caithness; and they missed their way among the darkening hills. Instead of going north they wandered due west up the Oykell.

For two days and two nights they were without food and shelter. There were few houses in that land, and no roads; it had been a backward year, and the snow was still far down on the slopes, the bogs were full, and every stream was an icy torrent. With starving and hunted men the sense of direction soon disappears, one stretch of sodden bent is like another, and presently the hills lose their features and become a mere blur to the wearied eye. Somehow the three struggled over the watershed, where the streams began to flow to the Atlantic. It is possible that they believed that they

---

[1] The authorities for the Carbisdale campaign are Gordon of Sallagh, Balfour and Monteith. Murdoch and Simpson (289–321) have provided an admirable reconstruction, in which they have used also local tradition and Taylor's MS. account of the parish of Assynt from the Dunrobin papers.

were twenty miles farther north and beginning the descent towards Scourie. But they were now in desperate case for food, and they resolved to separate and take different roads on the chance of stumbling on help. Sir Edward Sinclair, the Orcadian, was never heard of again ; somewhere in the wilderness he died of famine, and only the foxes and the eagles could tell of his end.[1] On the third day Montrose was given bread and milk at the shieling of Glaschyle. His enemies were already beating the glens, and a party reached the hut while Montrose was indoors, but he was hidden by the shepherd under a trough. On departing, he regretted that he had put his host in danger, and " determined never to do the like again to avoid death, of which, he thanked God, he was not afraid." [2] He was now some thirty miles from the scene of the battle.

But the hue-and-cry was out against him. The laird of Assynt was a certain Neil Macleod, a young man of twenty-two and a member of a sept, the " seed of John the Grizzled," with a dark record for deeds of blood. He had married a daughter of Monro of Lemlair, whom Montrose had hitherto looked upon as an ally, and he had himself been protected by Seaforth, and seems to have passed for something of a royalist. His brother-in-law sent him a letter bidding him search his country for fugitives, and " chiefly James Graham," [3] and Neil was no laggard in the business. One of his men found the famished wanderer on the confines of Assynt, and Montrose, when he heard his master's name, probably asked to be taken to him. He thought that he had much to hope for from a Macleod and a son-in-law of Lemlair. On the evening of the 30th of April

---

[1] Gordon of Sallagh makes Kinnoull accompany Montrose and perish with Sinclair. Now George, the third earl, had died in Orkney three months before, and William, the fourth earl, did not die, but lived to escape from Edinburgh castle in 1654 and for more than twenty years after. So, unless we interpolate a fourth earl of whom nothing else is known, we must reject Sallagh's story. It is probable that he did not know about the death of the third earl in Orkney, and, observing that after Carbisdale William received the title, assumed that his predecessor had died in the flight to Assynt. For the other view, see S. R. Gardiner, *Athenæum*, Nov. 11, 1893.

[2] *Miscellany* (S.H.S.), I., 223.

[3] Gordon of Sallagh, 555.

he was brought to the castle of Ardvreck, which still
stands on the northern shore of Loch Assynt. There
he found Neil, and there he met, too, the surviving
Sinclair, who had been brought in by Neil's gillies. But
from Assynt he got no kindness. The head of the viceroy was worth sufficient gold to set up for good his
impoverished family. Montrose asked to be sent to
Orkney, and offered him money, but Neil was resolute,
knowing well that the Estates would outbid the fugitive.
He dispatched an express with the happy news to Leslie,
who had now arrived at Tain, and confined the prisoners
in the cellars of his castle. A few days later, on the
4th of May, Holbourn arrived at Ardvreck, and Montrose was committed to his hands.

Carbisdale, like Philiphaugh, was a surprise and a
rout rather than a battle. It was the first action which
Montrose ever fought with a superiority in numbers,
for he had 1,200 men as against Strachan's 660 ; but
the only contest was between the 220 Covenant troopers
and Montrose's 40 horse and 400 foreigners. Further,
infantry in those days, unless of exceptional quality or
magnificently posted, had little chance against even a
weak body of cavalry ; so for the purpose of the battle
we may rule out all the foot who were struggling in
the flats, and say that the contest lay between Lisle's
40 gentlemen volunteers and Strachan's horse. There
could never have been any doubt as to the issue, and,
though Strachan deserves all credit for a bold feat of
arms, yet his task was easy. Montrose was doomed
when he left the heights of Craigcoinichean, and he left
them, as we have seen, because of the defective information of his local scoutmaster. But indeed he was lost
long before, during the days when he waited for the
Mackenzies who never came. He failed because, instead of pushing on with all speed to Badenoch, he
wasted time on a half-hearted clan. If Neil Macleod
was the immediate cause of Montrose's fate, his patron,
Seaforth, was the ruin of the campaign ; and Seaforth's
indecision was due beyond doubt to the two-faced

tactics of Charles. On the 2nd of May, the day on
which Montrose's doom was sealed, the king signed
with the Covenanters the draft of the Treaty of Breda.

The name of the laird of Assynt lives in Scottish
history with that of Sir John Menteith, who sold
Wallace. It is remembered as the solitary case of a
Gael who betrayed a suppliant for gold. Ian Lom, the
bard of Keppoch, has left bitter verses on the " stripped
tree of the false apples, Neil's son of woeful Assynt."
He made little of his infamy. His lands were raided by
Glengarry, the Macleods, and the penitent Mackenzies.
After the Restoration he was a good deal in gaol, and
was twice tried for his life. His castle was burned, and
no children survived to bear his name. He was awarded
25,000 pounds Scots for his services, of which 20,000
were to be paid in coin and the rest in oatmeal. It
does not appear that he ever got the money, but
the receipts for the meal were long extant, and Highland tradition is positive that two-thirds of it were
sour.[1]

---

[1] The question of Assynt's guilt is exhaustively examined by Murdoch and
Simpson (App. XIII.) who decide against him on every count. There can be no
question about his surrender of the fugitives, but I cannot find it proved that he
had ever served under Montrose, though Montrose probably assumed him to be
friendly from his knowledge of his connection with Seaforth and Lemlair. For
his later fate see M. and S. *loc. cit.*, and for a defence see *Trans. of the Gaelic
Society of Inverness*, xxiv., 374, etc. Ian Lom's verses are worth quoting
(*Cumha Mhontroise* in Mackenzie's *Beauties of Gaelic Poetry* (1841), 50 ; the
translation is by Sheriff Nicolson :

' I'll not go to Dunedin
Since the Graham's blood was shed,
The manly, mighty lion
Tortured on the gallows.

That was the true gentleman,
Who came of line not humble.
Good was the flushing of his cheek
When drawing up to combat.

His chalk-white teeth well closing,
His slender brow not gloomy !—
Though oft my love awakes me,
This night I will not bear it.

Neil's son of woeful Assynt,
If I in net could take thee,
My sentence would condemn thee,
Nor would I spare the gibbet.

If you and I encountered
On the marshes of Ben Etive,
The black waters and the clods
Would there be mixed together.

If thou and thy wife's father,
The householder of Leime (Lemlair ?)
Were hanged both together,
'Twould not atone my loss.

Stript tree of the false apples,
Without esteem, or fame, or grace,
Ever murdering each other
'Mid dregs of wounds and knives !

Death-wrapping to thee, base one !
Ill didst thou sell the righteous,
For the meal of Leith,
And two-thirds of it sour ! "

CHAPTER XVII

THE CURTAIN FALLS

(*May* 1650)

> No man kills his enemy, therefore, that his enemy might have a better life
> in heaven ; that is not his end in killing him : it is God's end. Therefore he
> brings us to death, that by that gate he might lead us into life everlasting. And
> he hath not discovered, but made, that Northern passage, to passe by the frozen
> Sea of calamity and tribulation to Paradise, to the heavenly Jerusalem.
>
> JOHN DONNE.

I

NOW that the last blow had been struck, and only death remained, the oppression was lifted from
Montrose's soul. The " fey " mood had passed, and
his spirit was enlarged. The touch of haughtiness, which
his contemporaries remarked in him, the self-assurance
necessary for one whose daily bread was peril, had
gone from him ; courtesy he had never lost, but he
recovered the modest simplicity which Clarendon had
approved long ago in Oxford. Once more he is the clear-
sighted and constant patriot, the great gentleman who, in
the hour of deepest degradation, can meet the taunts of
his enemies with a smiling face, the Christian who has
compassion upon the frailty of mankind. For six years
his name had terrified his opponents, and as their hold
upon the nation had declined, so had their nerve and
courage. The news of his landing in the north had shaken
the Estates to their foundation. The crowning mercy
of Carbisdale was at first scarcely believed, and when
Strachan himself arrived post-haste to claim his reward,
their exultation of relief knew no bounds. Mixed with
it was the zest of coming revenge. Their tormentor

had been marvellously delivered into their hands, and
we can judge of their past trepidation by the punishment they devised. The measure of their vengeance is
the measure of their fear.

It is not easy to judge Charles with either patience
or fairness, the master was so immeasurably smaller
than the servant. In the compost of graces and infirmities which made up his character, a fine sense of
honour had no part, since for that some spiritual discipline is required. He was an engaging creature of
impulse, with a tolerant humour which could laugh at
himself as well as at others, with the courage which
comes from a good constitution and a high vitality, and
which could face misfortunes with equanimity—both
his own and his friends'. But it is almost certain that,
before signing the Treaty of Breda, this "gentle,
innocent, well-inclined prince" (so he seemed to Baillie)[1]
had convinced himself, with his ready optimism, that
he had made provision for the safety of his captain-
general. On the 5th of May he wrote to Montrose,
bidding him lay down his arms and disband his men.
He seems to have received assurances from the Scottish
commissioners of an indemnity for the royalist army.
On the 8th of May he wrote to the Estates asking that
Montrose and his forces should be allowed to leave the
country in safety. A private letter was also written to
the viceroy, telling him that 12,000 rix-dollars were at
his call in Sir Patrick Drummond's hands. Sir William
Fleming, a cousin of Montrose's, had further orders,
dated the 12th of May, written apparently after some
rumour of Carbisdale had reached the king. These
latest instructions were not to deliver the letter of the
8th of May to Parliament unless Montrose was still unbeaten and at the head of a reasonable force; if he
had been defeated, the letter was to be concealed.
Apparently Charles did not want to ask for grace for his
captain-general from the Estates if he was a fugitive;
he trusted to his private arrangement with the Scottish
commissioners. It is a tangled story, but it is incon-

[1] III., 88.

ceivable that the king hoped to conceal or disavow his
complicity in the invasion. This was already clear from
the published letter of the 12th of January, which every
one in Scotland knew of, and from his personal letter of
the 5th of May to Montrose, which was delivered and
read to the Estates. Still another letter, dated the
12th of May, was also read to Parliament, in which
Charles disclaimed all responsibility for Montrose's
doings.[1] But it is impossible to believe that the king,
who was no fool, and had the rest of the correspondence
in his memory, could have been guilty of so futile and
purposeless a piece of treachery by which no one could
be deceived. It is more likely that this was a fabrica-
tion of Will Murray, Argyll's emissary, with the view
of alienating from the now Covenanted king the last
remnants of royalist respect in Scotland and Cavalier
support in England. Base and heartless as was Charles's
conduct, it is incredible that it reached the height of
perfidy which Argyll and Loudoun would have had the
world believe.[2]

To Montrose royal duplicity and Covenanting intrigues had become matters of little moment. For him
the long day's task was nearly done, and the hour of
unarming had struck. He was led in triumphant
progress by his captors through the length of Scotland,
but the triumph was not theirs. On the 5th of May
Holbourn hurried him from Ardvreck by way of Inver-
shin to Skibo, on the north side of the Kyle. A night
was spent there, and the lady of the castle, finding
that the rank of the prisoner was not sufficiently recognized, is said to have beaten Holbourn about the head
with a leg of mutton and had Montrose given the seat
of honour.[3] He was ferried over the Kyle, and on the
8th delivered to David Leslie at Tain. Thence next

---

[1] Balfour, IV. It is to be noted that the king's letter of this date, printed
in *Charles II. and Scotland in 1650*, 103, has an altogether different tenor.

[2] This paragraph embodies the impression left on my mind by reading the
letters, which are in the *Wigton Papers* (Maitland Club). The whole of the
complicated question has been exhaustively examined by Lang (III., 221–226).
Gardiner (*Commonwealth and Protectorate*, I., 190, etc.) takes the view set out
above.

[3] Taylor's " Assynt " in *Dunrobin MSS.*

morning he was carried by way of Dingwall to Brahan
castle. On the following day he was at Beauly, and
we have the record of Mr. James Fraser, afterwards
Lovat's chaplain, and then a boy of sixteen, who now
joined the march. The viceroy sat " upon a little shelty
horse, without a saddle, but a quilt of rags and straw,
and pieces of rope for stirrups, his feet fastened under
the horse's belly, with a tether and a bit halter for a
bridle." [1] It was a mode of progress which was later
endured by many saints of the Covenant, notably Mr.
Donald Cargill. He still wore peasant's clothes, on his
head was a montero cáp, and around his shoulders a
ragged, old, reddish plaid. The fatigue and privations
of the past week had induced a high fever. At Muir-
town, near Inverness, he begged for water, and there the
crowd from the town came out to gaze on him. The
two ministers of Inverness also appeared, and showed
in their behaviour a decency unusual in their profession ;
one of them, Mr. John Annand, had been a former
acquaintance of the prisoner. At the bridge-end an
old woman railed at him and reminded him of the houses
which had been burned when he besieged the town.
" Yet he never altered his countenance, but with a
majesty and state beseeming him kept his countenance
high." [2]

The magistrates met him at the cross, where they
had set up a table of refreshments. He was offered
wine, and mixed it with water. Fraser saw the other
prisoners drinking heartily under a forestair, and remarked among them Sir John Hurry, " a robust, tall,
stately fellow, with a long cut in his cheek." Hurry
was the true soldier of fortune, own brother to Dugald
Dalgetty, and throughout his varied career and many
changes of side he preserved a certain disarming audacity
and humour. As was said of a more famous Sir John,
the world could have better spared a better man. The
provost, Duncan Forbes of Culloden, a courteous member
of an honourable house, said on taking leave : " My lord,

[1] *Wardlaw MS.*, 353.
[2] *Ibid.*, 354.

I am sorry for your circumstances." That night the company were lodged at Castle Stewart, on the road to Nairn.

On the way through Moray many friends came to greet him, college companions at St. Andrews, and loyalists such as Pluscardine, whose clan had so grievously failed him. At Elgin he was greatly cheered by the sight of an old college friend, Mr. Alexander Somers, the minister of Duffus. His well-wishers conveyed him over Spey, and on the 11th he halted at Keith, where he lay on straw in a tent set up in the fields. The next day was the Sabbath, and he attended the ministrations of Mr. William Kinanmond, who preached from the favourite Covenanting text of the hewing of Agag and the Amalekites. He violently abused the prisoner, till he disgusted even his Covenanting hearers. " Rail on, Rabshakeh," was his victim's only reply. " All honest men," says Fraser, " hated Kinanmond for this ever after." [1]

On the 13th the prisoner reached Pitcaple castle, the home of an Engager, John Leslie, whose wife was a kinswoman of Montrose.[2] The quicker road to the south through Mar was not taken, probably through fear of a rescue by the Farquharsons, and the route chosen was one by which Montrose had often led his swift armies. Now he traversed the scene of his victories with a herald pacing before him, proclaiming : " Here comes James Graham, a traitor to his country." He was probably at Fordoun on the 14th, and on the 15th he reached Southesk's castle of Kinnaird. There he saw his two younger children, Robert and Jean. When he left them he left the last slender ties which still bound him to earth. His wife and his eldest son were gone ; his best friends had perished on the scaffold ; the great comradeship was broken, and its members dead or on their way to death ; his cause, the clean and sane ideals he had championed, was undone ; death had no terrors for one who had nothing to live for, and who had faced

---

[1] *Wardlaw MS.*, 355.
[2] M. and S., 318 *n.*

it so often with a lover's gaiety. His words might have
been those of Kent in *Lear*:

> " I have a journey, sir, shortly to go ;
> My master calls me, I must not say no."

On the night of the 15th he halted at the house of
Grange, a property of the Durhams, five miles from
Dundee. Here there seems to have been an attempt
as at Pitcaple, to assist him to escape. The lady of the
house plied the guards with strong ale and brandy, and
they, being Highlanders of Lawers's regiment, willingly
succumbed. But the outer guards had not been tam-
pered with, and the fugitive was discovered by a trooper
of Strachan's horse.[1] Next day he entered Dundee,
and to the eternal credit of that staunchly Covenanting
town, which, moreover, had suffered more than most
at Montrose's hands, he was received with sympathy
and respect. " The whole town expressed a great deal
of sorrow for his condition, and presented him with
clothes and all other things suited to his place, birth,
and person." [2] We have no record of the two days'
march across Fife. No doubt the ministers flocked to
upbraid him, and the heroes who had returned from
Tippermuir and Kilsyth came to stare at one who had
given them little cause to love him. From Dysart or
Kirkcaldy the company took ship for Leith, and reached
it about four o'clock on the afternoon of Saturday the
18th. On the same day and at the same port arrived
Sir William Fleming, with the king's letter of disband-
ment.

The Covenanters had made ample preparation to
receive the prisoner. They knew that what they had
to do must be done quickly. The viceroy must be dead
before the king's coming to Scotland, or trouble would
follow ; a party, now royalist in policy, could not put
to death one who carried the royal commission. Further, the Commonwealth had never shown any bitterness
against the great captain, and might interdict those of

---

[1] *Memorie of the Somervilles.*   [2] *Wardlaw MS.*, 355.

the Estates who favoured Cromwell from the kind of
vengeance which Cromwell as a rule preferred to leave
to his Maker.   There were magnanimous men, too, in
all parties in Scotland, who resented the unsoldierly
treatment of a soldier, and there were his many friends
in foreign courts, especially in the court of France, who
would be certain to plead for him if time were allowed.
Such an appeal was actually sent at the instigation of
Cardinal de Retz, signed by the young king, Louis the
Fourteenth,[1] in which it was eloquently urged that
Montrose had always acted within the terms of his royal
commission, and therefore could not be condemned by
those who now acknowledged the royal authority.   But
the appeal arrived after the deed had been done.
Argyll and Loudoun were not the men to tarry when it
was a matter of getting rid of a rival so formidable and
so feared.

Immediately upon the news of Carbisdale, the
Estates had met to consider the question of punishment.
In a time of civil confusion nice questions of legality are
out of place, and the condemnation of Montrose was as
legal as any other act of the Parliament then sitting
in Scotland.   He had been attainted and outlawed in
1644, and there had been no reversal of the sentence.[2]
A commission was appointed to decide on the details of
the penalty, and on the 17th of May it made its report.[3]
The captive was to be met at the gates by the officers
of justice and the hangman, and conducted with every
circumstance of ignominy to the Tolbooth.   Thereafter
he was to be hanged on a gibbet—not beheaded, as was
the custom with State prisoners—with Wishart's book
and a copy of his own last declaration tied around his
neck.   Thus would be fulfilled the words of the prophet
Rothes, and he would be " lifted up above the rest in
three fathoms of a rope."   After death the head was
to be struck off and placed on a spike on the Tolbooth ;
the body dismembered, and the limbs fixed in public

---

[1] Monteith, 517.   M. and S., App. XII., 1.
[2] The Earl of Argyll, in 1685, was in the same position.
[3] Balfour, IV., 12.

places in Stirling, Glasgow, Perth, and Aberdeen. If he
repented of his misdeeds, the ban of excommunication
would be removed, and the body buried in Greyfriars
churchyard; if not, it would go to the felons' pit
on the Boroughmuir. It was piously hoped that the
common folk of Edinburgh, who had lost kith and kin
in his wars, would await his entrance and show their
hatred with filth and stones. For this purpose his
hands were to be pinioned behind his back.

The afternoon was clear and chilly, such as is common
on the shores of the Firth in late May. The magistrates
of Edinburgh met him at Leith, and the procession was
formed, the other prisoners on foot, and Montrose himself mounted on a cart-horse. His face was drawn and
wasted with fever, and his grey eyes burned with an
unnatural brilliance. The good folk of Dundee had
given him clothes more suited to his condition than those
he had worn when captured, and he bore himself among
the hostile crowd with a gentle dignity. A smile, it is
said, flickered about his mouth, not of scorn but of
peace. When he passed the Watergait, where the
faubourg of the Canongate began, in which stood the
houses of the nobility, he found awaiting him the officers
of justice, the hangman, and a hangman's cart drawn
by four horses. He was shown the sentence of the
Estates and read it carefully, saying that he was sorry
that the king, whose commission he bore, should be so
dishonoured. Then he entered the cart, and was tied
to a high seat with cords across his breast and arms.
The hangman wore his red bonnet, but Montrose,
according to his sentence, must ride uncovered.

Slowly, in the bright evening, the procession moved
up the ancient Via Dolorosa of Scottish history.[1] The
street was lined by a great crowd—the dregs of the
Edinburgh slums, the retainers of the Covenanting lords,
ministers from far and near—all the elements most
bitterly hostile to the prisoner. But to the amazement

---

[1] We have three accounts of Montrose's entry into Edinburgh: that of
James Fraser in the *Wardlaw MS.*; that of the *Wigton Papers*; and the report
to Mazarin of a French resident in Edinburgh, M. de Graymond, Napier, II.,
781 and App. IV

of the organizers of the spectacle there was no sign of
popular wrath. Rather there was silence, a tense air
of sympathy and pity and startled admiration. The
high pale countenance set up in that place of public
scorn awed the mob into stillness. " In all the way,
there appeared in him such majesty, courage, modesty,
and even somewhat more than natural, that these
common women who had lost their husbands and
children in his wars, and who were hired to stone him,
were, upon the sight of him, so astonished and moved
that their intended curses turned into tears and
prayers." [1] In the strained quiet, broken only by ex-
cited sobs, there was one jarring note. Lady Jean
Gordon, Lord Haddington's widow, Argyll's niece and
Huntly's daughter, is said to have laughed shrilly and
shouted a word of insult from the balcony where she
sat. A voice cried out of the crowd that the right
place for her was in the hangman's cart to expiate
her sins.[2]

In the lodgings along the Canongate the Covenant
chiefs were assembled to witness the degradation of
their enemy. In the balcony of Lord Moray's house
Lord Lorn sat with his young bride, Lady Mary Stewart,
the same man who, thirty-five years later, was himself
to go to a not inglorious scaffold. Inside the house,
with the shutters half-closed, stood Argyll with Loudoun
and Wariston. Montrose, as he passed, caught a glimpse
of the anxious, unhappy face which he knew so well, and
for the first time for long the two men looked into each
other's eyes. . . . The shutters were closed and the
faces disappeared. There was an English soldier in the
crowd who observed the incident and cried : " It was
no wonder they started aside at his look, for they
durst not look him in the face these seven years
bygone." [3]

It is the last we shall see of Argyll. What he thought

[1] *Wigton Papers.*
[2] There seems to be no contemporary evidence for the vices with which
the writer in the *Wigton Papers* charges the lady. See Willcock, *The Great
Marquess,* 232 n.
[3] *Wigton Papers.* Graymond to Mazarin, Napier, II., 839.

in that moment we can only guess. In his letter to
Lothian, written on the day of the execution, he reflects
that Montrose had " got some resolution how to go out
of this world, but nothing at all how to enter into
another." [1] But there must have been more in that
subtle mind than this pious platitude, for in Montrose
he looked upon his stark opposite, and in his enemy's
downfall he could read the presage of his own. If
Montrose had failed, so had he, and with a far more
complete failure. Of all that he had built nothing had
any hope of permanence. The theocracy on which his
power was founded was crumbling beneath him. A
mind of his calibre cannot have been bemused by the
ministerial dreams of Presbyterian dominance in Britain ;
he had fleeting visions of political moderation and religious tolerance which were denied to his colleagues.
But, playing with the skill of the adroit politician for
immediate gains, he had been too successful ; he had
won in the short game only to find that his victory
made the larger purpose for ever impossible. The
Solemn League hung round his neck like a millstone.
He had summoned spirits from the deep which he could
not control. He had allied himself with the English
Parliament, and discovered too late that he was being
ground between rival fanaticisms. That very year he
was to call his associates " madmen," [2] and for the rest
of his life, in his intrigues with Charles and his intrigues
with Cromwell, he was to be no more than a distracted
politician, without creed or comfort. Nothing remained
to him but the sombre religion which he had acquired
long before at the Glasgow Assembly, and which at any
rate taught him how to die.

As Montrose passed the cross he saw the new gallows
standing ready to receive him—that gallows which was
to earn the name of the " Ministers' Altar." About
seven o'clock he reached the Tolbooth. His bonds were
cut, and as he descended from the cart he gave the
hangman the customary drink-money. Scarcely was he

---

[1] Kirkton, *Hist. of the Church of Scotland*, 124 *n.*
[2] *Cal. S. P., Dom.* (Aug. 28, 1650), 310.

inside the prison when a deputation from the Estates,
with its retinue of ministers, arrived to interrogate
him. He refused to answer, for indeed he was very
weary with travel and sickness, and at last his tor-
mentors withdrew. His parting words to them were
a jest. " The compliments they had put upon him
that day," he said, " had proved something tedious."
He was still young—not yet thirty-eight.[1]

II

Next day, being the Sabbath, there was a great
preaching. From every pulpit in the city the clergy
thundered against the excommunicate, James Graham,
and no less against the mob which had refused to stone
him. The prisoner was visited by a deputation of
ministers and members of Parliament, among them
Sir James Stewart of Coltness, the Provost of Edinburgh, who was responsible for the details of the
execution, and who, though a staunch Covenanter, had
protested against its barbarity—" so much butchery
and dismembering." [2] They got no satisfaction. He
told them that " if they thought they had affronted
him the day before by carrying him in a cart they were
much mistaken, for he thought it the most honourable and joyful journey ever he made ; God having
all the while most comfortably manifested Himself to
him, and furnished him with resolution to overlook the
reproaches of men, and to behold Him for whose cause
he suffered." [3]

He was given no peace. At eight o'clock on the
Monday morning his persecutors returned to the attack.
Mr. James Guthrie, Mr. Mungo Law, Mr. Robert Traill,
and others were no doubt bound in duty to visit an
erring member of their own communion, and they hoped
to extract some confession from him which could be

---

[1] *Wardlaw MS.* ; *Wigton Papers* ; Wishart, Part II. ; *Montrose Redivivus* ;
Balfour, IV.
[2] *Coltness Papers*, 30. Napier, II., 797.   [3] *Wigton Papers.*

used to efface the profound impression that his appearance had made on the people of Edinburgh. They charged him at a venture with imaginary personal vices, of which he had none. Then they accused him of taking up arms against his country, of using Irish troops, and of shedding Scottish blood. He replied, as Wodrow's informant told him, in a manner " too airy and *volage*, not so much suiting the gravity of a nobleman." [1] Using their own armoury, he reminded them that David, in the cave of Adullam, had gathered together an odd fighting force ; and as for bloodshed, he declared " if it could have been thereby prevented, he would rather it had all come out of his own veins." Lastly, they charged him with a breach of the Covenant, and his answer was ready. " The Covenant which I took I own it and adhere to it. Bishops, I care not for them. I never intended to advance their interests. But when the king had granted you all your desires, and you were every one sitting under his vine and his fig tree—that then you should have taken a party in England by the hand, and entered into a League and Covenant with them against the king, was the thing I judged my duty to oppose to the yondmost." Mr. James Guthrie then touched on the excommunication, and said that since the prisoner showed himself obdurate it must remain. With the strange arrogance of his kind, he had the " fearful apprehension that what is bound on earth God will bind in heaven." Montrose replied gently that he would gladly be reconciled to the Church of Scotland, but that he could not call that his sin which he accounted to have been his duty.

When the ministers left him he was given a little bread dipped in ale for his breakfast, but he was not allowed a barber to shave him. At ten o'clock he was taken before the bar of Parliament to hear his sentence. It was common knowledge that he had acted under the

---

[1] *Wodrow MSS.* in the National Library of Scotland. Napier, II., 785, etc. The informant was a Mr. Patrick Simson, for whom see Warrick, *Moderators of the Church of Scotland, 1690–1740* (Edinburgh, 1913). He had been for some time chaplain at Inveraray, and had formed his notions of deportment on Argyll. His *Spiritual Songs* are almost the worst religious verse in the language.

king's credentials, and therefore nothing in the nature
of a trial could be allowed on the question of the Carbisdale campaign, since it was difficult for Loudoun and
Argyll to deny a mandate for which they had the royal
evidence. The Chancellor seems to have harped on the
incidents of the Highland wars, mingled with violent
denunciations of the viceroy's person. Since his arrival
in Edinburgh Montrose had been provided, probably
by the Napier ladies, with clothes worthy of his rank.
When he stood up before his accusers in Parliament, he
wore a suit of fine black cloth, with a richly laced scarlet
cloak to his knee ; on his head was a black beaver hat
with a silver band ; and on his legs stockings of carna-
tion silk.[1] His bearing was modest but " unmoved and
undaunted " ; his face was haggard, unshaven, and
very pale,[2] and he often sighed. He replied to his
accusers in a speech, happily preserved,[3] in which he
repeated the substance of his many declarations—his
loyalty to the true Covenant, his abhorrence of the
Solemn League. " How far religion has been advanced
by it this poor distressed kingdom can witness." War
could not be waged without the shedding of blood, but
he had repressed all disorders as soon as they were
discovered. " Never was any man's blood spilt but
in battle ; and even then, many thousand lives have I
preserved. And I dare here avow, in the presence of
God, that never a hair of Scotsman's head that I could
save fell to the ground." His last campaign had been
" by his Majesty's just commands, in order to accelerate
the treaty betwixt him and you : his Majesty knowing
that, whenever he had ended with you, I was ready
to retire upon his call." He asked to be judged " by
the laws of God, the laws of Nature and nations, and
the laws of this land." But he knew that the plea

---

[1] Relics of these garments belonged to the Napier family till 1912. They
are now, along with his George and his Garter riband, in the possession of
the Duke of Montrose.

[2] Balfour, IV., 16.

[3] Summaries of the speech are in the *Wardlaw MS.*, Wishart, and Balfour ;
but the simplicity of the *Wigton Papers* seems to embody the actual words of
Montrose.

was vain, so he appealed to a higher tribunal—" to the
righteous Judge of the world, who one day must be
your Judge and mine, and who always gives out righteous judgments." He had said his say ; he had fulfilled
the proud boast which he had made to Parliament nine
years before : " My resolution is to carry along fidelity
and honour to the grave." His judges had no answer.
Loudoun replied with abuse, and Wariston read the
sentence, which Montrose heard on his knees. We
are told that he lifted up his head as the grim words
were uttered, and looked Wariston calmly in the
face.

He was taken back to the Tolbooth, where all
day he was tormented by ministers. According to
one account, he had a talk apart with Mr. Robert
Baillie ; [1] if so, that honest and perplexed soul can
scarcely have been happy about the business, and it
is remarkable that in his voluminous writings he never
mentions this final scene. To the magistrates who
visited him he said : " I think it a greater honour to
have my head standing on the ports of this town for
this quarrel, than to have my picture in the king's
bedchamber. I am beholden to you that, lest my
loyalty should be forgotten, you have appointed five
of the most eminent towns to bear witness of it to
posterity." [2] The captain of the town guard was the
famous Major Weir,[3] the warlock of Edinburgh legend,
who afterwards expiated his many crimes at the stake.
By his orders the guard were always in the prisoner's
room, and filled it with tobacco smoke, which Montrose,
unlike his father, could not abide. None of his friends
were allowed to come near him. Nevertheless, we are
told, in spite of fever and pain and the imminence of
death, he continued his devotions unperturbed, and
slept as peacefully as a child. That last night, like
Sir Walter Raleigh, and much in the same strain, he,

[1] Mr. Robert Traill's *Diary*, Napier, II., 789–790.
[2] *Wigton Papers.*
[3] He had served in the Covenanting army against Montrose in 1644–45 as a
major in Lanark's regiment. See Roughead, *Twelve Scots Trials*, 43, 45.

who had so long forsaken the Muse, returned to his old
love. These lines were written amid the smoke and
wrangling of the guards :

> " Let them bestow on every airth a limb,
> Then open all my veins, that I may swim
> To Thee, my Maker, in that crimson lake ;
> Then place my parboiled head upon a stake,
> Scatter my ashes, strew them in the air.—
> Lord ! Since Thou knowest where all these atoms are,
> I'm hopeful Thou'lt recover once my dust,
> And confident Thou'lt raise me with the just." [1]

On Tuesday morning, the 21st of May, he rose for
the last time. Like the Spartans before Thermopylæ,
he combed his long locks for death. The usual concourse of ministers and politicians was in his cell, and
Wariston reproved him for his care of the body. " My
head is still my own," was his answer. " To-night,
when it will be yours, treat it as you please." Presently he heard the drums beating to arms, and was
told that the troops were assembling to prevent any
attempt at a rescue. He laughed and cried : " What,
am I still a terror to them ? Let them look to themselves ; my ghost will haunt them."

He was taken about two in the afternoon by the
bailies down the High Street to the Mercat Cross, which
stood between the Tolbooth and the Tron Kirk—that
dolorous road which Argyll and Wariston and James
Guthrie were themselves to travel. He still wore the
brave clothes in which he had confronted Parliament ;
nay, more, he had ribbons on his shoes and fine white
gloves on his hands. James Fraser, who saw him,
wrote : " He stept along the streets with so great state,
and there appeared in his countenance so much beauty,
majesty, and gravity as amazed the beholder, and
many of his enemies did acknowledge him to be the
bravest subject in the world, and in him a gallantry
that braced all that crowd." Another eyewitness,

---

[1] Voltaire refers to these lines in his *Essai sur l'Histoire générale,* and adds :
" C'était un des plus agréables esprits qui cultivassent alors les lettres, et l'âme
la plus héroïque qui fût dans les trois Royaumes."

John Nicoll, the notary public, thought him more
like a bridegroom than a criminal.[1] An Englishman
among the spectators, a Commonwealth agent, wrote
an account to his masters. " It is absolutely certain
that he hath overcome more men by his death, in
Scotland, than he would have done if he had lived.
For I never saw a more sweeter carriage in a man in
all my life." [2]

The scaffold was a great four-square platform, breast-
high, and on it a 30-foot gallows had been erected. On
the platform stood the ministers, Mr. Robert Traill and
Mr. Mungo Law, still bent on getting a word of confession or penitence. They were disappointed, for Montrose did not look at them. He was not allowed to
address the mob, which surged up against the edge of
the scaffold—a privilege hitherto granted to the meanest
criminals ; but he spoke apart to the magistrates and
to a few of the nearer spectators. A boy called Robert
Gordon [3] sat by and took down his words in some kind
of shorthand, and the crowd, with that decency which
belongs to all simple folk, kept a reverent silence.
The Estates were afraid lest he should attack the
king and spoil their game, but he spoke no word of
bitterness or reproach ; rather—*splendide mendax*—he
praised Charles's justice. It was the testament of a
man conscious of his mortal frailty, but confident in
the purity of his purpose and the mercy of his God.

" I am sorry if this manner of my end be scandalous to any good
Christian here. Doth it not often happen to the righteous according
to the way of the unrighteous ? Doth not sometimes a just man
perish in his righteousness, and a wicked man prosper in his wicked-
ness and malice ? They who know me should not disesteem me for
this. Many greater than I have been dealt with in this kind. But
I must not say but that all God's judgments are just, and this
measure, for my private sins, I acknowledge to be just with God,
and wholly submit myself to Him.

" But, in regard of man, I may say they are but instruments.

[1] Nicoll, *Diary of Public Transactions, etc., 1650–67* (Bannatyne Club),
12, etc.
[2] Napier, II., 805.
[3] Son of Sir Robert Gordon of Gordonstoun, the author of the *History of the
Earldom of Sutherland.*

God forgive them, and I forgive them. They have oppressed the poor and violently perverted judgment and justice, but He that is higher than they will reward them.

" What I did in this kingdom was in obedience to the most just commands of my sovereign, and in his defence, in the day of his distress, against those who rose up against him. I acknowledge nothing, but fear God and honour the king, according to the commandments of God and the just laws of Nature and nations. I have not sinned against man, but against God ; and with Him there is mercy, which is the ground of my drawing near unto Him.

" It is objected against me by many, even good people, that I am under the censure of the Church. This is not my fault, seeing it is only for doing my duty, by obeying my prince's most just commands, for religion, his sacred person, and authority. Yet I am sorry they did excommunicate me ; and in that which is according to God's laws, without wronging my conscience or allegiance, I desire to be relaxed. If they will not do it, I appeal to God, who is the righteous Judge of the world, and will, I hope, be my Judge and Saviour.

" It is spoken of me that I should blame the king. God forbid ! For the late king, he lived a saint and died a martyr. I pray God I may end as he did. If ever I would wish my soul in another man's stead, it should be in his. For his Majesty now living, never any people, I believe, might be more happy in a king. His commandments to me were most just, and I obeyed them. He deals justly with all men. I pray God he be so dealt withal that he be not betrayed under trust, as his father was.

" I desire not to be mistaken, as if my carriage at this time, in relation to your ways, were stubborn. I do but follow the light of my conscience, my rule ; which is seconded by the working of the Spirit of God that is within me. I thank Him I go to heaven with joy the way He paved for me. If He enable me against the fear of death, and furnish me with courage and confidence to embrace it even in its most ugly shape, let God be glorified in my end, though it were in my damnation. Yet I say not this out of any fear or mistrust, but out of my duty to God, and love to His people.

" I have no more to say, but that I desire your charity and prayers. I shall pray for you all. I leave my soul to God, my service to my prince, my goodwill to my friends, my love and charity to you all. And thus briefly I have exonerated my conscience." [1]

There is a tradition that during the morning there had been lowering thunder-clouds and flashes of lightning, but that as Montrose stood on the scaffold a burst of sunlight flooded the street. When he had finished speaking, he gave money to his executioner, and prayed

[1] *Wardlaw MS.*, 359–362. There are versions of the speech in Wishart, and in the *Wigton Papers*.

silently for a little. His arms were pinioned, and he
ascended the ladder with that stately carriage which
had always marked him. His last words were : " God
have mercy on this afflicted land ! " Tears ran down
the hangman's face as he pushed him off, and we are
told that a great sob broke from the crowd. They had
cause to sob, for that day there was done to death such
a man as his country has not seen again.

According to the sentence, the body was cut down
after three hours and the limbs distributed among the
chief towns. The remains in Aberdeen must have
caught the eye of Charles when he arrived a few weeks
later. The trunk was buried beside the public gallows
on the Boroughmuir.[1] The head was placed on a spike
on the west face of the Tolbooth, and eleven years later
was taken down to make room for the head of Argyll.[2]

III

There was to be another funeral besides that
melancholy scene by lantern light among the marshes
of the Boroughmuir. After the Restoration, one of
Charles's first acts was to give public burial to the
remains of his great captain. On January 4, 1661, the
Scots Parliament resolved on " an honourable reparation
for that horrid and monstrous barbarity in the person
of the great Marquis of Montrose." [3] The trunk was
solemnly taken up from the Boroughmuir,[4] and the limbs

---

[1] On the spot occupied by the factory of Thomas Nelson and Sons, where
this volume was printed.

[2] On account of rumours that the head was to be stolen by Montrose's friends,
" a new cross prick of iron to cross the former prick " was added six days after
the execution (Nicoll, *Diary*). Cromwell had the limbs taken down in Glasgow,
Stirling, Perth, and Aberdeen. The Aberdeen " member " was laid in Huntly's
vault till 1661, when it was moved to Edinburgh for the second funeral (M. and
S., App. XIV.). There was a story recorded by Sir Edward Walker that
after Dunbar Cromwell caused the head to be removed from the Tolbooth
(Douglas, *Cromwell's Scotch Campaigns*, 121 *n.*), but it remained till 1661, when
James Fraser saw it taken down. One Thomas Binning, mariner, serving as a
gunner at the Castle, who had a regard for Montrose's memory, tried to have it
shot down, but the ball only knocked off part of the stone support of the spike,
which in its fall " killed a drummer and a soldier or two." " Providence,"
Captain Binning piously reflected, " had ordered that head to be taken down
with more honour." See Binning, *A Light to the Art of Gunnery*, 1675.

[3] *Mercurius Caledonicus*, ed. by Saintserf. Jan. 4, 1661.

[4] Nicoll, *Diary*, 316.

gathered from the several towns, a ceremony attended
by " the honest people's loud and joyful acclamations."
The remains, wrapped in fine linen in a noble coffin, lay
in state in the Abbey Kirk of Holyrood from the 7th
of January to the 11th of May. On the latter date
took place the great procession to St. Giles's.[1] First
rode Sir Harry Graham, Montrose's half-brother, carrying the arms of his house. Then followed the Graham
kinsmen with their different standards—Duntroon,
Morphie, Cairnie, Monzie, Balgowan, Drums, Gorthie ;
and Black Pate of Inchbrakie, who had been with Montrose on the August afternoon in Atholl when the curtain
rose upon his campaign, bore his insignia of the Garter.
The body was carried by fourteen earls, including the
men, or the sons of the men, who had betrayed him—
such as Seaforth, and Home, and Roxburgh, as well as
old opponents like Eglinton and Callander. Twelve
viscounts and barons bore the pall, among them Strathnaver, the son of the Sutherland who had locked the
gates of the north after Carbisdale. The young Montrose and his brother, Lord Robert, followed the coffin,
and in the procession were representatives of almost
every Scottish house. Argyll's friend and Montrose's
brother-in-law, Rollo, was there, and Marischal, who
had held Dunnottar against him, and Tweeddale, who
had voted for his death. There, too, were the faithful
friends who had not failed him—Maderty and Frendraught and the Marquis of Douglas, and old Napier's
grandson. The morning had been stormy, but as the
procession moved from Holyrood the sun shone out
brightly, as it had done at his end. The streets were
lined with the trainbands, who fired their volleys, while
the cannon thundered in reply from the castle, wherein
lay Argyll under sentence of death. The nobles of
Scotland, according to their wont, had moved over to
the winning side. The pageant was an act of tardy
justice, and it pleases by its dramatic contrasts, but it
had small relevance to Montrose's true achievement.
He was as little kin to the rabble of the Restoration as

[1] *A Relation of the True Funeralls*, 1661, Napier, II., App. III.

to the rabble of the Covenant. The noble monument which now marks his grave in the ancient High Kirk of Scotland is a more fitting testimony, for it has been left to modern days to recognize the greatness of one who had no place in his generation.

The fate of his heart is a curious romance, like the tale of that ring which Marie Antoinette gave to Axel Fersen. Shortly after the execution young Lady Napier sent her servants by night to the grave on the Borough-muir, and had the heart taken from the body. It was skilfully embalmed, and placed in a little egg-shaped case of steel made from the blade of his sword.[1] This in turn was enclosed in a gold filagree box, which had been given to her husband's grandfather by a Doge of Venice. She sent the box to the young Marquis of Montrose on the Continent, who duly restored the heart to the body in 1661 at the second funeral.[2] The casket after a time passed out of the possession of the family. It was recognized in a Dutch collection by a friend of the fifth Lord Napier, who procured it for him. Napier bequeathed it on his death to his daughter, who had married a Johnston of Cairnsalloch, an officer of the East India Company. It was carried to India, and on the way out was struck by a shot in a battle with a French squadron off Cape Verd Islands, and the gold filagree box was shattered. But the adventures of the case were not ended. It remained for some time in the Johnstons' house at Madura, where the natives came to reverence it as a talisman. It was stolen, and was purchased by a tributary chief of the Nawab of Arcot, in whose treasury it long lay. The young Johnston in a hunting expedition happened to save his life, and the chief in gratitude restored the relic to his family.[3] It was brought home to Europe by the elder Johnstons

---

[1] The heart of Lord Capel was treated in the same way and presented to Charles II. after the Restoration.

[2] This is clear from the Lord Lyon's accounts (see Mr. J. C. Robbie's paper in the *Book of the Old Edinburgh Club*, I.). The heart was embalmed by a chirurgeon on May 11, 1661. On this point Napier's story (II., App. I.) must be amended.

[3] See Mr. Stephen Wheeler's articles in the Allahabad *Pioneer*, May 13 and August 9, 1920.

in 1792, and, as they travelled overland through France, they heard of the edict of the Revolution Government requiring the surrender of all gold and silver trinkets. Mrs. Johnston entrusted it to an Englishwoman at Boulogne till it could be sent to England, but the lady died soon afterwards, and in the troubled days that followed the relic disappeared. Since then it has been lost to the world. Some day, perhaps, an antiquary, rummaging in some back street in a French town, may come on a casket of Indian work, and opening it find the little egg-shaped case. It would be a precious discovery, for it once held the dust of the bravest of Scottish hearts.

CHAPTER XVIII

"A CANDIDATE FOR IMMORTALITY"[1]

Truly I know not whether to mervaile more, either that he in that mistie time could see so clearly, or that wee in this cleare age walke so stumblingly after him. SIR PHILIP SIDNEY.

I

MONTROSE founded no school and left no successor. He was a lonely figure in his day, and for almost two centuries his bequest remained unnoted and unshared. Cromwell, indeed, came north into Scotland the same year, and enforced one part of his message. Dunbar was the avenging of Philiphaugh and Carbisdale, and the heavy hand of the greatest of Englishmen was laid on the strange edifice which had been built out of the rubble of the Middle Ages. The nine years of the English occupation saw the plain man raising his head once more. Sir Alexander Irvine of Drum was moved to tell the Moderator of the Assembly that his wild charges were " but undigested rhapsodies of confused nonsense," [2] and none could gainsay him. Monk bade the ministers of Perth leave politics alone and " preach the gospel of Jesus Christ," which, the chronicler adds, " it seems is not their business." [3] Wariston had the " strange thought " that, like Hamilton and Montrose, Cromwell would ere long be brought to public justice in Edinburgh,[4] but no such fate befell the great iconoclast. He enforced his views on religious toleration, and did his best to curb the appetite of the

---

[1] The phrase is Wishart's, from the last sentence of his book.
[2] *Scotland and the Commonwealth* (S.H.S.), 354.
[3] *Ibid.*, 7.
[4] *Diary*, II., 24.

Kirk for witch-finding. He made an attempt at uniting
Scotland and England, reduced taxation, established
free trade with the south, took the sting out of excommunication by preventing any civil penalties attending it, and finally, to the infinite comfort of the lieges,
suppressed the General Assembly. For the first time
for generations even-handed justice was done between
all classes. And, as we know from Mr. Robert Law, the
spiritual life of the country, long bound under the
desolate frosts of faction, began to put forth hopeful
shoots.

Cromwell passed, and the king who had so cheerfully
betrayed his servant came to his own again. The old
strife was renewed of nobles and king and Kirk, and
again the commons of Scotland were the victims. One
thing had indeed been gained—the impossible theocracy
had perished. The Kirk, as always happens, having
asked too much, was to get less than her due, and the
spiritual liberty which she had denied to others in her
heyday was now to be denied to herself. The later
Covenanters, whose sufferings have left so dark a
memory among their countrymen, fought for a cause
similar only in name to that of their predecessors before
1660. They resisted a despotic " bond " imposed on
them by the Government to the outraging of their consciences, as Montrose had resisted the " bond " of
Guthrie and Wariston. The men who suffered on the
western moorlands, though his name was anathema to
them and they revered his executioners, yet stood con-
fusedly on the principles for which he died. The best
of them asked for that spiritual liberty he had pled for,
and resisted that constraining of men's consciences he
had warred against. But the evil had been wrought.
Fanaticism had raised a counter-fanaticism, and the
struggle had to continue till both were dead of their
wounds. The way was prepared for the long lack-lustre
régime of eighteenth-century Scotland, when the Kirk
was ossified into a thing of forms and dogmas, and civil
government sank to a dull and corrupt servitude to
the powers of the moment. The spiritual fires of the

Covenant had burned too murkily to be allowed to last, and the clear flame of Montrose had gone from a world that was not worthy of it. We can look back upon that tangled era and judge both parties without bitterness. Argyll's monument stands close to Montrose's in St. Giles's, and the most fervent admirer of the latter can admit the value of the tradition bequeathed by the founders of the Kirk. But it must not be forgotten that that tradition, which has at once educated and ennobled their countrymen, was a by-product, and was never the chief aim of the pre-1660 Covenanters. For that enduring work, the liberty of the Church and the elevation of the lowliest citizen to the dignity of an immortal soul, Montrose laboured as zealously as they. In their declared and paramount objects, which were the establishment of a theocracy above any civil power and an inquisition over every man's conscience, they failed utterly, and in their failure brought their land to the last misery and degradation.

The history of Scotland was written first by the divines and then by the Whigs, so it is small wonder that Montrose has fared badly. A kind of literary convention arose, according to which the most pagan of Edinburgh lawyers, when he took pen in hand, thought it his duty to pay tribute to the Solemn League and its abettors. It is only within recent generations that the balance has been redressed.[1] Hagiology is not an exact science, and that of the Covenant, born in frenzy and confusion, and nurtured in bitterness, has not withstood the slow sapping of a fuller knowledge and a more critical temper; yet it was able for the better part of two centuries to hide from his countrymen the rarity and majesty

---

[1] Burnet, as the Hamilton champion, was of course hostile (cf. *Hist. of his Own Time* (1724), I., 38). Later writers, like Laing, Brodie, and Hill Burton, have been uniformly unfavourable, and Hallam repeats baseless charges without examination. Even Hume Brown, for so just a writer, is curiously carping in his references. To Charles Knight, Montrose was only a skilful actor "playing his heroic rôle to perfection"; Godwin considered that "he possessed the temper of the commander of a gang of pirates"; to Mackenzie he was a "vain-glorious butcher"; to Dr. Burns, the editor of Wodrow, he is "that infamous ruffian but eminent loyalist." The reaction began with Lingard and Lord Stanhope, and the most recent historians, such as Gardiner and Lang and Mathieson, have done ample justice to "the most sympathetic figure in Scottish history."

of Montrose's character. But popular tradition was more just. The fame of the great marquis in the Lowlands seems always to have been attended by a kind of respect. Stories of his humanity, his beauty, and his tragic fate were handed down—a curious interlude in a memory of blood and suffering. Lowland legend never gave him the name of " persecutor," and he never sat at that grim tavern-board in hell with the " fierce Middleton, and the dissolute Rothes, and the crafty Lauderdale."[1] It would be strange if he had, for these were the men who brought him to his death. To royalist and Jacobite Scotland he became an almost mythical figure, little understood, and valued chiefly, perhaps, as the legendary victor over the Campbells. " The banes of a loyal and a gallant Grahame hae long rattled in their coffin for vengeance on thae Dukes of Guile and Lords for Lorn."[2] As for Celtic Scotland, she has taken him to her heart. Sir Ewen Cameron of Lochiel " had Montrose always in his mouth." In the account of the proceedings of the Estates on December 3, 1689, it is recorded : " That which gave the late Viscount of Dundee so much credit with, and authority over them, though he understood not their language nor was of their country, was his name and relation to the great Marquis of Montrose, for whose memory these Highlanders have all imaginable respect and veneration, and believe that fortune and success was entailed on that name of Graham."[3] To the Highlands he was their chosen knight, the only Lowlander who has ever entered the sacred circle of Gaelic folk-tale and song. Under him the Celt reached his apotheosis, and for one short year held the Saxon in the hollow of his hand. Clan rivalries have been forgotten in the homage to a racial hero. Said an old gillie on the Beauly : " My name is Campbell, but my heart is with the great Montrose."[4]

On the political side Montrose was a modern man, as

---

[1] " Wandering Willie's Tale " in *Redgauntlet.*
[2] Garschattachin in *Rob Roy.* Sir Walter took the phrase from some satirical verses of Alexander Craig, quoted in Scotstarvet's *Staggering State of Scots Statesmen.*
[3] Terry, *John Graham of Claverhouse,* 12 *n.*   [4] Lang, III., 117 *n.*

modern as Burke and Canning, and speaking a language far more intelligible to our ears than that of the Butes and Dundases of a later Scotland. The seventeenth century produced two curiously premature characters in the great Marquis and Sir George Mackenzie ; [1] but Mackenzie, lawyer-like, made a sharp distinction between theory and practice, and while his theory was modern his practice was of the Dark Ages ; whereas Montrose knew no cleavage between thoughts and deeds. Most great men have been in advance of their day. Some have had the insight to see several stages ahead and have tried to expedite the wheel of change ; some have thrown out ideas which were to fructify afterwards in a form of which they did not dream. Montrose was before his time, not from paradox or from hurry, but because almost alone in his age he looked clearly at the conditions of all government, and, having formed his conclusions, was not deterred by prudence or self-interest from acting upon them. As we have seen, he was notably free from contemporary prejudices. He had none of the current belief in Divine Right ; he had no excessive reverence for a king as such, and very little for a nobility ; he would not have shrunk from the views of Cromwell's Ironsides as to the historical origin of the peerage, which so scandalized the decorous soul of Richard Baxter.[2] He was willing to accept any form of government, provided it fulfilled the requirements which are indispensable in all governments ; and these he defined with an acumen and a precision which cannot be challenged.

Statesmanship demands two gifts—the conception of wise ends and the perception of adequate means. The first Montrose possessed in the highest degree, the second scarcely at all. He was a most fallible politician, and he was without skill in the game of parliamentary intrigue. He did not read the temper of the people with the accuracy of Argyll, or the possibilities of the moment with the profound sagacity of Cromwell. He was an

---

[1] For an acute study of Mackenzie's modernism, see Andrew Lang, *Sir George Mackenzie : His Life and Times* (1909).

[2] *Reliquiæ Baxterianæ* (1696), 51.

optimist about his dreams; he saw the Lowland peasantry looking for a deliverer, when they regarded him as a destroyer; he did not understand the depths of the antipathy of Saxon to Celt, or how fatally the use of Alasdair's men prejudiced his cause; he looked for loyalty in quarters which knew only self-interest, and courage among those who had it not. Practical statesmanship works essentially by compromises, accepting the second or third best as an instalment, and by slow degrees leading the people to acquiesce in an ideal which they have come to regard as their own creation. It must judge shrewdly the situation of the moment, and know precisely what elements therein are capable of providing the first stage in the great advance. It must have infinite patience, and infinite confidence in the slow processes of time.

Such a gift Montrose did not possess—indeed it may be questioned whether the problem before his age permitted of such evolutionary methods. There was no material to his hand in the shape of a nation at least partially instructed or a group of like-minded colleagues. But he was a statesman, if it be the part of statesmanship to see far ahead and to stand for the hope of the future. He stood for the Scottish democracy against those who would have crushed it and those who betrayed it with a kiss. In views and temperament it is not easy to find his parallel. He had Marlborough's contemptuous superiority to parties, but he lacked his passionless Olympian calm. With his kinsman Claverhouse— *Montrosio novus exoritur de pulvere phœnix* [1]—he had little in common except the power of leadership. There is some resemblance to Ireton in political creed, in his scorn of abstractions, and his belief in the need of a strong central government, monarchical, parliamentary, or both; [2] he shared the same view with Strafford, but, unlike him, he did not come to regard monarchical and parliamentary authority as mutually exclusive. He never relinquished his doctrine of a just balance, and if

---

[1] *Grameid* (S.H.S.), 40.
[2] For Ireton's opinions, see the *Clarke Papers, passim.*

in his last years he was compelled to put the emphasis on the royal power, it was for the same reason as Sir Thomas More was forced into opposition to Henry VIII—because the balance had been unduly depressed.

The truest kinship is perhaps with the troubled humanity of Cromwell. The Lord Protector fought for " the poor godly people "; Montrose for the plain folk without any qualification. Both were tolerant, both were idealists, striving for something which their age could not give them. Montrose had one obstacle in his way above all others, and that was Scotland. Her jealous nationalism was not ripe, even had the century been ripe, for his far-sighted good sense. She was still hugging to her breast her own fantastic creations, her covenants, her barren survivals, her peculiar royalism, still prepared to sacrifice peace and fortune to her pride. If Cromwell shipwrecked upon the genial materialism of England, Montrose split upon the rock of the sterile conservatism of his own land. Scotland was not ready for civic ideals or luminous reason. She had not found the self-confidence which was to give her a far truer and deeper national pride. She had still to tread for long years the path of coarse and earthy compromises, lit by flashes of crazy quixotry, till through suffering and poverty she came at last to find her own soul. Montrose was in advance of his age, he was in advance of England at her best, but he was utterly and eternally beyond the ken of seventeenth-century Scotland. Yet of the two great idealists he has had the happier destiny. Cromwell, brilliantly successful for the moment, built nothing which lasted. Except for his doctrine of toleration, he left no heritage of political thought which the world has used. The ideals of Montrose, on the other hand, are in the warp and woof of the constitutional fabric of to-day.

The moderate man is slow to appeal to arms. He sees too clearly the values on both sides to commit himself readily to that desperate hazard. But in a revolution it may be the only way. If men's passions are deeply stirred there must be recourse to the last and sternest arbitrament. In such a crisis it is the soldier who turns the scale, whether it be Cæsar's army of Gaul, or the Puritan New Model, or Washington's militia, or Napoleon's Grande Armée, or Garibaldi's Thousand, or Lincoln's citizen levies. A Holles or a Vane may dream his dreams, but it is Cromwell who brings his into being. Montrose both courted and warred against revolution. He desired to preserve the monarchy as against its anarchical assailants, but he was as ardent a revolutionary as Lilburne in his crusade against the existing régime in Scotland, with its dull tyranny of kirk and nobles. For there is a moderation which is in itself a fire, where enthusiasm burns as fiercely for the whole truth as it commonly does for half-truths, where toleration becomes not a policy but an act of religion. Such inspired moderation is usually found in an age of violent contraries. Henri IV. of France possessed it, as did William the Silent. Montrose, like Henri, was the supreme moderate of his age; and, like Henri, he realized that it needs a fiery soul to enforce moderation in a rabble of fanatics and debauchees. In such a strife, the ultimate word can only be spoken by one who is willing to make the ultimate sacrifice. To enter into the kingdom of the spirit a man must take his life in his hands, as martyr or as soldier.

II

As a soldier Montrose ranks by common consent with the greatest of his age, with Cromwell and Condé. The historian of the British army has described him as " perhaps the most brilliant natural military genius disclosed by the Civil War." [1] Like Cromwell, he seems to have learned his art rather by intuition than by experience, for, till his great campaign, his only training was the inglorious Bishops' War. He had never, like Leven or David Leslie, served under eminent foreign

---

[1] Fortescue, *Hist. of the British Army*, I., 228. Sir John Fortescue's other comment, " a woman in emotion and instability," is hardly appropriate to one of the most patient and resolute of military commanders.

generals; he was as unprofessional as Rupert, and, like him, he had that natural eye for country and dispositions, that power of quick resolution and that magnetism of leadership, which discomfited the more prosaic commanders who found themselves his opponents. He had learned the lesson of which his friend, the Cardinal de Retz, has given a famous epitome : " Il n'y a rien dans le monde qui n'ait son moment décisif ; et le chefd'œuvre de la bonne conduite est de connaître et de prendre ce moment."

It has been sometimes urged that it is easy to overpraise Montrose's military capacity, since he usually fought against inferior troops and incompetent generals, and that on the only occasion on which he met a commander of ability and a seasoned army he was defeated. But the argument does not bear examination. The men he scattered at Tippermuir and Aberdeen were, it is true, raw levies, though present in great numerical superiority ; but they were precisely the men with whom he had been victorious in his first campaign, and his conquering Highlanders were of the race which he had routed in 1639, when they fought under Aboyne. At Inverlochy he had against him the best disciplined of the Highland clans, and Auchinbreck had ten times his own experience of war. At Dundee and Auldearn and Alford he faced regular cavalry and foot, the pick of the men who had won renown under Leven in England ; and Hurry and Baillie had a high repute among the commanders of the day. Philiphaugh and Carbisdale are too much unlike normal battles to be made the basis for any judgment of one side or the other. No doubt Montrose's Highland and Irish troops, nourished on beef and game, were of a more stalwart physical type than the Lowland second line. But the regular Covenant foot were stout fellows, and they had the priceless advantage of a strict discipline and freedom from the endless clan jealousies. So far as equipment went, Montrose won his victories in the face of crushing odds. His army was always a fluid thing ; after every success a large part of it departed with their booty to their homes; more than half his time was spent in the work of shepherding back to his standard the volatile clans.[1] Under such conditions it is hard to make a plan of campaign, and harder still to execute it.

As a strategist he showed an extraordinary eye for country. The tangled passes of the Grampians, little known except in patches to the different clans, were grasped by him as a geographical whole, and he arranged his marches accordingly. He had a boldness, too, which staggered even those inured to mountain warfare, and his flank march before Inverlochy seemed both to friends and foes outside the limits of human power. His incredible speed was a further strategical advantage, for he could march over twenty miles in a single night among snowy mountains, as in his pursuit of Argyll in December 1644; or in thirty-six hours cover sixty miles, with fighting between, as at Dundee. This swiftness, indeed, was apt to be a snare to him. He despised his slower antagonists, and was twice almost caught—at Fyvie and Dundee—before the final surprise came at Philiphaugh. For strategy in the widest sense he was given no scope. He could not plan a campaign to correspond with the king's in England, for his hands were tied by the composition of his army; his Highlanders would not fight south of the Highland Line, and deserted in droves after each victory. In such circumstances there could be no continuity of purpose, and the marvel is that Kilsyth was ever fought. But it is clear that Montrose was fully alive to the need of the larger strategical intention, and that it was only the lack of response from the English side that confined him to mountain warfare. With a force such as Charles repeatedly frittered away, he would have swept these islands from Sutherland to Devon.

In tactics he had in a supreme degree the gift of suiting his scheme of battle to his material, using his horse now as mounted infantry and now as cavalry,

---

[1] Claverhouse had the same trouble up to the eve of Killiecrankie (*Memoirs of Locheill*, 237, etc.). So had Stonewall Jackson with Ashby's horse in the Valley Campaign of 1862 (Henderson, *Stonewall Jackson*, I., 333).

and getting full value from the impetuous Highland charge. His power of rapid decision never failed him, and in the stress of fight he could keep his head and alter his arrangements at the shortest notice. As proofs, we have the sudden strengthening of the left wing at Aberdeen, and his rapid dispositions in the hurry of the surprise before Auldearn, as well as the marvellous retreat from Dundee. At leisure he could dispose a battle with great skill, as at Alford, and could defy the ordinary rules of war with success, as at Kilsyth. Kilsyth is, indeed, an interesting case, for there is every reason to believe that Montrose deliberately chose what seemed to be the worse position. He was probably convinced that the Covenanters, finding themselves with the hill in their favour, would take some foolish risk and so play into his hands, and he counted on the power of his Highlanders to charge up a slope and arrive unwearied at the top. He knew, too, the value of the sudden word in the strain of battle to turn the tide, and his insight into the hearts of fighting men was at least as great a factor in his success as his tactical skill.

More notable than even his gifts for strategy and tactics was his unique power of leadership. He discerned the fighting value of the clans, and welded into an army the most heterogeneous materials on earth. Hitherto it had seemed impossible to band two minor septs together for one purpose for more than a week; Montrose united the whole central Highlands in a campaign of a year's duration. Nor did he win this strange authority by any pandering to the vices of savage warfare. Except for the sack of Aberdeen, there is no stain on his record. He refused to turn the captured cannon on the fugitives at Tippermuir; he tried to check the slaughter after Inverlochy; he punished looting severely, as at Glasgow; he observed scrupulously the etiquette of war; he never put a prisoner to death, not even when his dearest friends were being murdered by the Estates. He did not stoop, as his opponents did, to the methods of the dirk and the ambuscade. It should be remembered that he was no fire-eating giant like Alasdair, but a slim young man of middle height, somewhat grave and courtly in his manner, and fonder of a book than a drinking-bout. Yet no iron-fisted Hercules ever kept a wilder force in a sterner discipline. The man who, at Dundee, could draw off half-tipsy troops in the middle of a sack in the face of a superior enemy, and lead them, weary as they were, for thirty miles in the thick of night to the safety of the hills, had miraculous gifts as a leader. We may search for long in the annals of war to find an equal achievement.

Cromwell also had that moral authority which fused the forces under him into a single weapon for his hand to direct. But Cromwell, except at Dunbar, fought with numbers on his side, and he had the supreme advantage that his men were largely bound already by the tie of a strong religious faith. For Montrose there was no such aid to discipline. It was personal authority, and personal authority alone, that kept Gordon and Macdonald in the same firing line. The two great captains were fated never to meet, and their relative prowess must remain in the realm of hypothesis. The chief historian of the epoch rates Montrose the higher. " On the battlefield Montrose had all Cromwell's promptness of seizing the chances of the strife, together with a versatility in varying his tactics according to the varying resources of the enemy, to which Cromwell could lay no claim, while his skill as a strategist was certainly superior to that of his English contemporary." [1] Probably the judgment is just. At any rate, we can say that Montrose performed feats not inferior to Cromwell's best, with weaker resources and against greater odds.

Scale must not be confused with kind. Since Montrose's day the technical equipment of the soldier has been inconceivably enlarged, armies have grown into armed nations, the advance in the variety and precision of weapons has made every problem more intricate. But modern inventions, which make levies of millions possible, have provided in an equal ratio the

[1] Gardiner, *Civil War*, II., 351.

facilities for leading them. Military genius remains in its essentials the same, and it is still possible in this respect to compare the soldiers of all ages, and to rank one who commanded a few thousands in a moorland war among the masters of the art. In virtue of his achievement, Montrose must stand as the foremost Scottish man of action—perhaps the only Scot who approaches the confines of that small inner circle of the profession of arms, which, among men of our own blood, contains no other names than Marlborough, Wellington, and Lee.

III

Few careers have such romantic unity. In one aspect he is the complete paladin, full of courtesy and grace, a Volcker of Alsace with his sword-fiddlebow, whose every stroke is a note of music. He wins fights against odds, and scribbles immortal songs in his leisure, and dies in the end like some antique hero, with the lights burning low in the skies and the stage darkened. In another he is the thinker, who read, as no one else did, the riddle of his times, and preached a doctrine of government which had to wait for nearly two hundred years till it found an audience. In that fierce seventeenth century, when men died for half-truths or less, when the great forces of the State were apt to be selfish competitors for material gain, and the idealists were driven into the wilds or overseas—in that gross and turbid age he lit the lamp of pure duty and pure reason. There were those who followed duty, but it was too often blindly. There were those who loved reason, but they either retired from the struggle or, like Falkland, fought with the air of martyrs rather than of soldiers. Montrose was armed and mailed Reason, Philosophy with its sword unsheathed. He is a far rarer type than the quietist who has fascinated historians, or than the grim Ironside, " the most formidable of combinations, the practical mystic." He had all the grave lucidity of a Falkland, but he had none of his sad despair, for he went out joyfully to do battle for his faith. He was as stubborn and passionate in his cause as any Ironside, but he was no fanatic; he was not even any kind of mystic. He saw life clearly and calmly, and his spiritual force did not come, as it often comes, from a hectic imagination or a fevered brain. The springs of his being were a pellucid reasonableness of soul, joined to a power of absorption in duty which is commonly found only in the ranks of fanaticism.

It is a figure which must always haunt those who travel the rough roads of Scottish history. We see him in the brave clothes which still dazzle us in his portraits, the long, north-country face, the broad brow, the inscrutable grey eyes. He is thinking, wondering, brooding on the needs of his land, while others are preying on them. Then he reaches his conclusions, and, with something between the certainty of the thinker and the enthusiasm of the boy, he sets out on his desperate errand. We see him in battle, a flush on his cheek, a youthful ardour in his eye, but his mouth set like iron. We see him among his friends, conquering all hearts with his wit and grace. We see him in triumph and in failure, careless of self, his course set unfalteringly towards his dreams, carrying, in Keats's words, " an awful warmth about his heart like a load of immortality." He is always very human, very much the man, for Alasdair and his kerns would never have followed the ordinary dreamer. And then, when the last blow has been struck, he has neither fears nor reproaches. Clearly and reasonably he states his defence, and when it is flouted and he is condemned to a shameful death, he takes it meekly, knowing something of the fallibility of mankind. The Edinburgh mob is awed into a hush by his appearance; his enemies declared that it was his fine clothes and noble looks; more truly we may read it as that inward vision which is the beatitude of the pure in heart.

No great cause is ever lost or ever won. The battle must always be renewed and the creed restated, and the old formulas, once so potent a revelation, become

only dim antiquarian echoes. But some things are
universal, catholic, and undying—the souls of which
such formulas are the broken gleams. These do not age
or pass out of fashion, for they symbolize eternal things.
They are the guardians of the freedom of the human
spirit, the proof of what our mortal frailty can achieve.
Of this happy company Montrose is one. His qualities
in the retrospect seem to be drawn to a fine edge of
burning light. But, as we wonder and revere, there
comes a voice from behind the flame, and awe is changed
to wistfulness; for it is a voice of comradeship and joy
and youth which " sweetly torments us with invitations
to his own inaccessible homes."

APPENDIX

MONTROSE ON "SOVEREIGN POWER"[1]

"Noble Sir,—

" In the letter you did me the honour to send me, you move a question in two words, to give a satisfactory answer to which requires works and volumes, not letters. Besides, the matter is of so sublime and transcendant a nature as is above my reach, and not fit for subjects to meddle with—if it were not to do right to sovereign power in a time when so much is said and done to the disgrace and derogation of it. Nevertheless, to obey your desire, I will deliver my opinion : First, concerning the nature, essential parts, and practice of the supreme power in government of all sorts. Secondly, I will shew wherein the strength and weakness thereof consists, and the effects of both. Thirdly, I will answer some arguments and false positions maintained by the impugners of royal power ; and that without partiality, and as briefly as I can :

" 1. Civil societies, so pleasing to Almighty God, cannot subsist without government, nor government without a sovereign power, to force obedience to laws and just commands, to dispose and direct private endeavours to public ends, and to unite and incorporate the several members into one body politic, that with joint endeavours and abilities they may the better advance the public good. This sovereignty is a power over the people ; above which power there is none upon earth ; whose acts cannot be rescinded by any other; instituted by God, for His glory and the temporal and eternal happiness of men. This is it that is recorded so oft, by the wisdom of antient times, to be sacred and inviolable; the truest image and representation of the power of Almighty God upon earth; not to be bounded, disputed, meddled with at all by subjects; who can never handle it, though never so warily, but it is thereby wounded, and the public peace disturbed. Yet it is limited by the laws of God and Nature; and some laws of nations; and by the fundamental laws of the country; which are those upon which sovereign power itself resteth, in prejudice of which a king can do nothing; and those also which secure to the good subject his honour, his life, and the property of his goods.

This power—not speaking of those who are kings in name only, and in effect but *Principes Nobilitatis* or *Duces Belli*, nor of the arbitrary and despotic power, where one is head and all the rest slaves, but of that which is sovereign over all free subjects—is still one and the same, in points essential, wherever it be, whether in the person of a monarch, or in a few principal men, or in the Estates of the people. The essential points of sovereignty are these: To make laws; to create principal officers; to make peace and war; to give grace to men condemned by law; and to be the last to whom appellation is made. There be others, too, which are comprehended in those set down; but because majesty doeth not so clearly shine in them they are here omitted. These set down are inalienable, indivisible, incommunicable, and belong to the sovereign power primitively in all sorts of governments. They cannot subsist in a body composed of individuities; and if they be divided amongst several bodies, there is no government; as if there were many kings in one kingdom, there should be none at all; for whosoever should have one of these, were able to erase their proceedings who have all the rest; for the having them negative and prohibitive in that part to him belonging, might render the acts of all the others invalid, and there would be a superiority to the supreme, and an equality to the sovereign power,

which cannot fall in any man's conceit that hath common
sense; in speech it is incongruity, and to attempt it in
act is pernicious.

" Having in some measure expressed the nature of
supreme power, it shall be better known by the actual
practice of all nations, in all the several sorts of government, as well Republics and Monarchies.

" The people of Rome—who were masters of policy,
and war too, and to this day are made patterns of both
—being an Estate popular, did exercise, without control-
ment or opposition, all the forenamed points essential to
supreme power. No law was made but by the people;
and though the Senate did propone and advise a law
to be made, it was the people that gave it sanction; and
it received the force of law from their command and
authority, as may appear by the respective phrases of
the propounder—*Quod faustum felixque sit, vobis popu-
loque Romano velitis jubeatis.* The people used these
imperative words, *Esto sunto*; and if it were refused,
the Tribune of the people expressed it with a *veto*. The
propounder or adviser of the law was said *rogare legem*,
and the people *jubere legem*. The election of officers
was only made by the people, as appears by the ambitious buying and begging of suffrages, so frequent among
them upon the occasions. War and peace was ever
concluded by them, and never denounced but by their
Feciales and with commission from them. They only
gave grace and pardon; and for the last refuge, delin-
quents, and they who were wronged by the sentence of
judges and officers, *provocabant ad populum.*

" So it was in Athens, and to this day among the
Switzers and Grissons, the Estate of Holland, and all
Estates popular. In Venice, which is a pure aristocracy,
laws, war, peace, election of officers, pardon and appellation, are all concluded and done in *Conciglio maggiore,*
which consists of principal men who have the sovereignty.
As for the *Pregadi,* and the *Conciglio di dieci,* they were
but officers and executors of their power; and the duke
is nothing but the idol to whom ceremonies and compliments are addressed, without the least part of sove-

reignty. So it was in Sparta ; so it is in Lucca, Genoa, and Ragusa, and all other Aristocracies ; and, indeed, cannot be otherwise without the subversion of the present government.

" If, then, the lords in Republics have that power essential to sovereignty, by what reason can it be denied to a prince in whose person only, and primitively, resteth the sovereign power, and from whom all lawful subaltern power, as from the fountain, is derived ?

" 2. This power is strong and durable when it is temperate ; and it is temperate when it is possessed (with the essential parts aforesaid) with moderation, and limitation by the laws of God, of Nature, and the fundamental laws of the country. It is weak when it is restrained of these essential parts ; and it is weak also when it is extended beyond the laws whereby it is bounded ; which could never be any time endured by the people of the western part of the world, and by those of Scotland as little as any. For that which Galba said of his Romans is the humour of them all—*nec totam libertatem nec totam servitutem pati possunt*—but a temper of both. Unwise princes endeavour the extension of it—rebellious and turbulent subjects the restraint. Wise princes use it moderately ; but most desire to extend it, and that humour is fomented by advice of courtiers and bad counsellors, who are of a hasty ambition, and cannot abide the slow progress of riches and preferments in a temperate government. They persuade the arbitrary with reflexion on their own ends ; knowing that the exercise thereof shall be put upon them, whereby they shall be able quickly to compass their ends ; robbing thereby the people of their wealth, the king of the people's love due to him, and of the honour and reputation of wisdom. The effects of a moderate government are religion, justice, and peace ; flourishing love of the subjects towards their prince, in whose hearts he reigns ; durableness and strength against foreign invasions and intestine sedition ; happiness and security to king and people. The effect of a prince's power too far extended is tyranny—from the

king, if he be ill; if he be good, tyranny or a fear of it
from them to whom he hath entrusted the managing of
public affairs. The effect of the royal power restrained
is the oppression and tyranny of subjects; the most
fierce, insatiable, and insupportable tyranny in the
world; where every man of power oppresseth his neighbour, without any hope of redress from a prince despoiled
of his power to punish oppressors.

The people under an extended power are miserable, but
most miserable under the restrained power. The effects
of the former may be cured by good advice; satiety in
the prince; or fear of infamy; or the pains of writers; or
by some event which may bring a prince to the sense of
his errors; and when nothing else can do it, seeing the
prince is mortal, patience is a sovereign and dangerless
remedy in the subject; who in wisdom and duty is
obliged to tolerate the vices of his prince as they do
storms and tempests, and other natural evils which are
compensated with better times succeeding. It had been
better for Germany to have endured the encroachments
of Ferdinand, and after his death rectified them before
they had made a new election, than to have brought
it to desolation, and shed so much Christian blood
by unseasonable remedies and opposition. But when a
king's lawful power is restrained, the politic body is in
such desperate estate that it can neither endure the
disease, nor the remedy, which is force only. For
princes' lawful power is only restrained by violence, and
never repaired but by violence on the other side; which
can produce nothing but ruin to prince or people, or
rather to both. Patience in the subject is the best
remedy against the effects of a prince's power too far
extended; but when it is too far restrained, patience
in the prince is so far from being a remedy, that it
formeth and increaseth the disease; for patience, tract
of time, and possession, makes that which was at first
robbery, by a body that never dies, at last a good title,
and the government comes at last to be changed.

"To procure a temperate and moderate government,
there is much in the king and not a little in the people.

For let a prince command never so well, if there be not a correspondent obedience there is no temper. It is not the people's part, towards that end, to take upon them to limit and circumscribe royal power; it is Jupiter's thunder which never subject handled well yet; not the people's part to determine what is due to a prince, what to his people. It requires more than human sufficiency to go so even a way betwixt the prince's prerogative, and the subject's privilege, as to content both, or be just in itself. For they can never agree upon the matter; and where it hath been attempted, as in some places it hath, the sword did ever determine the question, which is to be avoided by all possible means. But there is a fair and justifiable way for subjects to procure a moderate government, incumbent to them in duty; which is, to endeavour the security of Religion and just Liberties, the matter on which the exorbitancy of a prince's power doth work; which being secured, his power must needs be temperate, and run in the even channel.

" ' But,' it may be demanded, ' how shall the people's just liberties be preserved if they be not known, and how known if they be not determined to be such ?' It is answered, the laws contain them; and the Parliaments, which ever have been the bulwarks of subjects' liberties in monarchies, may advise new laws against emergent occasions which prejudge their liberties; and so leave it to occasion, and not prevent it by foolish haste in Parliaments, which breeds contention, and disturbance to the quiet of the State. And if Parliaments be frequent, and rightly constituted, what favourite counsellor or statesman dare misinform or mislead a king to the prejudice of a subject's liberty, knowing he must answer it upon the peril of his head and estate at the next ensuing Parliament, and that he shall put the king to an hard choice for him, either to abandon him to justice, or, by protecting him, displease the estates of his kingdom ? And if the king should be so ill advised as to protect him, yet he doth not escape punishment that is branded with a mark of public infamy, declared enemy to the State, and incapable of any good amongst them.

3. " The perpetual cause of the controversies, between the prince and his subjects, is the ambitious designs of rule in great men, veiled under the specious pretext of Religion and the subject's Liberties, seconded with the arguments and false positions of seditious preachers : 1st, that the king is ordained for the people, and the end is more noble than the mean ; 2nd, that the constituter is superior to the constituent ; 3rd, that the king and people are two contraries, like the two scales of a balance—when the one goes up the other goes down ; 4th, that the prince's prerogative and the people's privilege are incompatible ; 5th, what power is taken from the king is added to the Estates of the people. This is the language of the spirits of division that walk betwixt the king and his people, to separate them whom God hath conjoined; which must not pass without some answer ; to slide upon which sandy ground these giants, who war against the gods, have builded their Babel.

" To the 1st : It is true that the true and utmost ends of men's actions, which is the glory of God and felicity of men, are to be preferred to all means directed thereunto. But there is not that order of dignity among the means themselves, or mid instruments compounded together. If it were so, and a man appointed to keep sheep, or a nobleman to be tutor-in-law to a pupil of meaner quality, the sheep should be preferred to the man, and the pupil to his tutor. To the 2nd : He that constituteth so as he still retaineth the power to reverse his constitution, is superior to the constituted in that respect ; but if his donation and constitution is absolute and without condition, devolving all his power in the person constituted, and his successors, what before was voluntary becomes necessary. It is voluntary to a woman to chuse such an one for her husband, and to a people what king they will at first ; both being once done, neither can the woman nor the people free themselves, from obedience and subjection to the husband and the prince, when they please. To the 3rd : In a

politic consideration, the king and his people are not
two, but one body politic, whereof the king is the head.
And so far are they from contrariety, and opposite
motions, that there is nothing good or ill for the one
which is not just so for the other. If their ends and
endeavours be divers, and never so little eccentric,
either that king inclineth to tyranny, or that people to
disloyalty—if they be contrary, it is mere tyranny or
mere disloyalty. To the 4th : The king's prerogative
and the subject's privilege are so far from incompati-
bility, that the one can never stand unless supported
by the other. For the sovereign being strong, and in
full possession of his lawful power and prerogative, is
able to protect his subjects from oppression, and maintain their liberties entire ; otherwise, not. On the other
side, a people, enjoying freely their just liberties and
privileges, maintaineth the prince's honour and prerogative out of the great affection they carry towards
him ; which is the greatest strength against foreign
invasion, or intestine insurrection, that a prince can
possibly be possessed with. To the 5th : It is a mere
fallacy ; for what is essential to one thing cannot be
given to another. The eye may lose its sight, the ear
its hearing, but can never be given to the hand, or foot,
or any other member ; and, as the head of the natural body may be deprived of invention, judgment, or
memory, and the rest of the members receive no part
thereof, so subjects, not being capable of the essential
parts of government properly and primitively belonging
to the prince, those being taken from him, they can
never be imparted to them, without change of the
government and the essence and being of the same.
When a king is restrained from the lawful use of his
power, and subjects can make no use of it—as under a
king they cannot—what can follow but a subversion of
government—anarchy and confusion ?

"Now, to any man that understands these things
only, the proceedings of these times may seem strange,
and he may expostulate with us thus :

" Noblemen and gentlemen of good quality, what do you mean ? Will you teach the people to put down the Lord's anointed, and lay violent hands on his authority to whom both you and they owe subjection, and assistance with your goods, lives, and fortunes, by all the laws of God and man ? Do ye think to stand and domineer over the people, in an aristocratic way— the people who owe you small or no obligation ? It is you, under your natural prince, that get all employment pregnant of honour or profit, in peace or war. You are the subjects of his liberality ; your houses decayed, either by merit or his grace and favour are repaired, without which you fall in contempt ; the people, jealous of their liberty, when you deserve best, to shelter themselves will make you shorter by the head, or serve you with an ostracism. If their first act be against kingly power, their next act will be against you. For if the people be of a fierce nature, they will cut your throats ; as the Switzers did of old ; you shall be contemptible. ; as some of antient houses are in Holland, their very burgomaster is the better man ; your honours —life— fortunes stand at the discretion of a seditious preacher !

" And you, ye meaner people of Scotland—who are not capable of a Republic, for many grave reasons— why are you induced by specious pretexts, to your own heavy prejudice and detriment, to be instruments of others' ambition ? Do ye not know, when the monarchical government is shaken, the great ones strive for the garland with *your* blood and *your* fortunes ? Whereby you gain nothing ; but, instead of a race of kings who have governed you two thousand years with peace and justice, and have preserved your liberties against all domineering nations, shall purchase to yourselves vultures and tigers to reign over your posterity ; and yourselves shall endure all those miseries, massacres, and proscriptions of the Triumvirate of Rome, (till) the kingdom fall again into the hands of One, who of necessity must, and for reason of State will, tyrannize over you. For kingdoms acquired by blood and violence are by the same means retained.

"And you great men—if any such be among you so blinded with ambition—who aim so high as the crown, do you think we are so far degenerate from the virtue, valour, and fidelity to our true and lawful sovereign, so constantly entertained by our ancestors, as to suffer you, with all your policy, to reign over us? Take heed you be not Æsop's dog, and lose the cheese for the shadow in the well.

"And thou, seditious preacher, who studies to put the sovereignty in the people's hands for thy own ambitious ends—as being able, by thy wicked eloquence and hypocrisy, to infuse into them what thou pleasest—know this, that this people is more incapable of sovereignty than any other known. Thou art abused like a pedant by the nimble-witted nobleman. Go, go along with them to shake the present government; not for thy ends to possess the people with it, but, as a cunning tennis-player lets the ball go to the wall, where it cannot stay, that he may take it at the bound with more ease.

"And whereas a durable peace with England—which is the wish and desire of all honest men—is pretended, surely it is a great solecism in us to aim at an end of peace with them, and overthrow the only means for that end. It is the King's Majesty's sovereignty over both that unites us in affection, and is only able to reconcile questions among us when they fall. To endeavour the dissolution of that bond of our union is nowise to establish a durable peace; but rather to procure enmity and war betwixt bordering nations, where occasions of quarrel are never wanting, nor men ever ready to take hold of them.

"Now, sir, you have my opinion concerning your desire, and that which I esteem truth set down nakedly for your use, not adorned for public view. And if zeal for my Sovereign and Country have transported me a little too far, I hope you will excuse the errors proceeding from so good a cause of

"Your humble servant,
"MONTROSE."

INDEX

INDEX

ABERDEEN, Montrose's first visit to,
81 ; second visit, 81–82 ; occupation of, by Montrose, 97–100 ;
first battle of, 101–104 ; 158, 191 ;
second battle of, 199–203, 390–
392 ; sack of, 203–205 ; 219, 231,
232 ; Nathaniel Gordon's raid
upon, 233 ; burial of Lord Gordon
in, 258 ; 294, 368, 378.
Aberfeldy, 191.
Abernethy on Spey, 206, 252.
Aboyne, James Gordon, Viscount,
101–103, 107, 155, 158, 161, 169,
171, 176, 198, 213, 242, 243, 248,
256, 257, 262, 264, 270, 281, 282,
283, 300, 301, 304, 331, 390. *See
also* Huntly, Marquis of.
Acts, the Black, 46 ; Act of Classes,
347 ; Act Rescissory, 88 ; Act of
Revocation, 66, 74.
Adwalton Moor, 158.
Agnew, James, of Lochnaw, 289.
Airlie, James Ogilvy, first Earl of, 116,
117, 123, 156, 198, 199, 204, 210,
215, 225, 232, 264, 270, 284, 289,
292, 300, 301, 312.
Airth, 267.
Alford, battle of, 254, 255, 258, 262,
390, 392.
Allan Water, 267.
Alloa, 266.
Almond, Lord. *See* Callander, Earl
of.
Amisfield. *See* Charteris of Amis-
field.
Angers, 40.
Angus, 96, 117, 196, 198, 232, 243,
302 ; Earl of, *see* Douglas,
Marquis of.
Annand, Mr. John, 364.
Annandale, James Murray, second
Earl of, 132, 275.
Antrim, Randal Macdonnell, first
Marquis of, 79, 95, 96, 117, 158,
160, 162, 163 n., 168, 173, 176,
180, 312.

Appin, 211, 220, 221, 263. *See also*
Stewarts of Appin.
Arbroath, 238.
Ardnamurchan, 180, 191.
Ardvreck castle, 258, 263.
Argyll, Archibald Campbell, eighth
Earl and first Marquis of, at St.
Andrews College, 36, 37 ; 79, 80 ;
at Glasgow Assembly, 84, 86, 88 ;
character of, 89–94 ; controversy
with Montrose, 107, 111, 115, 116 ;
commission of " fire and sword "
granted to, 117, 118, 119 ; 123,
124, 127 ; accused by Stewart of
Ladywell, 128, 129, 130, 132 ;
the " Incident," 133, 134 ; becomes a marquis, 135 ; political
aims, 142 ; at General Assembly
of 1642, 153, 154 ; 155, 156, 157,
162, 168, 169, 173, 176, 178, 180,
181, 185 n., 190, 191 ; reaches
Perth after Tippermuir, 196–197 ;
200, 205 ; at Fyvie, 206, 207, 208,
209, 210, 212 ; power in the
Highlands, 214, 215 ; at Inveraray, 217, 218, 219, 220 ; at
Inverlochy, 221, 223, 224, 225,
229, 230, 240, 251, 253 ; at
Alford, 257, 261 ; at Kilsyth, 267,
271, 279 ; at Philiphaugh, 283,
291, 295, 296 ; 302, 304, 305, 308 ;
opposes " Engagement," 322,
324, 325, 326, 332, 334, 345, 347 ;
at Montrose's trial and execution, 363, 367, 369, 372 n., 373,
375 ; death, 378, 379, 384, 391.
Articles of Perth, the, 49, 50, 70, 87.
Arundel, Lord, 94, 95.
Ashburnham, John, 319.
Atholl, 116, 117, 168, 181, 182, 206,
210, 241, 242, 251, 252, 262, 300,
302, 304, 349 ; John Murray, first
Earl of, 117, 119, 128 ; John,
second Earl, 182.
Auchterarder, 84, 112.
Augustine, St., 54, 59.

Auldearn, battle of, 244, 245, 250, 252, 256, 257, 258, 277, 390, 392.
Austerlitz, battle of, 250.

BACON, Nicholas, 141.
Badenoch, 96, 168, 181, 182, 188, 206, 210, 232, 252, 256, 263, 352.
Baillie, Mr. Robert, 62, 72, 75, 79, 84, 87, 95, 103, 104, 105, 112, 113, 124, 170, 174, 188, 203, 206, 218, 219, 229, 307, 322, 330, 332, 362, 374 ; Sir William, of Lamington, 218 ; Major-Gen. William, of Letham, 211, 218, 219, 225, 230, 234, 235, 237, 238, 239, 240, 242, 249, 251, 252, 253, 254, 255, 256, 257, 258, 259, 270, 271, 325, 348, 390.
Balcanquhal, Dr., Dean of Durham, 109.
Balcarres, Alexander Lindsay, first Earl of, 257, 258, 267, 269, 270, 271, 312, 325.
Balmerino, John Livingstone, second Lord, 70, 78, 128.
Balveny, 95, 209, 252.
Baxter, Mr. Richard, 59, 386.
Beauly, 306, 364, 385.
Bellie, Kirk of, 232.
Bellièvre, Pompone de, 320.
Benderloch, 214, 221.
Ben Nevis, 224.
Bergen, 318, 343.
Berwick, 283.
Biggar, 291.
Binning, Mr. Hugh, 19 n., 62 ; Captain Thomas, 378 n.
Bishops' War, the, 168, 176, 190, 205, 283, 289, 294.
Blackadder, Captain, 489.
Blair, Mr. Robert, 62, 230, 298, 326, 330.
Blair-in-Atholl, 182, 191, 210, 211, 215, 216, 251, 299.
Bog of Gight (Gordon castle), 102, 205, 232, 254, 300, 303, 306.
Bonar Bridge, 353.
Bothwell, 274, 275, 277, 279, 281.
Boyd, Mr. Robert, eighth Lord, 78, 119, 124 ; Mr. Robert, 62 ; Mr. Zachary, 274, 336.
Braemar, 211, 233, 301, 302.
Brahan castle, 351, 353, 364.
Brandenburg, Elector of, 339.
Brander, Pass of, 215, 220.
Breadalbane, 214, 216, 217.
Brechin, 85, 234, 236, 238, 334.
Breda, 337 ; Treaty of, 359, 360, 362.
Brentford, Patrick Ruthven, Lord, 338.
Bridlington Bay, 115.

Broadmeadows, 290.
Browne, Sir Thomas, 18.
Brussels, 324, 326, 327.
Buccleuch, Francis Scott, second Earl of, 172, 285.
Buchan, 177, 207, 216.
Buchanan, Sir George, 302 ; Mr. George, 38, 56, 70, 140.
Buchanan castle, 302.
Buchanty, 191.
Buckle, H. T., 57, 61 n.
Bunyan, John, 22, 26, 54, 350.
Burke, Edmund, 144, 145, 386.
Burleigh, Robert Arnot, second Lord (Balfour of), 115, 191, 196, 198, 201, 231, 253, 262, 267, 269, 271.
Burnet, Gilbert, Bishop of Salisbury, 40, 41, 42, 43 n., 86, 109, 124, 151, 323 n., 324 n., 325, 331 n. ; Sir Thomas, of Leys, 199.

CALLANDER, James Livingstone, first Earl of, 119, 131, 173, 176, 211, 324, 325, 379.
Calvin, John, 26, 27, 28, 46, 52, 54, 55.
Calvinism, 17, 25, 146.
Cambridge Platonists, the, 146.
Cameron clan, the, 96, 211, 215, 225, 226, 227, 263 ; Sir Ewen, of Lochiel, 222 n., 266 n., 299 n., 385.
Campbell clan, the, 158, 212, 213, 214, 218, 219, 222, 226, 227 ; Lady Mary, 157 n. ; Campbell of Ardchattan, 220 ; of Ardkinglass, 304 ; Sir Duncan, of Auchinbreck, 219, 225, 227, 390 ; of Crinan, 251 ; Patrick, of Edinample, 216 ; Sir Robert, of Glenorchy, 214, 216 ; Sir Mungo, of Lawers, 249 ; of Lochow, 214.
Cant, Mr. Andrew, 81, 82, 130, 134, 199, 293 n., 298.
Capel, Lord, 23, 380.
Carbisdale, battle of, 201 n., 294, 353, 356, 358, 361, 367, 382, 390.
Careston castle, 238.
Cargill, Mr. Donald, 36, 364.
Carisbrooke castle, 322, 324.
Carleton, Sir Dudley, 337.
Carlisle, 171, 175, 176, 179, 182, 183, 188, 193, 242, 251, 260, 301 ; James Hay, second Earl of, 337.
Carlyle, Thomas, 16, 29.
Carmichael, Mr. Frederick, 192.
Carnegie, James, Lord (afterwards second Earl of Southesk), 85, 97 n., 275 : see also Southesk, Earl of ; Lady Magdalen, see Montrose, Marchioness of.

Carnwath, Robert Dalziel, second Earl of, 133, 161, 170, 172, 230, 301.

Carron, river, 353, 354, 355.

Cassilis, John Kennedy, sixth Earl of, 118, 128, 265, 271, 325, 332.

Castle Campbell, 266.

Castle Stewart, 365.

Chalgrove Field, 158, 233.

Chanonry castle, 351, 353.

Charles I., King, 24, 28, 40 ; rebuffs Montrose, 43, 47, 49, 56, 65 ; attempts Tithe Reform, 66 ; ecclesiastical innovations in Scotland, 68, 71, 72, 73, 76, 77, 78, 79, 80, 83, 86, 88, 91, 94, 100, 101, 103, 104, 106, 107 ; character of, 108 ; meeting with Montrose, 109 ; 110, 113, 114, 115, 120, 121, Montrose's letter to, 125 ; last visit to Scotland, 130, 131, 132, 133, 134, 144 ; outbreak of Civil War, 152, 154, 155, 156, 158 ; receives Montrose at Oxford, 160, 169 ; Montrose's letter to, after Inverlochy, 228, 229 ; 240, 250 ; defeated at Naseby, 259 ; 273, 277, 279, 302 ; orders Montrose to disband, 307, 308, 309, 310, 311, 318 ; handed over by Scots army to English Parliament, 320, 321 ; at Carisbrooke castle, 322, 323 ; execution of, 328, 329.

Charles II., King, 322, 324 n., 326, 327, 330, 332, 333, 334, 335, 338, 340, 343, 344, 345, 346, 347, 350, 358, 361, 362, 363, 378.

Charteris, of Amisfield, 275, 287, 288.

Chillingworth, William, 26, 57, 58, 60, 146.

Christian IV., of Denmark, 318.

Christian of Brunswick, 337.

Christiania, 318.

Christina of Sweden, Queen, 341.

Clan Diarmaid. See Campbell, clan of.

Clan Donald. See Macdonald, clan of.

Clarendon, Edward Hyde, first Earl of, 22, 23, 41 n., 42, 43 n., 58 n., 68, 74, 91, 93, 108, 120, 134 n., 143, 162, 169, 180, 308, 323 n., 325, 327, 329, 330, 333, 339 n., 340, 361.

Claverhouse. See Graham of Claverhouse.

Clavering, Colonel, 174.

Clyde, river, 96, 177, 274, 275, 291, 292.

Cochrane, Colonel, 124, 169.

Coke, Sir Edward, 141.

Coleridge, S. T., 134.

Colkitto. See Macdonald, Sir Alasdair.

Colquhoun, Sir John, of Luss, 35, 40.

Comrie, 242.

Condé, Louis de Bourbon, Prince de, 114 n, 320, 324, 389.

Connel, 220.

Conway, Edward, Viscount, 120, 337.

Corgarff castle, 253.

Cornbury, 162.

Corrieyairack, 223 n.

Cotton, Charles, 19 n.

Coupar-Angus, 196, 235.

Covenant, the National, 73–76, 77, 79, 83, 98, 107, 109, 112, 119, 144, 148, 149, 173, 278, 372–373. See also Solemn League and Covenant.

Cowley, Abraham, 95.

Craigcoinichean, 353, 354, 355, 358.

Craigton, 262.

Cranstoun, 282.

Crathes, 199.

Craven, William, Earl of, 337.

Crawford, Ludovic Lindsay, sixteenth Earl of, 133, 161, 169, 171, 174, 230, 276, 281, 286, 289, 292, 306, 311, 312, 313, 319, 348.

Crawford-Lindsay. See Lindsay, Earl of.

Crianlarich, 216.

Crichton, of Frendraught. See Frendraught, Viscount.

Crieff, 242.

Cromwell, Oliver, 52, 54, 55, 57, 60, 76, 122, 127, 143, 150, 185, 186, 195, 202, 229, 248, 259, 285, 295, 308, 321, 322, 326, 331, 332, 333, 335, 342, 349, 350, 367, 370, 378 n., 382, 383, 386, 388, 389, 393 ; Richard, 141 ; Lord, 337.

Cryne's Cross Mounth, 199.

Cumbernauld Bond, the, 119, 124, 130, 173.

Cunningham, Thomas, of Campvere, 330 n.

Dalziel, "Captain Francis," 170, 171 ; Sir John, 290, 292, 303.

Dee, river, 102, 199, 243, 251, 252, 253, 262, 303.

Diarmaid, clan. See Campbell, clan of.

Dick, William, of Braid, 40.

Dickson, Mr. David, 81, 82, 85, 86, 109, 130, 196 n., 326, 330.

Digby, George, Lord (second Earl of Bristol), 162, 163 n., 229, 259, 273, 285, 286, 300, 301, 302, 303, 307, 329.

Don, river, 205, 206, 244, 254, 255, 257.

Donald the Fair, 182.
Donaldson, Margaret, 195.
Donne, John, 17, 18, 19, 24, 25, 38 n., 54, 55, 60, 241, 242, 336.
Dorislaus, Dr., 339.
Douglas, William, first Marquis of, 41, 96, 275, 281, 284, 289, 290, 292, 300, 379; of Cavers, 249; Sir Thomas, 342, 351, 355; Mr. Robert, 62.
Drum. See Irvine of Drum.
Drumminor castle, 300.
Drummond, James, Lord (son of Earl of Perth), 192, 193, 194, 275; David, Master of Maderty, 191, 193; Sir James, 210; Sir John, 191; John, of Balloch, 256, 304, 305, 313, 351; Sir Patrick, 362; William, of Hawthornden, 70, 136, 138 n., 139, 140 n., 176; Major, 246, 248.
Dullatur, 271.
Dumfries, 172, 173, 175, 178, 196, 301.
Dunavertie, 293.
Dunbar, battle of, 204, 283, 393.
Dunbeath, 339 n., 351.
Dundee, 196, 198, 234–236, 239, 240, 297, 355, 366, 368, 390, 391, 392, 393; Viscount, see Graham, John, of Claverhouse.
Dunfermline, Charles Seton, Earl of, 107, 207.
Dunglass, 101.
Dunkeld, 209, 210, 235, 263, 264.
Dunnottar castle, 103, 234, 379.
Dunrobin castle, 352, 356 n.
Duns, 103.
Dunyveg, 179.
Dupplin, Lord. See Kinnoull, third Earl of.
Durham, 169.
Durham, Mr. James, 62.

EDGEHILL, battle of, 23, 154, 183 n., 185 n., 248.
Eglinton, Alexander Montgomery, sixth Earl of, 265, 275, 325, 326, 379.
Elcho, David, Lord (afterwards second Earl of Wemyss), 191, 192, 193, 194, 200, 253, 267, 325.
Elgin, 231, 232, 244, 252.
Elizabeth, Queen, 15, 16, 48, 58; Queen, of Bohemia, 335–338; Princess, of the Palatine, 338.
Elphinstone, Sir George, of Blythswood, 35.
Engagement, the, 322–325.
Erskine, John, Lord (afterwards fourth Earl of Mar), 275, 283, 290, 300, 302; of Dun, 85.

Essex, Robert Devereux, third Earl of, 183 n.
Eythin, James King, Lord, 345.

FAIRFAX, Thomas, Lord, 158, 170, 176, 250.
Falkland, Lucius Cary, second Viscount, 22, 23, 27, 28, 58, 95, 394.
Farquharson, clan of, 211, 256, 263, 302, 365; Donald, 203, 208 n., 233, 247, 259.
Ferdinand IV., Emperor, 323, 324.
Fettercairn, 234.
Fielding, Basil, 40.
Fife, 153, 200, 265, 266, 267, 271, 366.
Fincastle, 302.
Findlater, James Ogilvy, first Earl of, 243.
Fleming, John, Lord (afterwards third Earl of Wigton), 275, 290; Sir William, 362, 366.
Fontenoy, battle of, 250.
Forbes, Master of, 101; Bishop, 69; Duncan, of Culloden, 364, 365; Sir William, of Craigievar, 202, 209 n.
Fordoun, 262, 368.
Forres, 244.
Forrett, Mr. William, 35, 36, 195, 232.
Fortescue, Sir John, 139; Sir J. W., 389 n.
Forthar, house of, 117, 267 n.
Fox, Charles James, 60; George, 26, 63.
Franck, Richard, 204.
Fraser, clan of, 305; Lord, 201; Mr. James, 364, 365, 368 n., 375, 378 n.
Frederick III., of Denmark, 339, 342.
Frendraught, James Crichton, Viscount, 98, 201, 351, 356, 379.
Fuller, Thomas, 308 n.
Fyvie, battle of, 207, 208, 291.

GALASHIELS, 287 n.
Gala Water, 284, 286, 287 n.
Gardiner, S. R., 66, 93, 99, 173, 237, 239 n., 264, 345 n., 393.
Gillespie, Mr. George, 88; Mr. Patrick, 230.
Gladsmuir, 286.
Glaschyle, 357.
Glasgow, 35, 36, 83, 266, 274, 277, 280, 296, 302, 368, 378 n., 392.
Glasgow Assembly, the, 83–89, 173, 333, 370.
Gledstanes of Whitelaw, 249.
Glencairn, William Cunningham, ninth Earl of, 89, 102, 172, 265, 271.
Glencoe, 211, 215, 221.

Glen Dochart, 216.
Glen Etive, 220.
Glenisla, 117.
Glen Muick, 243, 252.
Glen Nevis, 211, 224
Glenorchy, 217.
Glen Roy, 223.
Glenshee, 301, 311.
Glen Shira, 218.
Glen Turritt, 223.
Godolphin, Sidney, 23.
Gordon, clan of, 168, 181, 198, 207, 208, 213, 231, 232, 235, 236, 241, 242, 301, 304, 305, 306, 331; George, Lord, 99, 100, 198, 209 n., 231, 241, 242, 243, 245, 247, 248, 252, 253, 254, 256, 258, 259, 270, 313; James, of Rothiemay, 99; James, of Rynie, 247, 249, 256; Colonel John, 339; John, 236; Lord Lewis (afterwards third Marquis of Huntly), 102, 198, 200, 201, 231, 236, 262, 300, 301, 304, 306, 331, 349; Nathaniel, 199, 201, 202, 205, 209 n., 231, 233, 253, 256, 257, 271, 275, 276, 277, 282, 295, 298; Patrick, of Ruthven, 177, 179, 203, 233, 258, 259, 292, 294; Sir Robert, of Gordonstoun, 376 n.; Robert, 376; of Buckie, 254; of Buthlaw, 222 n.; of Straloch, 98, 99. See also under Aboyne, Viscount; Huntly, Marquis of; Haddington, Countess of; and Sutherland, Earl of.
Gothenburg, 340, 341 n., 343.
Graham, family of, 34; John, Lord, 195, 215, 232; Lady Dorothea, 37, 157 n.; Sir Harry, 176 n., 313, 339, 351, 352, 353, 356, 379; Lord James (see Montrose, second Marquis of); Lady Jean, 365; Lady Katherine, 40; Lady Lilias, 35; Lady Margaret, 35; Mr. John, of Auchterarder, 128; John, of Claverhouse (Viscount Dundee), 224, 250, 385, 387, 391 n.; Patrick, of Inchbrakie, 36, 177, 179; Patrick, younger, of Inchbrakie (Black Pate), 182, 183, 188, 191, 241, 263, 297, 304, 305, 379; Lord Robert, 251, 365, 379; Sir Richard, of Netherby, 171, 176; of Gorthie, 312, 379; of Morphie, 39, 40, 379.
Grange, 366.
Grant, clan of, 181, 206, 231, 232, 305, 317; Laird of, 231, 232.
Gray, Colonel Thomas, 318, 351.
Graymond, M. de, 368 n.

Grenville, Sir Bevil, 23.
Gun, Colonel (afterwards Sir William), 101, 102, 103.
Gunnersen, Jens, 313.
Gustavus Adolphus, 41, 43, 81, 95, 185, 186, 194, 218, 338, 341.
Guthrie, Andrew, 297, 298; Major David, 313, 355; Mr. James, 62, 89, 92, 230, 326, 371, 372, 375, 383; Mr. William, of Fenwick, 62.
Guthry, Bishop Henry, 129.
Gwynne, Captain John, 351 n.

Haddington, Countess of (Lady Jean Gordon), 369.
Hague, The, 328, 332, 335, 339.
Haldane, Major, 269, 271.
Hales, John, 26, 49, 52, 58, 146.
Haliburton, Mr. George, 195.
Halkerton castle, 234.
Halket, Colonel Robert, 353, 355.
Hamburg, 318, 319, 339, 343.
Hamilton, James, third Marquis and first Duke of, 40; character of, 42; intrigues against Montrose, 43; commissioned to treat with the Covenanters, 79, 80, 81; at Glasgow Assembly, 83, 84, 85, 86, 89, 91, 92, 94, 95, 96, 97; arrives in Forth, 100, 101, 107, 109; with the king in Edinburgh, 130, 131, 132, 133, 134, 153, 154, 155, 156, 158; imprisoned by the king, 160, 161; 169 n., 312 n.; leads the Engagers, 321, 323, 324 n.; defeated at Preston, 325; death, 331, 382; Sir Alexander, 187, 197 n.; Ann, Countess of, 42, 101. See also Lanark, Earl of.
Hampden, John, 22, 24, 27, 158, 233, 349.
Hareheadshaw, 286.
Harlaw, battle of, 211.
Harrington, James, 60.
Hartfell, James Johnston, first Earl of, 172, 275, 297.
Hay, Sir Francis of Dalgetty, 351; Colonel James, 201, 210; William, see Kinnoull, Earl of.
Henderson, Mr. Alexander, 62, 72, 80, 81, 85, 87, 88, 89, 91, 107, 110, 121, 122, 134, 146, 147, 148, 156, 157, 159.
Henri IV. of France, 389.
Henrietta Maria, Queen, 155, 156, 160, 317, 318, 319, 321, 322, 326, 327, 335, 340, 348.
Henrietta, Princess, of the Palatine, 338.

Henry VIII., King, 388.
Henry, Prince of Wales, 167, 336.
Hereford, siege of, 259, 282.
Herries, John, Lord, 172.
Hobbes, Thomas, 23 n., 140.
Holbourn, Major-Gen., 271, 348, 358, 363.
Holland, Lord, 94, 95.
Hollinbush, 267.
Home, James, third Earl of, 119, 161, 275, 277, 284, 379.
Honthorst (Gherardo dalle Notte), 89, 336, 337.
Hooker, Richard, 19, 26, 51, 140.
Hope, Sir Thomas, 72.
Hopton, Sir Ralph (afterwards Lord), 23, 155, 158, 229, 337.
Hotham, Sir John, 152.
Howell, James, 75.
Hume, Colonel, 270.
Huntly, George Gordon, second Marquis of, opposes Covenant, 79, 81 ; character of, 89, 90, 91, 95, 96, 97 ; quarrel with Montrose, 98, 99, 100 ; 104, 107, 116, 117, 123 ; meets Montrose, 156, 158, 161, 168 ; heads a rising, 173, 178, 181, 198, 199 ; jealousy of Montrose, 205, 208 n., 231, 232, 242 ; withdraws clan from Royalist army, 252, 253, 254, 256, 262 ; withdraws Aboyne, 281, 282 ; declines to assist Montrose, 301, 303, 305, 306, 311, 314 ; death, 371.
Hurry, Major-Gen. Sir John, 219, 230, 234, 237, 238, 239, 240, 242, 243, 245, 246, 249, 250, 251, 259, 265, 312, 313, 348, 351, 355, 364, 390.
Hyde, Edward. See Clarendon, Earl of.

Inchbrakie. See Graham of Inchbrakie.
"Incident," the, 132, 135.
Inglis, Lord President, 75 n.
Innerpeffray, 40.
Inveraray, 214, 217, 218.
Inverlochy, battle of, 157 n., 221, 222, 224, 225, 227, 230, 232, 294, 390.
Inverness, 220, 244, 249, 304, 305, 306, 331, 364.
Inverquharity. See Ogilvy of Inverquharity.
Inverurie, 98, 101.
Ireton, Major-Gen. Henry, 22, 387.
Irvine, Sir Alexander, of Drum, 276, 382 ; Alexander, younger, of Drum, 301.
Islay, 179, 180.

Jackson, Stonewall, 391 n.
Jaffray, Alexander, 203.
James VI. and I., King, 46, 47, 48, 50, 139.
Jameson, the painter, 39, 89.
Janssen, Cornelius, 338.
Jedburgh, 285.
Jermyn, Henry, Lord, 273, 319, 335.
Johnston, Sir Archibald, of Wariston, 73, 75, 78, 80, 85, 87, 89, 92, 121, 134, 156, 159, 296, 326, 341, 369, 374, 375, 382, 383 ; Sir William, 351 ; Colonel, 103.
Joyce, Cornet, 321.

Keats, John, 15, 395.
Keith, 254, 365.
Kelso, 284.
Kenmure, family of, 19, 91.
Keppoch. See Macdonald of Keppoch.
Ker, Lord, 133 ; Colonel Robin, 310, 311.
Kilcumin, 221, 222, 232.
Kildrummie, 205.
Kilgraston, 265.
Killiecrankie, battle of, 224, 250, 391 n.
Kilmartin Glassary, 216.
Kilpont, John, Lord (son of seventh Earl of Menteith), 191, 193, 196, 197, 200.
Kilsyth, battle of, 267-271, 283, 312, 348, 391, 392.
Kinanmond, Mr. William, 365.
Kincardine, 35, 37, 136, 150, 305.
Kinghorn, Earl of, 37, 98, 119.
Kinnaird, 37, 39, 195, 365.
Kinneil, 133.
Kinnoull, George Hay, first Earl of, 69 ; George, second Earl of, 107, 161 ; George, third Earl of, 196, 204, 210, 332, 338, 339, 340, 342 ; William, fourth Earl of, 292, 351, 357.
Kinnudie, 246.
Kintail, 181, 214, 249.
Kintore, 12, 33, 205.
Kintyre, 90, 96, 180, 216, 292 n.
Kirkton, Mr. James, 67.
Kirkwall, 339, 343, 351.
Knox, John, 22, 26, 44, 45, 46, 48, 49, 50, 55, 56, 57, 65, 68.
Kyle of Sutherland, 352, 353, 354.

Lachlan, Captain, 292, 295.
Lairg, 352.
Lambert, General, 325.
Lambie, Mr. John, 36, 40.
Lanark, William, Earl of (afterwards second Duke of Hamilton), 79, 89, 133, 159, 160, 161, 265, 266, 267,

268, 271, 313 *n.*, 322, 325, 326, 332, 333, 334, 335, 349.
Langdale, Sir Marmaduke, 301, 325.
Langport, battle of, 187.
Laud, Archbishop, 24, 25, 26, 52, 61, 69, 70, 71, 78, 86, 88, 122, 147.
Lauderdale, John Maitland, second Earl and first Duke of, 134, 322, 327, 332, 333, 334, 338, 385.
Law, Mr. Mungo, 225, 371, 376; Mr. Robert, 149, 383.
Lee, General Robert E., 394.
Leighton, Archbishop, 62, 63.
Leipsic, battle of, 185, 194.
Lennox, Duke of, 130, 131.
Lens, battle of, 324.
Leopold, Archduke, 324.
Leslie, Alexander, *see* Leven, Earl of; David (afterwards Lord Newark), 175, 186, 260, 274, 282, 283, 284, 285, 286, 287, 288, 289, 292, 293, 295, 300, 301, 302, 305, 325, 331, 342, 348, 351, 353, 358, 363, 389; John, of Pitcaple, 365; Patrick, 81.
Leven, Alexander, first Earl of, 89, 95, 96, 97, 99, 101, 103, 104, 107, 114, 118, 119, 120, 121, 122, 124, 130, 134, 155, 160, 161, 167, 170, 171, 172, 174, 176, 180, 187, 189, 197 *n.*, 205, 207, 209, 218, 226, 230, 234, 239, 250, 259, 260, 264, 273, 282, 294, 310, 320, 348, 389, 390.
Lilburne, John, 23, 57, 389.
Lindsay, John, Earl of, 37, 73, 119, 128, 153, 251, 252, 253, 254, 256, 259, 267, 269, 271, 283, 297.
Lindsay of the Byres, Lord. *See* Lindsay, Earl of.
Linlithgow, 275, 293; George, third Earl of, 275.
Linton, Lord (son of second Earl of Traquair), 275, 284, 286.
Lisle (or Lillie), Major, 313, 351, 354, 355, 358.
Lithgow, William, 38, 40.
Livingstone, Mr. John, 150.
Lochaber, 117, 168, 211, 214, 215 *n.*, 217, 218, 221, 230, 232.
Lochaline, 180, 206.
Loch Awe, 214, 217, 220.
Loch Dochart, 216.
Loch Earn, 197, 242, 301.
Loch Eil, 181, 225.
Loch Etive, 215, 220, 221.
Loch Fyne, 214, 218.
Lochiel. *See* Cameron of Lochiel.
Loch Leven, 221, 227.
Loch Ness, 221, 223.
Loch Shin, 352, 356.
Loch Sunart, 180.

Loch Tay, 216, 242.
Loch Tummel, 191.
Lorn, Archibald, Lord (afterwards ninth Earl of Argyll), 154, 367, 369.
Lothian, William Kerr, third Earl of, 107, 120, 153, 172, 196, 205, 208, 210, 211, 285, 291, 370.
Loudoun, John Campbell, first Earl of, 73, 75, 78, 107, 114, 131, 133, 134, 155, 271, 275, 322, 325, 326, 330, 363, 367, 369.
Louis XIV., 367.
Louise, Princess, of the Palatine, 338
Lovat, Lord, 243, 364.
Lucas, Sir Charles, 170.
Luther, Martin, 52, 53.

Macalain Dubh, Angus, 215.
MacBreck, Father, 216 *n.*, 217 *n.*, 221 *n.*, 222 *n.*
MacCulloch, Captain John, 174.
Macdonald, clan of, 158, 211, 217, 227; of Clanranald, 211, 264, 307; of Colonsay, 179; of Glengarry, 211, 262, 307; of the Isles, 211; of Keppoch, 211, 222, 224, 225, 359; of Sleat, 305, 307, 348.
Macdonald, Æneas, of Glengarry, 211; Sir Alasdair, 179, 182, 191, 192, 193, 194, 196, 197, 199, 200, 201, 202, 204, 206, 211, 215, 218, 220, 225, 232, 234, 236, 241, 243, 244, 245, 246, 247, 248, 249, 253, 254, 256, 262, 263, 269, 270, 271, 277, 279, 281, 307, 312, 387, 393; Angus, of Glengarry, 256, 257; Donald, of Moidart, 270; Donald Glas, of Keppoch, 211; Ian Lom, 222, 227, 359, 360; John, of Moidart, captain of Clanranald, 211, 215, 216; Sorley Boy, 179.
Macdonnells of Antrim, 180; Ranald Og, 215; James, 215.
Macdougal, clan of, 216.
Macgregor, clan of, 215, 216, 263; John, 84; Patrick, 91.
MacIans of Glencoe, 221.
Macildowie, Alan, 222 *n.*, 225.
Mackenzie, clan of, 120, 181, 241, 243, 305, 317, 331, 348, 349, 358, 360; Sir George, 36, 386; Thomas, of Pluscardine, 331, 348, 353, 365; of Applecross, 348. *See also* Seaforth, Earl of.
Mackinnon, Ranald, 247.
Maclean, clan of, 158, 211, 214, 215; Ewen, of Treshnish, 269, 270; Lachlan, of Duart, 262, 270; Murdoch, of Lochbuie, 262; of Coll, 304 *n.*

Maclear, John, 340, 343.
McClelland, Mr. John, 148 n.
Macleod, clan of, 317, 349, 359; Neil, of Assynt, 357, 358, 359, 360; of Skye, 305.
Macnab, clan of, 216, 263.
Maderty, John, second Lord, 275, 379.
Maidston, John, 122.
Maitland, F. W., 44, 51 n.
Manchester, Edward, second Earl of, 170, 229.
Mar, John Erskine, third Earl of, 96, 118, 119, 128, 166.
Marischal, William Keith, seventh Earl, 82, 101, 102 n., 104, 119, 156, 207, 208, 234, 379.
Marlborough, first Duke of, 387, 394.
Marston Moor, battle of, 175, 184, 185, 218, 229, 248.
Marstrand, 318.
Mauchline, 324.
Maurice, Prince, 163.
Maxwell, Bishop, 69.
May, Harry, 343.
Mazarin, Cardinal, 320.
Meldrum, Sir John, 189 n.
Melville, Mr. Andrew, 46, 47, 48, 57, 110; Mr. James, 37.
Melvin, Patrick, 313.
Menstrie, 267.
Menteith, 241, 268, 297, 302, 304; William Graham, seventh Earl of, 191; Sir John, 359.
Menzies, clan, 191, 216, 304; of Pitfoddels, 351, 355.
Methven, 179, 262, 265 n., 271.
Middleton, Major-General John, of Caldhame (afterwards Earl of), 283, 284, 300, 302, 305, 306, 307, 312 n., 313, 324, 325, 385.
Miereveldt, 366.
Mills of Drum, 199.
Milton, John, 18, 20, 22, 23, 25, 27, 54, 56, 140.
Mingary, 180, 206.
Monro, clan of, 353, 354, 355; General Sir George, 325, 326; General Sir Robert, 81, 279; of Achnes, 354; of Lemlair, 353, 357, 359 n.
Monteith, Robert, of Salmonet, 99, 206 n.
Montreuil (Montereul), Jean de, 307, 309, 310, 320.
Montrose, James Graham, fifth Earl and first Marquis of. Ancestry, 34–35; birth, 35; education, 35–38; marriage, 39; travels on the Continent, 40, 43; appearance and manners, 41; rebuff by the king, 43; supports National Covenant, 72–75; visits Aber-

deen, 81–82; at Glasgow Assembly, 85, 89; commands Covenant army in the north, 97, 99; quarrel with Huntly, 98–100; first battle of Aberdeen, 101–104; meeting with the king, 108; opposes Argyll's constitutional changes, 111; prepares Cumbernauld Bond, 119; letter to the king, 125–127; the "Plot," 128–132; the "Incident," 132–135; his political philosophy, 137–145; his discourse on Sovereign Power, 397–406; his religion, 146; opposes Solemn League and Covenant, 147–150; his poetry, 150–151; warns Henrietta Maria, 155; meeting with Alexander Henderson, 157; at Oxford with the king, 160; appointed lieutenant-general of the royal forces in Scotland, 163; at Newcastle's camp, 169; crosses the Border, 171–174; takes Morpeth, 174; meets Prince Rupert, 175; reaches the Highlands, 177; meets Alasdair Macdonald at Blair, 182–183; wins battle of Tippermuir, 191–196; wins second battle of Aberdeen, 200–203; sack of Aberdeen, 203, 205; falls ill in Badenoch, 206; meets Argyll at Fyvie, 207–208; at Balveny, 209; at Blair, 215; leads raid into Lorn, 215, 219; campaign of Inverlochy, 221–227; writes to the king, 227–228; receives submission of Seaforth, 231; death of Lord Graham, 232; drives Hurry out of Angus, 234; captures Dundee, 236, 237; retreat from Dundee, 237, 239; in Menteith, 242; wins battle of Auldearn, 245–250; wins battle of Alford, 255–258; his friendship with Lord Gordon, 258, 259; campaign of Kilsyth, 261–267; wins battle of Kilsyth, 267–272; occupies Glasgow, 274; summons a Parliament, 277; statement of policy, 278–280; campaign in the Borders, 281–286; battle of Philiphaugh, 286–290; negotiations with Huntly, 300–304; siege of Inverness, 305–306; ordered by the king to disband, 307–312; leaves Scotland, 313, 314; in Paris, 319; at Imperial Court, 323–324; corresponds with Prince Rupert, 327, 328; hears of death of the king, 328,

329 ; made Admiral of Scotland, 324 ; friendship with Elizabeth of Bohemia, 335–338 ; collects troops in northern Europe, 339–344 ; corresponds with Charles II., 344–346 ; arrives in Orkney, 351 ; lands in Caithness, 352 ; battle of Carbisdale, 354–356 ; captured in Assynt, 358 ; behaviour of Charles II., 363–371 ; trial, 371–374 ; execution, 375–378 ; the second funeral in 1661, 378, 380 ; story of his heart, 380–381 ; subsequent reputation, 382–385 ; his statesmanship, 385–388 ; as a soldier, 389–394 ; summary, 394–396.

Montrose, James, second Marquis of, 195, 199, 233, 251, 276, 379, 380 ; John, fourth Earl of, 34, 36 ; Magdalen, Marchioness of, 39, 302, 351 ; town of, 35, 39, 233, 303.

Moray, James Stewart, fourth earl of, 329, 369.

More, Sir Thomas, 388.

Morpeth, 174.

Morton, William Douglas, seventh Earl of, 171, 172 ; Robert, eighth Earl of, 339, 340, 342.

Morvern, 168, 181, 191, 211, 214.

Mucomir, 224.

Mugdock, 35, 302.

Mull, 211, 214.

Murray of Gask, Lord, see Tullibardine, Earl of ; Sir Gideon, 249 n. ; Mr. Robert, of Methven, 73, 74, 128, 134, 195 n. ; Will (afterwards first Earl of Dysart), 134, 152, 153, 154, 363 ; William, 297, 298 ; Murray of Philiphaugh, 249.

Musgrave, Sir Philip, 229, 273, 325.

Napier, Archibald, first Lord, of Merchiston, 35, 40, 43 n., 69, 113, 124, 128, 129, 132, 136, 157, 251, 275, 289, 290, 302, 342 ; Archibald, second Lord, 242, 251, 256, 257, 266, 275, 276, 277, 290, 305, 312, 320, 332 ; Lady, 380 ; Lilias, 319 ; Mark, 118, 136, 152 n., 352 n. ; Master of, see Napier, second Lord.

Naseby, 259, 264.

Netherby, 176.

Nevoy, Mr. John, 62, 293, 296 n.

New Model Army, the, 185, 186, 187, 230, 264, 389.

Newburn, battle of, 120.

Newbury, battle of, 185 n.

Newcastle, William Cavendish, Marquis and first Duke of, 155, 162, 169, 170, 171, 174, 175, 176 ; town of, 101, 120, 121, 170, 196, 209, 283, 292, 313, 318, 320.

Newman, Cardinal, 27.

Nicholas, Sir Edward, 310, 329, 346.

Nicoll, John, 376, 378 n.

Nisbet, Sir Philip, 296.

Nithsdale, Robert Maxwell, second Earl of, 158, 161, 169, 171, 172, 301, 348.

Nowell, Dean, 58.

O'Cahan, Magnus, 208, 215, 225, 226, 256, 257, 281, 292, 295.

Ogilvy, James, Lord (afterwards second Earl of Airlie), 155, 157, 161, 169, 171, 176, 198, 212, 230, 276, 281, 282, 284, 286, 295, 296, 303, 311, 312, 331 ; Lady, 117 ; Alexander, of Inverquharity, 263, 296 ; Sir David, of Baldovie, 198, 264 ; Sir Thomas, 198, 226, 227 ; of Powrie, 276, 287, 301, 351, 355.

Ord of Caithness, 351, 352.

Orkney Isles, 339, 342, 343, 352, 355.

Ormonde, James Butler, first Duke of, 131, 327, 340, 346.

Oxford, 155, 156, 160–163, 169, 176, 309, 361.

Pacification of Berwick, 104.

Parliament, the Long, 115, 121 ; the Short, 114.

Peebles, 291.

Perth, 173, 178, 193, 194, 195, 196, 210, 261, 262, 263, 264, 368, 378 n., 382 ; John Drummond, second Earl of, 132, 191.

Petty, 304.

Philiphaugh, battle of, 204, 286, 288–290, 294, 299, 356, 358, 382, 390, 391.

Pitcairne, Mr. Patrick, 239 n.

Pitcaple castle, 365.

" Plot," the, 128–132.

Pluscardine. See Mackenzie of Pluscardine.

Porter, Endymion, 162.

Preston, battle of, 187, 325, 331, 333.

Primrose, Sir Archibald, 277.

Puritans, the, 24–27.

Pym, John, 121, 123.

Raleigh, Sir Walter, 18, 36, 42, 141, 374.

Ranke, L. von, 86, 88.

Rattray, 312.

Reay, Donald Mackay, first Lord, 169, 276, 301, 307, 331, 351, 356.

Regiments :
Argyll, 185 n., 270.
Balcarres, 235 n., 256, 257.
Buccleuch (Tweeddale), 283, 290 n.
Buchanan, 243 n.
Cassilis (Kyle and Carrick), 235 n., 252 n., 256.
Clydesdale, 283.
Crawford-Lindsay (Fife), 235 n., 252 n.
Dalhousie, 205 n., 283.
Eglinton, 283.
Fraser's Dragoons, 283.
Galloway, 283.
Glencairn (Ayr and Renfrew), 235 n., 256, 270.
Hume, 252 n., 254 n.
Kenmure, 283.
Kirkcudbright's Dragoons, 283, 288.
Lanark, 235 n., 256, 374 n.
Lauderdale (Midlothian), 235 n., 252 n.
Lawers, 205n., 235n., 243n., 246, 249.
Leven, 283.
Lothian (Teviotdale), 241, 242, 243 n., 249.
Loudoun, 235 n., 241, 243 n.
Middleton, 283.
Montgomery, 283.
Strathearn, 283.
Retz, Cardinal de, 41, 320, 367, 390.
Richmond, 175.
Ripon, Treaty of, 121.
Robertson, clan of, 182, 183, 232, 241 ;
Donald, Tutor of Struan, 182.
Roe, Sir Thomas, 337.
Rollo, Sir James, of Duncrub, 37, 157, 225, 379 ; Sir William, 157 n., 175, 201, 202, 205, 282, 295, 296.
Rosebery, family of, 277.
Roseneath, 214, 218, 219.
Ross, clan of, 353, 354, 355.
Rotherham, 282.
Rothes, John Leslie, sixth Earl of, 36, 73, 74, 79, 81, 85, 89, 91, 107, 367.
Rothiemurchus, 206.
Rowton Heath, battle of, 285.
Roxburgh, Robert Ker, first Earl of, 79, 96, 131, 133, 161, 172, 275, 277, 284, 379.
Rupert, Prince, 152 n., 158, 162, 175, 186, 202, 233, 247, 296, 324, 326, 327, 337, 339, 390.
Rutherford, Mr. Samuel, 19, 54, 62, 91, 156.

St. Andrews, 36, 37, 38, 153, 177, 296, 303, 365.
Saintserf, Thomas, 41, 249.
Savile, Lord, 121.
Schiehallion, 191, 242.

Scone, 121.
Scot, Sir John, of Scotstarvet, 35 n.
Scott, Sir James, of Rossie, 192, 193, 194 ; Sir Walter, 119, 129 n., 167 n., 192, 197, 246, 283 n., 287 n., 331, 385 ; Sir William, of Harden, 283 n.
Seaforth, George Mackenzie, second Earl of, 119, 181, 219, 220, 221, 222, 223, 231, 232, 243, 244, 249, 305, 307, 311, 312, 313 n., 331, 338, 343, 348, 358, 379.
Selden, John, 147.
Selkirk, 286, 287 n., 288, 289.
Seton, George, Lord, 275.
Sibbald, Colonel, 176, 209.
Simson, Mr. Patrick, 372 n.
Sinclair, John, seventh Lord, 37, 173, 332 ; Sir Edward, 356, 357 ; Sir John, of Dunbeath, 152 ; Alexander, of Brims, 356, 358.
Skene, 243, 244.
Skibo castle, 352, 363.
Slain-Man's-Lee (Philiphaugh), 355.
Smith, Mr. William, 352 n.
Socinus, 53.
Solemn League and Covenant, the, 122, 147, 148, 159, 160, 229, 232, 235, 242, 245, 370, 373, 384.
Somers, Mr. Alexander, 365.
Somerville of Drum (tenth Lord Somerville), 174.
Sophia, Princess, of the Palatine (Electress of Hanover), 337, 338.
Southesk, David Carnegie, first Earl of, 39, 85, 96, 161, 251.
Southwell, 309.
Spalding, John, 99, 100, 203, 204, 233, 242.
Spean, river, 273, 274.
Spey, river, 206, 209, 243, 252, 304, 306, 354.
Spottiswoode, Archbishop, 69, 79 ; John, 313 ; Sir Robert, 163 n., 169, 212, 277, 285, 286, 295, 297, 298, 299, 313.
Stanhope, Lord, 113 n., 152 n., 384 n.
Stewart, Adjutant, 289, 292, 293 ; James, of Ardvoirlich, 196, 197 ; Archibald, of Blackhall, 128, 129 ; Sir James, of Coltness, 371 ; John, of Ladywell, 128–129 ; Walter, of Traquair, 128, 129, 130 ; of Grandtully, 128.
Stewarts of Appin, 211, 221 ; of Balquhidder, 304.
Stirling, 173, 261, 266, 267, 368, 378 n. ; Earl of, 267 ; Sir George, of Keir, 128, 129, 157, 251, 275 ; Lady, 173.
Stonehaven, 102, 224, 313.

Stormont, Lord, 36, 128.
Strachan, Colonel Archibald, 348, 353, 354, 355, 358, 366.
Strafford, Thomas Wentworth, first Earl of, 95, 96, 114, 122, 123, 131, 140, 143, 387.
Strathavon, 205, 208 *n.*, 233.
Strathbogie, 95, 205, 207, 209, 232, 243, 251, 252, 262, 300, 303.
Strathearn, 191, 192.
Strathnaver, 174, 198, 300, 356.
Strath Oykell, 353, 356.
Struther, Mr. William, 146 *n.*
Suckling, Sir John, 95.
Sutherland, John Gordon, thirteenth Earl of, 243, 244, 351, 352, 353, 379.
Sydserf (or Saintserf), Bishop, 69.

TAIN, 35, 38, 303.
Tarff, river, 223.
Tawney, R. H., 24 *n.*
Taylor, Jeremy, 26, 52, 56, 60, 156.
Tertullian, 52, 53.
Thirty Years' War, the, 247, 336.
Thomas Aquinas, St., 52, 59.
Thurso, 352.
Tippermuir, battle of, 192–195, 199, 216, 226, 232, 275, 390, 392.
Tithes question, 16, 65, 66, 69.
Tomintoul, 205.
Tournai, 324.
Traherne, Thomas, 224.
Traill, Mr. Robert, 62, 371, 376.
Traquair, John Stewart, second Earl of, 79, 91, 96, 107, 109, 110, 111, 113, 130, 154, 155, 161, 172, 176, 275, 284, 286, 287 *n.*, 288, 291.
Tullibardine, Patrick, third Earl of, 102, 192 *n.*, ; James, fourth Earl of, 192, 193, 262, 267, 271, 298.
Tullibelton, 177, 178, 182, 272.
Turner, Sir James, 173, 180, 292 *n.*, 309, 325, 331.
Turnham Green, battle of, 155.
Turriff, 97, 101, 233.
Tweed, river, 119, 120, 177, 281, 283, 284, 287, 291.

Tweeddale, John Hay, first Earl of, 379.
Tyndrum, 216.

ULSTER, 180. *See* Macdonald, Sir Alasdair, and Antrim, Marquis of.
Uxbridge, Treaty of, 229.

VANE, Sir Harry, the younger, 115, 143, 158.
Verney, Sir Edmund, 23, 28, 95.
Voltaire, 52, 375 *n.*

WALLER, Edmund, 95 ; Sir William, 158.
Wariston. *See* Johnston, Sir Archibald.
Warwick, Robert Rich, Earl of, 327 ; Sir Philip, 42, 108, 122.
Wedderburn, Bishop, 69.
Weir, Major, 374.
Weldon, Sir Anthony, 45.
Wellington, first Duke of, 394.
Wemyss, Mr. John, 110 ; Sir Patrick, 131.
Whichcote, Benjamin, 146.
Whigamore Raid, the, 326.
Whiteford, Colonel, 339 *n.*
Wigton, John Fleming, second Earl of, 37, 119, 146.
William the Silent, 54, 389.
Wishart, George, afterwards Bishop of Edinburgh, 124, 154, 188 *n.*, 189, 192, 212, 230, 239, 258, 276, 303, 304, 313, 314, 323, 329, 367.
Wodrow, Mr. Robert, 92, 136, 352 *n.*, 372.
Wood, Mr. James, 314.
Worcester, battle of, 185.
Wotton, Sir Henry, 38 *n.*, 336.

YARROW, river, 286, 290.
York, 155, 174, 175, 212 ; Duke of (James II.), 326, 334.
Ythan, river, 207.

ZUINGLIUS, 53.

THE END